SYMBOLIC COMPUTATION

Artificial Intelligence

Other titles in this series see pp. 427–428

Roland Hausser

Computation of Language

**An Essay on Syntax, Semantics
and Pragmatics in Natural
Man-Machine Communication**

Foreword by Dana Scott

Springer-Verlag Berlin Heidelberg GmbH

Roland Hausser
Laboratory for Computational Linguistics
Carnegie Mellon University
Pittsburgh, PA 15213, USA

CR Classification (1987): F.1, F.4, I.2.1, I.2.7, H.3–4, J.2, J.4–5, C.1.2

Library of Congress Cataloging-in-Publication Data
Hausser, Roland R.: Computation of Language / Roland Hausser. p. cm.–(Symbolic computation. Artificial intelligence) Bibliography: p. Includes index.
ISBN 978-3-642-74566-9   ISBN 978-3-642-74564-5 (eBook)
DOI 10.1007/978-3-642-74564-5

1. Artificial intelligence. 2. Programming languages (Electronic computers) 3. Machine theory. I. Title. II. Series. Q335.H39 1989 006.3–dc 20 89-32338 CIP

© Springer-Verlag Berlin Heidelberg 1989
Softcover reprint of the hardcover 1st edition 1989

2145/3140-543210 – Printed on acid-free paper

Foreword

The study of linguistics has been forever changed by the advent of the computer. Not only does the machine permit the processing of enormous quantities of text—thereby securing a better empirical foundation for conclusions—but also, since it is a modelling device, the machine allows the implementation of theories of grammar and other kinds of language processing. Models can have very unexpected properties—both good and bad—and it is only through extensive tests that the value of a model can be properly assessed. The computer revolution has been going on for many years, and its importance for linguistics was recognized early on, but the more recent spread of personal workstations has made it a reality that can no longer be ignored by anyone in the subject.

The present essay, in particular, could never have been written without the aid of the computer. I know personally from conversations and consultations with the author over many months how the book has changed. If he did not have at his command a powerful typesetting program, he would not have been able to see how his writing looked and exactly how it had to be revised and amplified. Even more significant for the evolution of the linguistic theory is the easy testing of examples made possible by the implementation of the parser and the computer-held lexicon. Indeed, the rule set and lexicon grew substantially after the successes of the early implementations created the desire to incorporate more linguistic phenomena.

As a general principle, the use of a computer not only forces the researcher to be more precise, but it also encourages him to be more ambitious. The use of the computer is an inspiration to thinking: once you pass a certain point of solidification of the implementation, you then find that whenever you get a new idea it is relatively easy to try it out. And we can share software and results with others, making independent verifications more feasible. I hope the fruits of the present work will be quickly tested in this way.

As the author explains in his preface, the book as a whole is divided into three parts, each of which has five chapters. This balance arose naturally as the shape of the essay emerged from the literary composition process. There are always many decisions to be made concerning the amount of detail that ought to be presented. Also, it is only after you start writing that you appreciate the strengths and weaknesses of your argument. Thus, over several months, the chapters split, moved, expanded, and contracted until the author was satisfied that the outline of the thesis he is putting forward was clear.

The emphasis in Part I is to give the general outlines of a theory of syntax, semantics, and pragmatics. As the author points out from the beginning, this theory did not arise from a preconceived theoretical standpoint: he was forced into it step by step by his efforts at implementation of a categorial grammar. After seeing what emerged from this work, he then realized that he could justify it on many other grounds. Once the main features of this justification are set out in Part I, the argument needs further underpinning, however. The mathematical mechanism of grammar construction is the topic of Part II of the book, where many results and comparisons with other approaches are presented.

I feel Roland Hausser is remarkably successful in showing that left-associative grammar is *practical*. I think he is also equally successful in showing in Parts I and II that the approach is *natural*. It seems to me to be a real discovery that the powerful rules are not so hard to write and are not too complex or prolix. Indeed, they are very, very compact. I strongly recommend that linguists take a hard look at these results, since I feel that the author has made a major advance in the technique of organization of grammatical information.

For example, the burden of resolving certain structural ambiguities, e.g., in "PP attachment," is clearly segregated from the problem of establishing surface grammatical form and made a matter of *semantic* not *syntactic* resolution. In the author's approach, this is a motivated redistribution of grammatical responsibility that leads to efficiencies—and naturalness—in parsing akin to those that result when syntax is relieved of the burden of anaphora resolution.

Aside from Hausser's arguments of naturalness, the basic idea, as I see it, is the balance and interplay he achieves in controlling the exploration of continuations through the information contained in his categories and the ways he transforms the categories in his rules. There are many different styles to do this, but the author has opted for straight-forward solutions close to traditional analyses. It took me a while to catch on to the idea of how his categories work, but after I did I had to agree that it is a powerful idea that ought to be open to much further exploitation. We also worked together with David Evans and a project team on lexicon development, and the use of the categories has proved to be very satisfactory.

The final section of the essay, Part III, returns to many old, and extensively discussed topics in philosophy of language. The nature of reference and the uncovering of the means of communication are well worn topics. What is new here, I believe, is the placing of the arguments in the context of a theoretical mechanism. Hausser is putting forward an integrated theory of how grammar, parsing, and the connections to semantic interpretation work. By having an explicit framework, he then is able to see what light is shed on the philosophical questions.

There are many other ways to develop the ideas present in this work. A left-associative approach to morphology and "word-grammar" is an obvious step, and some thought has been given to this. I myself would particularly like to see English punctuation incorporated into the grammar. Hausser assures me this will be easy, but I have to be convinced.

Of course, the parsing of *correct* sentences is an excellent thing to do, but we also have to give much more thought to *error analysis*. It will be clear from the many examples in the book that the approach can be adapted to doing this, but more software design is needed to make this actual and useful. It should also be clear that the parsing of phrases as well as sentences can be done. For uses in information retrieval that we have in mind, it will be essential to do this flexibly. For example, there are well known constructions with discontinuous constituents in English where the underlying concept has to be located by means of parsing.

Also, as everyone who works in natural-language processing knows, the lexicon is never large enough, and something will have to be developed to allow the parser to "guess" at the category of words not contained in the lexicon. This could be very useful in doing empirical work in expanding the lexicon. In general, lexicon construction is very labor intensive, and machine aids are badly needed to make the task easier. In any case, I am much encouraged that the NEWCAT Parser is turning out to be a real tool. The further evaluation of the method will also be easier when we have additional languages to try out. There already exists a sizable LA-grammar for German, which was put aside during the writing of this book. I hope the author can return to this project soon.

I think it must be emphasized that this is an *essay* and not an *exhaustive treatise*. Much more could (and has!) been said on many of the topics discussed here. The present book, however, is an attempt to establish a concept by making a real effort to explain how it fits into a philosophical and psychological point of view. But the attempt will fail if it is drowned in too much detail. If the basic concept is accepted, the elaboration can come later.

The conclusions in this book may be controversial, but the author has provided—in a pleasant, non-dogmatic way—a new platform for a fresh and rational discussion. I hope linguists and philosophers will take the trouble to understand his theory and continue the debate.

Dana Scott
Carnegie Mellon University
February, 1989

Author's Preface

My grandmother sometimes played dominoes[1] with me. Later I was struck by the idea that language worked very much like the pieces of this game. Each piece you add must be compatible with the previous one, and it in turn determines what can be added next. This is the idea of *possible continuations*.

Contemporary linguistic theory takes a different approach. It looks at language as a system of abstract sentence schemata: one gets a real sentence by replacing variables in the main schema with more elaborate sub-schemata, until finally the variables in the sub-schemata are replaced by actual words. This is the idea of *possible substitutions*.

What is the difference between the two approaches? The substitution approach is based on partially ordered replacements in abstract schemata: in a schema with several variables it does not matter in which order they are being substituted. The continuation approach, on the other hand, is based on the linear order of concrete pieces (word forms): the next piece can only be added at the end[2] of the sequence.

For many years I worked in the substitution paradigm. But in 1984, I was compelled to explore the idea of possible continuations. I had completed a book[3] on categorial grammar, and was working on a computational implementation of its rule system. Having expended much effort on a formal grammar which was more constrained, more complete, and as explicit as any Montague grammar I had seen, I was puzzled by the computational inefficiency of my system.

The possible substitutions in my categorial grammar permitted an extremely large number of derivations, most of which would eventually lead to dead ends. I searched for a principle to constrain the derivations, but none was found. Then I remembered the games of dominoes with my grandmother. Finally I sat down and started to experiment with the idea of translating my substitution system into a grammar of possible continuations.

---

[1]An ancient game played with twenty-eight small regular pieces of wood or ivory, divided into two equal spaces, each of which is either blank or marked from one to six spots. The players must match according to the number of dots on each half.

[2]While dominoes permits additions at both ends of the sequence, natural language is time-linear and permits addition only after the *last* word. Thus, regarding derivation order, natural language is even more constrained than dominoes.

[3]Hausser (1984a).

At first, this translation required some mental effort because I had to completely rethink the syntactic derivation process. An explicit statement of all possible continuations after each word of the sentence requires a more distributed packaging of the grammatical information than in a substitution system. But the basic intuitions of possible continuations are clear and firm: for any given "sentence start" one can easily determine which "next word" categories are grammatical, and which are not.

The resulting symbolic parallel distributed system of Left-Associative Grammar (LA-grammar) turned out to be powerful and efficient in the analysis of natural language. It was tested by building extensive systems for German and English. In 1986, I presented the results in a book[4] which shows how the traditional linguistic notions of valency, agreement, and word order function in a time-linear analysis of German and English.

Having demonstrated that the principle of possible continuations works well in the linguistic description of natural-language syntax, I turn now to the following questions: (i) What are the exact formal properties of the left-associative algorithm? (ii) How does the principle of possible continuations relate to the functioning of natural language in communication?

The main body of this book consists of an introduction, and three parts of five chapters each. Part I presents a general outline of a theory of syntax, semantics, and pragmatics; the linguistic, psychological, and computational arguments which support it; comparisons with other linguistic approaches; the handling of specific phenomena such as agreement, valency, word order, and pronouns; and the treatment of analysis and generation.

Part II presents the formal definition and theoretical analysis of the left-associative syntax, a subject matter which falls into automata theory and the theory of formal languages. Relating left-associative syntax to this large body of knowledge seems to be the best way to explain the computational and mathematical power of our new approach. The regular, context-free, and context-sensitive languages are reconstructed in LA-grammar, and questions of decidability and computational efficiency are explored in detail. The phrase structure grammars of numerous formal languages discussed in the literature are compared with explicitly defined, weakly equivalent LA-grammars, which illustrate how succinctly grammatical information may be formulated in the left-associative framework.

Part III deals with the philosophical aspect of language analysis, and describes our overall approach to communication. Topics are the theory of signs; the nature of reference; the role of ontology, truth, and the metalanguage; the function of a semantically interpreted language in a speaking robot; and the purpose of logic in natural-language analysis.

While the sequence of chapters proceeds according to a certain logic, the parts and chapters may be read separately as selfcontained presentations. In particular, the

---

[4]Hausser (1986).

philosophical discussion of Part III may be read independently of the formal results presented in Part II, though Part III explains the intended conceptual interpretation of the formal system. Part II may be read independently of Part I, though Part II provides the formal definitions underlying the syntactic analysis outlined in Part I.

A brief conclusion is followed by three appendices describing different aspects of ECAT. ECAT is an LA-grammar of a sizeable fragment of English, which is implemented in Lisp as a parser.

The parsers for English (ECAT) and German (DCAT) were originally developed at CSLI-Stanford in INTERLISP-D on a Xerox 1109 machine. After translation into Common Lisp, ECAT was substantially expanded. The Common Lisp version of semantically interpreted ECAT presented in this book was developed on an HP-9000 work station, but has been successfully brought up on Micro-VAXes, TI-explorers, and SUN work stations.

The parsers for the natural and formal languages described in this book are all running at the Laboratory for Computational Linguistics of Carnegie Mellon University. The sample derivations contained in the following pages are undoctored verbatim outputs of the parsers.

Acknowledgements

The research presented in this book was supported by a five year Heisenberg grant by the Deutsche Forschungsgemeinschaft, West Germany. During this time I visited the Philosophy Department of Stanford University (1983/4), the Center for the Study of Language and Information at Stanford (1984/6), the Department of Computer Science at Carnegie Mellon University (1986/7), and the Laboratory for Computational Linguistics at Carnegie Mellon University (1987/8). I am grateful to Julius Moravscik, Stanley Peters, Betsy Macken, John Perry, Jaime Carbonell, Masaru Tomita, David Evans, and Dana Scott for sponsoring my stays at their research institutions.

Portions of Chapters 3, 4, 6, and 7 were previously published in *Computers and Translation*. Passages in Chapters 14 and 15 were lifted from articles in the *Journal of Semantics*, *Conceptus* and *Language Research*. I wish to acknowledge my indebtedness to the editors of these journals. Otherwise, to the best of my recollection, no portions of the work have been previously published.

Edward Gibson, Stanley Peters, Stuart Shieber, Helmut Schwichtenberg, Dana Scott, and Masaru Tomita offered vigorous resistance, as well as constructive ideas, to various preliminary views and formulations, thus contributing greatly to the outcome of this book. But they are in no way responsible for the result.

I wish to thank Jaime Carbonell, Brian McWhinney, Teruko Mitamura, Sergei Nirenburg, Carl Pollard, and David Touretzky for helpful discussions and important suggestions. Crucial help with programming problems at various times was provided by Jaime Carbonell, Todd Kaufmann, Eric Nyberg, and Peter Shell. Johanna Seibt and Robert Carpenter provided detailed comments on the manuscript, which resulted in numerous corrections and improvements. I was fortunate in being able to discuss much of the material with the members of my seminars and lecture courses at the University of Munich.

The book was written between November 1, 1987 and September 30, 1988 at the Laboratory for Computational Linguistics, Carnegie Mellon University, Pittsburgh, Pennsylvania. The production of this book would have been virtually impossible without the LAT_EX software running on the workstations provided by CMU. I am grateful for access to the computing facilities of the Laboratory for Computational Linguistics and the Department of Computer Science.

I am indebted to Kathryn Gula, who created the many difficult pictures in LAT_EX. I am grateful to David Sours, who proofread and copyedited the text meticulously and with great skill. Also I would like to thank the editor at Springer-Verlag Heidelberg, Dr. Hans Wössner, for his support. The book was produced from a camera-ready copy supplied by the author.

Contents

We may say that in practically all speaking two things must have unremitting attention: the ideas and the words. In the former case, the sphere of subject matter is chiefly concerned; in the latter, that of expression.

Dionysious Halicarnassus
On Literary Composition, I.
(between 20 and 10 B.C.)

Introduction

Science is based on abstraction. Some aspects of the phenomena described are taken as fundamental, while others are purposely ignored, or relegated to an ancillary part of the theory. This strategy is as legitimate as it is necessary. But it is equally legitimate to question whether the current set of theoretical assumptions and descriptive goals is optimal for the continued progress of the science.

A case in point is the proper delineation of basic structure and use. This question arises in linguistics (Part I), automata theory (Part II), and philosophy of language (Part III). The following sections of the Introduction summarize the book in light of the distinction between *competence* and *performance* in linguistics (I), the distinction between the *declarative* and *procedural aspects* of the computation (II), and the distinction between *semantics* and *pragmatics* in philosophy (III).

I.

Let's consider the boundary between competence and performance in contemporary linguistics. Competence is defined as "the speaker-hearer's knowledge of his language," while performance concerns "the actual use of the language in concrete situations" (Chomsky 1965, p.4). The task of the linguist is to discover the competence grammar.

But what exactly is included in the "speaker-hearer's knowledge of his language"?

> To avoid what has been a continuing misunderstanding, it is perhaps worth while to reiterate that a generative grammar is not a model for a speaker or a hearer. It attempts to characterize in the most neutral terms the knowledge of the language that provides the basis for actual use of language by a speaker-hearer. When we speak of a grammar as generating a sentence with a certain structural description, we mean simply that the grammar assigns this structural description to the sentence. When we say that a sentence has a certain derivation with respect to a particular generative grammar, we say nothing about how the speaker or hearer might proceed, in some practical or efficient way, to construct such a derivation. These questions belong to the theory of language use—the theory of performance.
>
> Chomsky 1965, p. 9

In short, Chomsky's competence grammar is not *intended* to be applied directly in a system simulating natural-language communication. But shouldn't the "knowledge of the language that provides the basis for actual use" be such that a speaker-hearer (or a robot simulating a speaker-hearer) *could* proceed in a practical or efficient way to construct a derivation based on the competence grammar?

The structure of language reflects the functioning of language in communication. A grammar of natural language can only be descriptively and explanatorily adequate if it is structurally compatible with the **principles** of language use. We therefore adopt an alternative notion of competence which refers to language as a system functioning in communication, leaving to performance only accidental, implementation-dependent variations during operation. This notion of competence defines more broadly than Chomsky's what the speaker-hearer knows about his or her language .

What is required of a system that provides a model of natural-language communication?

> Two fundamental problems stand out: How do people map natural-language strings into a representation of their meaning? How do people encode thoughts in natural language? Because of a purported interest in the purely formal properties of language, linguists have consciously avoided both of these naturalistic problems.

> Schank and Abelson (1977), p. 7.

In other words, the grammar system has to provide an explicit bidirectional surface-meaning mapping. Syntactic well-formedness should be characterized by the rules which map meanings into linear surfaces, and vice versa.

However, the problem with contemporary competence grammars is not just a matter of "purported interest." Rather, the formalism of phrase structure grammar (PS-grammar), which Chomsky adopted from Post (1936), doesn't have the right structure for representing a bidirectional surface-meaning mapping. Chomsky's restrictive notion of competence, and the related arguments concerning innateness and learnability, serve to justify a type of grammar system which is inherently unsuitable for the simulation of natural-language communication.

A PS-grammar is designed to map a start symbol (usually called "S") into a string of terminal symbols. This process, based on the substitution of non-terminals by means of rewriting rules, is well motivated in its original context of recursion theory. But the structure of PS-grammar is incompatible with the principles language use: the speaker is not interested in exploring grammaticality by rewriting an S-node, but in mapping a given meaning into a corresponding surface.

For similar reasons, PS-grammar is unsuitable for direct parsing. Parsers for context-free PS-grammars cannot possibly apply the rules of the grammar directly because the rules of the grammar rewrite an initial start symbol, while the parser takes sentences as input. The standard solution to this dilemma consists of computational routines which reconstruct the grammatical analysis in an indirect way by building large intermediate structures which are not part of the grammar.

The Earley algorithm,[5] for example, constructs "state sets," the CYK algorithm[6] constructs "charts," and the Tomita parser[7] is based on precompiled "LR-tables." These state sets, charts, or tables are considered to be the "procedural aspect" of the computational analysis, while the PS-grammar which is being transformed into the intermediate structures is said to represent the "declarative aspect." Thus the central question of the correct boundary between basic structure (competence) and use (performance) reappears in automata theory as the dichotomy between the **declarative** and the **procedural** aspect of parsers (and generators).

Our objective is a competence grammar which describes the linguistic data in a well-motivated general manner, yet which can be used directly by a computational system simulating natural-language communication. A syntactic formalism used directly in parsing and generation eliminates the need for a "procedural" reconstruction of the grammar, ensures that the grammar used by parsers and generators is general and linguistically well motivated, and provides a computational testing ground for competence grammars with tremendous heuristic power.

II.

Many linguists, psychologists, and computer scientists have explored alternatives to Chomsky's approach, and have searched for models and algorithms which are better suited to a computational analysis of natural language. These systems may be divided into two groups.

The first group comprises theories which maintain the basic format of PS-grammar. They attempt to improve particular aspects of linguistic description by adding, rearranging, or eliminating components of Chomsky's original grammar(s). LFG,[8] for example, postulates an "F-structure"[9] in addition to the "C-structure"[10] generated by PS-grammar. GPSG,[11] on the other hand, eliminates the transformational component and extends the coverage of the PS-grammar by means of meta-rules.

This strategy has the initial advantage that many of the linguistic assumptions and results of the earlier system can be retained. Furthermore, the study of formal languages in automata theory is based to a large extent on the formalism of PS-grammar. Therefore, retaining PS-grammar as a basic part of the alternative grammar systems has facilitated using the standard tools of formal language analysis for the study of their mathematical and computational properties.[12]

---

[5]Early (1970).
[6]See Hopcroft and Ullman (1979), pp. 139 – 145.
[7]Tomita (1986).
[8]Lexical Functional Grammar, Bresnan (1984).
[9]F-structure stands for "functional structure."
[10]C-structure stands for "constituent structure."
[11]Generalized Phrase Structure Grammar, Gazdar et al. (1985).
[12]See Barton et al. (1987) for a computational analysis of LFG and GPSG.

But the fatal flaw of these "mild" alternatives is that their use of a PS-grammar makes them subject to the same objections as Chomsky's original grammar(s). Parsers and generators cannot use the rule system of GPSG or LFG directly, but must preprocess the rule system and/or reformulate it into intermediate structures (e.g., charts). This amounts to a substantial modification of the rule system, and constitutes an inefficient duplication of effort. Given the separation of the competence grammar and its "procedural" implementation, it is not surprising that central structures of contemporary competence grammars are often simply ignored in computational implementations.[13]

The second group comprises systems which grew directly out of the computational environment. Representative examples of this large and diverse group are Winograd (1972), Wilks (1975), and Schank et al. (1975). These systems implement surface-meaning mappings, but they do not constitute a general, well-defined, formal theory of natural-language grammar. The systems Marcus (1980) and McDonald (1984) are also primarily computational implementations, even though they maintain a notational resemblance with the dominant school of linguistics.

What is needed is a basic alternative to the formalism of PS-grammar. It should be equally general and simple, theoretically transparent, yet suitable for direct modeling of analysis and generation in natural language. The fundamental structural aspect missing in PS-grammar-based systems is the fact that language is inherently time-linear.

The formalism of Left-Associative Grammar (LA-grammar) analyzes a string word by word from left to right, and computes the possible continuations each time a "next word" has been added. LA-grammar is a new algorithm which resembles finite state automata, but accepts all and only the recursive languages. The rules of an LA-grammar are used directly in parsing and in generation.

This is possible because LA-grammar is **input-output equivalent** with parsers and generators. An LA-grammar used for analysis takes a sentence as input—like a parser; an LA-grammar used for generation computes possible continuations—like a generator. Thus LA-grammar achieves **absolute type transparency**:[14] all important properties of the derivation are handled declaratively in the grammar, while the procedural aspect of the computational analysis is no more than a straightforward application of the grammatical rules.

---

[13]For example, the LFG-based generation system running at the Center of Machine Translation at Carnegie Mellon University does not generate a C-structure. One could, of course, hook up a C-structure component, but it would be excess baggage without any function—the name "L(exical) F(unctional) G(rammar)" notwithstanding. The LFG parser for German running at the University of Stuttgart also worked initially without a C-structure, but one was added later.

[14]See Berwick & Weinberg (1984), p. 41.

III.

Characterizing the formal properties of the surface-meaning mapping requires an explicit theory of meaning. Our approach to semantics and pragmatics starts from the question: "How could model-theoretic semantics in the tradition of Tarski, Carnap, Kripke, and Montague be used in the design of a robot capable of communicating in natural language?"

Model theory—like PS-grammar—originated in the foundations of mathematical logic. Model-theoretic semantics—like Chomsky's competence grammar—abstracts from the *use* of language by the speaker-hearer. Thus the question arises as to which aspects of use should be incorporated into the structure of the formal system—not only concerning the boundary between linguistic competence and performance,[15] but also with respect to the boundary between model-theoretic semantics and a compatible theory of pragmatics.

The most important theoretical issue concerning the interaction of semantics and pragmatics is the ontological status of "meaning." Using the example of a simple robot that can recognize and name colors, we arrive at two basic distinctions: external (or **-constr**) versus internal (or **+constr**), as well as extensional (or **-sense**) versus intensional (or **+sense**) approaches to meaning.

After demonstrating that all four possible approaches to meaning (i.e., <-constr, -sense>, <-constr,+sense>, <+constr,-sense> and <+constr,+sense>) based on these two distinctions have been explored in the literature, it is shown that the computational modeling of communication requires a +constr approach. Furthermore, spontaneous reference to new objects, as well as non-literal uses of language, require a +sense approach.

Our <+constr,+sense> ontology is based on the assumption that signs have literal meanings which are used relative to the speaker-hearer's internal utterance context. Pragmatics in general, and reference in particular, is treated as a matching procedure between the literal meanings and the corresponding entities in the internal subcontext.

The construction of literal meanings is based on the principle of **surface compositionality**.[16] A surface-compositional grammar takes the word forms as the basic entities of the syntax, such that all syntactic and semantic properties of a sentence are a compositional result of the words in their particular surface order. A surface-compositional approach to syntax and semantics applies the Fregean Principle directly to the concretely given natural surface.

Assuming the system has this overall structure, our central task in pragmatics is the correct positioning of (the literal meaning of) the sign relative to the interpretation context. The primary fix-point of this positioning procedure is the Space-Time-

---

[15]See Moravscik (1974) for a discussion of the competence/performance distinction from a philosophical point of view.

[16]Hausser (1984a).

Agent-Recipient point (STAR-point) of origin of the sign. A secondary positioning is based on the time-linear structure of natural-language signs. Given the correct positioning of the signs relative to the interpretation context, the matching is explained in terms of specific properties of the individual signs.

The assumptions of surface-compositional semantics and time-linear syntax are similar insofar as they result in grammatical components which have considerably more systematic structure than conventional systems which do not make these assumptions. A linear syntax exhibits a completely regular tree structure based on concrete word forms, while a surface-compositional semantics is strictly homomorphic with the sequence of surface words.

In other words, each of the assumptions results in much simpler structures because the descriptive load of the respective components is greatly reduced. A time-linear syntax does away with semantically motivated constituent structures in the syntax, making room for the systematic derivation of semantic hierarchies. A surface-compositional semantics does away with aspects of language use in the semantics, making room for a systematic theory of pragmatics.

In fact, our internal matching approach to pragmatics is not possible without compositionally constructed literal meanings. The time-linear derivation order, furthermore, provides the basic constraint on the matching procedure. Thus the principles of surface-compositional semantics and time-linear syntax contribute directly to a new, highly structured approach to pragmatic interpretation.

Part I

Natural Language and Formal Grammar

1. Goals and Results

How do people transmit information with natural-language symbols? The literature in philosophy, linguistics, psychology, and artificial intelligence dealing directly or indirectly with this question is substantial. But it provides us only with partial answers based on a wide range of conflicting assumptions. The linguistic analysis presented in this book will clarify the basic issues, and provide a unified perspective of natural-language communication. Ultimately, it will lead to the design of a **natural-language communicating robot,** or NLC-robot.[1]

This particular approach to linguistic analysis leaves aside many of the topics central to contemporary analysis, such as "psychological reality", "innate core grammars," and "mental representations." Instead, computational simulation of natural-language communication is treated as an abstract information processing problem. Just as the ability to fly may be separated from birds and other animals, and treated abstractly as the problem of figuring out the correct physics for building an airplane, natural-language communication may be analyzed in terms of a formal theory of signs.

1.1 A Unified Perspective

Designing and constructing an NLC-robot guides us to seek the foundations of natural language in (i) the structure of the agents who use it, and (ii) the structure of the agents' interaction with their environment. In contemporary linguistics these aspects are mostly ignored; rather than explaining natural languages within the contexts where they are used, they are analyzed in terms of structures which are supposed to be innate. Contemporary philosophy of language, on the other hand, ignores these aspects for methodological reasons, chief among them a post-positivistic emphasis on "real objects."

But earlier work on natural language clearly recognized the central role of information processing occuring within the agent.

> Wir setzen voraus, daß die fremde Seele in demselben Verhältnis zur Außenwelt seht wie die unsrige, daß die nämlichen physischen Eindrücke in ihr die gleichen Vorstellungen erzeugen wie in der unsrigen, und daß diese Vorstellungen sich in der gleichen Weise verbinden. Ein gewisser Grad von Übereinstimmung in der geistigen und körperlichen Organisation, in der umgebenden Natur,

---

[1]The preference here is for NL "communication" rather than NL "processing," because analysis and computational reconstruction of personal **communication** is more central and more fruitful for a basic understanding of natural language than the **processing** of impersonal texts or records.

und den Erlebnissen ist demnach die Vorbedingung für die Möglichkeit einer Verständigung zwischen Individuen. Je größer die Übereinstimmung, desto leichter die Verständigung. Umgekehrt bedingt jede Verschiedenheit in dieser Beziehung nicht nur die Möglichkeit, sondern die Notwendigkeit des Nichtverstehens, des unvollkommenen Verständnisses oder des Mißverständnisses.

Translation:[2]

We presuppose that the other mind relates to the external world in the same way as our own, that the same physical sensations produce in it the same mental images as in our own mind, and that these mental images join together in the same way. A certain degree of correspondence in the mental and physical organization, in the surrounding environment, and in the experiences is therefore a precondition for the possibility of understanding between individuals. The better the correspondence, the easier the communication. Conversely, each difference in this connection implies not only the possibility, but the necessity of no understanding, of incomplete understanding, or of misinterpretation.

H. Paul (1920ᵛ), p. 15

To discover the general principles of natural-language communication, we must study how people transfer information by talking to people. Extracting information from books, or translating books, or proving mathematical theorems, or interacting with computers, constitute highly specialized forms of communication. These can only be understood within a general theory which explains the basic uses of language.

The most basic uses of natural language evolved in face-to-face communication. People talking with each other characteristically refer to the surrounding environment, as well as to each other. This action presupposes the ability of perception. Furthermore, normal communication requires that the hearer be able to interpret language signs from the perspective of the speaker and his utterance situation. As long as computers have no image of their communication partner(s) and other relevant features of the utterance situation, natural-language communication with computers will be extremely restricted.

At present, man-machine communication with the keyboard, the screen, and the commands of a programming language is cumbersome and requires special skills, such as programming and typing. Furthermore, this kind of information transfer is completely detached from the speaker and the utterance situation. A successful model of natural-language communication will lead to substantial improvements in the way people interact with computers.

The computational reconstruction of natural-language communication should be based at least partially on robots, rather than on conventional computers.[3] That's

---

[2]Provided by the author.

[3]The "need to integrate physical actions and linguistic actions into a single planning system" is illustrated in Appelt (1982).

because robots are defined as self-contained entities equipped with perception in addition to the usual electronic information-processing capabilities. This perception serves as the basis for elementary concepts from which complex concepts and meanings may be built with the robot's computational logic. Furthermore, the robot's orientation in time and space can and should be used as the basic structure for organizing perceptions in memory.

A possible danger associated with solutions embedded in, or arising from, the computational environment is epitomized by systems like ELIZA.[4] These systems simulate narrowly constrained aspects of high-level phenomena in an "interesting" way, but provide no basis for up-scaling, or for theoretical development of their parts. This danger can be avoided, however, by a thorough analysis of the assumptions and results of the pertinent theories in linguistics, philosophy and cognitive science. A careful evaluation of these theories may lead to a new system which is no less principled, but more empirical, and better attuned to the task of building an NLC-robot.

As we shall see, several central puzzles of natural language find a natural solution in the context of an NLC-robot. In particular, the concepts of literal meaning, elementary meaning, reference, context, vagueness, and metaphor can be reconstructed in a robot in a fairly simple and straightforward manner. Once we understand how natural language functions, any form of natural language—including large texts— will be equally susceptible to a complete computational interpretation.

1.2   Assumptions Accepted and Assumptions Rejected

Natural-language signs are based on a time-linear structure, and the use of natural-language signs involves a mapping from surfaces to meanings (in the case of the hearer) and from meanings to surfaces (in the case of the speaker). All other functions of natural language are dependent on—and influenced by—these input-output conditions. A theory of grammar cannot arrive at valid linguistic generalizations if its structure is incompatible with the input-output conditions of natural language.[5]

In Left-Associative Grammar (LA-grammar), communication-theoretic analysis translates into the following concrete assumptions:

1.2.1 The Basic Assumptions of LA-Grammar

- The natural-language grammar is defined as a system which constructs a decidable, bidirectional,[6] surface-meaning mapping.

---

[4]Weizenbaum (1966).

[5]An emphasis on the input-output conditions of natural language may be found already in Saussure (1915)—cf. his discussion of "language in the facts of speech" (chapter III). What is missing, however, is the linear time factor of language production and language analysis. For Saussure, time was only a historical dimension in the area of language change.

[6]I.e., from surfaces to literal meanings and from literal meanings to surfaces.

- The formal design of the surface-meaning mapping is based on (i) a time-linear derivation order, (ii) a simultaneous derivation of syntax and semantics, and (iii) a surface-compositional homomorphism between linear syntax and hierarchical semantics.

- Semantic representations (literal meanings) of sentences are defined as minimal databases.

- Pragmatic interpretation is defined as unification of the semantic representation and the internal utterance context.

- The grammar system must be "type-transparent" with respect to associated parsers.

Although linguists have stressed a need for structural constraints, no previous grammar system has been designed to accommodate a bidirectional surface-meaning mapping or a time-linear derivation order. Furthermore, a transparent relationship between grammars and parsers (type transparency) thus far has not been regarded as an important desideratum of linguistic analysis. At present, LA-grammar is the only linguistic theory where the central topics are (i) input-output conditions of speech, (ii) computational complexity, and (iii) type transparency between grammar and parser.

A formalization with a computational implementation constitutes a higher methodological standard than a formalization by itself, because there are many widely accepted formalizations which either cannot be implemented at all, or do not permit direct or efficient processing. That a theory is computationally well-suited may be demonstrated best by presenting a sufficiently elegant and comprehensive implementation.

The use of computers in the construction of large, procedurally adequate[7] grammars of natural language is desirable for methodological, heuristic and practical reasons. The implementation of the grammar must be fast because a linguist working on an expansion of the grammar has to be able to test individual sentences. Slow systems quickly frustrate empirical work.

The computational approach to synchronic analysis presented in this book does not abandon "linguistic generalizations." But the goal of a computational model of communication leads naturally to a set of requirements and assumptions which are either incompatible with, or unrelated to, the central assumptions of most contemporary theories of meaning and grammar.

In particular, this goal leads to a rejection of constituent structures in favor of semantic hierarchies suitable for pragmatic interpretation. Constituent-structure analysis is subject to empirical problems in connection with "discontinuous elements."[8] Furthermore, a constituent structure is not suitable for direct semantic and prag-

---

[7]This notion is explained in 2.4.1.
[8]See examples 2.1.2 and 3.3.4.

matic interpretation. Finally, a derivation order designed to generate the constituent-structure hierarchy, whether in a top-down or bottom-up fashion, is neither psychologically well-founded,[9] nor computationally efficient.[10]

In the context of modeling natural-language communication by an NLC-robot, the following suppositions are regarded as false.

1.2.2 Suppositions Which are False

1. Syntactic analysis of natural language must be based on constituent structure if it is to be explanatorily adequate (see Sections 2.1 and 5.1).

2. Meanings are not in the head; the surrounding environment ("the world") is full of meanings (see Sections 11.2 and 13.4).

3. Semantics describes the relationship between "language and the world" (see Sections 12.3 and 13.3).

4. The purpose of pragmatics is the interpretation of indexicals (see Sections 2.3 11.3).

5. Syntactic algorithms do not have to be decidable in order to be psychologically plausible (see Sections 2.4 and 6.5).

6. Grammars do not have to be type transparent, i.e., the derivational order of the grammar does not have to be suitable to serve as the computational derivation order as well (see Sections 3.5 and 8.1).

Some readers also may be looking for a discussion of the linguistic assumptions which are listed in 1.2.3, and which are central to Chomsky's theory of "Government and Binding."

1.2.3 Suppositions Which are Unproductive

1. The grammars of natural language are innate.

2. The learning of natural language by the child is based on a setting of parameters.

3. Syntactic analysis should be principle based rather than rule based.

These suppositions have no direct effect on empirical analysis in the context of constructing a talking robot.[11] Consequently, no attempt will be made either to support or refute them. Instead, we provide direct support for LA-grammar by showing that it satisfies the Criteria of Psychological Well-Foundedness (cf. 2.4.3).

---

[9]Violation of the Derivational Order Hypothesis 2.4.2.

[10]See Section 3.5.

[11]Also, they cannot be falsified, in the sense of Popper (1959).

1.3   Theory and Practice

The linguistic analysis presented in this book is formulated as a generative grammar. A generative grammar is a formal rule system which quasi-mechanically generates infinitely many well-formed expressions from a finite set of basic expressions with a finite set of rules.[12] A generative grammar for a natural language is called descriptively adequate, if it generates all sentences—and only sentences—which are accepted by the native speakers of that language. Examples of grammatical paradigms which subscribe to the approach of generative grammar are Categorial Grammar and Transformational Grammar.

What reasons may be given for using the generative approach in linguistics?

1.3.1 Reasons for Using the Generative Approach in Linguistics

1. The definition of a formal, quasi-mechanical rule system ensures the explicit formulation of linguistic hypotheses. This is desirable methodologically and useful heuristically.

2. Formalizing the structural principles of a natural language in the form of a generative grammar may be an essential step towards a computational implementation of the natural language.

However, formalizing a theory does not guarantee it will be suitable for implementation on a computer. Furthermore, the approach of generative grammar only provides a general format of description. Adoption of this format implies nothing about the content of the linguistic analysis. The various formal grammars proposed since the late 1950's for the analysis of natural languages differ profoundly along the following parameters:

1.3.2 Areas of Difference in Contemporary Schools

1. Linguistic analyses differ in the choice of syntactic categorization and associated rule systems;

2. Linguistic analyses differ in the relationship of syntax, semantics, and pragmatics and

3. Linguistic analyses differ in the relationship between theoretical linguistic analysis and computational implementation.

Thus, adherence to the methodology of generative grammar has not resulted in a consolidation of the theoretical foundations of natural-language analysis. On the contrary, the common ground of generative grammar has produced a wide range of different, highly theoretical frameworks with an average life span of about five years.

---

[12]The evolution of the notion "generative" is described by Hymes and Fought (1981), pp. 165 – 174, in the historical context of American Structuralism.

A positive consequence of the generative approach, at least initially, has been an invigorated interest in new empirical data. However, analysis of many sentences does not necessarily lead to scientific progress unless the analysis is based on sound theoretical premises. After all, medieval chemistry—alchemy—was also highly data-oriented.[13] So far, the generative approach has not produced data coverage that is coherent, complete, widely accepted, or practically useful.

What are the reasons that LA-grammar is not merely a scholastic mythology dressed up as a modern theory of language?[14] The notions used in LA-grammar are the traditional linguistic concepts of agreement, valency, and word order. Linguistic analysis in LA-grammar is motivated further by a strictly time-linear derivation order; by the requirement of an explicit, decidable, bidirectional surface-meaning mapping; and by principles of economy which are measured by computational complexity.

Efficiency of computation is appealing to those who have grown weary of ever-changing, highly abstract, and impractical linguistic theories. Although we can sympathize with these sentiments, we should not view natural-language processing (for the purpose of database queries, machine translation, etc.,) primarily as an engineering task. The history of machine translation has clearly shown that engineering alone cannot successfully tackle the problems posed by natural-language analysis. Even with the vastly improved computing power of today, no amount of money and manpower will accomplish the more ambitious goals of natural-language processing unless there is first a principled, detailed, and correct theory of natural-language communication.

LA-grammar evolved as part of a comprehensive theory of natural-language communication, based on a wide-ranging study of different approaches in philosophy of language (see Chapters 11 – 15). Furthermore, the formalism of LA-grammar originated from research which investigated whether phrase structure grammar (PS-grammar) or categorial grammar (C-grammar) is more suitable for the syntactic and semantic description of natural language.[15] As a brief introduction, let us summarize the main similarities and differences between LA-grammar and more familiar systems.

- LA-grammar is like a Finite State Automaton (cf. Section 8.2), or FA, except that in an FA a transition depends on the current state and the category of the next word. In LA-grammar, on the other hand, a transition depends on the current state, the category of the expression analyzed so far (called the

---

[13]Furthermore, the attempt to explain a wide variety of phenomena in terms of the four elements fire, water, earth, and air—as well as the promise of turning base metals into gold—constituted a fascinating intellectual challenge even to Isaac Newton, who devoted the latter part of his life to the study of alchemy.

[14]"All science may indeed be a mythology, but not all mythology qualifies as a science." Sowa (1984), p. 355.

[15]This question is the premise of Hausser (1984a).

sentence-start category), and the next word. The derivation of sentence-start categories in LA-grammar is the precondition for the definition of the **categorial operations**, which map a sentence-start category and a next-word category into a new sentence-start category.

- LA-grammar is like a Recursive Transition Network (cf. Section 8.3), an Augmented Transition Network[16] (cf. Section 8.3), a Multiple Path Syntactic Analyzer[17] (cf. Section 8.4), or a Deterministic Parser[18] (cf. Section 8.4), in that it analyzes the input from left to right and computes predictions. LA-grammar differs from all these systems, however, in that it computes the possible continuations for the **next word**, whereas the other systems compute predictions for **constituents**.

- LA-grammar differs from conventional parsers and generators in that (i) it is a general mathematical theory for the recursive languages, and (ii) the rules of the grammar are used directly by the parsing and generating algorithm. This absolute type transparency is possible because the mathematical formalism of LA-grammar is based on a strictly time-linear derivation order, which results in input-output equivalence with parsers and generators (as well as with the speaker-hearer).

- LA-grammar is like Categorial Grammar, except that (i) the derivation order is left-associative; (ii) the categories do not contain any "slashes" or other diacritic symbols for controlling syntactic composition; (iii) the left-associative rules define a finite state control structure by means of rule packages; and (iv) the categorial operations can be any total recursive function.

- LA-grammar is like Montague Grammar in that the semantic interpretation is derived simultaneously with the syntactic analysis. In fact, the derivation of the semantic analyses in LA-grammar is constrained by the homomorphism condition (Montague 1974). But LA-grammar differs from Montague Grammar because of the different surface syntax, and because the formalism of intensional logic is replaced by frame structures. The homomorphism between syntax and semantics is achieved in LA-grammar even though the syntactic and the semantic trees look very different. That's because the syntax is left-associative, while the semantics has a traditional hierarchical structure.

---

[16]Woods (1970).
[17]Kuno & Oettinger (1963).
[18]Marcus (1978).

1.4   Summary of the Formal Results

LA-grammar was developed simultaneously at the levels of (i) an algebraic and automata-theoretic characterization, (ii) abstract linguistic rules, and (iii) a concrete implementation. An LA-derivation analyzes or generates a sentence from left to right, always combining a sentence start and a next word into a new sentence start. The theoretical basis of this process is the use of complex categories which serve as abstract "buffers" to encode valency and agreement information.

LA-categories are defined as lists of category segments. Words are defined as ordered pairs, consisting of a surface and a category, e.g., *(give* (N D A V)). A left-associative rule r_i is an ordered pair $(co_i\ rp_i)$, where co_i is a categorial operation and rp_i is the rule package of r_i, containing the rules which can possibly apply after a succesfull application of r_i.

Left-associative rules are notated in the following form:

r_i: [CAT-1 CAT-2] $\Rightarrow$ [rp_i CAT-3]

The categorial operation co_i takes CAT-1 (representing the category of the current "sentence start") and CAT-2 (representing the category of the current "next word") as input, and derives CAT-3 (representing the category of the resulting sentence start) as output; co_i may be any total recursive function. Surface concatenation, or SC, is left implicit because of its completely regular nature. In the next combination, the rules in rp_i are applied to the sentence start resulting from r_i and a new "next word."

The categorial operation and the rule package represent two different aspects of syntactic combination, each of which is clearly motivated linguistically. The result category CAT-3 encodes a specific agenda for subsequent combination steps in terms of valency and agreement information. The rule package encodes which continuations are possible in general after the application of a particular rule.

The combination of a categorial operation and a rule package in a left-associative rule relate directly to the computational efficiency of the system.

> The overall computational cost of an A.I. production system is the combined rule application cost and control strategy cost. Part of the art of designing efficient A.I. systems is deciding how to balance these two costs.
>
> N. Nilsson (1980), p. 54

A rule application in LA-grammar is defined as a categorial operation on the input categories. The control structure, on the other hand, is defined by the interaction of rules and rule packages, and constitutes a finite state transition network. In LA-grammar rule application and control structure are both based on the linear order of the input string.

This new method of combining rule applications and control is not limited to the analysis of natural and formal languages. Rather, it has obvious applications as a general data-driven heuristic search method.

The most basic formal result in LA-grammar is that it generates all—and only—the recursive languages (Theorem 1, 6.5.1, and Theorem 2, 6.5.2). Furthermore, we shall see that the automata-theoretic hierarchy of regular, context-free, and context-sensitive languages is clearly reflected in the formalism of LA-grammar.

Specifically, **regular languages** are generated by LA-Grammar with rules using only empty categorial operations (Theorem 3, 7.1.1), e.g.,

$$r_i: [\epsilon \text{ CAT-2}] \Rightarrow [\text{rp}_i \ \epsilon]$$

Context-free languages are generated by LA-grammars with categorial operations which work only at the beginning of CAT-1 and CAT-3 (Theorem 4, 7.1.2), e.g.,

$$r_i: [(a \ X)(a)] \Rightarrow [\text{rp}_i \ (X)]$$

or

$$r_i: [(X)(a)] \Rightarrow [\text{rp}_i \ (a \ X)]$$

where X is a variable for sequences of category segments. And **context-sensitive languages** are generated by LA-grammars where the length of the categories is bounded by $C \cdot n$, where C is a finite constant and n is the length of a complete well-formed input expression (Theorem 5, 7.1.7).

A particularly interesting class of LA-grammars is the constant LA-grammars, or C-LAGs. The categorial operations of C-LAGs look at no more than k sentence-start category segments, for some constant k. Because of this property, the application of a rule may be taken as the "primitive operation" for purposes of complexity analysis. C-LAGs accept the regular, the context-free and most context-sensitive languages. We shall see that the class of C-languages is closed under union, concatenation, and Kleene closure (Theorem 6, 7.2.6).

Next we turn to questions of decidability. For arbitrary, context-free grammars it is undecidable whether the languages generated are ambiguous, in an inclusion relation, or equivalent. In LA-grammar, on the other hand, questions of ambiguity, emptiness, inclusion, and equivalence are decidable for a large subset of the C-LAGs which includes context-sensitive languages (Theorem 7, 9.2.11; Theorem 8, 9.2.13; Theorem 9, 9.3.8; and Theorem 10, 9.3.10). This class of decidable C-LAGs is called D-LAGs.

An investigation of possible sources of inefficiency in the design of LA-grammar leads to the notion of sound LA-grammars. We shall see that the elimination of certain well-defined redundancies does not affect generative capacity. Consequently, there exists a weakly equivalent sound LA-grammar for any LA-grammar which is not sound (Theorem 11, 9.5.11).

Finally, computational complexity is specified for the class of C-LAGs. Unambiguous C-LAGs are proven to parse in linear time (Theorem 12, 10.1.2)—a result which surpasses all previous general-purpose parsers, both in efficiency and in the size of the class of languages covered.[19] In the case of ambiguous C-LAGs, we distinguish between syntactic and lexical ambiguities. Sound syntactically ambiguous C-LAGs are shown to parse in n^2 (Theorem 13, 10.4.1). Because for any LA-grammar there exists a weakly equivalent sound LA-grammar (Theorem 11), any syntactically ambiguous C-language can be parsed in n^2. Finally, for any lexically ambiguous C-language, there exists a C-LAG which will "packed parse" it in linear time (Theorem 14, 10.5.12).

In summary, previous general purpose parsers achieve n^3 (packed-parsing) complexity for arbitrary context-free grammars. For an arbitrary C-language, on the other hand, there exists an LA-grammar (C-LAG) which which will packed-parse it in n^2.

The descriptive power and the computational efficiency of LA-grammar derives from a design which combines certain features of Finite State Automata with certain features of Categorial Grammar. Because of its relationship to Finite State Automata, LA-grammar resembles the "Markovian approach"[20] which was explored in the beginnings of natural-language processing. A conceptual approach which was proposed earlier, but did not succeed, is not necessarily wrong. Rather, the rediscovery—independent of the earlier tradition[21]—may be taken as an indication that the approach is a natural one. The reason it did not work before is that important ingredients were still missing (e.g., sentence-start categories and categorial operations).

1.5   Applications and Future Work

LA-parsers are input-output equivalent with LA-grammars, and use the rules of the grammars directly. Thus, there is neither preprocessing nor precompilation, which greatly facilitates debugging and expanding ("up-scaling") of complex natural-language grammars. Furthermore, the excellent theoretical complexity results for LA-grammar translate into extremely fast implementations. The linear analysis of any sentence in the current sample set (cf. Appendix C), including twenty word sentences with several syntactic ambiguities, takes no more than 0.2 seconds central processor time on a Hewlett-Packard 9000 work station.

LA-grammar has been implemented as a sizable fragment of English with a database semantics and a lexicon of 8,000 words (stems). The range of constructions covered is indicated in Appendix C. Furthermore, LA-grammar has been im-

---

[19]For example, the Earley algorithm is of complexity n^2 for unambiguous context-free grammars. The set of languages accepted by unambiguous context-free grammars is considerably smaller than that accepted by unambiguous C-LAGs.

[20]Markov (1954), Yngve (1955). A brief historical summary of Markov models may be found in Damerau (1971). See also Hutchins (1986).

[21]The time-linear derivation order and the computation of possible continuations on the level of "next words" was developed during the attempt to implement the categorial grammar defined in Hausser (1984a) as an efficient parser. The partial similarity with Markov models was realized later.

plemented for a fragment of German, but so far without frame-theoretic semantics, and with a lexicon of only about 800 words. The linguistic motivations behind the LA-grammars for English and German syntax are described in detail in Hausser (1986). Small LA-grammars have been written for Japanese, Polish, and French, as well as for numerous formal languages, many of which are defined and illustrated in the following chapters.

What are the next steps in the development of LA-grammar? One obvious requirement is expansion of the syntactico-semantic and lexical analysis to cover an entire natural language. Given the fact that LA-grammar scales up remarkably well, this task could be accomplished fairly quickly with favorable conditions.

But parallel to the quantitative development, we should begin with the implementation of the pragmatics. At present, the semantic representations (frame-theoretic icons) are generated on a sentence-by-sentence basis. What is needed next is a facility for embedding these structures into a knowledge base. This is again a theoretical task, which involves utilization of the sequential structure of the text, the correct pragmatic interpretation of quantifiers and pronouns, and the translation of grammatical case information into the correct pragmatic functions.

Like left-associative syntax and semantics, the theory of left-associative pragmatics should be developed on the basis of an experimental implementation. Before the first tentative pragmatic interpretation functions can be defined, however, construction of a temporally structured internal context and definition of a semantic hierarchy[22] is required. Once an initial "operating system of pragmatic interpretation" has been built, the syntactico-semantic facility of the grammar may be used automatically to expand the knowledge base (context) by parsing and interpreting larger and larger texts. This automated process of pragmatic interpretation will lead incrementally to a more sophisticated context representation.

It will also provide the data for more refined functions of pragmatic interpretation, and it will result in a simple, language oriented capability for inference and reasoning. As more experience is gathered in automatic pragmatic interpretation of frame-theoretic icons relative to a knowledge base, the inverse process of expressing database information in natural language can be approached. This requires that the context structure grows further to include a "pragmatic operating system for verbalization."

Modeling natural-language understanding and natural-language communication is not only revealing for further theoretical analysis, but also of tremendous practical value for a number of important applications, such as information retrieval,[23], database interfaces, content analysis, database maintenance and up-scaling, dialog systems, machine translation, and foreign language teaching.

---

[22]For a summary of the considerable cognitive science literature on this subject see Rumelhart (1977), pp. 219 f. See also Brachman (1979) for a review of data-structures called "semantic nets."

[23]See Salton and McGill (1983)

2. Grammar and Interpretation

This chapter presents basic criteria of adequacy for grammars. Section 2.1 explains the empirical limitations of constituent-structure analysis. Section 2.2 presents the basic theory of natural-language communication. Section 2.3 illustrates the process of understanding a sentence with a simple formal example. Section 2.4 presents the Criteria of Psychological Well-Foundedness. Section 2.5 shows that grammars within current paradigms of linguistic analysis are not psychologically well-founded.

2.1 Limitations of Constituent Structures

The problem of contemporary linguistics is not finding an analysis, but to find the **right** analysis. For a given string (sentence) a multitude of different structural analyses (tree structures) may be defined within a formal rule system. Until now grammarians have based their choice of a particular tree structure on intuitions which are inherently semantic. These semantically motivated trees are called "constituent structures." Constituent structures go back to the "immediate constituent analysis" of Bloomfield (1933).[1]

What started out as a piece of structuralist methodology[2] reappeared in transformational grammar as part of the "innate human language capability." Chomsky (1957) appeals to constituent structures in order to refute a "Markovian analysis" of natural language.[3] Instead, Chomsky argues for several abstract levels of grammatical analysis, which are motivated by linguistic intuition, and are claimed to result in a simplified description.[4]

---

[1]Bloomfield illustrates constituent analysis briefly with some simple sentences (op.cit., pp. 161, 167). But a more detailed application is presented under the heading of morphology (op. cit., pp. 209 f, 221 f). "The principle of immediate constituents will lead us, for example, to class a form like *gentlemanly* not as a compound word, but as a derived secondary word, since the immediate constituents are the bound form *-ly* and the underlying form *gentleman*" (op. cit., p. 210).

This example is also discussed in Harris (1951), pp. 278 – 280, who presents immediate constituents in a more technical style, based on the notions "sequence," "class," and "substitution." The methodology of substitution tests—again mainly in morphology—is due to Harris. Bloomfield uses "substitution" only as a phonological term.

[2]Bloomfield (1933), Wells (1947), Harris (1951), Bloch (1953). For a more recent discussion of syntactic hierarchies from the viewpoint of tagmemic grammar see Longacre (1983), pp. 273 f.

[3]"In short, the approach to the analysis of grammaticalness suggested here in terms of a finite state Markov process that produces sentences from left to right, appears to lead to a dead end." Chomsky (1957), p. 24.

[4]"If a language can be described in an elementary, left-to-right manner in terms of a single level (i.e., if it is a finite state language) then this description may indeed be simplified by the construction of such higher levels; but to generate non-finite state languages such as English, we need fundamentally different methods, and a more general concept of 'linguistic level'." Chomsky (1957), p. 25.

Constituent structures are formally defined as trees which fulfill the following two conditions:

2.1.1 The Definition of Constituent Structure

1. Words or constituents which belong together semantically are to be dominated directly and exhaustively by a node. Thus, *found a bone* in the sentence *Fido found a bone* is directly dominated by a node (e.g., VP), while there is no node that directly and exhaustively dominates *Fido found*.
2. The branches of a constituent-structure tree may not cross. This condition is also known as the "non-tangling condition."

Constituent structure analysis cannot directly account for sentences where two parts which belong together semantically are not adjacent in the surface. A classic example is "discontinous constituents" as illustrated in 2.1.2:

2.1.2 An Illustration of the Constituent-Structure Paradox

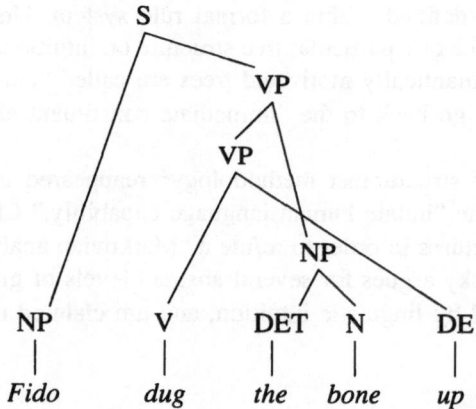

A tree like 2.1.2 is prohibited, because it violates the requirement that the lines of the tree may not cross. Yet an alternative tree without crossing lines would violate the assumption that parts which belong together semantically must be dominated directly and exhaustively by a node characterizing them as a constituent.

Given that expressions which belong together from the viewpoint of semantic intuition need not be adjacent in the surface, contemporary linguistic theories based on constituent structure are faced with a problem. How can they account for the facts of natural language?

2.1.3 Methods Employed to Circumvent the Constituent-Structure Paradox

1. Weakening of the first condition of 2.1.1:

(a) *Transformational approach.* Constituent-structure analysis applies only to "deep structures." Discontinuous surfaces are derived from the deep structures via transformations, whereby the surfaces do not obey the constituent-structure conditions.

(b) *Semantic feature component.* In GPSG and LFG, constituent-structure analysis is applied only where structurally possible. In problematic constructions a second mechanism, namely a semantic feature component, is used to express the semantic intuitions in question.

2. Weakening of the second condition of 2.1.1:

(a) *Tree-linking grammar.* By postulating three-dimensional trees, the non-tangling condition is effectively circumvented. However, this approach discards all linguistic constraints and mathematical knowledge based on the notions of precedence and dominance in traditional two-dimensional trees.

(b) *Orthogonal grammar.* Instead of requiring that constituents which belong together semantically must be dominated directly and exhaustively by a node, Orthogonal Syntax merely requires that they should be in a functor/argument relation, which means that they must be *adjacent* in the semantic representation. This attempt to save the basic intuitions of constituent-structure analysis is accommodated by the definition of a new kind of tree structure which separates the surface order (vertical dimension) and the semantic order (horizontal dimension).

We see that all syntactic proposals to circumvent the constituent-structure paradox amount to a principled weakening of the constituent-structure approach. Yet the basic assumptions of constituent structure have never been properly examined. Why should semantic hierarchies obey the conditions of 2.1.1? After all, building a semantic hierarchy is not identical with building a constituent structure. The real purpose of a semantic hierarchy is characterizing semantic relations for the purpose of pragmatic interpretation.

Once we accept this conclusion, we may look for an inherently syntactic principle to motivate the syntax, and an inherently semantic principle to motivate the semantics. But first we must have an understanding of what pragmatic interpretation is.

2.2 Basic Communication

The central task of linguistic analysis in the areas of synchronic syntax, semantics, and pragmatics is to explain the functioning of language in communication. In order to clarify the respective roles of the components of a grammar, let us consider the following question: What happens when a speaker utters a meaningful sentence, and the hearer understands it?

The answer depends on the non-verbal **context** of the speaker-hearer.

2.2.1 Definition of the Speaker-Hearer Context

> The *context* of the speaker is defined as an internal representation of what he or she perceives and remembers at the moment (or time interval) of the utterance. Similarly, the context of the hearer is a representation of what he or she perceives and remembers at the moment of interpretation of the utterance.[5]

This notion of context must be clearly distinguished from verbal context, such as "intensional" and "extensional" contexts (cf. Section15.4).

Our notion of context differs from that of other authors because it is defined as a speaker-hearer internal structure. Van Dijk (1977), for example, defines contexts as "courses of events" (op.cit., p. 192) which are speaker-hearer external. The question of whether the utterance context should be defined as a speaker-hearer internal structure or as part of the external environment is crucial for the theory of semantics and pragmatics, and is discussed in detail in Chapters 11 – 15.

The active part of the context, i.e., what the speaker-hearer is conscious of at a given moment, is called the **subcontext**.[6] The context and subcontext of speaker and hearer will differ inasmuch as they represent the minds of different persons. Furthermore, utterance and interpretation of a sign may occur at different times and places (cf. the postcard example in Section 11.3).

The context is built up from elementary concepts (based on elementary perceptions), complex concepts (i.e., mental structures based on elementary concepts), and relationships between concepts. To have a **language** means not only to have (i) a set of simple surfaces (words), and (ii) a syntactic mechanism for combining these word surfaces into complex surfaces, but also (iii) that a subset of the concepts (called word meanings) is firmly attached to the word surfaces.

To utter a meaningful sentence is to make an image of a relevant part of the speaker's subcontext. The speaker depicts part of his subcontext by building an image with word meanings. He cannot make a simple copy of the subcontext, because the only concepts he can use for the image are those which are attached to language surfaces, i.e., concepts which double as meanings.

The speaker transmits the image by uttering the **surfaces** attached to those meanings from which the image was constructed. The surface constitutes a sign which can be decoded by anybody who speaks the language. To be part of a language community is to share not only the same set of surfaces, but also the same set of associated meanings. Concepts in general, and meanings in particular, exist only in

---

[5]Hausser (1979b,c).

[6]McDonald et al. (1987) use the term "relevant portion of the situation" or RPS (op. cit., p. 161). We avoid the term "situation" because it is biased toward a description of the external world, rather than certain internal states of the speaker or the hearer. For a related discussion see Section 12.5.

the minds of the agents. In other words, the external tokens of signs consist solely of their surface. Only the internal counterparts of the signs' surfaces in the minds of the respective agents have meanings attached to them.

The hearer interprets the sign by going from the surfaces to the meanings, i.e., to the concepts attached to the surfaces in the hearer's mind. To understand a sentence is to unify the meaning structure expressed by the sign with the hearer's internal context. But the hearer's context may be a large system of different domains, memories, etc. A sign is properly interpreted only if its meaning is unified with the **correct** subpart of the hearer's context. Chapter 11 presents a theory of pragmatics which explains how the hearer deduces the correct "filing address" of a meaning from the STAR-point[7] of the sign, the time-linear structure of the sign, and the meaning types of the parts of the sign.

This explanation of the most basic principle of natural-language communication resembles the cognitive psychology approach of Anderson and Bower (1980),[8] but differs substantially from more traditional models of information transfer, which are based on the stimulus-response model of behaviorism[9] and/or try to make due with the concepts of the communication theory by Shannon and Weaver (1949). Eco's (1975) theory of semiotics, for example, attempts to explain natural-language communication on the basis of a "floating buoy model," and is formulated in terms of "code" originating from a "source," which is "transmitted" through a "channel" and decoded at a "destination." Similar models of communication are Grice's (1957) "bus bell model,"[10] and Dretske's (1981) "door bell model."

While our approach is compatible with an information-theoretic analysis `a la Shannon and Weaver (1949), it is not concerned with the mechanics of transferring a piece of code through communication channels, but with the process of **producing** and **understanding** meaningful signs. Our central notion of **depicting contextual substructures** is based on speaker-hearer internal databases, and a definition of language as an inherently two-level structure, comprising surface forms and literal meanings. These notions go beyond the basic assumptions of Shannon and Weaver (1949).

2.3   Database Semantics and Pragmatic Interpretation

Let us illustrate the functioning of natural language outlined above with a simple example. The relevant subcontext of the interpretation may be defined as a frame-theoretic database, for example 2.3.1.

---

[7]STAR-point stands for the Space-Time-Agent-Recipient point of origin of a sign.
[8]See pp. 103 f. of Anderson and Bower (1980).
[9]E.g., Quine (1960).
[10]See Section 11.2 for further discussion.

2.3.1 Definition of a Subcontext as a Database

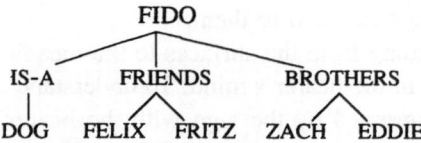

A **frame-name**, e.g., "FIDO," has zero or more **slots**, e.g., "IS-A," "FRIENDS," and "BROTHERS." These slots may have zero or more **fillers**, where the fillers may themselves be frame-names and may as such dominate other slots and fillers. 2.3.1 expresses that FIDO is a dog, has FELIX and FRITZ as friends, and ZACH and EDDIE as brothers. These semantic relations may also be expressed with model-theoretic semantics.[11] Consider 2.3.2:

2.3.2 A Model-Theoretic Representation of 2.3.1

Let $\mathcal{A}$ be a model-structure $(A,I,J,\leq,F)$.

$A =_{def} \{a_0, a_1, a_2, a_3, a_4\}$

$I =_{def} \{i_1\}$

$J =_{def} \{j_1\}$

$F(fido')(i_1, j_1) =_{def} a_0$

$F(felix')(i_1, j_1) =_{def} a_1$

$F(fritz')(i_1, j_1) =_{def} a_2$

$F(zach')(i_1, j_1) =_{def} a_3$

$F(eddie')(i_1, j_1) =_{def} a_4$

$F(dog')(i_1, j_1) =_{def} \{a_0\}$

$F(fido\text{-}friends')(i_1, j_1) =_{def} \{a_1, a_2\}$

$F(fido\text{-}brothers')(i_1, j_1) =_{def} \{a_3, a_4\}$

Technical details aside, 2.3.2 expresses the same facts as 2.3.1, though in a more cumbersome fashion. The inferences rendered by the model-theoretic definition are easily replicated within the frame-theoretic system. The latter approach has the advantage that the inferences can actually be used. A query like "Does Fido have brothers?" will elicit the correct response from a suitable implementation of 2.3.1, whereas an implementation of 2.3.2 would be much too cumbersome for practical use. In this book we will employ a frame-theoretic rather than model-theoretic formalism for the representation of contexts and literal meanings. But it should be understood that these frame-theoretic structures could also be presented model-theoretically.[12]

---

[11]The exact definitions of the intensional logic used in 2.3.2 are explicitly given in Section 15.5.

[12]Much of the discussion of semantics and pragmatics in Chapters 11 – 15 will be formulated in model-theoretic terms.

As an example of a literal meaning, consider 2.3.3.

2.3.3 The Semantic Representation of *Fido likes Zach*

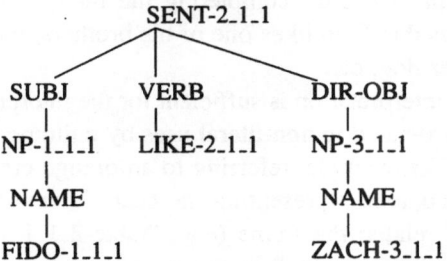

This kind of semantic analysis is called database semantics because the literal meaning of the sign is represented as a minimal database, called a **frame-theoretic icon**, which characterizes the semantic relations expressed in the sentence *Fido likes Zach*. Our notion of *database semantics* does not mean "a semantics for databases,"[13] but "a semantics expressed in the form of minimal databases."

The interpretation of the frame-theoretic icon 2.3.3 relative to the context-model 2.3.1 results in the new context-model 2.3.4.

2.3.4 The Context Model Resulting from Interpretation of 2.3.3

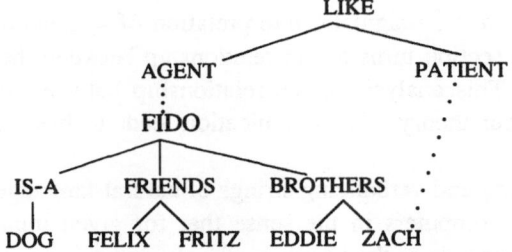

How does this new database come about? In a frame-theoretic icon like 2.3.3 we may distinguish two kinds of fillers: fillers like NP-1_1_1 which dominate other slots, and fillers like FIDO-1_1_1, which do not. Let us call the former kind "non-terminal fillers" and the later kind "terminal fillers." As the base[14] of a terminal filler we use the stem of the analyzed word form from which the frame was derived.

Consider now the pragmatic interpretation functions which lead to the construction of 2.3.4. One function, call it REF, takes the NP-frames in the frame-theoretic icon and establishes reference by relating the bases of the terminal fillers FIDO-1_1_1 and ZACH-3_1_1 to corresponding frame-names in the database 2.3.1. A second

---

[13] As, for example, in Sowa (1984), p. 302.

[14] For reasons explained in Section 3.4, semantic frame-names like FIDO-1_1_1 consist of two parts, namely the base, e.g., FIDO, and the index, e.g., -1_1_1.

function, call it REL, takes the verb-frame SENT-2_1_1 with its slots SUBJ and DIR-OBJ and builds a new frame in the context-model, which is called LIKE and has the slots AGENT and PATIENT, filled by FIDO and ZACH, respectively.[15] This process models understanding in that, after completing the interpretation of 2.3.3 relative to 2.3.1, the robot knows that Fido likes one of his brothers, that Zach is a dog, that Zach is liked by another dog, etc.

This simple approach to pragmatic interpretation is sufficient for the interpretation of literal use. Furthermore, it can be extended to non-literal uses by building a more sophisticated context representation. For example, referring to an orange crate with the word *table* requires a structured context, representing the hearer's environment at the utterance moment. After REF related the frame (e.g., "table-2_1_1") of the utterance token to the corresponding frame "table" in the (non-episodic) context, the correct reference comes about by a sequence of contextual inferences. These contextual inferences are triggered by the fact that the representation of the utterance situation does not contain a "table"-frame. Assuming this representation contains an "orange crate"-frame and a "baseball bat"-frame, the inference system will use properties dominated by these frames to determine the orange crate as the intended referent.

2.4   Criteria of Adequacy of Grammar

The previous section described the pragmatic interpretation of a meaning relative to an utterance context. This section turns to the relationship between the meaning and the surface of the sign. This analysis of the relationship between syntax and semantics in the context of our theory of communication leads to basic criteria of adequacy for grammar.

The process of understanding and verbalizing strings of natural-language symbols is analogous for people and computers in the sense that for given inputs certain outputs are derived. If the system is in the hearer mode, the input is an unanalyzed surface string[16] and the output a semantic interpretation based on syntactic analysis. If the system is in the speaker mode, the input is a semantic representation and the output a surface expression representing its meaning.

In other words, the interpretation of a sentence involves a "surface-meaning mapping" which takes unanalyzed surface strings as input and gives semantic representations as output. The verbalization of a meaning, on the other hand, involves a "meaning-surface mapping" which takes semantic representations as input and gives unanalyzed surface strings as output. A system which provides a surface-meaning mapping is input-output equivalent (I/O-equivalent) to an analyzer. A system which

---

[15]Since the frame-theoretic icon is build simultaneously with the left-associative derivation (cf. Section 3.3), pragmatic interpretation may commence during the syntactico/semantic analysis.

[16]I.e., a sequence of word forms, such as *Fido found a bone*.

provides a meaning-surface mapping is I/O-equivalent to a generator.

Combining these considerations with two other rather obvious demands on formal grammars, we arrive at the following criteria:

2.4.1 The Criteria of Procedural Adequacy

A grammar of natural language is procedurally adequate if and only if it

1. provides an explicit formal statement of the grammatical rules;[17]
2. provides a bidirectional surface-meaning mapping;
3. is inherently decidable.[18]

The next question is in which **order** the surface-meaning mapping is to be executed. Possible derivation orders used in conventional systems are left-to-right, right-to-left, top-down, bottom-up, left-corner, right-corner, etc. Which derivation order is the correct order for natural language?

Because the hearer understands the beginning of a sentence without knowing how it is going to be continued,[19] and because the speaker can decide in midstream how to continue a sentence,[20] the following hypothesis is psychologically motivated:

2.4.2 The Derivational Order Hypothesis

> The derivational order in the generation and interpretation of natural-language expressions is the time-linear order of the words in the surface.

Normal communication between speaker and hearer always involves a bidirectional surface-meaning mapping and always satisfies the Derivational Order Hypothesis. Therefore, these two structural principles constitute a necessary[21] part of the I/O-conditions of language use by the speaker-hearer. Note that we specify the I/O-conditions of language use in purely functional terms, without recourse to "innate ideas," or "universals" delimiting natural languages from formal languages.

---

[17]A methodological desideratum inherited from generative grammar in general. See Section 6.1.

[18]Peters & Ritchie (1973) showed that the *Aspects* model of transformational grammar (Chomsky (1965)) is equivalent to a Turing machine, and therefore not decidable. Similar results hold for GB, Montague Grammar, GPSG (Uszkoreit & Peters (1982), Shieber, Stucky, Uszkoreit & Robinson (1983)), and LFG. Note that we are talking about the *inherent* decidability of a rule system; of course, any rule system can be made decidable by adding artificial restrictions (for example, an arbitrary, but finite, limit on the number of embeddings in Transformational Grammar, "finite closure" in GPSG, or exclusion of "nonbranching dominance cycles" in LFG). For a related discussion regarding computational complexity see Barton et al. (1987), pp. 19 f. A summary of different criteria of adequacy in generative grammar may be found in the postscript by Wasow in Sells (1985).

[19]That the hearer is often able to *guess* the continuation, enabling him to complete the sentence before the speaker, provides additional support to a linear (or left-associative) approach to syntax.

[20]A limiting case of a continuation is the speaker's decision to break off and start over ('false starts'). "Speech is irreversible. That is its fatality. What has been said cannot be unsaid, *except by adding to it*: to correct here, is, oddly enough, to continue." (R. Barthes, 1986, p. 76).

[21]The bidirectional surface-meaning mapping and the time-linear derivation order constitute necessary, but not sufficient, I/O-conditions of language use. That is, while no natural-language use will violate these conditions, there may well be further constraints.

A grammar is I/O-equivalent to the speaker-hearer only if it satisfies both the Criteria of Procedural Adequacy[22] and the Derivational Order Hypothesis. Since it is unlikely that the grammatical structure of natural languages evolved without being compatible with the I/O-conditions of language use, it is important that formal grammars of natural language are designed to be I/O-equivalent to the speaker-hearer.

2.4.3 The Criteria of Psychological Well-Foundedness

A generative grammar is a psychologically well-founded model of the structure of natural language only if the grammar conforms to

1. the Criteria of Procedural Adequacy, and
2. the Derivational Order Hypothesis.

Given the widely acknowledged need for structural constraints in grammatical theory, linguists should welcome the challenge of designing psychologically well-founded grammars. The resulting systems, which are I/O-equivalent to people and computers, are well-motivated theoretically, and have a wide range of practical applications in natural-language processing.

2.5   Current Paradigms

The Criteria of Psychological Well-Foundedness demand that a generative grammar analyze natural language in a way which is compatible with the function of language in communication. Let us briefly consider whether today's grammars are psychologically well-founded.

Within generative grammar two paradigms may be distinguished:

1. *Categorial Grammar* (hence C-grammar,[23] e.g., Montague Grammar,[24] Orthogonal Grammar[25])

2. *Phrase-Structure Grammar* (hence PS-grammar,[26] e.g., Transformational Grammar,[27] GB[28] LFG,[29] GPSG[30])

---

[22]Only clauses 2 and 3 of the Criteria of Procedural Adequacy are relevant for I/O-equivalence with the speaker-hearer. Clause 1 is not specifically excluded, however, because the explicit formal statement of the grammatical rules is a methodological precondition for evaluating clauses 2 and 3 in a meaningful way.

[23]The formalism of C-grammar is based on Leśnieswki (1929) and Ajdukiewicz (1935). This formalism was first applied to the description of natural language by Bar-Hillel (1953).

[24]Montague (1974), Chapter 8, henceforth "PTQ."

[25]Hausser (1984a).

[26]The formalism of PS-grammar is based on the rewriting systems of Post (1936). This formalism was first applied to the description of natural language by Chomsky (1957).

[27]Chomsky (1965).

[28]Chomsky (1981).

[29]Bresnan (1984).

[30]Gazdar et al. (1985).

Grammars belonging to these paradigms differ in their rules, categories, and derivation orders.

Consider the derivational structure of an indirectly interpreting Montague system (PTQ), the most influential approach within the C-grammar paradigm.

2.5.1 The Derivational Structure of Montague Grammar

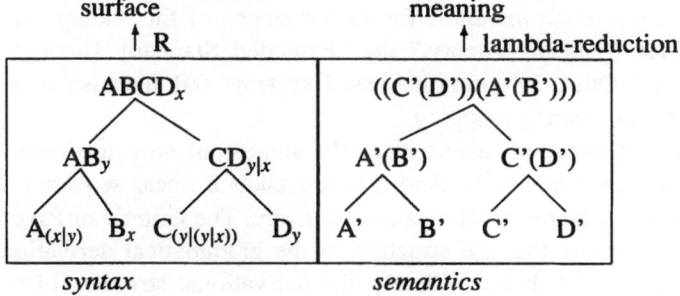

The grammatical derivation order of Montague Grammar is uniformly bottom-up. The syntactic and the semantic tree are derived simultaneously. Montague Grammar has a well-defined model-theoretic semantics, but there are no unidirectional mappings from the surface to the meaning or from the meaning to the surface. The reason is that both R (i.e., the mapping from the syntactic tree to the surface) and lambda-reduction (i.e., the mapping from the semantic tree to the reduced meaning formula) are defined in only one direction.[31] Other systems within the C-grammar paradigm fail likewise to provide a bidirectional surface-meaning mapping.

Next, consider the derivational structure of Government-Binding Theory (Chomsky (1981)), the most influential approach within the paradigm of PS-grammar.

2.5.2 The Derivational Structure of Government-Binding Theory

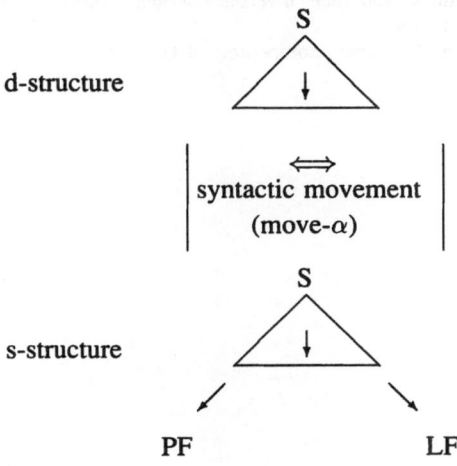

The grammatical derivation order of Government-Binding Theory is conceptually top-down. Input to the derivation is not a sentence or a meaning, but an abstract start-symbol S. The task of a parser based on such a grammar consists in finding a path from a given surface (PF or phonetic form) back to the start-symbol S. There is no representation of meaning. Instead, the d-structure and the LF (logical form) are suggested as input to a semantic component yet to be defined. Similar considerations hold *mutatis mutandis* for earlier stages of this theory, such as the "Revised Extended Standard Theory," the "Extended Standard Theory," and the "Standard Theory." Other PS-grammar based systems fail likewise to provide a bidirectional surface-meaning mapping.

A speaker, on the other hand, takes a hierarchical meaning structure and transduces it into a linear sequence of words. And a hearer takes a linear sequence of words and transduces it into a hierarchical meaning structure. The Criteria of Psychological Well-Foundedness require that the structure of the grammatical derivation mirrors this process in the speaker-hearer. Clearly, the derivational structure of the theory of Government and Binding as well as its numerous predecessors does not satisfy the Criteria of Psychological Well-Foundedness.[32]

Chomsky argues, however, that the purpose of these grammars is not really to model what the speaker-hearer does when communicating in natural language ("performance"), but to model the innate human language capacity ("competence"). Since the derivational structure of GB-theory is not compatible with the I/O-conditions of language use, Chomsky claims that the innate human language capacity evolved independently of language use. Given the general facts of nature, this is a highly unlikely assumption. A theory of language learning based on a derivational structure incompatible with the I/O-conditions of language use is psychologically implausible.

---

[31]R and lambda-reduction are many-one functions, and their inverses one-many relations. See Hausser (1984a), chapters 2 and 4, for further discussion.

[32]The same holds for the derivational structure of the current competitors of GB.

3. Outline of Left-Associative Grammar

This chapter outlines a grammar which satisfies the Criteria of Psychological Well-Foundedness. Section 3.1 presents a syntactic theory which satisfies the Derivational Order Hypothesis. Section 3.2 illustrates how the syntactic analysis of Left-Associative Grammar is displayed by the associated NEWCAT parsers. Section 3.3 describes a semantic interpretation for this syntax which satisfies the Criteria of Psychological Adequacy. Section 3.4 illustrates the system with the analysis of a "garden path sentence." Section 3.5 summarizes the descriptive, methodological and heuristic advantages of left-associative grammar.

3.1 Left-Associative Syntax

The first step in constructing a psychologically well-founded grammar—in the specific sense of 2.4.3—is the design of a syntax with a time-linear derivation order. The time-linear derivation order corresponds formally to the principle of left-associative combinations.[1] The left-associative derivation order is presented below in comparison with the conceptual derivation orders of C-grammar and PS-grammar.

3.1.1 Three Grammatical Derivation Orders

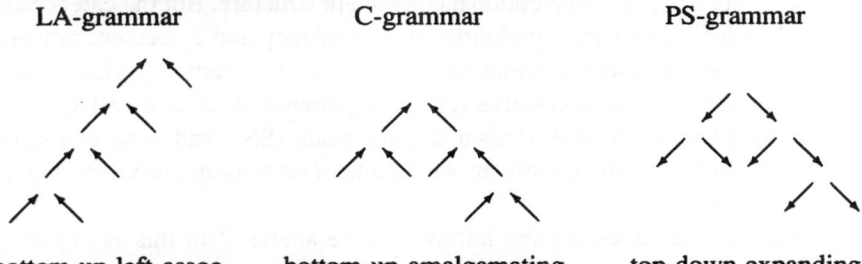

LA-grammar	C-grammar	PS-grammar
bottom-up left-assoc.	bottom-up amalgamating	top-down expanding

A grammar which uses the derivation order of left-associative combinations is called a left-associative grammar or LA-grammar. The grammatical derivation order of LA-grammar is completely regular and consists of combining a "sentence start" and a "next word" into a new sentence start. This grammatical derivation order reflects

---

[1] *"a+b+c can be interpreted as ((a+b)+c) or as (a+(b+c)). We say that + is left-associative if operands are grouped left to right as in ((a+b)+c)."* Aho & Ullman (1979), p. 47. Identification of the time-linear derivation order of language with the formal principle of left-associative combinations was first proposed in Hausser (1985).

the time-linear[2] production and interpretation of natural language (hypothesis 2.4.2). Moreover, it is well suited to double as the procedural derivation order (see Section 3.5).

LA-grammar evolved in the attempt to implement the Categorial Grammar defined in Hausser (1984a) as a parsing program. The relationship between Categorial Grammar and LA-grammar is illustrated in 3.1.2 and 3.1.3.

3.1.2 A Traditional Analysis in Categorial Grammar

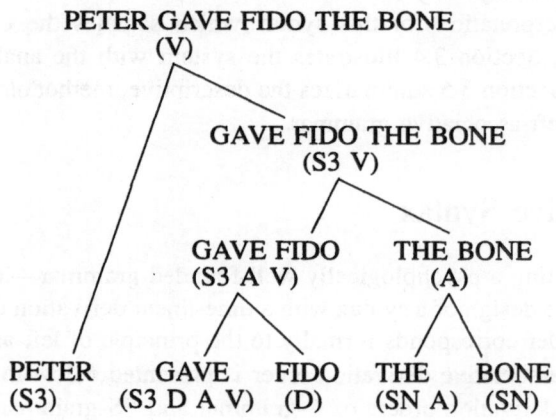

The tree structure 3.1.2 is a conventional constituent structure. But the categories are of a special variety in that they explicitly encode valency and agreement properties. *Peter* is a third-person singular nominative (S3); *gave* is a verb (V) which takes an (S3), a dative (D), and an accusative (A) as arguments; *Fido* is a dative (D); *the* is an accusative (A) which still needs a singular noun (SN); and *bone* is a singular noun (SN). As in Categorial Grammar, we assume a bottom-up derivation based on category cancelling.[3]

Next, consider the corresponding left-associative analysis[4] of this example:

---

[2]The time-linear derivation order characteristic of LA-grammar must be distinguished from Hockett's (1966) notion of a "linear generative grammar," which is simply a phrase structure grammar without transformations.

[3]A category segment X in the category (X Y Z) can be cancelled by a category (W) only if X and W *correspond*. In 3.1.2 and 3.1.3, category correspondence is defined in terms of *identity*: X in (X Y Z) corresponds to (W) only if X = W. The actual categorization of LA-grammar uses a more indirect notion of category correspondence, which results in a less transparent process of cancelling, but a linguistically much more economical analysis of word forms. See Chapter 4.

[4]The NEWCAT derivation of 3.1.3 is given in 3.2.2.

3.1.3 An Analysis in LA-Grammar

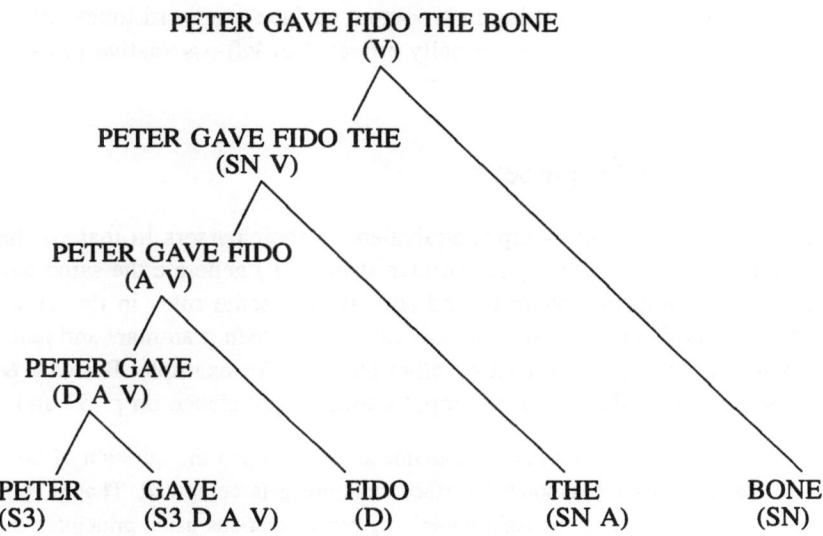

3.1.3 assigns the same categories as 3.1.2. But the left-associative analysis uses a completely regular procedure of combining a sentence start (ss) with a next word (nw) into a new sentence start. Within constituent-structure analysis, *Peter gave Fido the* is not acceptable as an intermediate expression because it violates the substitution tests on which constituent structure is conceptually and methodologically based. LA-grammar, on the other hand, is based on the quite different notion of **possible continuations**; an intermediate expression like *Peter gave Fido the* is accepted because it can be continued into a complete well-formed sentence.

The input to a left-associative rule is a sentence start *ss* and a next word *nw*. A sentence start $[(w_1 \; w_2 \; ... \; w_n)(cat_{ss})]$ is an ordered pair consisting of a list of word surfaces and a category. A next word $[w_{n+1} \; (cat_{nw})]$ is an ordered pair consisting of a word surface and a category. Categories in LA-grammar are defined as lists of category segments,[5] e.g., (S3 D A V).

3.1.4 The Form of Left-Associative Rules

$$r_i: [\text{CAT-1 CAT-2}] \Rightarrow [\text{rp}_i \; \text{CAT-3}]$$

A left-associative rule r_i consists of (i) a characteristic categorial operation, and a (ii) a rule package. The **categorial operation** specifies the possible input categories of the sentence start and the next word, and derives an output category. The **rule package** rp$_i$ of r_i lists the rules which may possibly apply after r_i was successful.

---

[5]See Section 6.2 for the algebraic definition of LA-grammar.

When a left-associative rule applies, the surface of the next word is appended to the surface of the sentence start. This completely regular procedure of Surface Concatention (SC)—resulting in an output surface one word longer than that of the input sentence start—is not formally reflected in left-associative rules, but handled implicitly.

3.2   NEWCAT parsers

LA-grammars are input-output equivalent to their parsers in that (i) they take the same input (i.e., an unanalyzed surface string), (ii) generate the same output (a left-associative syntactic analysis), and (iii) use the same rules in the same derivation order. The notion of input-output equivalence between grammars and parsers is much stronger here than when used by other authors. For example, Berwick & Weinberg (1984) introduce the notion of "input-output" equivalence on p. 57 and continue:

> Note that this definition of equivalence leaves open the question of how it is exactly that the annotated surface structure gets computed. That is, a parser could reconstruct the right underlying representations using principles entirely unrelated to the grammar and yet still be input-output equivalent to the grammar.

If the grammar takes an abstract S-symbol as input and the parser an unanalyzed surface, then the grammar and the parser are not input equivalent in our view. Furthermore, according to our definition (cf. Section 8.1), a grammar and a parser are output equivalent only if the grammar and the parser use the same rules in the same derivation order.

The components of our LA-parser, called NEWCAT, are a grammar, a rule-compiler, a lexicon written as a list of analyzed words, a function which turns the lexicon into a hash-table, and a motor. The motor, the rule-compiler, and the software for creating the lexicon hash-table are the same for all LA-grammars, no matter whether they describe formal or natural languages. In other words, LA-parsers for different languages differ solely in the rules of the grammar, and the definition of the words in the lexicon.

The NEWCAT parser uses Lisp translations of the rules of an LA-grammar.[6] As an example of such a translation consider 3.2.1, which compares the abstract formulation of a left-associative rule with its the actual Lisp source code.[7]

---

[6]Obviously, LA-grammar is not restricted to Lisp; the rules of an LA-grammar can be parsed in any general purpose programming language. For example, there exists a version of LA-grammar in Prolog.

[7]The rule r-2 is part of the LA-grammar for the context sensitive language $a^k b^k c^k$ defined in 6.4.3.

3.2.1 Abstract LA-Rule and Corresponding Lisp Source Code

1. Abstract formulation:
   r-2: [(bXc)(b)] $\Rightarrow$ [{r-2, r-3}(Xc)]

2. Source code:

```
(defrule r-2

  ;local-vars
  ()

  ;input-condition
  (and (eq (car ss-cat) 'b)
       (eq (car (last ss-cat)) 'c)
       (equal nw-cat '(b)))

  ;output-condition
  (cdr ss-cat)

  ;rule package
  (r-2 r-3))
```

The relation between the abstract rule and its translation into Lisp is perfectly transparent. The categorial operation of the rule is specified by the input and output conditions, while the rule package is specified as a list of rules.

The function *defrule* in 3.2.1 represents the rule-compiler,[8] which takes (i) a rule name, (ii) a (possibly empty) list of local variables, (iii) an input condition, (iv) an output condition and (v) a list of rules as input, and outputs an expression in which certain additional clauses common to all rules have been added. In other words, the rule-compiler takes care of the general format, and allows the grammar writer to concentrate on the linguistic content of the rules. The Lisp concepts required for the definition of LA-grammar rules within the general format of the rule compiler are simple and straightforward.[9]

A left-associative derivation begins with the rule package START, which contains all rules which may possibly apply at the beginning of a sentence. If a rule r_i in START is successful on the ordered pair consisting of the first two words, the rule

---

[8]The rule-compiler was implemented by Gerald Klix (University of Munich). For use on a PC, the LA-grammar shell was translated into PC-SCHEME because it is considerably smaller than Golden Common Lisp.

[9]At the University of Munich, students who had never used computers before mastered LA-grammar writing within a few weeks. The students were provided with 640 KB personal computers running PC-scheme, and the general shell of LA-grammar, i.e., the motor, the rule-compiler, and the hash-table function. The students needed more time to get acquainted with the general use of the computers, e.g., getting from Lisp into the editor and back, writing directories, etc., than to learn the Lisp concepts needed to write rules like 3.2.1.

package rp_i of r_i is applied to the output of r_i (a new sentence start) and the third word, etc.

Consider the NEWCAT derivation corresponding to 3.1.3:

3.2.2 *Peter gave Fido the bone.*

```
(z Peter gave Fido the bone \.)
Real time:     0.06 s
Run time:      0.06 s

    Linear Analysis:

    *START_0
    1
        (NH) PETER
        (N D A V) GAVE
    *NOM+FVERB_3
    2
        (D A V) PETER GAVE
        (N-H) FIDO
    *FVERB+MAIN_4
    3
        (A V) PETER GAVE FIDO
        (GQ) THE
    *FVERB+MAIN_4
    4
        (GQ V) PETER GAVE FIDO THE
        (S-H) BONE
    *DET+NOUN_2
    5
        (V) PETER GAVE FIDO THE BONE
        (V DECL) .
    *CMPLT_13
    6
        (DECL) PETER GAVE FIDO THE BONE .
```

Since the derivation trees of LA-grammar always have the same form, NEWCAT parsers use the format of structured lists which are homomorphic to left-associative trees.[10]

In a sentence with n words there are n-1 left-associative combinations. The syntactic analysis provided by the parser presents each combination step as a numbered **history section**:

```
    2
        (D A V) PETER GAVE
        (N-H) FIDO
    *FVERB+MAIN_4
    3
        (A V) PETER GAVE FIDO
```

History section 2 consists of

_____

[10]Structured lists are easier to print and much faster to display than tree structures.

1. the sentence start *Peter gave* of category (D A V);[11]

2. the next word *Fido* of category (N-H);[12]

3. the rule FVERB+MAIN.

Application of FVERB+MAIN to *Peter gave* and *Fido* results in the new sentence start "(A V) PETER GAVE FIDO", which is printed as the first line of the next history section. FVERB+MAIN cancelled the dative valency in the sentence start of history section 2 with the noun phrase *Fido*.

The rule in a history section serves two functions: it indicates which rule combined the previous *ss* and *nw*, and it indicates which associated rule package will be applied to the following *ss* and *nw*. For example, FVERB+MAIN combined the *ss* and *nw* in history section 2, while the rule package of FVERB+MAIN will be applied to the *ss* and *nw* in history section 3. The rule package of a rule X contains all rules which may possibly apply after X was successful.

Using Lisp as a simple formal language for writing grammar rules has a tremendous advantage. While writing a new rule, the grammar writer may use Lisp to see what the various parts of the definition are actually doing. After setting the variables ss-cat (sentence-start category) and nw-cat (next-word category) to specific values, one may test whether a particular clause of the input condition works as intended, whether the output condition produces the desired result, etc. This technique is also extremely effective for debugging.

Debugging is further aided by the fact that input is always parsed up to the point where there are no grammatical continuations (or no more next word). Consider the analysis of ungrammatical input in 3.2.3

3.2.3 Analysis of Ungrammatical Input: *The young man give Fido the bone.*[13]

```
(z the young man give Fido the bone \.)
Real time:     0.02 s
Run time:      0.00 s

ERROR
Ungrammatical continuation at: "GIVE"
    Linear Analysis:

    *START_0
    1
        (GQ) THE
```

---

[11]This category represents a V (sentential expression containing the finite verb) which still needs a D (dative) and an A (accusative) to become a complete sentence.

[12]N-H is the category segment representing the name of a non-human being, e.g., dog. The human/non-human distinction in proper names and nouns is needed for the choice between *who* and *which* in a possible relative clause. The category segment S-H (cf. *bone* in 3.2.1) represents a noun which denotes a non-human object. The category segment GQ (cf. *the* in 3.2.1) stands for a "general quantifier," i.e., an article which combines with nouns regardless of their grammatical number.

[13]Examples of ungrammatical sentences are marked with an asterisk (" * "), a convention which dates back at least to Bloomfield (1933).

```
    (ADJ)  YOUNG
*DET+ADJ_1
2
    (GQ)  THE  YOUNG
    (SH)  MAN
*DET+NOUN_2
3
    (S)  THE  YOUNG  MAN
```

There are two possible reasons which may cause a left-associative parse to stop before the end of the sentence is reached: either the input string is not well-formed and the grammar is adequate, or the input string is well-formed and the grammar is not yet adequate. In a new system under construction a parse will often fail on well-formed input, in which case a partial derivation (up to the defective transition) is extremely effective for locating the problem.

3.3   Semantic Interpretation

The second step in the construction of a psychologically well-founded grammar is the construction of a bidirectional mapping between natural-language surfaces and their meanings. How can we get from a linear, left-associative syntax to a semantic hierarchy which characterizes the grammatical relations and is suitable for a pragmatic interpretation relative to a context?

Richard Montague (1930 – 1971) pioneered a method of semantic interpretation where the syntactic analysis and the semantic derivation are derived simultaneously. Unfortunately, Montague used hierarchical structures not only for the semantic representation, but for the syntax as well. Since the grammatical derivation order of Montague's categorial syntax is defined to mirror constituent structure, it violates the Derivational Order Hypothesis.[14]

Semantically interpreted LA-grammar, on the other hand, combines a linear syntax with a hierarchical semantics, as illustrated schematically in 3.3.1.

3.3.1 Building a Semantic Hierarchy during a Left-Associative Parse

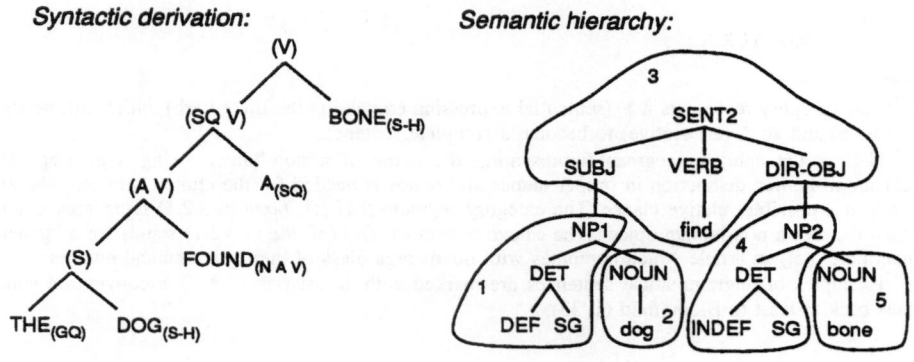

Each subtree in the semantic hierarchy of 3.3.1 corresponds to (and is derived from) a word in the surface. The semantic hierarchy in 3.3.1 is built up in following left-associative order:

$1 + 2 \rightarrow (1, 2)$

$(1, 2) + 3 \rightarrow (1, 2, 3)$

$(1, 2, 3) + 4 \rightarrow (1, 2, 3, 4)$

$(1, 2, 3, 4) + 5 \rightarrow (1, 2, 3, 4, 5)$

In other words, the semantic representation of word 1 is combined with the semantic representation of word 2, resulting in the subtree (1,2). Then the subtree (1,2) is combined with the semantic representation of word 3 into the subtree (1,2,3), etc.

The semantic derivation in LA-grammar resembles Montague Grammar in that

1. the semantic hierarchy is constructed simultaneously with the syntactic derivation; and

2. semantic representations are homomorphic with the syntactic analysis.

Without going into the details of Montague's algebraic definition,[15] the homomorphism in question may be described as follows:

3.3.2 The Homomorphism between Syntax and Semantics

1. For each syntactic category there is a corresponding semantic object.[16]
2. For each syntactic operation there is a corresponding semantic operation.

Montague's homomorphism condition may be read as a mathematical interpretation of the Principle of Compositionality or Fregean principle.

3.3.3 The Fregean Principle

The meaning of a complex expression is a function of the meaning of its parts and their mode of composition.

If a syntactic analysis and the associated semantic representation are homomorphic, then the Fregean Principle is intuitively satisfied: the meaning of the parts is established by the first condition of 3.3.2, while the composition of meanings is linked systematically to the syntactic composition by the second condition.

The systematic correlation between syntax and semantics according to the homomorphism condition may be technically vacuous, however. For example, an identity mapping in the syntax (e.g., $A \Rightarrow A$) with a corresponding semantic operation like $A' \Rightarrow A'(B')$ does not violate the letter of Montague's homomorphism condition. The same holds for syncategorematic operations in the syntax, e.g., $A \bullet B \Rightarrow A\ C\ B$

---

[14]Since Montague Grammar doesn't construct a bidirectional surface-meaning mapping, it also fails to satisfy the Criteria of Procedural Adequacy (2.4.1).

[15]See Montague (1974), pp. 222 – 246.

[16]E.g., a semantic type or a kind of model-theoretic denotation.

with a corresponding semantic operation A'• B' ⇒ A'(B'). We therefore adopt the Principle of Surface Compositionality,[17] which strengthens the homomorphism to link only proper syntactic compositions (e.g., A • B ⇒ A B) with proper semantic compositions (e.g., A' • B' ⇒ A'(B')).

Having established the general properties of the surface-meaning mapping in LA-grammar, let us turn to the intuitive interpretation of the semantic interpretation. Consider the linear (syntactic) and hierarchical (semantic) analysis of a sentence with a discontinuous construction.

3.3.4 *Fido dug the bone up.*

```
* (z Fido dug the bone up \.)

    Linear Analysis:

    *START
    1
        (N-H) FIDO
        (N A UP V) DUG
    *NOM+FVERB
    2
        (A UP V) FIDO DUG
        (GQ) THE
    *FVERB+MAIN
    3
        (GQ UP V) FIDO DUG THE
        (S-H) BONE
    *DET+NOUN
    4
        (UP V) FIDO DUG THE BONE
        (UP NP) UP
    *FVERB+MAIN
    5
        (V) FIDO DUG THE BONE UP
        (V DECL)  .
    *CMPLT
    6
        (DECL) FIDO DUG THE BONE UP  .

Hierarchical Analysis:

(SENT-2_5_9
  (SUBJ ((NP-1_5_9 (NAME (FIDO-1_5_9)))))
  (VERB (DIG-2_5_9))
  (DIR-OBJ ((NP-3_5_9 (REF (DEF-3_5_9 SG-4_5_9)) (NOUN ((BONE-4_5_9))))))
  (DISCONTINUOUS-ELEMENT ((UP-5_5_9))))
```

The hierarchical analysis in 3.3.4 is the semantic representation. It may be displayed automatically in the form of a tree if a suitable tree printer is available.

---

[17]Hausser (1984a).

3.3.5 The Frame-Tree Isomorphic to the Hierarchical Analysis of 3.3.4

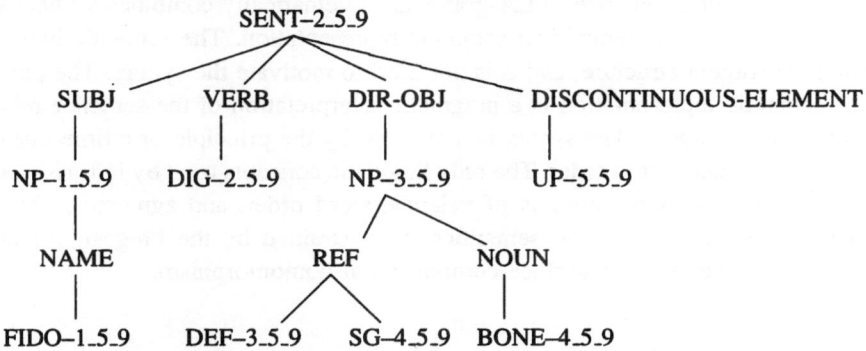

The tree structure 3.3.5 looks very much like a phrase-structure tree, which is pleasing to the eye of linguists in that tradition. But 3.3.5 was not generated as a phrase structure (and has no specific linear ordering). Rather, the formal system maps the linear syntactic analysis into a frame-theoretic database which is suitable for pragmatic interpretation relative to a knowledge base. This database happens to have a hierarchical structure which may be *displayed* as the tree 3.3.5. Since the primary structure is a minimal database, no modification of 3.3.5 is needed for pragmatic interpretation.[18] The pragmatic interpretation of 3.3.5 consists roughly in incorporating the minimal database (called a frame-theoretic icon of the literal meaning) into a larger knowledge base representing the utterance context.

The semantic nature of the database represented in 3.3.4 may be emphasized by changing from the linguistic[19] terminology of 3.3.5 to the logical categories of 3.3.6.

3.3.6 A Frame-Tree like 3.3.5, but with Logical Categories

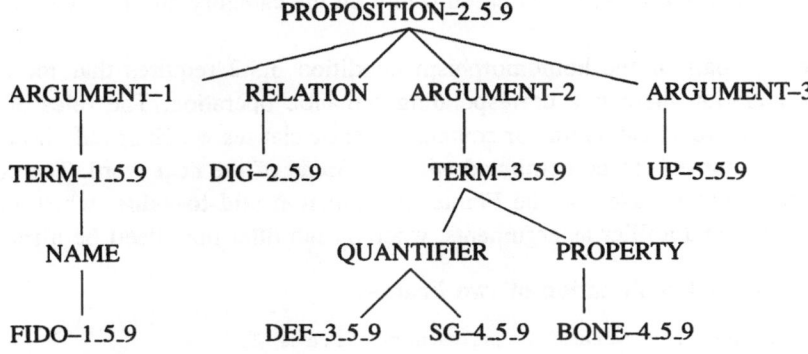

---

[18]For example, we don't have to build a minimal database from the tree, because the structure was built as a database in the first place.

[19]That the hierarchial analyses of LA-grammar use slot names like SUBJ, DIR-OBJ, etc., is partly a concession to popular usage, and partly intended to distinguish the semantic representation from the syntactic analysis, which uses cases.

3.3.5 and 3.3.6 are equivalent from a frame-theoretic point of view.

The analysis of a sentence in LA-grammar systematically combines a linear syntactic analysis with a hierarchical semantic representation. The semantic hierarchy is not a constituent structure, and it is not used to motivate the syntax. The purpose of the semantic representation is a pragmatic interpretation of the sentence relative to an utterance context. The syntax is motivated by the principle of a time-linear or left-associative derivation order. The only linguistic concepts used by left-associative syntax are the traditional notions of valency, word order, and agreement. The relationship between syntax and semantics is constrained by the Fregean Principle, formally implemented as a surface-compositional homomorphism.

3.4 An Example

Let us consider the details of a simultaneous syntactico-semantic derivation in LA-grammar. The first clause of the homomorphism condition 3.3.2 is implemented in terms of a systematic generation of semantic frames from analyzed word forms. An analyzed word form consists of a surface, a category, and a stem.

For example, the analyzed word forms ("THE" (GQ) THE) and ("FOUND" (N A V) FIND) are mapped into the frames illustrated in 3.4.1.

3.4.1 Printing the Frames NP-1_1_1 and SENT-3_1_1 as Trees

```
     NP–1_1_1                           SENT–3_1_1
       /                                   /
     REF                     SUBJ      VERB
      /                                   |
   THE–1_1_1                           FIND–3_1_1
```

The derivation of a word-frame is based solely on the category and the stem of the word.

The second part of the homomorphism condition 3.3.2 requires that for each syntactic operation there is a corresponding semantic operation. The rules of semantically interpreted LA-grammar contain semantic clauses which specify how the sentence-start frame is to be combined with the frame of the next word. The combination of frames is based on the FrameKit[20] function **add-to-value**, which takes a frame, a slot, and a filler as arguments, whereby the filler may itself be a frame.

3.4.2 Schematic Combination of two Frames

```
(add-to-value 'frame-1 'slot-name 'frame-2)
```

For example,

(add-to-value 'NP-1_1_1 'noun (newfr (car (lexit "dog"))))

---

[20]Carbonell and Joseph (1986), Nyberg (1988).

adds the frame derived from "dog" to the slot 'noun' of NP-1_1_1.[21] The result is shown in 3.4.3.

3.4.3 Combining a Determiner Frame with a Noun Frame

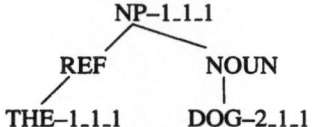

A frame-name like NP-1_1_1 consists of a base (e.g., NP) and an index (e.g., 1_1_1). Different instances of frames with the same base are distinguished by different indices. This is important to control the addition of values to slots.

The index of a frame has three digits. The first represents the number of the word from which the frame or the filler has been generated,[22] the second is the copy-number of the frame, and the third is the number of the sentence in a text.

If a sentence has several constituents of the same category, the frames with the same base are distinguished by different word-numbers (first digit of the index). If a sentence start is ambiguous, the frames of each reading are distinguished by different copy-numbers (second digit of the index). It is necessary to distinguish frames in the semantic representations of different readings to insure that semantic additions specific to a certain reading are limited to that reading.[23] Let us illustrate this point by considering the crucial derivation step in a "garden path" sentence.

Garden path sentences are constructions where two readings are maintained in parallel, and the less expected reading survives. The sentence start *The man read* has only one reading, but *The man read a* has two readings: the indefinite article could be the beginning of the direct object to *read*, as in *The man read a book*, or it could be the beginning of the subject of a subordinate clause without a complementizer, as in *The man read a book was given to Mary*.[24]

3.4.4 Syntactic and Semantic Analysis of *The man read*

```
* (z the man read)

Linear Analysis:

    *START_0
    1
        (GQ) THE
        (SH) MAN
```

---

[21] If a slot does not yet exist, *add-to-value* will create it.

[22] The first digit also shows which word contributed what to the semantic representation. For example, the filler "SG-4" (for singular) in 3.3.5 has the word-number 4, because this aspect of the noun phrase was determined by word 4.

[23] This distinction of frames representing different readings is based on a frame copying function which was written by Jaime Carbonell as an addition to the FrameKit software.

[24] This sentence has the same meaning as *The man read that a book was given to Mary*.

```
*DET+NOUN_2
2
    (S) THE MAN
    (N SC V) READ
*NOM+FVERB_3
3
    (SC V) THE MAN READ
```

Hierarchical Analysis:

```
(SENT-3_3_3
 (SUBJ ((NP-1_3_3 (REF (THE-1_3_3 SG-2_3_3)) (NOUN ((MAN-2_3_3))))))
 (VERB (READ-3_3_3)))
```

LA-grammar rules add the next-word frame to copies of the sentence-start frame, leaving the original for possible other rules (in the case of an ambiguous continuation). In our example, the original sentence-start frame is SENT-3_3_3.[25] The next combination step is ambiguous because two rules in the rule package of NOM+FVERB accept the new input pair, namely FVERB+MAIN and START-SUBCL.

FVERB+MAIN in the first reading of 3.4.5 below copies the sentence-start frame SENT-3_3_3 into SENT-3_4_4[26] and adds the next-word frame as a direct object. Next START-SUBCL applies to the input pair. It copies the original sentence-start frame SENT-3_3_3 into SENT-3_5_4 and adds the next-word frame as the beginning of a subclause without a complementizer.

3.4.5 Syntactic and Semantic Analysis of *The man read a*

```
* (z the man read a)

2    Linear Analysis:

    *START_0
    1
        (GQ) THE
        (SH) MAN
    *DET+NOUN_2
    2
        (S) THE MAN
        (N SC V) READ
    *NOM+FVERB_3
    3
        (SC V) THE MAN READ
        (SQ) A
    *FVERB+MAIN_4
    4
        (SQ V) THE MAN READ A
```

---

[25]The first digit of SENT-3_3_3 is "3" because this frame is derived from the third word in the sentence, i.e. *read*.

[26]The third index digit in 3.4.5 is 4 rather than 3 because 3.4.5 is a new derivation, for the sake of demonstration, thus incrementing the sentence counter by 1.

Hierarchical Analysis:

```
(SENT-3_4_4
 (SUBJ ((NP-1_4_4 (REF (THE-1_4_4 SG-2_4_4)) (NOUN ((MAN-2_4_4))))))
 (VERB (READ-3_4_4))
 (DIR-OBJ ((NP-4_4_4 (REF (A-4_4_4 SG-4_4_4))))))
```

1   Linear Analysis:

```
    *START_0
    1
        (GQ) THE
        (SH) MAN
    *DET+NOUN_2
    2
        (S) THE MAN
        (N SC V) READ
    *NOM+FVERB_3
    3
        (SC V) THE MAN READ
        (SQ) A
    *START-SUBCL_8
    4
        (SQ $ V) THE MAN READ A
```

Hierarchical Analysis:

```
(SENT-3_5_4
 (SUBJ ((NP-1_5_4 (REF (DEF-1_5_4 SG-2_5_4)) (NOUN ((MAN-2_5_4))))))
 (VERB (READ-3_5_4))
 (DIR-OBJ ((SENT-4_5_4
            (SUBJ (NP-4_5_4 (REF (A-4_5_4 SG-4_5_4)))))))))
```

In the case of an ambiguous sentence start like 3.4.5 or an ambiguous sentence the readings are numbered and printed in sequence, beginning with the highest number.[27]

Example 3.4.5 shows that LA-grammar handles "garden path" sentences without look-ahead or backtracking. The system simply proceeds in a breadth-first, bottom-up manner, computing all possible continuations at each combination step. This is the technique of "anticipating splits."

As an example of a complete hierarchical analysis consider 3.4.6.

3.4.6 Semantic Analysis of *The man read a book was given to Mary.*

```
(PROPOSITION-10_17_6
 (MOOD (DECLARATIVE-10_17_6))
 (PROP-CONTENT
  ((SENT-3_17_6
    (SUBJ ((NP-1_17_6 (REF (THE-1_17_6 SG-2_17_6)) (NOUN ((MAN-2_17_6))))))
    (VERB (READ-3_17_6))
    (DIR-OBJ
     ((SENT-4_17_6
       (SUBJ
```

---

[27]In this way the number of readings is apparent when the first parse appears on the screen.

```
   ((NP-4_17_6 (REF (A-4_17_6 SG-4_17_6)) (NOUN ((BOOK-5_17_6))))))
   (AUX ((BE-6_17_6)))
   (PASSIVE-PREDICATE
    ((NFV-7_17_6
      (PAST-PART (GIVE-7_17_6))
      (PREPOSITIONAL_OBJ
       ((PREP-8_17_6
         (PREPOSITION (TO-8_17_6))
         (PREPOSITIONAL-ARG ((NP-9_17_6 (NAME (MARY-9_17_6)))))))))))))))))
   )))))
```

Due to the linear nature of natural language, the number of parallel readings is usually quite small. The first word after completion of the object noun phrase in 3.4.5 will determine which of the two readings must be discarded: if we continue *The man read a book* with *was*, the first reading is discarded; if we continue with a period, the second is discarded.[28]

3.5   Two Fallacies of Constituent Structure

While all constituent structures are semantic hierarchies, not all semantic hierarchies are constituent structures. The first fallacy of constituent-structure based PS- and C-grammars is that they build semantic hierarchies (constituent structures) which are intended to motivate syntactic structures, but are unsuitable for pragmatic interpretation. They therefore necessitate definition of an additional semantic component, which partly duplicates the constituent structure.

The second fallacy is that constituent-structure based grammars build their hierarchies in a manner where the grammatical derivation order is defined to mirror the hierarchical structure. This conceptual derivation order is incompatible with the input-output conditions of natural-language speech, and therefore psychologically implausible. Furthermore, a derivation order defined to reflect a constituent structure cannot double as the procedural derivation order of parsers.

Most linguists, however, refuse to be concerned with these aspects of their grammars, declaring it to be a "procedural" problem. Constituent analyses are presented as abstract representations of the human language capability, and often are suggested to be "innate" or "universal." The "competence/performance" dichotomy is used to claim that the only thing which matters for the competence grammar is the structure of the tree, whereas the process by which it is constructed is irrelevant.

We should keep in mind, however, that the conceptual separation of generative grammars and their parsers in terms of the "declarative-procedural dichotomy" was not originally intended; rather, this separation was adopted in reaction to the computational difficulties created by constituent-structure analysis:

---

[28]At present, LA-grammar treats all possible continuations as equal. However, as explained in Hausser (1986), p. 50, a weighing of readings based on the order of rules in the rule packages would be straightforward.

Miller and Chomsky's original (1963) suggestion is really that grammars be realized more or less directly as parsing algorithms. We might take this as a methodological principle. In this case we impose the condition that the logical organization of rules and structures incorporated in the grammar be mirrored rather exactly in the organization of the parsing mechanism. We will call this *type transparency*.

Berwick & Weinberg, (1984), p. 39.

In the constituent-structure based competence grammars of today, derivation order is not treated as part of theory. Yet generative grammars are defined as quasi-mechanical rule systems. Thus, in their actual implementation some derivation order has to be assumed. What is the structural reason behind the claim that the particular choice of a grammatical derivation order is of no theoretical importance in constituent structure based systems?

Consider a set of PS-grammar rules:

3.5.1 A Small Phrase-Structure Grammar

S → NP + VP
NP → DET + N
VP → V + NP

These rules generate a small set of hierarchical structures in a **partial** top-down order. The order is partial because the rules do not tell us whether to first expand the NP or the VP. In other words, whether the hierarchical structure is built from left-to-right, or right-to-left, or any other "horizontal" order happens to be conceptually irrelevant in constituent-structure systems.

Furthermore, the arrows in rules may be reversed, which will result in a bottom-up derivation order. In summary, the rules in 3.5.1 may be used to build a hierarchy in top-down left-to-right, top-down right-to-left, bottom-up left-to-right, and bottom-up right-to-left orders, as well as any mixture of these orders. Similar considerations hold for a corresponding C-grammar.

In comparison, consider the derivation order of LA-grammar. Left-associative rules of the form

$$r_i: [CAT\text{-}1 \ CAT\text{-}2] \Rightarrow [rp_i \ CAT\text{-}3]$$

do not impose a total derivation order. But the non-deterministic aspect of LA-grammar is much more restricted than in constituent-structure based systems. For one, the arrow of LA-rules cannot be reversed. Furthermore, the system provides no possibility of top-down expansion. Thus, LA-grammar is based conceptually on a **left-to-right bottom-up** derivation order.

The only indeterminacy in the derivation order of LA-grammar is in the choice of a rule from the current rule package. For example, in the combination illustrated in 3.5.2, all the rules in the rule package *FVERB+MAIN will be applied to the following *ss-nw* pair, but the order of their application is left to the implementation.

3.5.2 A Rule Package and its Input

```
*FVERB+MAIN
4
    (GQ V)  PETER GAVE FIDO THE
    (S-H)  BONE
```

The choice between a breadth-first or a depth-first implementation in LA-grammar depends on whether the system is used for interpretation (analysis) or verbalization (generation). During analysis, a breadth-first approach which follows all possible syntactic analyses in parallel is the most efficient and the most natural.[29] During interpretation, on the other hand, only a single rule is chosen from the current rule-package (depth-first—or rather depth-only). The choice is controlled by the pragmatic strategy for approaching a particular goal node.[30]

In summary, the strictly time-linear derivation order of LA-grammar is psychologically well-motivated, and serves as the backbone of syntactic, semantic, and pragmatic interpretation. This derivation order is equally suited for generation and analysis. The only difference between generation and analysis is that in generation the next word is picked from the lexicon, whereas in analysis the next word is given by the input string.

Furthermore, the left-associative derivation order can be used directly by a NEW-CAT parser. LA-grammar achieves "absolute type transparency"[31] because it is strongly input-output equivalent to its generators and its parsers (see Section 8.1). That a NEWCAT analysis is both a declarative grammatical analysis and a trace of the computation, results from a design which treats the linguistic analysis and the computation as different aspects of the same (left-associative) structure. This design has several advantages.

3.5.3 Advantages of Using the Grammar Rules in the Parser

- Improvements in the linguistic analysis of the syntax translate directly into a faster computation.
- Analysis of the computation (tracing) provides excellent heuristics for arriving at a better (i.e., more minimal) syntactic theory.

---

[29]While the present LA-parser is designed as a bottom-up breadth-first system, a bottom-up depth-first backtracking implementation is theoretically possible (and actually running in a Prolog version of LA-grammar). A depth-first implementation applies the first rule in the rule package, and, if successful, goes on to the next combination right away. When a depth-first derivation encounters an ungrammatical continuation, it backtracks and applies the respective second rules in the rule packages, etc. But a truly parallel breadth-first approach is conceptually and computationally optimal (see Section 4.1).

[30]See Sections 5.4 and 5.5 for further discussion.

[31]Berwick & Weinberg (1984), p. 41.

3.5.4 Advantages of Using a Left-Associative Derivation Order

- Because of the linear nature of left-associative derivations, it is easy to add new constructions to LA-grammars and their parsers (up-scaling).

- For the same reason, bugs in the grammar can be isolated quickly.

- The left-associative derivation order is equally suitable for analysis (breadth-first) and generation (depth-only).

The speed of NEWCAT in the analysis of natural language depends not only on the inherent efficiency of LA-grammar[32] but also on the empirical linguistic fact that the number of possible readings at each left-associative combination step is quite small. At certain points in a sentence, a combination may produce several sentence-start readings, but most of them will be eliminated at the next combination step.[33] LA-grammars and NEWCAT parsers take advantage of the inherently time-linear nature of natural language.

---

[32] The computational complexity of LA-grammer is analyzed in Chapter 10.
[33] See the analysis and discussion of a "garden path" sentence in Section 3.4.

4. Continuations in Natural Language

This chapter describes techniques of linguistic analysis in LA-grammar. The systems discussed are ECAT, an LA-grammar of English, and DCAT, an LA-grammar of German.[1] Section 4.1 explains the overall structure of ECAT. Section 4.2 discusses the handling of modifier agreement in English and German. Section 4.3 deals with the phenomenon of valency in English. Section 4.4 explains the handling of word order on the basis of the categorization and the control structure. Section 4.5 discusses the syntactic and semantic nature of pronouns.

4.1   Scheduling Access to Grammatical Information

Traditional analysis of natural language outside of generative grammar is based on three basic concepts: (i) valency, (ii) agreement, and (iii) word order. This approach to natural language has a long tradition. Consider the following quotation from the second century A.D., referring to ancient Greek.

> The fundamental cause of ungrammaticality...lies in the following. Of the parts of speech (a) some are inflected for case and number—e.g., the noun and all other words that take number with case; (b) some have the categories of person and number, e.g., verbs and pronouns; (c) some are inflected for gender, e.g., the above-mentioned nouns and whatever else can make a distinction of gender. Finally, (d) some are not inflected for any of these categories, namely those which have only a single form, such as conjunctions, prepositions, and almost all the adverbs. (13)
>
> The first [three] classes of words, changed according to their respective inflectional patterns into the required concordance ... are marked for association with whatever word they are construed with, say plural with plural... (14)
>
> When words have been subclassified ... according to their proper applicational positions, they act by means of their grammatical correctness as restraints on words which, for whatever reason, have by chance come into a position where they don't belong. (22)
>
> Apollonious Dyscolus, Book III[2]

---

[1]For a detailed description of these systems see Hausser (1986). The present versions differ in some details of linguistic description, and in the switch from INTERLISP-D to Common Lisp.

[2]See Householder (1981).

Apollonius[3] of Alexandria describes the local combinatorics of ancient Greek in minute detail. For instance, "the article is unacceptable in construction with *amphoteroi* ('both'), being forbidden both by ordinary usage and by supporting argument. This shows that *amphoteroi* is not the same as *duo* ('two'), since, when needed the article can be placed before *duo*, as well as all other numbers, but not before the word in question."[4]

This kind of knowledge is completely internalized by the native speaker-hearer: even though (s)he is not consciously aware of them, (s)he obeys the rules of morphology and word order with all their exceptions infallibly and without effort. But as an explicit statement of fact, this kind of information is hard to remember, especially when there are so many such details. Thus it is legitimate and necessary for linguists to go beyond the details of morphology and explain natural language in a more conceptual manner.

The ancient grammarians approached this task by carefully justifying the order in which the parts of speech (noun, verb, participle, article, pronoun, preposition, adverb, conjunction) are listed in the grammar. The argument is based mainly on the idea that when language was first invented the parts of speech became necessary in a particular order.[5] The classical order of the parts of speech is maintained in most traditional grammars of today, but it is not taken seriously as a functional explanation of natural language.

A second attempt to explain syntactic structure conceptually was made in modern times in the form of constituent-structure analysis. The idea to analyze sentences into sub-sentences, sub-sentences into clauses, clauses into phrases, and phrases into words constitutes a natural complement to the details of morphology and gives rise to generative syntax. But it sets aside most of the information contained in the concrete surface and analyzes sentences as abstract frames, derived from a start symbol by means of substitutions.

Thus when the NP and VP nodes in the deep structure of constituent-structure grammars have finally been mapped into the abstract forms (stems) of actual words, the details of agreement, valency, and word order are still unresolved. Transformations are required to adjust the word order, features "percolate up the tree," and "filters" are used for a belated treatment of the concrete facts abstracted from within the deep structure derivation.

> The introduction of filtering devices into the model of grammar has sometimes drawn misconceived criticism. In particular, some have felt that it is a priori wrong to first generate a wide range of structures only to filter out

---

[3]The surname *Dyscolus*— "the difficult"—can be "explained in three ways, either (a) because the elliptical and compressed nature of his style makes difficult reading, (b) because he was a cantankerous or argumentative person, or (c) because he used to pose rare and difficult words to ancient game-show contestants (who were rival grammarians)." Householder (1981), p. 5.

[4]Op.Cit., Book I, 71.

[5]Householder (1981), p. 9.

most of them later. But the appeal of this view is inspired by a procedural interpretation of the model. If the model were a production model (a model of how speakers actually generate sentences), excessive reliance on filtering devices could (indeed, should) be frowned upon. However, since the model linguists are developing is a competence model (a model of what speakers of a language know about it) no such considerations apply. The only valid criteria for evaluating filters, like any other component of grammar, are the degree to which they correctly characterize and explain grammatical phenomena and the degree to which they add to the overall elegance of the theory of grammar.

Riemsdijk and Williams (1986, p. 157)

The syntax of natural languages—including English—runs on the concrete cog wheels and gears of morphology. A linguistic approach which abstracts away from these details is subject to the danger of misappropriating their proper function.

LA-grammar proposes a third way to make conceptual sense of the details of natural language. The task is approached in the form of a syntactic procedure which at each point in the sentence calls up only those details of the grammar which can possibly be relevant at that point. This syntactic procedure is based on the time-linear nature of natural language. The principle of possible continuations constitutes a specialized method for describing local compatibilities based on morphology. In addition, this approach to syntax provides all the information needed for a simultaneous derivation of semantic hierarchies (as explained in Sections 3.3 and 3.4).

Like PS-grammar, LA-grammar separates the aspects of phrase structure (semantic hierarchy) on the one hand, and morphologically based valency and agreement structure (linear analysis) on the other. But whereas PS-grammar generates sentences on the basis of phrase structure rules and deals with the details of morphology later, LA-grammar generates sentences on the basis of highly structured, analyzed word forms, deriving semantic hierarchies at the same time.

In summary, possible continuations constitute a scheduling structure which is equally suitable for the handling of morphologically based combinatorics and for the derivation of semantic hierarchies. It is inherently simple, linguistically illuminating, psychologically plausible, computationally efficient, as well as compatible with the input-output conditions of speech, and absolutely type-transparent in natural-language processing.

In the syntactic analysis of natural language, LA-grammar proceeds in three steps. First, it translates the morpho-syntactic properties of each word form into a straightforward categorization. Second, it codes local compositions (of sentence starts and next words) into categorial operations which are based on agreement and valency properties. Third, it organizes the categorial operations into a simple control structure, based on rules calling rule packages.

These three ingredients are expressed jointly in the schema of left-associative rules:

$$r_i: [CAT\text{-}1 \ CAT\text{-}2] \Rightarrow [rp_i \ CAT\text{-}3]$$

The lexical categorization of the words is represented by CAT-2, the categorial operation by the mapping of CAT-1 and CAT-2 into CAT-3, and the control structure by linking rp_i to r_i.

ECAT presently consists of the following sixteen rules:

4.1.1 The Rules of ECAT

1. det+adj	5. prep+np	9. add-nom	13 cmplt
2. det+noun	6. add-verb	10. fverb+nom	14. noun+pnm
3. nom+fverb	7. start-inf	11. main&w+aux	15. start-relcl
4. fverb+main	8. start-subcl	12. wh+verb	16. cont-compound

The rules of ECAT conform to the general format of LA-grammar. For example, rule 10 has the following declarative formulation:[6]

4.1.2 Declarative Formulation [7] of the Rule FVERB+NOM

FVERB+NOM: [(seg1 seg2 Y seg3) (seg4 X)]

$$\Rightarrow [*FVERB+NOM (seg5 \ seg2 \ X \ Y \ seg3)]$$

where
    seg1 ε {s1, s3, n, nom, nm}
    seg2 ε {b, m, do, hv}
    seg3 ε {v, vi}
    seg4 ε {gq, pq, sq, adj, nh, n-h, s, p, s1, s3, p1, p3, wh, w-h}
and
    if
    seg4 ε {gq, pq, sq, adj}
    then seg5 = seg4
    else
    seg5 = 0
and
    *FVERB+NOM = {fverb+main, nom+fverb, det+noun, det+adj,
                   add-verb, wh+verb, cmplt}

ECAT presently uses 63 category segments like S1, S3, N, etc. These category segments are listed and explained in Appendix A. They represent grammatical properties like number, case, etc., which are encoded in the morphology of the natural language described.

---

[6]Note the specification of category correspondence by explicit definition rather than by the principle of identity (see footnote 4 in Section 2.1). The categorial operations defined by left-associative rules are much more powerful than the cancelling schemas of Categorial Grammar.

[7](X) and (Y) are variables for sequences. For example, if (X) = (1 2 3), then (a b X c) = (a b 1 2 3 c).

How much exactly is covered by the current ECAT grammar? At present, no grammatical system, including ECAT, provides a complete analysis of English. The grammatical coverage of ECAT is extensive, but if we take an arbitrary newpaper article and try to parse it with ECAT, the system will very likely encounter an untreated syntactic construction.

A comparison of the descriptive coverage of ECAT with the whole of the English language is difficult because there exists no complete list of the syntactic constructions of English. This is because such a taxonomy is highly theory-dependent. Of the partial grammatical descriptions by different schools of syntactic analysis, none has been generally accepted as conclusive.

A comparison of ECAT with other grammars of English is also difficult because the empirical coverage of different incomplete grammars will have different strength and weaknesses. The best way to indicate the coverage of a partial system is by way of a set of sample sentences. The set of sample sentences indicating the current coverage of ECAT is given in Appendix C. These examples, which were added gradually to the set in the course of extending the grammar, are used to automatically test the grammar after the incorporation of new constructions.

Given the wide range of constructions indicated in Appendix C, the LA-grammar for English is surprisingly small. The source code of the current ECAT syntax is 25 kilobytes. The compiled code is less than that, i.e., there is no trade-off of space to increase run-time efficiency.

The control structure of ECAT, defined by rules calling rule packages, is given here below in a simplified form:

4.1.3 The Control Structure of ECAT
(Disregarding Rules 1, 2, 13, 14, 15, and 16)

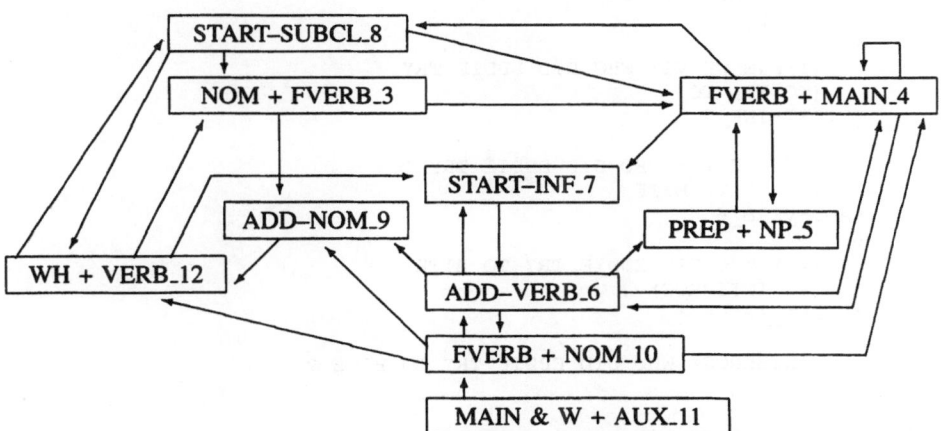

This representation identifies a state with the *name* of a rule package (cf. 8.3.3). The content of the rule package associated with a rule is indicated by the arrows going out of a rule-box. The rules 3, 10, and 11 are listed in the rule package of START and may apply at the beginning of a sentence. The rules 3, 4, 6, and 10 list CMPLT in their rule packages and may complete a sentence. Based on these facts we establish "proper paths" within the network. For example, sequence (11, 10, 12, 7, 6) is a proper path, exemplified by the derivation 4.1.4. Another proper path is the sequence (10, 6, 7, 6, 4), exemplified by the derivation 4.1.5.

4.1.4 Derivation Exemplifying the Rule Path '0,11,10,12,7,6,13'

Who[8] did Eddie try to bite?

```
* (z Who did Eddie try to bite ?)
*** Lex Lookup
Real time:      0.02 s
Run time:       0.00 s

*** Parse Timings
Real time:      0.06 s
Run time:       0.06 s

 Linear Analysis:

   *START_0
   1
      (WH) WHO
      (N DO V) DID
   *MAIN&W+AUX_11
   2
      (N DO WH VI) WHO DID
      (N-H) EDDIE
   *FVERB+NOM_10
   3
      (DO WH VI) WHO DID EDDIE
      (NOM INF&N V) TRY
   *WH+VERB_12
   4
      (INF&N WH VI) WHO DID EDDIE TRY
      (TO NP) TO
   *START-INF_7
   5
      (INF WH VI) WHO DID EDDIE TRY TO
      (NOM A V) BITE
   *ADD-VERB_6
   6
      (VI) WHO DID EDDIE TRY TO BITE
      (VI INTERROG) ?
   *CMPLT_13
   7
      (INTERROG) WHO DID EDDIE TRY TO BITE ?


Hierarchical Analysis:

(FRAMES_SWITCHED_OFF)
```

4.1.5 Derivation Exemplifying the Rule Path '0,10,6,7,6,4,13'
Did Eddie try to bite Fido?

```
*  (z Did Eddie try to bite Fido ?)

*** Lex Lookup
Real time:     0.00 s
Run time:      0.00 s

*** Parse Timings
Real time:     0.04 s
Run time:      0.04 s

    Linear Analysis:

    *START_0
    1
        (N DO V) DID
        (N-H) EDDIE
    *FVERB+NOM_10
    2
        (DO VI) DID EDDIE
        (NOM INF&N V) TRY
    *ADD-VERB_6
    3
        (INF&N VI) DID EDDIE TRY
        (TO NP) TO
    *START-INF_7
    4
        (INF VI) DID EDDIE TRY TO
        (NOM A V) BITE
    *ADD-VERB_6
    5
        (A VI) DID EDDIE TRY TO BITE
        (N-H) FIDO
    *FVERB+MAIN_4
    6
        (VI) DID EDDIE TRY TO BITE FIDO
        (VI INTERROG) ?
    *CMPLT_13
    7
        (INTERROG) DID EDDIE TRY TO BITE FIDO ?

Hierarchical Analysis:

(FRAMES_SWITCHED_OFF)
```

The concept of proper paths may be used to compute the time-complexity of a given grammar. Furthermore, representation 4.1.3 may be used as the floorplan of a micro-coded or hardwired natural language grammar (e.g., an ECAT-chip).

---

[8]This sentence is a variant of *Whom did Eddie try to bite?*, which is also accepted by the parser. The version presented in 4.1.4 was chosen as the more interesting one, because it involves the ambiguous sentence start *Who(m) did.*

Alternatively to the representation 4.1.3, we may identify a state with the *content* of a rule package. This equivalent representation is given in 4.1.6 (for the German parser DCAT) in the form of a "Masterscope graph."[9]

4.1.6 The Initial Part of the MASTERSCOPE Graph of DCAT

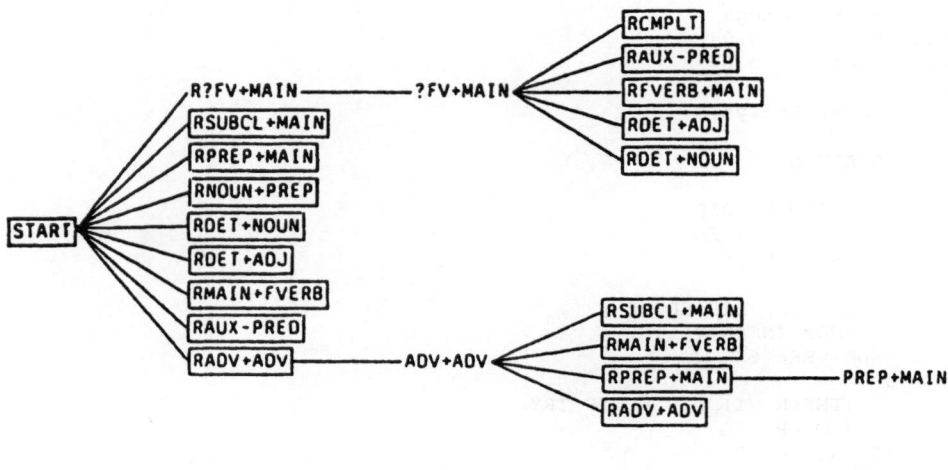

Window Image

4.1.6 shows that LA-grammar (and the associated parsers) have a highly parallel nature. In theory, the rules of a rule package apply in parallel to the ss-nw pair. A genuinely parallel architecture will make it possible to utilize the inherent parallelism of LA-grammar, resulting in a system which is even faster than the present sequential implementation.

4.1.6 shows furthermore that LA-grammar is also of a highly distributed nature, Each rule is called by many rule packages. Thus the categorial operation of a rule provides a local transition in many types of constructions.

After building a larger LA-grammar for a natural language, it is interesting heuristically to see how specific rules behave across several hundred sample derivations. This is accomplished with a program which analyzes the applications of specified rules in all the derivations produced by wholesale parsing of an example set.[10] A small detail illustrating this kind of rule analysis is given in 4.1.7.

---

[9]"Masterscope" is part of Interlisp-D and displays the structure of programs in terms of function calls. Left-Associative Grammar was initially developed in Interlisp-D on a Xerox 1109.

[10]This software was written with the help of Eric Nyberg (Carnegie Mellon University).

4.1.7 The Behavior of the ECAT Rule DET+ADJ in a Large Sample Set

```
The rules calling *DET+ADJ_1:
(*FVERB+NOM_10 *ADD-NOM_9 *START_0 *PREP+NP_5 *DET+ADJ_1
 *FVERB+MAIN_4 *DET+NOUN_2 *START-SUBCL_8)

The ss-categories accepted by *DET+ADJ_1:
((GQ DO WT VI)  (GQ $ WT VI)  (GNQ)  (GQ)  (GQ V)  (SQ)  (GNQ A V)
 (SQ TO V)  (GQ BY V)  (SQ V)  (PQ V)  (GQ DO VI)  (WQ)  (WQ VI)
 (GQ A VIMP)  (GQ $ WS V)  (GQ $ V)  (GQ TO* DO WT VI)  (GQ TO* VI)
 (GQ TO V)  (GQ INF&A V))

The nw-categories accepted by *DET+ADJ_1:
((ADJ)  (B)  (INT)  (MST)  (SADJ)  (MR))

The output-categories generated by *DET+ADJ_1:
((GQ DO WT VI)  (GQ $ WT VI)  (GNQ)  (GQ)  (GQ V)  (SQ)  (GNQ A V)
 (SQ TO V)  (GQ BY V)  (SQ V)  (PQ V)  (GQ DO VI)  (WQ)  (WQ VI)
 (GQ A VIMP)  (GQ $ WS V)  (GQ $ V)  (GQ TO* DO WT VI)  (GQ TO* VI)
 (GQ TO V)  (GQ INF&A V))

The rules called after *DET+ADJ_1:
(*DET+NOUN_2 *DET+ADJ_1)

;--------------------EXAMPLE 1
;--------------------EXAMPLE 2
;--------------------EXAMPLE 3
;--------------------EXAMPLE 4
;--------------------EXAMPLE 5
;--------------------EXAMPLE 6
;--------------------EXAMPLE 7
;--------------------EXAMPLE 8
;--------------------EXAMPLE 8
;--------------------EXAMPLE 9
;--------------------EXAMPLE 10

;Previous rule:
 *FVERB+NOM_10
;Input categories:
 ((GQ DO WT VI) (ADJ))
;Result:
 ((GQ DO WT VI) ("WHO" "DOES" "THE" "YOUNG"))
;Next rule:
 *DET+NOUN_2


;Previous rule:
 *ADD-NOM_9
;Input categories:
 ((GQ $ WT VI) (ADJ))
;Result:
 ((GQ $ WT VI) ("WHO" "DOES" "THE" "YOUNG" "DOG" "BELIEVE" "THAT"
                "THE" "BEAUTIFUL"))
;Next rule:
 *DET+NOUN_2

;--------------------EXAMPLE 11
;--------------------EXAMPLE 12
```

```
;-------------------EXAMPLE 13
;-------------------EXAMPLE 14
;-------------------EXAMPLE 15
;-------------------EXAMPLE 16

;Previous rule:
 *START_0
;Input categories:
 ((GNQ) (ADJ))
;Result:
 ((GNQ) ("JOHN'S" "BEAUTIFUL"))
;Next rule:
 *DET+NOUN_2

;-------------------EXAMPLE 17
```

Relative to a given set of over 400 analyzed examples, the rule analyzer specified the actual input and output categories, the rules calling DET+ADJ, and the rules called by DET+ADJ. Then the individual transitions from which this information was collected are listed. We see that DET+ADJ did not apply in the first nine examples, but fired twice in example ten, etc. This kind of diagnostic is orthogonal to the linear analysis of examples, and provides a sound, empirical basis for deciding whether a certain new type of transition should be handled by a new rule, or incorporated into an existing one.

The parallel distributed architecture of LA-grammar was developed independently of the related work in cognitive psychology called parallel distributed processing, or PDP. Differences between the two theories exist insofar as LA-grammar is a symbolic system designed for the linguistic analysis of high-level structures[11] in natural language, while PDP emphasizes a subsymbolic approach designed for the psychological (or even neurological) explanation of low-level learning phenomena.[12]

Second, seriality in PDP systems comes about mainly as a consequence of resource limitation: because there are only a limited number of processors, the information has to be channelled through them sequentially.

> Since it is patterns of activations over a set of units that are the relevant representational format and since a set of units can only contain one pattern at a time, there is an enforced seriality in what can be represented.

> Rumelhart, Smolensky, McClelland, and Hinton (1986), p. 7.

In LA-grammar, on the other hand, seriality is a primary structure provided by the time-linear nature of the input.

Third, connectionist parallelism assumes a strong interaction between different parallel paths. In LA-grammar, parallel paths come about only in the case of an

---

[11]The analysis of LA-grammar is relatively high level in that it operates with fully analyzed word forms.

[12]Smolensky (1986).

ambiguity. The primary aspect of parallel processing in LA-grammar consists in the fact that the rules in a rule package are fired simultaneously at each combination step. The independence of different readings in LA-grammar results from two structural properties of the system: (i) different readings at a certain point in a derivation are associated with different positions in the control structure (because different rules have applied), and/or (ii) different readings are characterized by different sentence start categories.

The advantage of PDP systems is a high degree of robustness: they can even make sense out of seriously deficient input. LA-grammar, on the other hand, shows the brittleness typical of abstract symbolic systems. The advantage of LA-grammar, however, is a highly efficient handling of structures which are far too complicated for the PDP method. It may well be worth-while, however, to explore the possibility of combining the two approaches, in order to increase the robustness of LA-grammar, and to extend the PDP approach to phenomena which are too large to work without abstraction.

4.2   Agreement

Having described the overall structure of LA-grammar, let's turn to certain basic details of syntactic analysis. Two expressions in natural language are said to be in *agreement* if they must have the same categorial property in some common parameter, e.g., they have to agree in number, or gender, or person, etc. Agreement may occur in connection with the cancelling of a valency position (cf. Section 4.3), or with an optional modifier. This section concentrates on the latter form of agreement.

In LA-grammar agreement features are coded into the category (using a special category segment, for example "k").

4.2.1 Rule Schemata for Handling Agreement

1. r_i: [(X k Y)(k')] $\Rightarrow$ [rp$_i$ (X k Y)]

2. r_i: [(k Y)(k')] $\Rightarrow$ [rp$_i$ (k Y)]

3. r_i: [(X k)(k')] $\Rightarrow$ [rp$_i$ (X k)]

4. r_i: [(k')(X k Y)] $\Rightarrow$ [rp$_i$ (X k Y)]

5. r_i: [(k')(k Y)] $\Rightarrow$ [rp$_i$ (k Y)]

6. r_i: [(k')(X k)] $\Rightarrow$ [rp$_i$ (X k)]

The argument position represented by segment k is restricted to values of category (k'). Since the k segment is not canceled in the output, more words with the k' agreement feature may be added.[13] In the first three schemata, the modifier follows the modified; in the last three schemata the modifier precedes the modified.

To illustrate the treatment of different kinds of agreement in LA-grammar, let's compare the syntax of adjectives in English and German.

4.2.2 John bought a beautiful old house.

```
* (z John bought a beautiful old house \.)

*** Lex Lookup
Real time:     0.06 s
Run time:      0.00 s

*** Parse Timings
Real time:     0.82 s
Run time:      0.54 s

    Linear Analysis:

    *START_0
    1
        (NH) JOHN
        (N A V) BOUGHT
    *NOM+FVERB_3
    2
        (A V) JOHN BOUGHT
        (SQ) A
    *FVERB+MAIN_4
    3
        (SQ V) JOHN BOUGHT A
        (ADJ) BEAUTIFUL
    *DET+ADJ_1
    4
        (SQ V) JOHN BOUGHT A BEAUTIFUL
        (ADJ) OLD
    *DET+ADJ_1
    5
        (SQ V) JOHN BOUGHT A BEAUTIFUL OLD
        (S-H) HOUSE
    *DET+NOUN_2
    6
        (V) JOHN BOUGHT A BEAUTIFUL OLD HOUSE
        (V DECL) .
    *CMPLT_13
    7
        (DECL) JOHN BOUGHT A BEAUTIFUL OLD HOUSE .


Hierarchical Analysis:

(PROPOSITION-7_8_1
  (MOOD (DECLARATIVE-7_8_1))
```

---

[13]Because the variables X and Y may be empty, the first and the fourth schema are the most general. Which of the six schemata is used depends on the language and the construction in question.

```
(PROP-CONTENT
  ((SENT-2_8_1
    (SUBJ ((NP-1_8_1 (NAME (JOHN-1_8_1)))))
    (VERB (BUY-2_8_1))
    (DIR-OBJ
      ((NP-3_8_1
        (REF (A-3_8_1 SG-3_8_1))
        (ADJ
          ((ADJ-4_8_1 (ADJECTIVE (BEAUTIFUL-4_8_1)))
           (ADJ-5_8_1 (ADJECTIVE (OLD-5_8_1)))))
        (NOUN ((HOUSE-6_8_1)))))))))))))
```

The rule DET+ADJ used in history sections 3 and 4 is of the kind illustrated in
4.2.1 (rule type 2), and is defined as follows:[14]

4.2.3 Simplified Version of the ECAT rule DET+ADJ

DET+ADJ: [(seg1 X)(ADJ)] $\Rightarrow$ [*DET+ADJ (seg1 X)]
where seg1 ε {GQ, SQ, PQ}, and *DET+ADJ = {DET+ADJ, DET+NOUN}

We see that the addition of an adjective in English requires the occurrence of a
determiner segment in the sentence start category (CAT-1).[15]

The rule package *DET+ADJ contains the rule DET+ADJ; furthermore, the CAT-
1 of the rule DET+ADJ equals the CAT-3. Consequently, an arbitrary number of
adjectives may be added. The categorial environment for adding adjectives arises after a determiner and after an adjective. But once the noun is added by DET+NOUN,
the categorial environment for adjectives is lost.

4.2.4 Simplified Version of the ECAT rule DET+NOUN

DET+NOUN: [(seg1 X)(seg2)] $\Rightarrow$ [*DET+NOUN (X)]
where seg1 = GQ and seg2 ε {SH, S-H, PH, P-H}, or
seg1 = SQ and seg2 ε {SH, S-H}, or
seg1 = PQ and seg2 ε {PH, P-H},
and *DET+NOUN = {NOM+FVERB, FVERB+MAIN, START-RELCL, ...}

The rule DET+ADJ (4.2.3) illustrates categorial *correspondence* on the basis of
an explicit definition: seg1 corresponds to ADJ if seg1 is either a GQ (general
quantifier like *the*), an SQ (singular quantifier like *every*), or a PQ (plural quantifier
like *all*).

Adjectives in English exhibit no morphological variation, and are not subject to
special agreement restrictions. Adjectives in German, on the other hand, arise in
four morphological flavors, characterized by the endings -E, -EN, -ES, and -ER.[16]

---

[14] The category segments GQ, SQ, and PQ stand for "general quantifier"(e.g., *the*), "singular
quantifier" (e.g., *every*) and "plural quantifier" (e.g., *all*), respectively. The linguistic interpretation of
all ECAT category segments is explained in Appendix A1.

[15] In mass noun constructions, like *John drinks red wine*, the adjective is treated as a determiner.

[16] Adjectives ending in -EM are disregarded because they incorporate a determiner function.

Furthermore, there are agreement restrictions which depend on number, gender, case, and definiteness of the noun phrase. Rather than using the possible constellations of these parameters,[17] the agreement of German adjectives is based on the endings, which are used as the agreement feature, and coded into the determiner.

Compare for example the lexical analyses of *das*, *ein*, and *dem*.

4.2.5 Lexical Analysis of Different German Determiners

```
("DAS" (S3 NS -E) DEF-SG (A NS -E) DEF-SG)

("EIN" (S3 MS -ER) INDEF-SG (S3 NS -ES) INDEF-SG (A NS -ES) INDEF-SG)

("DEM" (D MS -EN) DEF-SG (D NS -EN) DEF-SG)
```

Lexical entries in LA-grammars of natural languages are defined as a list consisting of the surface form of the entry (in double quotes), followed by a sequence of readings, each defined as a pair consisting of a category and a frame name. For example, "DAS" has two readings, namely (S3 NS -E) DEF-SG and (A NS -E) DEF-SG.

The category of the first reading characterizes "DAS" as a third person singular nominative (S3) which may take a neuter singular noun (NS) and adjectives ending in -E. The category of the second reading represents an accusative (A) which may take a neuter singular noun (NS) and adjectives ending in -E. The categories of "EIN", on the other hand, show that one nominative reading takes a masculine singular noun (MS) and an adjective ending in -ER, while a second nominative reading and the accusative take neuter singular nouns (NS) and an adjectives ending in -ES.

Given this categorization of the determiners in German, agreement is based on *identical* segments in adjectives and nouns.

4.2.6 Lexical Analysis of German Adjectives and Nouns

```
("SCHOENE" (-E) SCHOEN)

("ALTE") (-E) ALT)

("SCHOENES" (-ES) SCHOEN)

("SCHOENEN" (-EN) SCHOEN)

("BUCH" (NS) BUCH)

("TISCH" (MS) TISCH)
```

---

[17]If we followed a traditional parameter approach, these four distinctions would amount to a total of 48 categories for the four adjective forms of German: two numbers times three genders times four cases times two definiteness distinctions. See Hausser (1986) for a detailed discussion of exhaustive versus distinctive categorization.

Based on this categorization, the formulation of the DCAT rules DET+ADJ and DET+NOUN is straightforward.

4.2.7 Simplified Version of the DCAT rule DET+ADJ

DET+ADJ: [(X seg1)(seg1)] $\Rightarrow$ [*DET+ADJ (X seg1)]
where seg1 ε {-E, -EN, -ES, -ER}, and *DET+ADJ = {DET+ADJ, DET+NOUN}

4.2.8 Simplified Version of the DCAT rule DET+NOUN

DET+NOUN: [(X seg1 seg2)(seg1)] $\Rightarrow$ [*DET+NOUN (X)]
where seg1 ε {MS, FS, NS, MG, NG, P, PD}, seg2 ε {-E, -EN, -ES, -ER},
and *DET+NOUN = {MAIN+FVERB, FVERB+MAIN, START-RELCL, ...}

Consider the derivation of *das schöne Buch* in 4.2.9. The parser forms the Cartesian product of all readings of *das* and *schöne*, resulting in two category pairs: [(S3 NS -E) (-E)] and [(A NS -E) (-E)]. The rule DET+ADJ in the rule package *START fires on both pairs, resulting in two readings. These two readings are continued by the rule DET+NOUN, which is called by the rule package *DET+ADJ.

4.2.9 *das schöne Buch*

```
*  (z das schoene Buch)

*** Lex Lookup
Real time:     0.12 s
Run time:      0.00 s

*** Parse Timings
Real time:     0.10 s
Run time:      0.04 s

2    Linear Analysis:

    *START
    1
        (A NS -E) DAS
        (-E) SCHOENE
    *DET+ADJ
    2
        (A NS -E) DAS SCHOENE
        (NS) BUCH
    *DET+NOUN
    3
        (A) DAS SCHOENE BUCH

Hierarchical Analysis:

(FRAMES_SWITCHED_OFF)


1    Linear Analysis:
```

```
*START
1
    (S3 NS -E) DAS
    (-E) SCHOENE
*DET+ADJ
2
    (S3 NS -E) DAS SCHOENE
    (NS) BUCH
*DET+NOUN
3
    (S3) DAS SCHOENE BUCH
```

Hierarchical Analysis:

(FRAMES_SWITCHED_OFF)

The derivation of *ein schönes Buch* is analogous, except for the different agreement between the adjective and the determiner. The categorial analysis exhibited in the above derivation, and the categorial operation of the DCAT rule DET+ADJ, make it obvious that a determiner in German may be followed by an arbitrary number of adjectives, provided that they have the proper ending. An instance of improper agreement is illustrated in 4.2.10.

4.2.10 *dem schönen alte Buch*

`* (z dem schoenen alte Buch)`

```
*** Lex Lookup
Real time:    0.00 s
Run time:     0.00 s

*** Parse Timings
Real time:    0.06 s
Run time:     0.06 s


ERROR
"Ungrammatical continuation at:" "ALTE"
    Linear Analysis:

    *START
    1
        (D NS -EN) DEM
        (-EN) SCHOENEN
    *DET+ADJ
    2
        (D NS -EN) DEM SCHOENEN
```

Hierarchical Analysis:

(FRAMES_SWITCHED_OFF)

A particularly interesting case is relative clause agreement. Consider example 4.2.11.

4.2.11 *John kissed the girl who slept.*

```
* (z John kissed the girl who slept \.)

*** Lex Lookup
Real time:    0.04 s
Run time:     0.00 s

*** Parse Timings
Real time:    0.52 s
Run time:     0.42 s

    Linear Analysis:

    *START_0
    1
        (NH) JOHN
        (N A V) KISSED
    *NOM+FVERB_3
    2
        (A V) JOHN KISSED
        (GQ) THE
    *FVERB+MAIN_4
    3
        (GQ V) JOHN KISSED THE
        (SH) GIRL
    *DET+NOUN_2
    4
        (V) JOHN KISSED THE GIRL
        (WH) WHO
    *START-RELCL_15
    5
        (WS V) JOHN KISSED THE GIRL WHO
        (N V) SLEPT
    *NOM+FVERB_3
    6
        (V) JOHN KISSED THE GIRL WHO SLEPT
        (V DECL) .
    *CMPLT_13
    7
        (DECL) JOHN KISSED THE GIRL WHO SLEPT .

Hierarchical Analysis:

(PROPOSITION-7_7_2
  (MOOD (DECLARATIVE-7_7_2))
  (PROP-CONTENT
   ((SENT-2_7_2
     (SUBJ ((NP-1_7_2 (NAME (JOHN-1_7_2))))))
     (VERB (KISS-2_7_2))
     (DIR-OBJ
      ((NP-3_7_2
        (REF (THE-3_7_2 SG-4_7_2))
        (NOUN ((GIRL-4_7_2)))
        (REL-CLAUSE
         ((COMP-5_7_2
           (COMP ((WHO-5_5_2)))
```

```
(SENT ((SENT-6_7_2 (SUBJ ("NP-3_7_2"))
                   (VERB (SLEEP-6_7_2)))))))))))))))))
```

The choice of the complementizer *who* versus *which* depends on whether the referent of the head noun is human. This distinction is coded into the lexical category of English nouns.

4.2.12 Lexical Analysis of Human versus Non-Human Nouns in English

```
("GIRL" (SH) GIRL)
```

```
("CAT" (S-H) CAT)
```

The category segment SH stands for "singular human," while S-H stands for "singular non-human."

Because the category of the noun is used to cancel the determiner segment, it does not become part of the sentence-start category, as shown in history sections 3 and 4 of 4.2.1. Thus the sentence-start category (V) does not contain the agreement information necessary for handling relative clauses. But the information is still available in the "next word" of history section 3.[18]

The solution is to treat the history as part of the sentence start category. This is possible because the output of LA-grammar rules for natural language specify (i) the new rule package, (ii) the surface of the resulting sentence start, (iii) the category of the resulting sentence start, (iv) the frame-name of the resulting sentence start, and (v) the history of the derivation. The raw output of the rule DET+NOUN is illustrated in 4.2.13.

4.2.13 Analysis of *THE MAN* Prior to Pretty-Printing

```
((*DET+NOUN_2
  (("THE" "MAN")
      (S)
      ((#:NP-1_2_4))
      1 (*START_0 ("THE") (GQ) ("MAN") (SH)) 2)))
```

Given this structure, we may define a "generalized category," consisting of the current sentence start category and the current derivational history, e.g., [(S), 1 (*START_0 ("THE") (GQ) ("MAN") (SH))]. While most rules use only the sentence-start category, there are certain phenomena (such as relative clause agreements) where the categorial operation of the rule depends also on the history. Definition of a procedure searching for a preceding head noun with proper agreement properties, for example, is straightforward because of the completely regular nature of derivational histories.

The agreement distinction in question is illustrated in 4.2.14 and 4.2.15:

---

[18]Earlier versions of DCAT and ECAT handled agreement of relative clauses by carrying the noun segments along in the category. This resulted in an untidy cluttering of the categories, and was not easily extendable to the handling of conjunction and gapping.

4.2.14 *The man who*

```
* (z the man who)

*** Lex Lookup
Real time:     0.00 s
Run time:      0.00 s

*** Parse Timings
Real time:     0.28 s
Run time:      0.12 s

    Linear Analysis:

    *START_0
    1
        (GQ) THE
        (SH) MAN
    *DET+NOUN_2
    2
        (S) THE MAN
        (WH) WHO
    *START-RELCL_15
    3
        (WS S) THE MAN WHO
```

```
Hierarchical Analysis:

(NP-1_3_5
  (REF (THE-1_3_5 SG-2_3_5))
  (NOUN ((MAN-2_3_5)))
  (REL-CLAUSE ((COMP-3_3_5 (COMP ((WHO-3_3_5)))))))
```

The difference between *who* and *which* is coded in the respective categories (WH) and (W-H). In 4.2.14, WH agrees with SH in history section 1. But in 4.2.15, START-RELCL cannot find a compatible antecedent for *which*.

4.2.15 **The man which*

```
* (z the man which)

*** Lex Lookup
Real time:     0.04 s
Run time:      0.00 s

*** Parse Timings
Real time:     0.10 s
Run time:      0.08 s


ERROR
"Ungrammatical continuation at:" "WHICH"
    Linear Analysis:

    *START_0
    1
```

```
     (GQ)  THE
     (SH)  MAN
 *DET+NOUN_2
 2
     (S)  THE MAN
```

```
Hierarchical Analysis:
```

```
(NP-1_2_6
 (REF  (THE-1_2_6 SG-2_2_6))
 (NOUN  ((MAN-2_2_6)))))
```

The option of using the derivational history as part of a generalized category is especially valuable for the treatment of constructions with "long-distance antecedents," such as extraposed relative clauses, conjunction, and gapping. But it raises the generative power of LA-grammars for natural language to the level of B-LAGs:[19]the length of the derivational history is bounded by the length of the input parsed, but there is no finite constant delimiting the steps of the categorial operation searching for the antecedent.

4.3   Valency

An expression is called a **valency carrier** if it has one or more argument positions which must be filled by certain types of expressions in order to be complete. For example, the verb form *eats* is a valency carrier with a nominative position for a third person singular noun phrase and an accusative position. The accusative position may be filled by any kind of noun phrase which is not restricted to nominative (such as *I* or *he*).

The valency properties of a valency carrier are expressed in LA-grammar by means of the lexical categorization. For example, *eats* is analyzed as ("EATS" (S3 A V)). Thereby, 'S3' represents a nominative position restricted to third person singular, 'A' represents the accusative position, and 'V'—for verb—is the result category, i.e., the category which results once all valencies have been saturated.

The restriction of valency positions to certain kinds of argument expressions constitutes a kind of agreement, but valency goes beyond modifier agreement (cf. Section 4.2) in that there may be only one filler per valency position. The relation between valency carriers and their arguments is handled in LA-grammar by rules of the following structure:

4.3.1 Basic Rule Schemata Illustrating the Handling of Valency

1. r_i: $[(k')(X\ k\ Y)] \Rightarrow [rp_i\ (X\ Y)]$

2. r_i: $[(k')(k\ Y)] \Rightarrow [rp_i\ (Y)]$

3. r_i: $[(k')(X\ k)] \Rightarrow [rp_i\ (X)]$

4. r_i: $[(X \ k \ Y)(k')] \Rightarrow [rp_i \ (X \ Y)]$

5. r_i: $[(k \ Y)(k')] \Rightarrow [rp_i \ (Y)]$

6. r_i: $[(X \ k)(k')] \Rightarrow [rp_i \ (X)]$

The valency position k is restricted to arguments of category (k'). The addition of such an argument results in cancellation of the valency position. In the first three schemata the argument precedes the valency carrier; in the remaining schemata the argument follows the valency carrier.

Consider 4.3.2 as an example.

4.3.2 *John eats*

```
* (z John eats)

*** Lex Lookup
Real time:      0.02 s
Run time:       0.02 s

*** Parse Timings
Real time:      0.06 s
Run time:       0.06 s

    Linear Analysis:

    *START_0
    1
        (NH) JOHN
        (S3 A V) EATS
    *NOM+FVERB_3
    2
        (A V) JOHN EATS

Hierarchical Analysis:

(SENT-2_2_15
 (SUBJ ((NP-1_2_15 (NAME (JOHN-1_2_15))))))
 (VERB (EAT-2_2_15)))
```

We see that the nominative position in the valency carrier is cancelled in history section 2. Furthermore, the categorial operation is of type 2 in 4.3.1. The result of applying NOM+FVERB is the sentence start *John eats*, which still has an open accusative valency position.

As in the case of optional modifiers, the correspondence between k and k' may be based on explicit definition in the rules, or on the identity of the category segments involved. We see in example 4.3.2 that the agreement between the valency position and its filler does not depend on the identity of the category segments involved, but rather on explicit correspondence definitions in the rule NOM+FVERB.

---

[19] See Chapter 7.

The agreement of the nominative and the finite verb in English is based on the following categorization of noun phrases and finite verbs.

4.3.3 Lexical Analysis of Elementary Noun Phrases and Finite Verbs in English

```
("I" (S1) I)

("YOU" (SP2) YOU)

("HE" (S3) HE)

("SHE" (S3) SHE)

("IT" (N-H) IT)

("WE" (P1) WE)

("THEY" (P3) THEY)

("JOHN" (NH) JOHN)

("FIDO" (N-H) FIDO)

("AM" (S1 B V) BE)

("ARE" (NM B V) BE)

("IS" (S3 B V) BE)

("WAS" (S1 B V) BE (S3 B V) BE)

("WERE" (N B V) BE)

("HAVE" (NOM HV V) HAVE)

("HAS" (S3 HV V) HAVE)

("HAD" (N HV V) HAVE)

("EAT" (NOM A V) EAT)

("EATS" (S3 A V) EAT)

("ATE" (N A V) EAT)

("EATING" (B A) EAT)

("EATEN" (HV A) EAT)

("GIVE" (NOM D A V) GIVE (NOM A TO V) GIVE)

("GIVES" (S3 D A V) GIVE (S3 A TO V) GIVE)

("GAVE" (N D A V) GIVE (N A TO V) GIVE)

("GIVING" (B D A) GIVE (B A TO) GIVE)
```

```
("GIVEN" (HV D A) GIVE (HV A TO) GIVE)
```

The interpretation of the category segments used in 4.3.3 is explained in the alphabetical listing of Appendix A.1. Recall that lexical entries in LA-grammars of natural languages are defined as a list consisting of the surface form of the entry (in double quotes), followed by a sequence of readings, each defined as a pair consisting of a category and a frame name (word stem).

Given this categorization, the agreement between the nominative (argument) and the finite verb (valency carrier) is captured by the following definition of the rule NOM+FVERB:

4.3.4 Simplified Version of the ECAT rule NOM+FVERB

> NOM+FVERB: [(seg1)(seg2 X)] $\Rightarrow$ [*NOM+FVERB (X)]
> where seg1 = S1 and seg2 ε {S1, N, NOM}, or
> seg1 ε {SP2, P1, P3, P} and seg2 ε {NM, N, NOM}, or
> seg1 ε {NH, N-H, S3, S} and seg2 ε {S3, N}.
> and *NOM+FVERB = {FVERB+MAIN, ADD-VERB, START-INF, ...}

Next consider this example:

4.3.5 *The man has eaten an apple.*

```
* (z The man has eaten an apple \.)

*** Lex Lookup
Real time:     0.10 s
Run time:      0.02 s

*** Parse Timings
Real time:     0.56 s
Run time:      0.48 s

    Linear Analysis:

    *START_0
    1
        (GQ) THE
        (SH) MAN
    *DET+NOUN_2
    2
        (S) THE MAN
        (S3 HV V) HAS
    *NOM+FVERB_3
    3
        (HV V) THE MAN HAS
        (HV A) EATEN
    *ADD-VERB_6
    4
        (A V) THE MAN HAS EATEN
        (SQ) AN
    *FVERB+MAIN_4
    5
        (SQ V) THE MAN HAS EATEN AN
```

```
    (S-H) APPLE
*DET+NOUN_2
6
    (V) THE MAN HAS EATEN AN APPLE
    (V DECL) .
*CMPLT_13
7
    (DECL) THE MAN HAS EATEN AN APPLE .
```

Hierarchical Analysis:

```
(PROPOSITION-7_7_20
 (MOOD (DECLARATIVE-7_7_20))
 (PROP-CONTENT
  ((SENT-3_7_20
    (SUBJ ((NP-1_7_20 (REF (THE-1_7_20 SG-2_7_20)) (NOUN ((MAN-2_7_20))))))
    (AUX (HAVE-3_7_20))
    (PREDICATE
     ((NFV-4_7_20
       (PAST-PART (EAT-4_7_20))
       (DIR-OBJ
        ((NP-5_7_20 (REF (A-5_7_20 SG-5_7_20)) (NOUN ((APPLE-6_7_20)))))))))
  )))))
```

The categorial operations of this example exhibit three different kinds of relations between a valency carrier and its argument.

In history section 2, the argument (S) precedes the valency carrier (S3 HV V), resulting in (HV V). This categorial operation corresponds to schema 2 in 4.3.1. Note that the argument is a *complex* noun phrase.

In history section 3, we encounter a type of valency not contained in the basic schemata of 4.3.1: the sentence start of category (HV V) is combined with the non-finite verb of category (HV A) into (A V). This kind of valency-based composition has numerous structural alternatives, which are illustrated schematically in 4.3.6.

4.3.6 Basic Rule Schemata Illustrating Valency-Based Composition

1. r_i: [(k X)(k' Y)] $\Rightarrow$ [rp$_i$ (X Y)]

2. r_i: [(k X)(Y k')] $\Rightarrow$ [rp$_i$ (X Y)]

3. r_i: [(X k)(k' Y)] $\Rightarrow$ [rp$_i$ (X Y)]

4. r_i: [(X k)(Y k')] $\Rightarrow$ [rp$_i$ (X Y)]

5. r_i: [(k X)(k' Y)] $\Rightarrow$ [rp$_i$ (Y X)]

6. r_i: [(k X)(Y k')] $\Rightarrow$ [rp$_i$ (Y X)]

7. r_i: [(X k)(k' Y)] $\Rightarrow$ [rp$_i$ (Y X)]

8. r_i: [(X k)(Y k')] $\Rightarrow$ [rp$_i$ (Y X)]

The composition in history section 3 corresponds to schema 1 of 4.3.6.

The third type of relation between a valency carrier and its argument is illustrated in history section 4 of 4.3.5: the valency carrier (A V) is followed by the argument (SQ), resulting in (SQ V). This result category indicates that the argument is an incomplete noun phrase which requires a noun compatible with a singular quantifier. The noun phrase is completed by calling DET+NOUN and DET+ADJ in the rule package of FVERB+MAIN.

4.3.7 Simplified Version of the ECAT rule FVERB+MAIN

> FVERB+MAIN: [(seg1 X)(seg2)] $\Rightarrow$ [*FVERB+MAIN (seg3 X)]
> where seg1 ε {D, A, SC}, seg2 ε {NH, N-H}, and seg3 = nil, or
> seg1 ε {D, A, SC}, seg2 ε {GQ, SQ, PQ}, and seg3 = seg2, or
> seg1 ε {TO, BY}, seg2 = seg1, and seg3 = NP,
> and *FVERB+MAIN = {DET+ADJ, DET+NOUN, FVERB+MAIN,
> PREP+NP ...}

The type of valency cancellation defined in FVERB+MAIN corresponds roughly to schema 5 of 4.3.1.

4.4   Word Order

The large number of different possible schemata for categorial operations is one reason for the descriptive power of LA-grammar. But each natural language uses only certain kinds of categorial operations. The characteristic kinds of categorial operations used by a natural language constitute an obvious typology of that language.

English, for example, is a language with a fixed word order. This fact is reflected by categorial operations of the following structure:

4.4.1 The Categorial Operations Characteristic of English

1. r_i: [(k')(k X)] $\Rightarrow$ [rp$_i$ (X)]   (e.g., NOM+FVERB)

2. r_i: [(k X)(k')] $\Rightarrow$ [rp$_i$ (X)]   (e.g., FVERB+MAIN)

The two schematic rules are different in that the valency carrier follows the argument in the first rule, but precedes the argument in the second. The two rules are similar, however, in that the valency position to be filled (cancelled) is always the *first* segment of the category of the valency carrier. Thus the categorial operations in question translate the order of the argument positions (in the valency carrier category) into a corresponding rigid word order.

A second factor in the handling of word order is the control structure. The system defined in 4.4.2 produces a rigid word order solely on the basis of certain rules calling certain other rules, without any reliance on the categorial structure.

4.4.2 A Schematic Rule System Illustrating the Handling of Rigid Word Order

r-1: $[(X)(a)] \Rightarrow [\{r\text{-}2\} \ (X)]$
r-2: $[(X)(b)] \Rightarrow [\{r\text{-}3\} \ (X)]$
r-3: $[(X)(c)] \Rightarrow [rp\text{-}3 \ (X)]$

These rules insure that an 'a' is followed by a 'b', and a 'b' is followed by a 'c'. This order is encoded by the content of the rule packages. The handling of English word order resembles the formal properties illustrated in 4.4.2 insofar as NOM+FVERB calls FVERB+MAIN, but not vice versa.

As an example illustrating the handling of English word order consider 4.4.3. The sentence start *John gave Mary* is ambiguous. On one reading Mary is a dative, as in *John gave Mary a book*. On the other reading Mary is an accusative, as in *John gave Mary to her mother*. Furthermore, the first reading must be followed by an accusative, while the second reading must be followed by a *to*-phrase.

These structural properties are handled in terms of a lexical ambiguity of *gave*, expressed in the alternative categories (N D A V) and (N A TO V).

4.4.3 *John gave Mary*

```
* (z John gave Mary)

*** Lex Lookup
Real time:     0.02 s
Run time:      0.00 s

*** Parse Timings
Real time:     0.24 s
Run time:      0.24 s

2    Linear Analysis:

    *START_0
    1
        (NH) JOHN
        (N A TO V) GAVE
    *NOM+FVERB_3
    2
        (A TO V) JOHN GAVE
        (NH) MARY
    *FVERB+MAIN_4
    3
        (TO V) JOHN GAVE MARY


Hierarchical Analysis:

(SENT-2_5_2
  (SUBJ ((NP-1_5_2 (NAME (JOHN-1_5_2)))))
  (VERB (GIVE-2_5_2))
  (DIR-OBJ ((NP-3_5_2 (NAME (MARY-3_5_2))))))
```

1   Linear Analysis:

```
*START_0
1       .
    (NH) JOHN
    (N D A V) GAVE
*NOM+FVERB_3
2
    (D A V) JOHN GAVE
    (NH) MARY
*FVERB+MAIN_4
3
    (A V) JOHN GAVE MARY
```

Hierarchical Analysis:

```
(SENT-2_4_2
  (SUBJ ((NP-1_4_2 (NAME (JOHN-1_4_2)))))
  (VERB (GIVE-2_4_2))
  (INDIR-OBJ ((NP-3_4_2 (NAME (MARY-3_4_2))))))
```

We see that the different grammatical roles (DIR-OBJ versus INDIR-OBJ) of *Mary* are correctly specified in the respective semantic hierarchies. Furthermore, the result categories (TO V) versus (A V) encode the correct expectations for the next continuation.

Next consider the categorial operations characteristic of German. German has a relatively free word order. This fact is reflected by categorial operations of the following structure:

4.4.4 The Categorial Operations Characteristic of German Main Clauses

1. r_i: $[(k)(X \ k \ Y)] \Rightarrow [rp_i \ (X \ Y)]$ (e.g., MAIN+FVERB)

2. r_i: $[(X \ k \ Y)(k)] \Rightarrow [rp_i \ (X \ Y)]$ (e.g., FVERB+MAIN)

These rules correspond to the schemas 1 and 4 in 4.3.1. They differ in that the valency carrier follows its argument in the first rule, but precedes in the second. The rules are similar, however, in that the valency position can be anywhere in the category of the valency carrier as long as the argument and the valency position are represented by *identical* segments. Thus the categorial operations in question are not bound by the order of the argument positions (in the valency carrier category).

The DCAT rules MAIN+FVERB and FVERB+MAIN are formulated as follows:

4.4.5 A Simplified Version of MAIN+FVERB and FVERB+MAIN in DCAT

MAIN+FVERB: $[(\text{seg1})(\text{v } X)] \Rightarrow [\{\text{FVERB+MAIN}\} (\text{v } Y)]$
where seg1 ε {n, d, a},[20] seg1 ε X, and Y = X − {seg1}
FVERB+MAIN: $[(\text{v } X)(\text{seg1})] \Rightarrow [\{\text{FVERB+MAIN}\} (\text{v } Y)]$
where seg1 ε {n, d, a}, seg1 ε X, and Y = X − {seg1}

The free ordering of noun phrases encoded by these rules is illustrated by the following derivations of *Der Mann sah die Frau* and *Die Frau sah der Mann*.

4.4.6 *Der Mann sah die Frau.*

```
* (z Der Mann sah die Frau \.)

*** Lex Lookup
Real time:     0.04 s
Run time:      0.00 s

*** Parse Timings
Real time:     0.18 s
Run time:      0.12 s

    Linear Analysis:

    START
    1
       (S3 MS -E) DER
       (MS) MANN
    DET+NOUN
    2
       (S3) DER MANN
       (V S3 A) SAH
    MAIN+FVERB
    3
       (V A) DER MANN SAH
       (A FS -E) DIE
    FVERB+MAIN
    4
       (V FS -E) DER MANN SAH DIE
       (FS) FRAU
    DET+NOUN
    5
       (V) DER MANN SAH DIE FRAU
       (V DECL) .
    CMPLT
    6
       (DECL) DER MANN SAH DIE FRAU .

Hierarchical Analysis:

(FRAMES_SWITCHED_OFF)
```

---

[20]The segments n, d, a, and v represent a nominative, dative, accusative, and verb, respectively. The handling of adverbs is omitted for the sake of simplicity.

4.4.7 *Die Frau sah der Mann.*

```
*  (z Die Frau sah der Mann \.)

*** Lex Lookup
Real time:     0.02 s
Run time:      0.02 s

*** Parse Timings
Real time:     0.24 s
Run time:      0.22 s

    Linear Analysis:

    START
    1
        (A FS -E) DIE
        (FS) FRAU
    DET+NOUN
    2
        (A) DIE FRAU
        (V S3 A) SAH
    MAIN+FVERB
    3
        (V S3) DIE FRAU SAH
        (S3 MS -E) DER
    FVERB+MAIN
    4
        (V MS -E) DIE FRAU SAH DER
        (MS) MANN
    DET+NOUN
    5
        (V) DIE FRAU SAH DER MANN
        (V DECL)  .
    CMPLT
    6
        (DECL) DIE FRAU SAH DER MANN .


Hierarchical Analysis:

(FRAMES_SWITCHED_OFF)
```

But the word order of German is not completely free: in main clauses the finite verb has to be in second position. This is handled in part by the control structure technique illustrated in 4.4.2: MAIN+FVERB calls FVERB+MAIN, but not vice versa. Furthermore, MAIN+FVERB requires a non-verbal constituent and a finite verb as input (in that order), while FVERB+MAIN requires as input a sentence start containing a finite verb and (the beginning of) a non-verbal constituent.

This point is illustrated in 4.4.8.

4.4.8 *Der Mann die Frau sah.*

```
* (z Der Mann die Frau sah)

*** Lex Lookup
Real time:    0.00 s
Run time:     0.00 s

*** Parse Timings
Real time:    0.04 s
Run time:     0.04 s


ERROR
"Ungrammatical continuation at:" "DIE"
    Linear Analysis:

    START
    1
        (S3 MS -E) DER
        (MS) MANN
    DET+NOUN
    2
        (S3) DER MANN


Hierarchical Analysis:

(FRAMES_SWITCHED_OFF)
```

While the order of 4.4.8 is ungrammatical in German main clauses, it is grammatical in subordinate clauses. The latter allow noun phrases and adverbs in any order, but require the finite verb in final position. A valency carrier at the end of the clause requires yet two more types of categorial operations, called "argument adding" and "wholesale cancelling," which are illustrated in 4.4.9.

4.4.9 *Weil der Mann die Frau sah,*

```
* (z Weil der Mann die Frau sah)

*** Lex Lookup
Real time:    0.02 s
Run time:     0.02 s

*** Parse Timings
Real time:    0.16 s
Run time:     0.16 s

    Linear Analysis:

    START
    1
        (ADCL V) WEIL
        (S3 MS -E) DER
    SUBCL+MAIN
    2
        (ADCL V S3 MS -E) WEIL DER
```

```
    (MS)  MANN
DET+NOUN
3
    (ADCL V S3)  WEIL DER MANN
    (A FS -E)  DIE
SUBCL+MAIN
4
    (ADCL V S3 A FS -E)  WEIL DER MANN DIE
    (FS)  FRAU
DET+NOUN
5
    (ADCL V S3 A)  WEIL DER MANN DIE FRAU
    (V S3 A)  SAH
SUBCL+LASTVERB
6
    (ADCL)  WEIL DER MANN DIE FRAU SAH ,
```

Hierarchical Analysis:

(FRAMES_SWITCHED_OFF)

Next consider a language like Latin or Polish, where the verb and its arguments can occur in any order. This type of word order is handled by the following rule system:

4.4.10 A Schematic Rule System Illustrating the Handling of Free Word Order

r-1: $[(X)(seg1)] \Rightarrow [\{r\text{-}1, r\text{-}2\} (X\ seg1)]$
where $\{X\} \cap \{v\} = \emptyset$ [21] and $seg1\ \varepsilon\ \{n, d, a\}$.
r-2: $[(X)(Y\ v)] \Rightarrow [\{r\text{-}3\} (Z\ v)]$
where $\{X\} \cup \{Y\} \cup \{n\ d\ a\} = \{n\ d\ a\}$ and $Z = \{X\} \cap \{Y\}$.
r-3: $[(X)(seg1)] \Rightarrow [\{r\text{-}3\} (Y)]$
where $v\ \varepsilon\ \{X\}$, $seg1\ \varepsilon\ \{n\ d\ a\}$, and $Y = \{X\} - \{seg1\}$.

Finally consider the case of local ambiguities, like the one described in 3.4.4 and 3.4.5, where the noun phrase *a book* in *The man read a book* can be either the direct object of the main clause, or the subject of a reduced complement—as in *the man read a book was given to Mary*. At first glance, one might assume that the parsing of such constructions would require 'look-ahead.'

But this is not the case. Instead of look-ahead, such constructions are treated equivalently by a local ambiguity which **anticipates** all possible continuations. Which of the parallel readings is the correct one is decided when the derivation gets to the words which disambiguate the construction. Thus a '.' results in discarding the second reading of example 3.4.4, while a 'was' results in discarding the first.

Local ambiguities, which are common in some languages (e.g., Japanese), are handled by rule systems like the following:

---

[21]I.e., the cat-1 does not contain a 'v', which means that the sentence start hasn't yet incorporated the verb.

4.4.11 A Schematic Rule System Illustrating Anticipating Splits

r-1: $[(X)(a)] \Rightarrow [\{r\text{-}2,r\text{-}3\} \ (X \ a)]$
r-2: $[(X \ a)(b)] \Rightarrow [\{r\text{-}4\} \ (X \ c)]$
r-3: $[(X \ a)(b)] \Rightarrow [\{r\text{-}5\} \ (X \ d)]$
r-4: $[(X \ c)(seg1)] \Rightarrow [rp\text{-}4 \ (Y)]$
r-5: $[(X \ d)(seg1)] \Rightarrow [rp\text{-}5 \ (Y)]$

In 4.4.11, the local syntactic ambiguity is created by r-2 and r-3, which (i) are both called by r-1, and (ii) both accept the same input. The local ambiguity is resolved during application of r-4 and r-5. Rule systems may create local ambiguities which run in parallel over arbitrarily many words. If a local ambiguity is not resolved when the end of the sentence is reached, the sentence is called syntactically ambiguous.[22]

4.5   Pronouns

Pronouns occur in various different syntactic categories. For example, *I*, *you*, *he*, *she*, *it*, etc., are noun phrases; *here*, *there*, *then*, etc., are adverbs; and *my*, *your*, *his*, etc., are determiners. The only pronouns that are really nouns in English are *one* and *ones*. The name pronoun is therefore unfortunate, and is replaced by pro-form.

As explained in Section 11.3, a pro-form may consist of several semantic components. For example, *he* combines the symbolic qualities 'male' and 'singular' with the indexical quality of a certain kind of pointer. In Hausser (1979a) these factors are expressed by the following formula of intensional logic:[23]

4.5.1 The Logical Analysis of *HE*

$$\lambda P \forall x \ \varepsilon \ [male(x) \ \& \ \Gamma_3]^1 P\{x\}$$

Thereby $\forall x \ \varepsilon \ [...]$ expresses an existential presupposition in terms of restricted quantification;[24] the superscript on $[...]^1$ expresses singular in terms of a definition resembling Russell's uniqueness condition; and Γ_3 is a context variable expressing the characteristic aspect of indexicality, i.e., third person.

In an extended system of ECAT, a frame-theoretic translation of logical analyses like 4.5.1 will be available as part of the word frame:

("HE" (S3) HE)
|
$$\lambda P \forall x \ \varepsilon \ [male(x) \ \& \ \Gamma_3]^1 P\{x\}$$

---

[22]See Section 7.3 for further discussion.
[23]See Section 15.2 and 15.5 for the logical definitions in question.
[24]Cf. Section 15.2.

This kind of componential analysis may be extended to all pro-forms. Consider, for example, the analysis of *we* in 4.5.2:

4.5.2 The Logical Analysis of *WE*

$$\lambda \mathcal{P} \forall x \; \varepsilon \; [\Gamma_1]^2 \mathcal{P}\{x\}$$

In 4.5.2 there is no gender specification, the superscript $[...]^2$ indicates plural, and the characteristic aspect of indexicality is Γ_1 (first person) rather than Γ_3.

4.5.1 and 4.5.2 illustrate the semantic aspect in the analysis of pro-forms: a small set of constants representing gender, the possessor relation, the singular/plural distinction, and a limited number of context variables to indicate different aspects of indexicality suffice to express the differences and similarities of various pro-forms. For example, *we* and *they* are alike except that they use different context variables (Γ_1 versus Γ_3). Or take *we* and *our*, which have the same context variable and the same number, but differ in their syntactic categories (*we* is a noun phrase, while *our* is a determiner), and in that *our* expresses a possessor relation.

4.5.3 The Logical Analysis of *OUR*

$$\lambda \mathcal{Q} \lambda \mathcal{P} \forall x \; \varepsilon \; [\mathcal{Q}(x) \; \& \; \forall y \; \varepsilon \; [\Gamma_1]^2 \; relate \; (x, \lambda \mathcal{P} \mathcal{P} \; \{y\}] \; \mathcal{P}\{x\}$$

This kind of logical semantic analysis may be developed to a high degree of descriptive detail. But the most interesting part in the semantic decomposition of pro-forms is their characteristic aspect of indexicality.

Consider, for example, the utterance *I am happy*. One part of this utterance is the structure of the sign, which is analyzed as follows:

4.5.4 The Syntactico-Semantic Analysis of *I am happy*.

```
*  (z I am happy \.)

Linear Analysis:

   *START_0
   1
       (S1) I
       (S1 B V) AM
   *NOM+FVERB_3
   2
       (B V) I AM
       (ADJ) HAPPY
   *ADD-VERB_6
   3
       (V) I AM HAPPY
       (V DECL) .
   *CMPLT_15
   4
       (DECL) I AM HAPPY .
```

Hierarchical Analysis:

```
(PROPOSITION-4_4_20
 (MOOD (DECLARATIVE-4_4_20))
 (PROP-CONTENT
  ((SENT-2_4_20
    (SUBJ ((NP-1_4_20 (PRO ((I-1_4_20))))))
    (AUX (BE-2_4_20))
    (PREDICATE ((ADJ-3_4_20 (ADJECTIVE (HAPPY-3_4_20)))))))))))
```

The syntactico-semantic analysis of this sentence is completely analogous to a similar sentence without a pro-form, e.g., *Peter is happy*. Apart from the difference in verb agreement, *I* functions just like *Peter*. The special property of the pro-form only comes into play through the **pragmatic** interpretion of 4.5.4 relative to a context.

The indexicality aspect of first person may be described informally as "refers to the speaker." But a concrete definition of this pragmatic interpretation function is possible only in a system which contains an explicit definition of internal context in addition to a syntactico-semantic analysis like 4.5.4.

Similar considerations hold for **anaphoric** uses of pro-forms. A pro-form is used anaphorically if it is *coreferential* with another phrase in the sentence. As an example consider 4.5.5:

4.5.5 *John slept after he ate an apple.*

```
* (z john slept after he ate an apple \.)

    Linear Analysis:

    *START_0
    1
        (NH) JOHN
        (N V) SLEPT
    *NOM+FVERB_3
    2
        (V) JOHN SLEPT
        (ADP SNP) AFTER
    *ADD-ADP_14
    3
        (SNP V) JOHN SLEPT AFTER
        (S3) HE
    *START-SUBCL_8
    4
        (S3 V) JOHN SLEPT AFTER HE
        (N A V) ATE
    *NOM+FVERB_3
    5
        (A V) JOHN SLEPT AFTER HE ATE
        (SQ) AN
    *FVERB+MAIN_4
    6
        (SQ V) JOHN SLEPT AFTER HE ATE AN
        (S-H) APPLE
    *DET+NOUN_2
    7
```

```
     (V)  JOHN  SLEPT  AFTER  HE  ATE  AN  APPLE
     (V DECL)  .
 *CMPLT_15
 8
     (DECL)  JOHN  SLEPT  AFTER  HE  ATE  AN  APPLE  .
```

```
Hierarchical Analysis:

(PROPOSITION-8_8_12
 (MOOD (DECLARATIVE-8_8_12))
 (PROP-CONTENT
  ((SENT-2_8_12
    (SUBJ ((NP-1_8_12 (NAME (JOHN-1_8_12)))))
    (VERB (SLEEP-2_8_12))
    (ADVERB
     ((PREP-3_8_12
       (ADV (AFTER-3_8_12))
       (PREPOSITIONAL-OBJ
        ((SENT-4_8_12
          (SUBJ ((NP-4_8_12 (PRO ((HE-4_8_12))))))
          (VERB ((EAT-5_8_12)))
          (DIR-OBJ
           ((NP-6_8_12 (REF (A-6_8_12 SG-6_8_12))
                       (NOUN ((APPLE-7_8_12)))))))))))))))))))))
```

The indexicality aspect of *he* differs from that of *I* in that *I* may be used only indexically, while *he* may be used indexically[25] as well as anaphorically. On the anaphoric reading, *he* is coreferential with its "antecedent" *John*, while on the indexical reading, *he* refers to some other person in the utterance context.

It was noted at least as early as 1963 by Lees and Klima that the anaphoric interpretation of pro-forms depends in part on the structure of the sentence. Compare 4.5.6 (which is equal to 4.5.5) and 4.5.7.

4.5.6 *John slept after he ate an apple.*

4.5.7 *% He slept after John ate an apple.*

As indicated by '%', 4.5.7 does not have the full range of pro-form interpretations. Although 4.5.7 is perfectly grammatical, it differs from 4.5.7 in that it does not permit an interpretation where *he* is coreferential with *John*. The sentences 4.5.8 and 4.5.9, on the other hand, both allow an anaphoric interpretation:

4.5.8 *After John ate an apple he slept.*

4.5.9 *After he ate an apple John slept.*

The structural reason for the different interpretation of 4.5.7 in contrast to 4.5.6, 4.5.8, and 4.5.9 may be formulated as follows:

---

[25]Our notion of "indexical" pronoun use refers to all non-anaphoric uses. Thus it covers what is sometimes called the "deictic" use of pronouns.

4.5.10 Coreference Restrictions on Anaphorically Used Pro-Forms

If the antecedent precedes the pro-form, coreference is possible. If the antecedent follows the pro-form, coreference is possible only if the antecedent is in a higher clause.

The notion of "higher clause"—and the concepts of preceding or following—are available for pragmatic interpretation in LA-grammar. Compare, for example, the hierarchical analysis of 4.5.5, which represents the structure of 4.5.6 and 4.5.7, with the hierarchical analysis of 4.5.11, which represents the structure of 4.5.8 and 4.5.9:

4.5.11 *After John ate an apple he slept.*

```
* (z After John ate an apple he slept \.)

    Linear Analysis:

    *START_0
    1
        (ADP SNP) AFTER
        (NH) JOHN
    *START-SUBCL_8
    2
        (NH ADP) AFTER JOHN
        (N A V) ATE
    *NOM+FVERB_3
    3
        (A ADP) AFTER JOHN ATE
        (SQ) AN
    *FVERB+MAIN_4
    4
        (SQ ADP) AFTER JOHN ATE AN
        (S-H) APPLE
    *DET+NOUN_2
    5
        (ADP) AFTER JOHN ATE AN APPLE
        (S3) HE
    *ADD-ADP_14
    6
        (S3) AFTER JOHN ATE AN APPLE HE
        (N V) SLEPT
    *NOM+FVERB_3
    7
        (V) AFTER JOHN ATE AN APPLE HE SLEPT
        (V DECL) .
    *CMPLT_15
    8
        (DECL) AFTER JOHN ATE AN APPLE HE SLEPT .


Hierarchical Analysis:

(PROPOSITION-8_15_13
 (MOOD (DECLARATIVE-8_15_13))
 (PROP-CONTENT
```

```
((SENT-6_15_13
  (ADVERB
   ((PREP-1_15_13
     (ADV (AFTER-1_15_13))
     (PREPOSITIONAL_OBJ
      ((SENT-2_15_13
        (SUBJ ((NP-2_15_13 (NAME (JOHN-2_15_13)))))))
        (VERB ((EAT-3_15_13)))
        (DIR-OBJ
         ((NP-4_15_13
           (REF (A-4_15_13 SG-4_15_13))
           (NOUN ((APPLE-5_15_13)))))))))))))))
    (SUBJ ((NP-6_15_13 (PRO ((HE-6_15_13))))))
    (VERB (SLEEP-6_15_13)))))))
```

The formulation of possible coreference relations between anaphorically used pro-forms and their antecedents in 4.5.10 is not complete, however, because of cases of obligatory "backward pronominalization." Only in 4.5.13 can *him* be coreferential with *John*, whereas in 4.5.12 a coreferential interpretation is not acceptable.[26]

4.5.12 % *Near John, he saw a snake.*

4.5.13 *Near him John saw a snake.*

```
*  (z near him John saw a snake \.)

   Linear Analysis:

   *START_0
   1
      (ADP SNP) NEAR
      (:S3) HIM
   *PREP+NP_5
   2
      (ADP) NEAR HIM
      (NH) JOHN
   *ADD-ADP_14
   3
      (NH) NEAR HIM JOHN
      (N SC V) SAW
   *NOM+FVERB_3
   4
      (SC V) NEAR HIM JOHN SAW
      (SQ) A
   *FVERB+MAIN_4
   5
      (SQ V) NEAR HIM JOHN SAW A
      (S-H) SNAKE
   *DET+NOUN_2
   6
      (V) NEAR HIM JOHN SAW A SNAKE
      (V DECL) .
   *CMPLT_13
```

---

[26]These examples are from Lakoff (1968).

```
7
    (DECL) NEAR HIM JOHN SAW A SNAKE .
```

Hierarchical Analysis:

```
(PROPOSITION-7_12_4
 (MOOD (DECLARATIVE-7_12_4))
 (PROP-CONTENT
  ((SENT-3_12_4
    (ADVERB
     ((PREP-1_12_4
       (ADV (NEAR-1_12_4))
       (PREPOSITIONAL-ARG ((S3-2_12_4 (PRO ((HE-2_12_4)))))))))
    (SUBJ ((NP-3_12_4 (NAME (JOHN-3_12_4)))))
    (VERB (SEE-3_12_4))
    (DIR-OBJ
     ((NP-5_12_4 (REF (A-5_12_4 SG-5_12_4)) (NOUN ((SNAKE-6_12_4)))))))))))
```

Further complications in describing the anaphoric use of pro-forms are illustrated by the following example:[27]

4.5.14 *The man who gave the paycheck to his wife is wiser than the man who gave it to his mistress.*

```
* (z the man who gave the paycheck to his wife is wiser than the man who
gave it to his mistress \.)
```

Linear Analysis:

```
*START_0
1
    (GQ) THE
    (SH) MAN
*DET+NOUN_2
2
    (S) THE MAN
    (WH) WHO
*START-RELCL_15
3
    (WS S) THE MAN WHO
    (N A TO V) GAVE
*NOM+FVERB_3
4
    (A TO S) THE MAN WHO GAVE
    (GQ) THE
*FVERB+MAIN_4
5
    (GQ TO S) THE MAN WHO GAVE THE
    (SH) PAYCHECK
*DET+NOUN_2
6
    (TO S) THE MAN WHO GAVE THE PAYCHECK
    (ADP NP) TO
```

---

[27]Karttunen (1977).

```
*FVERB+MAIN_4
7
    (NP S) THE MAN WHO GAVE THE PAYCHECK TO
    (GQ) HIS
*PREP+NP_5
8
    (GQ S) THE MAN WHO GAVE THE PAYCHECK TO HIS
    (SH) WIFE
*DET+NOUN_2
9
    (S) THE MAN WHO GAVE THE PAYCHECK TO HIS WIFE
    (S3 B V) IS
*NOM+FVERB_3
10
    (B V) THE MAN WHO GAVE THE PAYCHECK TO HIS WIFE IS
    (CADJ) WISER
*ADD-VERB_6
11
    (V) THE MAN WHO GAVE THE PAYCHECK TO HIS WIFE IS WISER
    (THAN NP) THAN
*ADD-ADP_14
12
    (NP V) THE MAN WHO GAVE THE PAYCHECK TO HIS WIFE IS WISER THAN
    (GQ) THE
*PREP+NP_5
13
    (GQ V) THE MAN WHO GAVE THE PAYCHECK TO HIS WIFE IS WISER THAN THE
    (SH) MAN
*DET+NOUN_2
14
    (V) THE MAN WHO GAVE THE PAYCHECK TO HIS WIFE IS WISER THAN THE
    MAN
    (WH) WHO
*START-RELCL_15
15
    (WS V) THE MAN WHO GAVE THE PAYCHECK TO HIS WIFE IS WISER THAN THE
    MAN WHO
    (N A TO V) GAVE
*NOM+FVERB_3
16
    (A TO V) THE MAN WHO GAVE THE PAYCHECK TO HIS WIFE IS WISER THAN
    THE MAN WHO GAVE
    (N-H) IT
*FVERB+MAIN_4
17
    (TO V) THE MAN WHO GAVE THE PAYCHECK TO HIS WIFE IS WISER THAN THE
    MAN WHO GAVE IT
    (ADP NP) TO
*FVERB+MAIN_4
18
    (NP V) THE MAN WHO GAVE THE PAYCHECK TO HIS WIFE IS WISER THAN THE
    MAN WHO GAVE IT TO
    (GQ) HIS
*PREP+NP_5
19
    (GQ V) THE MAN WHO GAVE THE PAYCHECK TO HIS WIFE IS WISER THAN THE
    MAN WHO GAVE IT TO HIS
```

```
        (SH) MISTRESS
   *DET+NOUN_2
   20
        (V) THE MAN WHO GAVE THE PAYCHECK TO HIS WIFE IS WISER THAN THE
        MAN WHO GAVE IT TO HIS MISTRESS
        (V DECL) .
   *CMPLT_13
   21
        (DECL) THE MAN WHO GAVE THE PAYCHECK TO HIS WIFE IS WISER THAN THE
        MAN WHO GAVE IT TO HIS MISTRESS .
```

Hierarchical Analysis:

```
(PROPOSITION-21_45_10
 (MOOD (DECLARATIVE-21_45_10))
 (PROP-CONTENT
  ((SENT-10_45_10
    (SUBJ
     ((NP-1_45_10
       (REF (THE-1_45_10 SG-2_45_10))
       (NOUN ((MAN-2_45_10)))
       (REL-CLAUSE
        ((COMP-3_45_10
          (COMP ((WHO-3_3_10)))
          (SENT
           ((SENT-4_45_10
             (SUBJ ("NP-1_45_10"))
             (VERB (GIVE-4_45_10))
             (DIR-OBJ
              ((NP-5_45_10
                (REF (THE-5_45_10 SG-6_45_10))
                (NOUN ((PAYCHECK-6_45_10)))))))
             (PREPOSITIONAL_OBJ
              ((PREP-7_45_10
                (PREPOSITION (TO-7_45_10))
                (PREPOSITIONAL-ARG
                 ((NP-8_45_10
                   (REF (HE-8_45_10 SG-9_45_10))
                   (NOUN ((WIFE-9_45_10)))))))))))))))))))))
    (AUX (BE-10_45_10))
    (PREDICATE
     ((CADJ-11_45_10
       (CADJ (WISE-11_45_10))
       (ADVERB
        ((NP-12_45_10
          (PRO ((THAN-12_45_10)))
          (PREPOSITIONAL-ARG
           ((NP-13_45_10
             (REF (THE-13_45_10 SG-14_45_10))
             (NOUN ((MAN-14_45_10)))
             (REL-CLAUSE
              ((COMP-15_45_10
                (COMP ((WHO-15_28_10)))
                (SENT
                 ((SENT-16_45_10
                   (SUBJ ("NP-13_45_10"))
                   (VERB (GIVE-16_45_10))
```

```
                    (DIR-OBJ ((NP-17_45_10 (PRO (IT-17_45_10)))))
                    (PREPOSITIONAL_OBJ
                     ((PREP-18_45_10
                        (PREPOSITION (TO-18_45_10))
                        (PREPOSITIONAL-ARG
                         ((NP-19_45_10
                            (REF (HE-19_45_10 SG-20_45_10))
                            (NOUN ((MISTRESS-20_45_10))))))))))))))))))))))))))))
  )))
```

Even though the interpretation of *it* in the second relative clause is related to the antecedent *the paycheck* in the first relative clause, the pro-form is not **coreferential** with its antecedent.

Finally consider an instance of a Bach-Peters sentence:

4.5.15 *The man who deserves it will get the prize he wants.*

```
* (z the man who deserves it will get the prize he wants \.)

    Linear Analysis:

    *START_0
    1
        (GQ) THE
        (SH) MAN
    *DET+NOUN_2
    2
        (S) THE MAN
        (WH) WHO
    *START-RELCL_15
    3
        (WS S) THE MAN WHO
        (S3 SC-INF&N V) DESERVES
    *NOM+FVERB_3
    4
        (SC-INF&N S) THE MAN WHO DESERVES
        (N-H) IT
    *FVERB+MAIN_4
    5
        (S) THE MAN WHO DESERVES IT
        (N M V) WILL
    *NOM+FVERB_3
    6
        (M V) THE MAN WHO DESERVES IT WILL
        (NOM A V) GET
    *ADD-VERB_6
    7
        (A V) THE MAN WHO DESERVES IT WILL GET
        (GQ) THE
    *FVERB+MAIN_4
    8
        (GQ V) THE MAN WHO DESERVES IT WILL GET THE
        (SH) PRIZE
    *DET+NOUN_2
    9
        (V) THE MAN WHO DESERVES IT WILL GET THE PRIZE
```

```
        (S3) HE
    *START-RELCL_15
    10
        (S3 WS V) THE MAN WHO DESERVES IT WILL GET THE PRIZE HE
        (S3 SC-INF&N V) WANTS
    *OBJ+VERB_12
    11
        (V) THE MAN WHO DESERVES IT WILL GET THE PRIZE HE WANTS
        (V DECL) .
    *CMPLT_13
    12
        (DECL) THE MAN WHO DESERVES IT WILL GET THE PRIZE HE WANTS .


Hierarchical Analysis:

(PROPOSITION-12_22_14
  (MOOD (DECLARATIVE-12_22_14))
  (PROP-CONTENT
    ((SENT-6_22_14
      (SUBJ
        ((NP-1_22_14
          (REF (THE-1_22_14 SG-2_22_14))
          (NOUN ((MAN-2_22_14)))
          (REL-CLAUSE
            ((COMP-3_22_14
              (COMP ((WHO-3_3_14)))
              (SENT
                ((SENT-4_22_14
                  (SUBJ ("NP-1_22_14"))
                  (VERB (DESERVE-4_22_14))
                  (DIR-OBJ ((NP-5_22_14 (PRO (IT-5_22_14)))))))))))))))
      (AUX (WILL-6_22_14))
      (PREDICATE
        ((NFV-7_22_14
          (INF (GET-7_22_14))
          (DIR-OBJ
            ((NP-8_22_14
              (REF (THE-8_22_14 SG-9_22_14))
              (NOUN ((PRIZE-9_22_14)))
              (REL-CLAUSE
                ((SENT-10_22_14
                  (SUBJ ((NP-10_22_14 (PRO ((HE-10_22_14))))))
                  (VERB ((WANT-11_22_14)))
                  (DIR-OBJ ("NP-8_22_14")))))))))))))))
```

This example demonstrates two pro-forms whereby the second pro-form occurs in the antecedent of the first, and the first pro-form occurs in the antecedent of the second.

The crucial question at this point is: Should the relation between an anaphoric pro-form and its antecedent be treated in the syntax, the semantics, or the pragmatics? Within transformational grammar, the analysis of anaphoric pro-forms began with a syntactic treatment of reflexive pro-forms. For example, *John shaved himself* was transformationally derived from *John$_i$ shaved John$_i$*. This approach of syntactically stipulated coreference—based on coindexed, identical, underlying noun phrases—worked reasonably well for sentences like 4.5.6 – 4.5.9. But it ran into descriptive problems with other constructions, not least of them sentences like 4.5.14 and 4.5.15.

The current, most widely accepted syntactic approach to the interpretation of anaphoric pro-forms assumes "base-generated" pro-forms. Furthermore, it assumes that *"sentence grammar should properly be concerned, not with coreference, but with* **non-coreference***... The new insight is that it is simpler to specify where they cannot be coreferential."*[28]

The mechanism for specifying non-coreference is *"to assign indices freely...and subsequently filter out the unwanted cases of indexing."*[29] This mechanism is not only extremely inefficient, but the grammar's specification of non-coreference of pro-forms with other phrases in the sentence has no conceivable purpose.

The task in the interpretation of pro-forms, whether they are used indexically or anaphorically, is proper assignment of a **referent**, and this task is neither syntactic nor semantic. The fact that the semantic structure of the sign sometimes guides the pragmatic interpretation of pro-forms is no reason to change the syntax or the semantics of the grammar. Rather, given the hierarchical structures provided by the grammar, we have to define pragmatic interpretation functions which properly utilize these structures.

Consider what is required for the definition of the pragmatic interpretation functions for different aspects of indexicality. In the case of first person pro-forms like *I* or *my*, the interpretation function has to distinguish between different possibilities. If Mary hears Peter say "I am hungry," *I* refers to Peter in Mary's context representation; but if Mary herself utters this sentence, *I* refers to Mary. Thus interpretation of *I* depends on whether the sentence is being uttered or being heard. Another case to consider is direct speech, as in "Peter said: ' I am hungry.' "

On the other hand, the interpretation function for indexically used *third person* pro-forms, must be based on factors like recentness and saliency,[30] as well as on compatibility with the symbolic properties of the pro-form (e.g., number and gender). From here it is only a small step to the interpretation of *anaphorically* interpreted third person pro-forms. The structure of the semantic hierarchy is just one additional aspect to be taken into account by the interpretation function. The hierarchical structures of 4.5.5, 4.5.11, 4.5.13, 4.5.14, and 4.5.15 provide all that is needed for this purpose.

The treatment of pro-forms in LA-grammar proceeds on the assumptions that (i) the syntactic aspect of pro-forms consists solely in their category, (ii) the semantic aspect of pro-forms consists in their decomposition into symbolic and indexical parts, while (iii) the pragmatic aspect consists in the assignment of proper referents,

---

[28]Riemsdijk and Williams (1986, p. 199).
[29]Riemsdijk and Williams (1986, pp. 194,5).
[30]This aspect is part of the "Predictability Requirement for Pronouns" (Kuno 1972).

based on properties of the sign and properties of the utterance context. This approach covers indexical and anaphoric uses alike.[31]

Description of coreference between an anaphorically used pro-form and its antecedent is part of the theory of reference. And reference is a pragmatic phenomenon.

> In order to understand how pronouns work in a language, elucidating the semantic and discourse conditions that control them is as important as explaining the structural relations that must hold between the pronoun and the antecedent. Unfortunately, the former task has not received enough attention.

> Kuno (1987), p. 87

The task of handling pro-form reference highlights the importance of treating grammatical analysis as part of a comprehensive theory of communication. We cannot expect that a theory will render linguistically satisfactory formalizations of contextual phenomena if the grammar operates on a smaller basis of contextual information than the speaker does in daily life.

---

[31]Even the use of reflexive pro-forms can be explained in pragmatic terms. The inherently anaphoric use of reflexives is treated simply in terms of inherently anaphoric context variables (Hausser 1979a).

5. Analysis and Generation

This chapter analyzes the functionality of LA-grammar in analysis and generation. Section 5.1 illustrates the process of incremental pragmatic interpretation during analysis, and explains why constituent-structure analysis seems to have such a strong intuitive basis. Section 5.2 discusses the relation between the syntactic generation of strings and the notion of pragmatico-semantic generation, defined as a mapping from utterance meanings to surfaces. Section 5.3 describes the left-associative approach to analysis and generation based on the Linear Path Hypothesis. Section 5.4 explains three basic problems of generation, and illustrates possible ways to solve the Extraction Problem and the Connection Problem. Section 5.5 addresses the Choice Problem of generation.

5.1   Incremental Pragmatic Interpretation

In actual use, the sentences of natural language run by very quickly. We can permanently store natural language in the form of a tape recording or a written text, but that doesn't alter the fact that the primary interpretation always has the form of a continuous linear movement. This important structural property is represented in the characteristic derivation order of LA-grammar.

The methodology of constituent-structure analysis, on the other hand, is like anatomy. Before a sentence can be taken apart it (i) must be taken out of the utterance context, and (ii) the time-linear nature of live utterances must be abstracted away. This is because the linguist tries to discover the structure of the sentence by performing substitution and movement tests. The prime data are the intuitions experienced during these tests. But the tests are completely alien to the time-linear structure of language.

This section explains why constituent structure has no basic function in the semantic and pragmatic interpretation of natural language. It shows why the intuitions underlying constituent structure seem to be so strong. And it demonstrates how the intuitions underlying constituent structure are captured in LA-grammar.

Chapters 2 and 3 described language interpretation (analysis) in LA-grammar as a two-stage process:

1. The syntactico-semantic interpretation, consisting of building semantic hierarchies during the linear syntactic parse (cf. 3.3.1).

2. The semantico-pragmatic interpretation, consisting of the unification of the semantic hierarchy with the subcontext (cf. 2.3.1, 2.3.3, and 2.3.4).

The central structural property of this interpretation process is its time-linear nature— not only on the semantic level (deriving a literal meaning), but also on the pragmatic level (extending the subcontext). Since the hearer understands the initial part of an incoming sentence before it is completed, the pragmatic interpretation must take place more or less simultaneously with the left-associative syntactico-semantic analysis. In other words, the pragmatic interpretation is **linearly incremental** on the basis of the time-linear syntactico-semantic analysis.

Let's illustrate the relation between syntactico-semantic analysis in LA-grammar and an incremental pragmatic interpretation with an example. The sentence to be analyzed word by word is *The old bone was found.* In the course of examining the mapping from linear surfaces to extended subcontexts we will discuss what role, if any, constituent structures play in the process of analysis.

The first step in the analysis of the sentence in question consists of the syntactico-semantic composition of the first two words:

5.1.1 *The old*

```
* (z the old)

*** Lex Lookup
Real time:      0.00 s
Run time:       0.00 s

*** Parse Timings
Real time:      0.06 s
Run time:       0.06 s

    Linear Analysis:

    *START_0
    1
        (GQ) THE
        (ADJ) OLD
    *DET+ADJ_1
    2
        (GQ) THE OLD


Hierarchical Analysis:

(NP-1_2_2
  (REF (THE-1_2_2))
  (ADJ ((ADJ-2_2_2 (ADJECTIVE (OLD-2_2_2))))))
```

At this point a successful pragmatic interpretation of the partial semantic hierarchy relative to a well-defined subcontext in a natural communication situation is not likely.[1] This is because the head noun has not yet been added.[2]

---

[1] We disregard here the possible interpretation of adjectives as nouns, as in "The meek shall inherit the earth."

[2] It may be, however, that the utterance situation is so redundant that the expression *the old* provides

5.1.2 *The old bone*

```
* (z the old bone)

*** Lex Lookup
Real time:    0.00 s
Run time:     0.00 s

*** Parse Timings
Real time:    0.10 s
Run time:     0.10 s

    Linear Analysis:

    *START_0
    1
        (GQ) THE
        (ADJ) OLD
    *DET+ADJ_1
    2
        (GQ) THE OLD
        (S-H) BONE
    *DET+NOUN_2
    3
        (S) THE OLD BONE


Hierarchical Analysis:

(NP-1_3_3
 (REF (THE-1_3_3 SG-3_3_3))
 (ADJ ((ADJ-2_3_3 (ADJECTIVE (OLD-2_3_3)))))
 (NOUN ((BONE-3_3_3))))
```

At this point a pragmatic interpretation of *the old bone* is much more likely than in the previous stage. It may be, however, that additional modifiers, such as *which Zach tried to steal* or *under the table*, are added by the speaker. Whether such continuations function to assist in referential disambiguation—or as additional explications—depends entirely on the hearer's subcontext (see Sections 11.3 and 11.5).

Given the structure of the hierarchical analysis in 5.1.2, one might be tempted to recognize a constituent structure—but in a pragmatic rather than a syntactic function. Thus one might like to redefine a constituent as a hierarchical substructure which has all its lower nodes, and is therefore maximally equipped for pragmatic reference relative to a subcontext.

But when does the hearer know during analysis that a substructure has been completed? In 5.1.2, for example, the speaker might still add a relative clause. In a left-to-right word-by-word analysis, completion of a hierarchical substructure is

---

the hearer with sufficient clues to relate the NP-frame of 5.1.1 to the correct contextual counterpart. After all, pragmatic interpretation depends at least as much on the state of the hearer's internal subcontext as on the meaning structure of the sign.

always determined in hindsight.

In other words, the syntactico-semantic derivation results in hierarchical sub-structures, but—unlike constituents—they have no function as intermediate entities of the syntactic derivation. Furthermore, since the point of an incremental pragmatic interpretation is the processing of incomplete semantic structures, postulation of constituents in the pragmatics would be self-defeating.[3]

That constituents have no function in the incremental build-up of semantic hierarchies is illustrated in the following LA-derivation, which shows the addition of the auxiliary.

5.1.3 *The old bone was*

```
* (z the old bone was)

*** Lex Lookup
Real time:     0.00 s
Run time:      0.00 s

*** Parse Timings
Real time:     0.18 s
Run time:      0.16 s

    Linear Analysis:

    *START_0
    1
        (GQ) THE
        (ADJ) OLD
    *DET+ADJ_1
    2
        (GQ) THE OLD
        (S-H) BONE
    *DET+NOUN_2
    3
        (S) THE OLD BONE
        (S3 B V) WAS
    *NOM+FVERB_3
    4
        (B V) THE OLD BONE WAS


Hierarchical Analysis:

(SENT-4_4_4
 (SUBJ
  ((NP-1_4_4
    (REF (THE-1_4_4 SG-3_4_4))
    (ADJ ((ADJ-2_4_4 (ADJECTIVE (OLD-2_4_4)))))
    (NOUN ((BONE-3_4_4))))))
  (AUX (BE-4_4_4)))
```

---

[3]Please remember that constituents can be of arbitrary length. If pragmatic interpretation were limited to constituents—defined as *complete* subhierarchies—the interpretation process would be held up indefinitely.

The build-up of this partial hierarchy[4] is not based on the composition of complete parts (constituents), but rather on the time-linear order of the surface. We can see, however, why constituent structure has such a strong foundation in the intuition of the linguist. If we take the string "the old bone was" and perform a substitution test on the NP, rendering, *the big old bone was* or *it was* or *the bone which Zach ate was*, then everything in the hierarchical analysis of 5.1.3 remains constant except for the NP-frame, which varies systematically with the different substitutions. In a movement test, on the other hand, the NP-frame representing *the old bone* would always stay the same.

In other words, constituents appear in LA-grammar as those semantic structures which either leave everything else unchanged in a substitution test, or which remain themselves unchanged in a movement test. There is a considerable difference between a system which is based on constituent structures—in that all intermediate structures must be constituents (at least at the deep-structure level)—and a system which exhibits something like a constituent structure as the automatic effect of certain test operations.

Let's return to example 5.1.3. What does the addition of the auxiliary mean for the incremental pragmatic interpretation? It characterizes the noun phrase as complete and assigns it the grammatical-subject function. However, a direct reference to a corresponding structure in the subcontext—such as a property or relation—must wait until the next composition.

5.1.4 *The old bone was found*

```
*  (z the old bone was found)

*** Lex Lookup
Real time:    0.00 s
Run time:     0.00 s

*** Parse Timings
Real time:    0.30 s
Run time:     0.24 s

    Linear Analysis:

    *START_0
    1
        (GQ)  THE
        (ADJ) OLD
    *DET+ADJ_1
    2               .
        (GQ)  THE OLD
        (S-H) BONE
    *DET+NOUN_2
```

---

[4]The transition from 5.1.2 to 5.1.3 requires construction of the higher frame SENT-4_4_4, to which the NP-1_4_4 frame is attached as the subject, and the BE-4_4_4 frame as the auxiliary. Derivation of the next-word frame, and the composition of the sentence-start frame and the next-word frame—performed by the rule NOM+FVERB_3—is controlled by the respective syntactic categories.

```
3
    (S)  THE  OLD  BONE
    (S3  B  V)  WAS
*NOM+FVERB_3
4
    (B  V)  THE  OLD  BONE  WAS
    (HV  SC)  FOUND
*ADD-VERB_6
5
    (BY  V)  THE  OLD  BONE  WAS  FOUND
```

```
Hierarchical Analysis:

(SENT-4_5_5
 (SUBJ
  ((NP-1_5_5
    (REF  (THE-1_5_5  SG-3_5_5))
    (ADJ  ((ADJ-2_5_5  (ADJECTIVE  (OLD-2_5_5)))))
    (NOUN  ((BONE-3_5_5))))))
 (AUX  (BE-4_5_5))
 (PASSIVE-PREDICATE  ((NFV-5_5_5  (PAST-PART  (FIND-5_5_5))))))
```

5.1.4 shows that the active/passive alternative is decided immediately after the addition of the auxiliary. This information is important for an incremental pragmatic interpretation because it determines whether the grammatical subject functions as the agent. In 5.1.4, the pragmatic interpretation consists of asserting the *find*-relation in the subcontext—with the node represented by *the old bone* functioning as the patient. Whether 5.1.4 is complete or not is up to the speaker—the left-associative rules permit a completing continuation (adding a punctuation sign) as well as several types of non-completing continuations.

According to Chomsky, constituent structure is part of the speaker-hearer's competence, defined as the implicit knowledge of the structure of the language. But in addition to the intuitions of constituent structure, the speaker-hearer has strong intuitions about the possible continuations at each point in a sentence. Indeed, the intuitive reality of possible continuations is always present in speech, whereas the intuitions of constituent structure are based on operations which never occur naturally in communication. Since LA-grammar explicitly describes both kinds of intuitions, constituent structure,[5] and possible continuations, it is a competence grammar which accounts for a considerably broader range of intuitive phenomena than the grammars by Chomsky.

---

[5] The *precise* intuitions of constituent structure are difficult to determine, and therefore controversial. Fillmore (1968), for example, proposes a constituent structure without a VP-node. Since LA-grammar analyzes constituent structures as a derived phenomenon, their ultimate "true" nature is much less important than in systems which use intermediate constituents for motivating syntactic structure and claim that constitent structures reflect the innate human language capability. Though a hierarchical analysis like that of 3.3.4 is not a constituent structure in the narrow sense of definition 2.1.1, we claim that it (i) captures the relevant intuitions in an acceptable manner and (ii) provides a suitable basis for pragmatic interpretation.

5.2   The Generation Paradox

The illustration of an incremental linear pragmatic analysis in Section 5.1 resembles the "match and identify" process of Anderson and Bower (1980, Chapter 6)—except for a small but important difference in the order of the incremental process. The terminal symbols in the linguistic deep structures of Anderson and Bower are ordered from left-to-right according to logical conventions, whereas our incremental pragmatic interpretation is ordered according to the sequence of the words in the surface.

For example, the sentence *In the park a hippie sang* is represented by Anderson and Bower as a tree with the terminal symbols [park] [past] [hippie] [sing]. The symbol [past] is fronted in their deep structure because it is treated as a modifier of the basic proposition [hippie] [sing]. On the other hand, our linearly incremental pragmatic interpretation encounters the [past] marker at the end as part of the verb analysis.[6]

Given the tentative and general nature of Anderson and Bower's deep structures, we may assume that their "match and identify" procedure could process a deep structure hierarchy equally well in the surface order[7] as in a logical order. Furthermore, we will provide linguistic reasons why adherence to the concretely given surface order is desirable (Section 5.4). But first let's discuss the general nature of analysis and generation from the viewpoint of syntax, semantics, and pragmatics.

A natural language may be regarded as a set of uninterpreted strings, or as a semantically interpreted means of communication. Therefore, we may distinguish a *syntactic* and a *semantic-pragmatic* aspect in generation and in analysis.

The syntactic aspect of **generation** covers the formal derivation of a surface structure from a *start symbol*. The pragmatico-semantic aspect of generation consists of mapping a multidimensional *meaning structure* into a linear surface.

The syntactic aspect of **analysis**, on the other hand, covers the derivation of a *syntactic analysis* from an unanalyzed input string. The semantico-pragmatic aspect of analysis consists of mapping the input string into an *extended subcontext*.

The difference between a syntactic (or narrow) and a pragmatico-semantic (or wide) interpretation of generation is schematically indicated in 5.2.1.

5.2.1 Two Possible Domain-Range Structures of GENERATION

1. *syntactic* generation:
   start symbol $\Rightarrow$ analyzed surface

2. *pragmatico-semantic* generation:
   subcontext $\Rightarrow$ analyzed surface[8]

---

[6]In this example, the [past] marker arises as part of the lexical analysis of the verb. The present implementation does not consider tense, but it can be added easily in the generation of lexical frames.

[7]I.e., in the manner indicated in Section 5.1.

We see that the generation mappings in 5.2.1 have different domains, but the same range.

The corresponding distinction in analysis is presented in 5.2.2:

5.2.2 Two Possible Domain-Range Structures of ANALYSIS

1. *syntactic* analysis:
   unanalyzed linear surface $\Rightarrow$ analyzed surface

2. *semantico-pragmatic* analysis:
   unanalyzed linear surface $\Rightarrow$ extended subcontext

We see that the analysis mappings in 5.2.2 have the same domains, but different ranges.

A crucial question for the theory of syntax is the relation of syntactic generation and syntactic analysis. In traditional systems, syntactic generation and analysis are associated conceptually with different derivation orders within the syntax. In PS-grammar, for example, generation is identified with *top-down expansion* of the rewriting rules, while *bottom-up amalgamation* of the rewriting rules (with inverted arrows) is identified with analysis.[9]

In LA-grammar, on the other hand, the syntactic aspects of analysis and generation are not treated as inverse processes. Rather, the only difference between syntactic analysis and generation is the source of the *next word*.[10] Thus analysis and generation in LA-grammar are based on the same syntactic rules in the same derivation order.

A crucial question for the theory of communication is the relation between the *syntactic* aspect and the *semantico-pragmatic* aspect of generation, as well as of analysis. Without going into the overall set-up of specific grammar systems, we can tell from the different domain-range structures in 5.2.1 and 5.2.2 that the connection between syntactic and semantico-pragmatic analysis is more easily established than the corresponding connection in the case of generation. Because the two analysis mappings have the same domain, the semantico-pragmatic aspect of analysis may be defined as an extension of the syntactic aspect.

In the case of generation, on the other hand, the domains seem to be different. In PS-grammar, for example, syntactic generation is based on expanding an abstract start symbol (S-node) into a phrase-structure tree by means of recursive rewriting rules. The start symbol is the same for all sentences. Consequently the syntactic aspect of generation in PS-grammar is completely separated from the pragmatico-semantic aspect of generation. The reason is obvious: the domain of syntactic generation, based on expanding an abstract S-node, is incompatible with the domain of pragmatico-semantic generation—no matter how "meanings" may be defined.

---

[8]The mapping from an analyzed surface to an unanalyzed linear string is trivial; it consist in deleting everything except for the sequence of word surfaces.

[9]See 3.5.1.

[10]See Section 8.1.

But if the domain of syntactic generation (abstract S-node) is distinct from the domain of pragmatico-semantic generation (meaning to be expressed), it is impossible to use the grammatical rules for mapping the meaning into a syntactic form. In PS-grammar, for example, neither the generation mode nor the analysis mode of the rule system can be used for pragmatico-semantic generation. The generation mode uses the same S-node for all sentences of the language, and the analysis mode requires a surface string as input.

This problem is called the **Generation Paradox** of constituent-structure based grammars.[11] The dual characterization of generation in terms of two different mappings (cf. 5.2.1) suggests that the Generation Paradox can only be resolved by establishing an inherent connection between the two domains. Is it possible to relate the syntactic start symbol to the subcontext?

5.3   The Linear Path Hypothesis

Given that a text is a linear sequence of sentences, and that a sentence is a linear sequence of words, we view the hearer's understanding of a text as a **path** through the subcontext which is triggered by—and which is simultaneous with—the time-linear sequence of icons and indices (cf. Section 11.1) coded by the natural-language surface.

5.3.1 Schema of Natural-Language Understanding (Analysis)

$$\text{Surface:} \quad w1 \rightarrow w2 \rightarrow w3 \rightarrow w4 \rightarrow w5 \rightarrow w6 \ldots$$
$$\downarrow \quad \downarrow \quad \downarrow \quad \downarrow \quad \downarrow \quad \downarrow$$
$$\text{Subcontext:} \quad \bullet \rightarrow \bullet \rightarrow \bullet \rightarrow \bullet \rightarrow \bullet \rightarrow \bullet \ldots$$

Left-associative analysis maps a surface into a meaning, but the surface is not treated as something analyzed prior to the interpretation. Rather, the syntactico-semantic analysis of the surface and the pragmatic reconstruction of the utterance meaning evolve simultaneously in the form of a two-level path.[12]

When we say that analysis involves a mapping from a linear surface to a multidimensional meaning structure, then this does not necessarily imply a *deserialization*. The incremental pragmatic interpretation described in Section 5.1 shows that the

---

[11]For a background discussion see Hausser (1984a), pp. 170 – 193.

[12]As explained in Chapter 11, the pragmatic interpretation process either routes the path through nodes already existing in subcontext (reference to entities known by the hearer), or it builds new nodes which accommodate the meaning structure coded by the language sign. At some points the pragmatic interpretation process may be unsure about the proper direction of the next step, such as in the case of ambiguities; but occasional hesitations and even corrections (backtracking) are not in conflict with the assumption that the utterance meaning is essentially a path through a (speaker-hearer internal) knowledge base.

non-linear meaning structure can be "covered" in a sequential manner. Thereby the entry and the exit point of the path through the hierarchy need not be the highest node (root) or one of the lowest nodes (leaves). But the sequence of points in the path must be strictly ordered.

Let's turn next to generation in LA-grammar. In LA-grammar the start symbol is the first word; it is continued into a complex expression by means of left-associative continuation rules. Furthermore, a word in LA-grammar is analyzed as a two-level structure, consisting of a surface and a literal meaning. Thus the initial word of a sentence establishes a connection between the domains of the two different generation mappings.

If we assume that generation is the inverse of analysis, then the apparent discrepancy between syntactic and pragmatico-semantic generation (Generation Paradox) finds a natural solution in LA-grammar:

5.3.2 Schema of Natural-Language Verbalization (Generation)

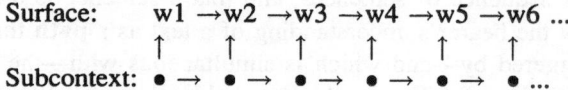

Left-associative generation maps a meaning into a surface, but the meaning is not treated as something given prior to the verbalization. Rather, the meaning and the surface evolve simultaneously in the form of a two-level path.[13]

When we say that generation involves a mapping from a multidimensional meaning structure to a linear surface, this does not necessarily imply a *serialization*, in the sense of finding a natural order for an unordered hierarchical structure. Instead we may assume that a "thought" is a linear path through a meaning structure, and that the sequential aspect of this path is reflected directly by the surface.

Our concept of incremental generation is based on the sequential choice of local goals. After the thought focus arrived at node A, the next goal, node B, is selected. The transition to node B may consist of several steps which are controlled by node A as well as node B. The strategy for building a linguistic bridge between two nodes will often proceed in a manner where the modifiers of the head (e.g., number, definiteness, adjectives) are verbalized before the head itself.

The schemata 5.3.1 and 5.3.2 characterize analysis and generation as inverse processes. But the overriding time-linear nature of each results in a "flattening" of the contrast between top-down and bottom-up computation usually associated with inversion of a procedure. Furthermore, we may well conceive of mixing the respective vertical directions indicated in 5.3.1 and 5.3.2.

---

[13]The assumption of generation as a two-level path does not exclude the use of templates, such as "How are you?", which may be triggered as a whole when the path traverses particular nodes.

In the interpretation of an ambiguous sentence, for example, a reading may be excluded from further consideration on the basis of the incremental pragmatic interpretation, a process involving an up-arrow during analysis. During generation, on the other hand, the transition from one node to another may be bridged by the continuation rules of the language, a process involving down-arrows during generation.

The "Linear Path Hypothesis" underlying 5.3.1 and 5.3.2 is appealing for a number of reasons. First, it leads to a direct correspondence between the meaning structure and its verbalization in language. This provides the basis for high computational efficiency.[14] Second, in contrast to conventional generation systems which subscribe to the "conduit metaphor" (Reddy 1979), it does not assume a separation between the processes of "deciding what to say and how to say it" (Appelt 1982, p.8). Third, it explains the cohesion of texts and dialogs in terms of the structure of the underlying knowledge base (see Section 5.4).

However, given that the nature of thought is still an unresolved research issue in psychology[15]and represented by a wide range of diverse assumptions in computational linguistics,[16]it is perhaps noteworthy that the Linear Path Hypothesis is not a *necessary* precondition for solving the Generation Paradox in LA-grammar.

As a non-linear alternative to the linear generation scheme 5.3.2, consider 5.3.3:

5.3.3 Schematic Representation of Non-Linear Generation in LA-Grammar

output:	w_1	w_2	w_3	w_4	w_5	*unanalyzed linear surface*
LA-syntax: $\Rightarrow$	w_1	w_2	w_3	w_4	w_5	*analyzed surface*
	$\uparrow$	$\uparrow$	$\uparrow$	$\uparrow$	$\uparrow$	*inverse lexical look-up*
	f_1	f_2	f_3	f_4	f_5	*word-frames*

pragmatic preprocessing

$\Uparrow$

input: meaning
                structure

---

[14]"Generator designs gain efficiency according to the directness by which they move from situations to utterances." (McDonald et al. 1987, p. 165)

[15]For varying approaches to the "spreading activation theory" of semantics, see Collins and Loftus (1975); Ratcliff and McKoon (1981); Anderson (1983); Rumelhart, Smolensky, McClelland, and Hinton (1986).

[16]Summaries of different viewpoints regarding generation may be found in McKeown (1985).

Assuming that the meaning structure is a complex frame, pragmatic preprocessing will derive from it an unordered set of subframes such that each subframe corresponds to a set of surface word forms of the natural target language. From this unordered set of word forms the standard syntactic apparatus of LA-grammar will generate all surface structures derivable from it. The simultaneously derived semantic hierarchies may then be used to pick the linear analysis with the semantic hierarchy closest to the input meaning.

The set-up illustrated in 5.3.3 is not subject to the Generation Paradox because the domains of syntactic generation and pragmatico-semantic generation are connected: whatever first word is chosen by the linear syntactic derivation, its meaning will be in the set of frames produced by the pragmatic preprocessing. Once the first word has been chosen by the pragmatics, the syntactic generation system is ready to compute the possible continuations.

But the non-linear approach of 5.3.3 raises a number of problems. It seems unlikely that the speaker would generate a whole set of sentences, and then look for the one fitting his underlying meaning best. Such a strategy is not only highly inefficient, but violates the spirit of the Derivational Order Hypothesis (2.4.2). Furthermore, the approach of 5.3.3 differs considerably from the incremental pragmatic analysis process described in Section 5.1; therefore, it violates the natural assumption that analysis and generation are complementary processes.

5.4   The Extraction Problem of Generation

In contrast to the behaviorists, who defined thought as "non-verbal speech," we view speech as verbalized thought. The problem of natural-language generation is that we need a relatively clear idea of what the thoughts are.

In standard knowledge representations two aspects may be distinguished: (i) *semantic hierarchies* based on predicates like *is-a* and *is-part-of*; and (ii) *episodic connections* between the various nodes of the semantic hierarchy. The link between nodes A and B may be stronger than the link between nodes B and A, but the overall structure is a network which can be traversed in many different directions. The problem is that such semantic networks,[17] even with inheritance, demons, views, and defaults are essentially static structures, whereas thoughts evolve dynamically.

What is needed for generation is a general procedure which answers the following questions:

---

[17]See Brachman (1979) for a summary.

5.4.1 Three Basic Problems of Natural-Language Generation

1. **Extraction Problem**: How does the meaning, used as input to the generation system, come about?

2. **Connection Problem**: Given a meaning structure for several sentences, what decides the proper order of the sentences, so that the result is a connected text?

3. **Choice Problem**: Which word selection and phrasing produces the rhetorically most appropriate rendering of a given meaning structure and what determines that choice?

The first problem is most central because the method of solving it is likely to influence solutions to the other two. But the literature of computational linguistics does not present a coherent treatment of the Extraction Problem.

Some authors simply exclude it from consideration, and start from meaning structures defined *ad hoc* which they consider reasonable. Other authors provide solutions which are closely connected to specific generation tasks, such as machine translation,[18] dialog,[19] and generation of text from a database with an inherently regular[20] or preprocessed[21] structure.

Let's consider whether it is more fruitful to assume that the complex meaning structure underlying a sentence is lifted out of the knowledge structure as a whole, or in the form of a linear path through the knowledge base. A standard knowledge base is defined as a network structure which is inherently non-sequential. Therefore, a substructure extracted from such a network as a whole, e.g., by taking all nodes dominated by a particular node, is inherently non-sequential. Thus if the meaning of each sentence is extracted in a wholesale fashion, the generation component is faced with the problem of how to properly serialize the nodes in the substructure.

Furthermore, the generation component must account for the fact that certain sentence sequences are *connected* while others are not. For example, compare 5.4.2 and 5.4.3.

---

[18]Machine translation is harder and easier than natural-language generation from a knowledge base. It is easier because the source language provides clearly defined meanings; thus the Extraction Problem is largely avoided in machine translation. It is harder because the relation between the underlying meaning and the surface has to be managed for two (or more) natural languages, and not just for one. Use of a knowledge base as the interlingua in machine translation is explored in Nirenburg, Raskin, and Tucker (1987).

[19]Carbonell (1981) uses a specialized goal structure to determine the meanings to be verbalized.

[20]McKeown (1985).

[21]Mann and Thompson (1987).

5.4.2 A Connected Sentence Sequence

Zach ate a bone. The bone was found by Fido.

5.4.3 An Unconnected Sentence Sequence

Zach ate a bone. Fido found the bone.

If utterance meanings are just a network of nodes, then there is no reason why the continuation in the second sentence of 5.4.2 is more appropriate than that in 5.4.3. But if utterance meanings are extracted in the form of a path, resulting in an *ordered sequence* of nodes, then the phenomenon of text cohesion may be explained as follows:

The path through a contextual substructure has an **entry point** and an intended **exit point**. Two sentences A and B are connected if the exit point of A is "near" the entry point of B. The function of different surface serializations in natural language is to supply alternative entry and exit points in the pragmatic interpretation. Thus the Linear Path Hypothesis provides not only for a highly structured method of extraction, it establishes a close relation between the Extraction Problem and the Connection Problem by treating them as different aspects of the same procedure.

As an example of alternative entry and exit points consider the active/passive distinction. The active construction corresponds to the following path through a contextual substructure:[22]

5.4.4 The Path verbalized by *Fido has found the bone*.

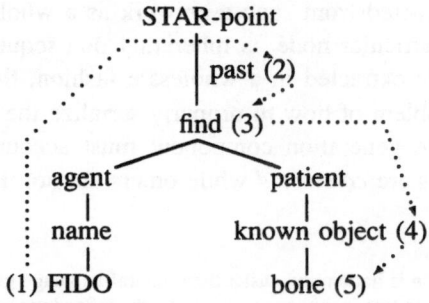

----

[22]Speculation about the underlying structure of language has always been part of linguistics. It appears to different degrees in the "theme/rheme" distinction of Functional Sentence Perspective (Firbas 1964, Daneš 1974, Sgall 1974, Sgall et al. 1986), the concepts of "deep structure" and "universal base" in Transformational Grammar (Chomsky 1965, 1981), in the notions of "directed action," "non-directed action," and "ascription" in Systemic Grammar (Halliday 1967), and the "deep cases" of Case Grammar (Fillmore 1968, 1977).

The *passive* is based on exactly the same substructure as the *active*, but the entry and the exit are reversed.

5.4.5 The Path verbalized by *The bone was found by Fido.*

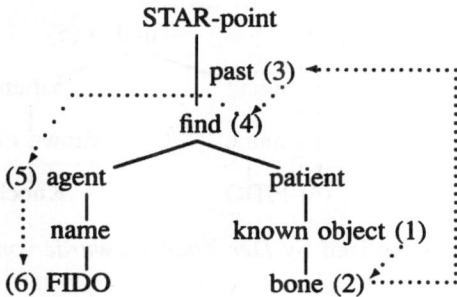

The choice of the overall sequence in the surface is motivated by the underlying entry and exit points. But the linguistic details of the traversal are determined by the syntax of the language. For example, the agent in 5.4.5 can be accessed from the verb only via the preposition *by*.

Furthermore, English requires that the non-finite verb follows directly after the auxiliary, whereas in German the sentence corresponding to 5.4.4 is constituted by the following traversal of the database:

5.4.6 The Path verbalized by *Fido hat den Knochen gefunden.*

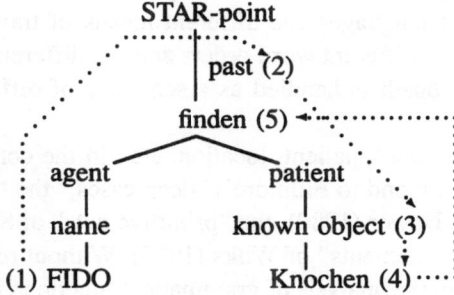

The possible path from a given entry to an intended exit may vary from language to language. For example, the traversal illustrated in the English example 5.4.5 can be expressed in German alternatively as in 5.4.7 and 5.4.8.[23]

---

[23]The reason for "the abundance of passive constructions in Modern English" (Mathesius 1928, p. 63) is that the fixed word order of English does not provide general syntactic means similar to 5.4.7 for inverting underlying entry and exit points. Constructions like *That book I haven't got in my library* or *This argument I can't follow* (Mathesius 1928) present alternatives to the passive version which resemble 5.4.7. But they require heavy stress and are mostly restricted to spoken English.

5.4.7 The Path verbalized by *Den Knochen hat Fido gefunden.*

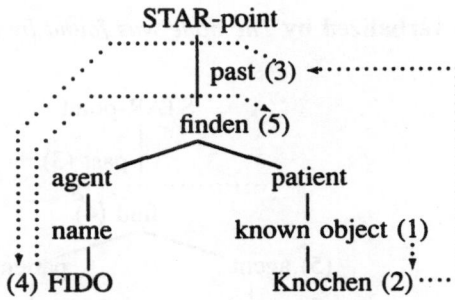

5.4.8 The Path verbalized by *Der Knochen wurde von Fido gefunden.*

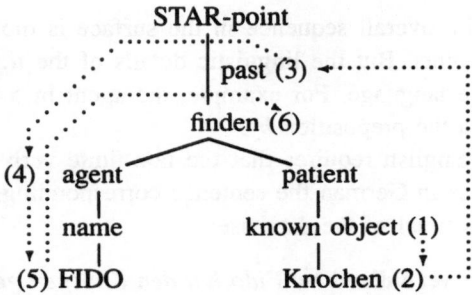

The problem of translation from one language into another results largely from the fact that different languages use different means of traversing a given subcontext. These consist in (i) different word orders and (ii) different degrees of incorporation, i.e., whether a subpath is handled as a sequence of different words or in the form of one word.[24]

The notions of agent, patient, location, etc., in the context representation used in 5.4.4 – 5.4.8 correspond to Fillmore's "deep cases," the "predicates" and "relations" of Anderson and Bower (1980), the "primitive acts" of Schank and Abelson (1977), and the "semantic elements" of Wilks (1975). Without reference to a systematic underlying structure, the analysis of grammatical functions is limited to the comparison of corresponding constructions in different languages, or to different constructions in the same language.[25]

We have seen that the context structure underlying 5.4.4 – 5.4.8, in conjunction

---

[24]E.g., handling of tense in the finite main verb or as a complex consisting of a finite auxiliary and a non-finite main verb.

[25]For example, characterization of the "subject-function" as a nominative used as the theme, or statements like "the prepositional phrase functions as the agent" remain more or less anecdotal without a systematic theory of the context structure.

with our path concept of utterance meaning, provides the basis for a unified solution to the Extraction and the Connection problems. The design of a linguistically and psychologically well-motivated, computationally efficient, language-independent knowledge base is essential for the successful modeling of natural-language analysis and generation, and requires the cooperation of linguists, psychologists, and computer scientists.

5.5 Remarks on the Choice Problem

The general principles of grammatical function must be based on a theory of *context structure*. But this is not the only requirement for a principled explanation of the functioning of language. There must also be a *procedure to extract* the utterance meaning from the context. And there must be a *goal structure* to guide the extraction procedure. These three aspects are closely connected, and should be implemented as an integrated system.

Our notion of utterance meaning as a path through the knowledge base provides the basis for a simple, highly structured extraction procedure. It also constitutes a simple method for characterizing the cohesion of a text in terms of the connectedness of the entry and exit points of the path segments represented by the sentences.

Furthermore, the concept of a path through a knowledge base provides an important structural basis for the design of the goal structure. Just as the local terrain influences how a mountain climber guides his steps, and results in continuous readjustments of his short-term goal structure, the design of the goal structure required for natural-language generation systems must rely in part on the structure of the subcontext.

Next, let's show how the path concept relates to the **choice problem** of generation.[26]

> When you compare the language produced by people to the text produced by existing language generation programs, one thing becomes immediately clear: people can say the same thing in various ways to achieve various effects, and generators cannot.

> E.H. Hovy (1987), p. 3

As pointed out by Hovy, the choice of how a certain meaning is conveyed in language depends on factors like the conditions of the conversational atmosphere (setting); the speaker's emotional state and knowledge of (or interest in) the topic; the hearer's emotional state and knowledge of (or interest in) the topic; the speaker-hearer relationship in terms of depth of acquaintance, relative social status, and emotion; and interpersonal goals such as affecting the hearer's opinion of the topic.[27]

---

[26]Cf. 5.4.1.
[27]See also Bolinger (1968), p. 261.

These are clearly important factors influencing the way things are said. For example, if the speaker is under great stress, (s)he will be brief, as in "A doctor—quick!" The question is how much of the variations in style are a matter of conscious choice, and how much is an automatic reflection of the momentary state of the speaker's subcontext.

The momentary state of the subcontext is not like a particular room in a large house, but more like what can be seen in a landscape from a specific perspective under specific lighting conditions.[28] The speaker's emotional state, his or her attitude towards the hearer, etc., may be analyzed as contributing directly to how the speaker sees the world at that moment.

Differences in style may therefore be partly explained as differences in the state of the subcontext which directly influence the nature of the path, and are thus reflected in language automatically. In other words, the style of how we express ourselves in language may be determined more by our adopting a particular attitude (affecting the subcontext as a whole) than by a conscious choice as to how to do a particular phrasing. Furthermore, most of the time the speaker doesn't even have an option, but uses language in a spontaneous manner which directly reflects his or her momentary state.

The view of generation as a two-level path through the subcontext suggests an efficient method for scheduling lexical look-up and controlling the choice of words. This is another important aspect of style. Consider a system which generates language from non-sequential meaning structures (e.g. 5.3.3.). Since such meaning structures don't indicate which node is going to be verbalized first, the system has to provide a strategy for arriving at a suitable serialization. This strategy will depend in part on the selection of words. Thus, word selection must precede serialization, which means that lexical look-up has to be complete before the syntactic structure of the sentence is determined and the utterance can begin.

On the other hand, if the meaning structure is sequential to begin with—in accord with the Linear Path Hypothesis—then word selection will not be wholesale, but incremental in the order of the nodes in the path. This incremental lexical look-up is psychologically well-motivated, and computationally economical.

The notion of a locally controlled word selection does not exclude global parameters influencing lexical look-up. General properties of the subcontext—such as the attitude towards the hearer—may affect lexical selection as a whole, as in the selection of the correct honorifics in Japanese.

Finally, the view of generation as a path through a contextual substructure suggests a natural place for handling the spontaneous coining of new words (neologisms). Consider the following examples:

5.5.1 Example of a Neologism

John already webstered this word.

---

[28]I.e., certain links in the network are "lit up" while the others remain inactive.

5.5.2 Corresponding Standard Phrasing

John already looked up this word in Webster's New Collegiate Dictionary.

We may picture the subcontext underlying both utterances as follows:

5.5.3 Knowledge Representation underlying 5.5.1 and 5.5.2

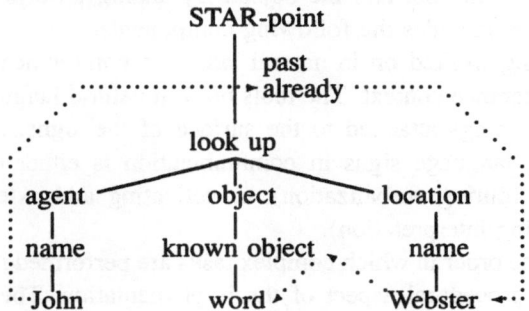

In order to solve his task of depicting this meaning structure, the speaker may take the lexical stem associated with the location and make a verb out of it (as indicated in 5.5.3), rather than following the more conventional route via *look up*.

This suggestion does not explain why **John worded the Webster's* would not be an acceptable neologism.[29] But it does provide a natural location for a theory dealing with the formation of new words. The location is natural because it provides (i) a clearly defined purpose for the new word in the form of a particular node transition and (ii) a clearly defined set of syntactic alternatives in the form of the possible continuations specified by the grammar for the transition in question.

Defining generation as a two-level path through the subcontext is a simple hypothesis, intended to contribute to an explanation of "the orientational and perspectival structuring of the message."[30] In combination with a suitable goal structure it provides a uniform basis for approaching the problems of extraction, connectness, and choice. The assumption of a sequential path provides more structure than wholesale extraction.

Furthermore, we have a linguistically and psychologically well-motivated theory of grammar closely compatible with this approach to generation. At each point in the sentence, the grammar specifies exactly which syntactic rules may be applied next, and for each of these rules, what the syntactic categories of the next word may be. Given a goal node, the pragmatics of generation consists of choosing a rule (e.g., FVERB+MAIN, DET+NOUN, etc.) from the current rule package and a suitably

---

[29]Obviously, the spontaneous coining of new words is controlled by the grammar. Furthermore, the particular use illustrated in 5.5.3 occurs also without a neologism. Consider for example *Would you mind if I crack this window?* in the context of a car ride, meaning "Would you mind if I open this window a crack?"

[30]Fillmore (1977), p. 60.

categorized next word, such that the resulting syntactic composition gets the system closer to the goal node.

In summary, the task of natural language communication resembles the use of a tool. Three basic aspects may be distinguished: (i) the structure of the tool, (ii) the structure of the object being worked on with the tool, and (iii) the purpose of the interaction between the tool and the object. By analogy, we proposed that the use of natural language includes the following components.

The object being worked on in natural language communication is the speaker-hearer internal utterance context. The tools used in natural language communication are the literal meanings attached to the surface of the signs. And the most basic purpose of using language signs in communication is either depicting a contextual substructure (during verbalization), or activating and extending a contextual substructure (during interpretation).

Furthermore, the order in which complex tasks are performed is not a minor aspect to be left to the procedural aspect of the implementation. The theory of *possible continuations* is based on the assumption that the naturally given order of a task should also be the theoretical derivation order. If there are alternative routes through a given task, they must be specified by the theory.

Part I outlined the theory of possible continuations, and applied it to natural language. In Part II, we turn to the formal definitions of this theory.

Part II

Algebraic and Automata-Theoretic Characterization

6. The Left-Associative Algorithm

This chapter presents the formal definition of left-associative syntax. A formal definition is the precondition for the analysis of generative capacity (Chapter 7), automata theoretic characterization (Chapter 8), and the analysis of computational complexity (Chapter 10).

Section 6.1 provides the background by comparing formal and conceptual properties of PS-grammar, C-grammar, and LA-grammar. Section 6.2 presents the algebraic definition of left-associative syntax. Section 6.3 explains the formal nature of left-associative derivations. Section 6.4 illustrates the formal definition with an example, the LA-grammar for the context-sensitive language $a^k b^k c^k$.[1] Section 6.5 presents proof that LA-grammar generates all—and only—recursive languages.

6.1 Basic Concepts of PS-, C-, and LA-Grammar

The main paradigms of generative grammar since the late 1950's have been Phrase Structure Grammar (PS-grammar) and Categorial Grammar (C-grammar).[2] Study of the different descriptive and heuristic potential of PS-grammar and C-grammar is not only interesting in its own right, but also important for a deeper understanding of LA-Grammar.

As a background for the algebraic definition of LA-grammar in Sections 6.2 and 6.3, let us compare the basic formal concepts of PS-grammar and C-grammar with those of LA-grammar. The notions under consideration are

1. the characteristic **rule schemata,**

2. the specific definitions of **syntactic categories,**

3. the underlying notions of a **word,**

4. the intuitive concepts of a **complex expression,** and

5. the interpretation of **tree structures.**

These five notions are intimately related within a system of grammar: The rules are based on categories. The categories reflect how the basic and complex expressions are viewed intuitively. The interpretation of the trees depends on the definition of

---

[1]This language is often called $a^n b^n c^n$. We use k instead of n because n is also used to indicate the length of strings.

[2]See also Sections 2.1 and 2.5 above.

rules and categories. The formal nature of the categories reflects their use in certain rule schemata, etc.

The brief comparison of the basic concepts in this section cannot do justice to the different traditions, heuristics, descriptive goals, types of linguistic generalizations, and sub-schools associated with PS-grammar and C-grammar. It is simply intended as a summary.[3] We begin with a comparison of the different types of **rule schemata** employed by the three systems under consideration.

The formalism of PS-grammar is based on the rewriting systems of Post (1936). Rewriting rules have the following form:

6.1.1 The Schema of a Phrase-Structure Rewriting Rule

$$A \rightarrow B\ C$$

By replacing (rewriting) the symbol A with B and C, this rule generates a tree structure with A dominating B and C. Conceptually, the derivation order of rewriting rules is top-down.

The formalism of C-grammar is based on the categorial-canceling rules of Leśnieswki (1929) and Ajdukiewicz (1935). Categorial-canceling rules have the following form:

6.1.2 The Schema of a Categorial Canceling Rule

$$\alpha_{(Y|X)} \bullet \beta_{(Y)} \Rightarrow \alpha\beta_{(X)}$$

This rule schema combines α and β into $\alpha\beta$ by canceling the Y in the category of α with the corresponding category of β. The result is a tree structure with $\alpha\beta$ of category X dominating α and β. Conceptually, the derivation order of categorial-canceling rules is bottom-up.

The formalism of LA-grammar is based on rules of the following form:

6.1.3 The Schema of a Left-Associative Rule

$$r_i: [\text{CAT-1 CAT-2}] \Rightarrow [rp_i\ \text{CAT-3}]$$

A left-associative rule r_i maps a sentence start (represented by its category CAT-1) and a new word (represented by its category CAT-2) into the rule package rp_i and a new sentence start (represented by its category CAT-3). LA-rules differ from C-rules as follows:

1. The rules of C-grammar specify (i) a categorial operation and (ii) a **surface composition**.

2. The rules of LA-grammar specify (i) a categorial operation and (ii) a **rule package**.

---

[3]For an in-depth comparison of PS-grammar and C-grammar see Hausser (1984a).

The composition of *surfaces* is specified explicitly by the C-rules because a functor may precede or follow its argument:

$$\alpha_{(Y/X)} \bullet \beta_{(Y)} \Rightarrow \alpha\beta_{(X)}$$
$$\alpha_{(Y\backslash X)} \bullet \beta_{(Y)} \Rightarrow \beta\alpha_{(X)}$$

In LA-grammar, on the other hand, surface composition is of a completely regular nature, and therefore implicit in the LA-rules.

The rule package in the output of an LA-rule readies the algorithm for the next left-associative composition: if the categorial operation of rule r_i is successful, the rule package rp_i is applied to the pair consisting of the new sentence start and the next word. Thus, categorial compatibility is not absolute in LA-grammar; a sentence start and a next word can be combined only if (i) there is a rule which accepts their respective categories, and (ii) this rule happens to be in the rule package activated by the last composition. The control structure defined in the rule packages of LA-grammar represents a major difference from C-grammar, where any two expressions can be combined if their surfaces are adjacent and their categories are compatible.[4]

Next consider the different kinds of categories used in PS-grammar, C-grammar, and LA-grammar. In PS-grammar categories are *combinatorially opaque*[5] in that they do not have an internal structure which is combinatorially meaningful.[6] Instead the combinatorics of PS-grammar are encoded in a large number of rewriting rules: the combinatorial properties of an expression are characterized in terms of those PS-rules which mention the category representing the lowest node dominating this expression.

The categories of C-grammar, on the other hand, are *combinatorially transparent* in the following sense: they have an internal structure which gives a precise characterization of the combinatorial properties of the expressions which have this category. For example, $\alpha_{(Y|X)}$ can combine only with argument expressions of category (Y), or with higher functor expressions of category $((Y \mid X) \mid Z)$. Thus, the combinatorics of C-grammar are encoded in the categories, while the rules of C-grammar consist of a few general schemas which interpret the structure of the categories.

The categories of LA-grammar are related more closely to the structured categories of C-grammar than they are to the primitive categories of PS-grammar. But

---

[4]The fact that C-grammar encodes the combinatorics in the categories alone leads to serious problems in applications of C-grammar to natural language: it either requires differentiation of categories at the price of numerous lexical ambiguities (as witnessed by the categorial grammar of English presented in Hausser (1982, 1984a), or it results in enormous numbers of spurious syntactic ambiguities (as witnessed by systems like Lambek (1958) and Geach (1972)). Both alternatives are computational untractable. LA-grammar, on the other hand, avoids these problems by encoding only valency and agreement into the categories, while word order is handled by means of the control structure constituted by the interaction of rules and rule packages.

[5]Hausser (1984a, p. 36.)

[6]X-bar theory generates PS-categories from 4 or 5 basic symbols (N, A, V, P, and INFL), and 3, 4, or 5 bar levels. But the categorial structure provided by X-bar theory fails to provide a basis for a combinatorial or a denotational interpretation.

while C-grammar generates an infinite set of "complex categories" from a small finite set of "basic categories," LA-grammar distinguishes between category **segments**, defined as atoms, and **categories**, defined as lists of segments. The category segments are used to encode valency and agreement information, whereas word order is handled by the network of LA-rules. The simple list structure of LA-categories is distinct from C-categories with their different slashes (e.g.," / " versus " \ ") and other diacritic symbols used to control different kinds of surface composition. Furthermore, LA-categories do not specify the functor-argument structure of expressions by means of bracketing.

Next, consider the different notions of a **word** in PS-grammar, C-grammar and LA-grammar. PS-grammar distinguishes "terminal" and "non-terminal" symbols, whereby words are defined as the terminal symbols. Terminal symbols are those which cannot be rewritten and therefore occur as the "leaves" of the phrase-structure tree. The non-terminal symbols, on the other hand, are the root of the tree and all nodes between the root and the leaves (or words).

In C-grammar, the definition of words is not based on a distinction between terminal and non-terminal symbols. Rather, each language expression consists of two parts, a **surface** and a **category**. The category is usually written as a subscript to the surface (cf. 6.1.2). Words are defined as expressions with an elementary surface, e.g., $\alpha_{(X)}$, while complex expressions consist of a sequence of surface expressions, e.g., $\alpha\beta_{(Y)}$.

In LA-grammar, a word is defined as an **ordered pair**, consisting of a surface and a category.[7] Words differ from sentence starts in that a word surface is an atom, while a sentence-start surface is a list. An expression with an elementary surface like *the* may be defined both, as a (next) word of the form "[the (GQ)]," and as a sentence start of the form "[(the)(GQ)]."

A **complex expression** generated by a PS-grammar is a **constituent**, i.e., a tree dominating a sequence of terminal symbols. The root of such a tree represents the category of the constituent. A constituent is justified methodologically in terms of **movement** and **substitution tests**. A complex expression is a constituent if it can be moved in the sentence, or replaced by another expression of the same category, without loss of grammaticality or change of the meaning structure. Intuitively, constituents are semantic units. C-grammar resembles PS-grammar in that its complex expressions are likewise defined as constituents.

In LA-grammar, on the other hand, complex expressions are not defined as constituents but as **sentence starts**. A sentence start is a sequence of one or more words which can be continued into a complete, well-formed sentence. While constituents are based on the notion of possible substitutions, sentence starts are based on the notion of **possible continuations**.

---

[7]In semantically-interpreted LA-grammars of natural language, words are defined as **ordered triples**, consisting of a surface, a category, and a stem, while sentence starts are defined as triples consisting of a surface, a stem, and a frame-name. See Section 3.3 and 3.4 above.

Finally, consider the different interpretations of **tree structures** in PS-grammar, C-grammar, and LA-grammar. The tree structures generated by PS-grammar and C-grammar are hybrids which simultaneously encode (i) certain semantic intuitions and (ii) a partial representation of the derivation order. Consider, for example, the following tree:

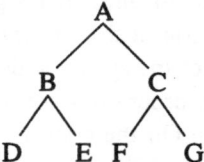

In PS-grammar, the semantic aspect of this tree resides in the fact that D and E are regarded as more closely related semantically than E and F. The derivational aspect, furthermore, resides in the fact that in a top-down derivation the expansion A → B + C must precede the expansions B → D + E and C → F + E. In a bottom-up derivation, on the other hand, the composition B + C → A must be preceded by the compositions D + E → B and F + G → C. In either case the derivation order is represented only partially because the tree does not indicate whether B or C has been expanded (or derived) first.

These considerations apply also to C-grammar (and any other constituent-structure based system). But C-grammar introduces an additional semantic distinction between **functors** and **arguments**. For example, while B and C are treated as equal "sisters" in PS-grammar, C-grammar specifies one as the functor and the other as the argument in terms of their respective categories.

In PS-grammar, the rewriting of A as B and C is grammatically legal if and only if there exists a suitable rewriting rule. The rewriting rule tells us that the expressions represented by B and C may be combined, but it doesn't say anything about the semantic relationship between the two expressions (except that the two expressions are related more closely semantically than are expressions whose categories do not appear on the right hand side of any rewriting rule).

In C-grammar, on the other hand, categorial compatibility is defined in terms of an asymmetric structure of the categories. From the beginning of C-grammar within the foundations of mathematics, this formal assymmetry of syntactically-compatible categories has been interpreted in semantic terms: if α is of category $(Y \mid X)$, then α is regarded semantically as a **function** with domain in Y and range in X. In other words, the combinatorially transparent categories of C-grammar are also **denotationally transparent**, in that their structure characterizes the domain/range structure of the semantic functions associated with the syntactic expressions.

Denotational transparency based on a syntactically-defined functor-argument structure provides an obvious basis for a straightforward semantic interpretation. But it has the disadvantage of imposing a non-linear derivation order on the syntax. Furthermore, a functor-argument-based syntax is not a necessary precondition for a systematic semantic interpretation of the surface. In short, the syntactic tree structure need not anticipate or forestall the semantic structure in order to be semantically interpretable — as illustrated in 3.3.1.

LA-grammar differs from both PS-grammar and C-grammar in that the tree structures generated during syntactic analysis or generation do not resemble semantic hierarchies in any way. Instead, left-associative trees are defined to reflect the derivation order completely, in contrast to trees in PS-grammar and C-grammar, which provide only a partial representation of the derivation order.[8]

The fact that the tree structure of the syntactic derivation in LA-grammar is determined by a time-linear derivation order does not mean that semantic considerations remain untreated in LA-grammar. On the contrary, extensive research in "database semantics" has shown that semantic hierarchies may be constructed simultaneously with the linear, syntactic derivation. The structure of these semantic hierarchies is generated directly from the syntactic categories and the categorial operations[9] of LA-grammar. The empirical problems characteristic of constituent-structure-based grammars arising in connection with discontinuous constituents[10] do not exist in semantically-interpreted LA-grammar.

6.2   The Mathematical Definition of Left-Associative Syntax

Left-associative grammars constitute a new class of formal objects for which we are going to give an algebraic definition. Let us recall some notation from set theory needed for this purpose. If X is a set, then X^+ is the "positive closure," i.e., the set of all concatenations of elements of X. X^* is the Kleene closure of X, defined as $X^+ \cup \epsilon$, where ϵ is the "empty sequence." The power set of X is denoted by 2^X . If X and Y are sets, then $(X \times Y)$ is the Cartesian product of X and Y, i.e., the set of ordered pairs consisting of an element of X and an element of Y. For convenience, we also identify integers with sets, i.e., $n = \{i \mid 0 \leq i < n\}$.

6.2.1 Formal Definition of Left-Associative Grammar[11]

A left-associative grammar (or LA-grammar) is defined as a 7-tuple $<W, C, LX, CO, RP, ST_S, ST_F >$, where

1. W is a finite set of *word surfaces*;
2. C is a finite set of *category segments*;
3. $LX \subset (W \times C^+)$ is a finite set comprising the *lexicon*;[12]
4. $CO = (co_0 ... co_{n-1})$ is a finite sequence of total recursive functions from $(C^* \times C^+)$ into $C^* \cup \{\perp\}$, called *categorial operations*.

---

[8]Because the left-associative derivation order is completely regular, the derivation tree is of no heuristic value and may be replaced by the structured lists characteristic of left-associative parsers.

[9]See Section 3.4.

[10]See Section 2.1.

[12]Since LX is finite, each w ϵ W is related by LX to a non-empty finite set of elements of C^+.

5. RP = (rp_0 ... rp_{n-1}) is an equally long sequence of subsets of n called *rule packages*.

6. ST_S = {(rp_s cat$_s$), ...} is a set of *initial states*, where each rp_s is a subset of n called a start rule package and each cat$_s$ ε C^+.

7. ST_F = {(rp_f cat$_f$), ...} is a set of *final states*, where each rp_f ε RP and each cat$_f$ ε C^*.

For theoretical reasons, the categorial operations are defined as total functions. In practice, the categorial operations are defined on easily-recognizable subsets of (C^* × C^+), where anything outside these subsets is mapped into the arbitrary "don't care" value {⊥}, making the categorial operations total.

To explain our intention in structuring grammars in the way just defined, we introduce the following auxiliary notions.

6.2.2 Definition of a Category

A *category* is an element of C^+.

In other words, a category is a sequence of non-empty category segments. For example, if N, D, A, V are category segments ε C, then (N D A V) is a category ε C^+.

6.2.3 Definition of a Categorized Word

A *categorized word* is an element of (W × C^+).

Thus, a categorized word is an ordered pair consisting of a word surface and a category. For example, if *gave* is a word surface ε W and (N D A V) is a category ε C^+, then [*gave* (N D A V)] is a categorized word ε (W × C^+).

The relation between the word surfaces in W and the categorized words in LX is called "lexical look-up." Lexical look-up is a one-many relation restricted as follows: w_i → (w_j c_k), for all w_i, w_j ε W, and all c_k ε C^+, is an instance of lexical look-up only if w_i = w_j. (w_i c_k), (w_i c_l), (w_i c_m), etc., are called the "lexical readings" of the word surface w_i ε W. For example, the word surface *gave* is mapped into the lexical readings [*gave* (N D A V)] and [*gave* (N A TO V)].

6.2.4 Definition of a Sentence Start

A *sentence start* is an element of (W^+ × C^*).

A sentence start is an ordered pair consisting of a sequence of word surfaces (called the "surface" of the sentence start) and a category. For example, if *John*, *read*, and *the* are word surfaces in W, and if GQ, V are category segments in C, then [(*John read the*) (GQ V)] is a sentence start consisting of the surface (*John read the*) ε W^+ and the category (GQ V) ε C^+.

---

[12]Please note that the details of Sections 6.2 – 6.5 differ from the corresponding definitions in Hausser (1988b).

6.2.5 Definition of Surface Concatenation

Surface concatenation is the function SC from $(W^* \times W)$ into W^+ such
that $SC((w_1 \ldots w_k), w_{k+1}) = (w_1 \ldots w_k \, w_{k+1})$, for all $w_j \, \varepsilon \, W$.

The function SC concatenates the surfaces of the input expressions[13] into the surface
of the resulting sentence start. This completely regular operation gives rise to the
name of Left-Associative Grammar.

6.2.6 Definition of a Left-Associative Rule

The i-th *left-associative rule* r_i is the ordered pair $(co_i \, rp_i)$.

A left-associative rule r_i takes a sentence start ss and a next word nw as input,
and applies the categorial operation co_i to the sentence category cat-1 and the next
word category cat-2. If the input condition of the categorial operation is satisfied
by (cat-1 cat-2), the application of r_i is successful and an output is derived. The
output consists of the pair [rp_i ss'], where rp_i is a *rule package* and ss' is a *resulting
sentence start*. If the input condition of the categorial operation is not satisfied by
(cat-1 cat-2), the application of rule r_i is not successful and no output is derived.

The rule package rp_i provided by the rule r_i contains all rules which may apply
after rule r_i was successful. A rule package is defined as a set of rule names, where
the name of a rule r_g is the place number g of its categorial operation co_g in the
sequence CO.[14] In practice, the rules are called by more mnemonic names, such as
"rule-g" or "Fverb+main."

The resulting sentence start ss' is derived as follows. If ss = (A_n cat-1) and nw
= (w_{n+1} cat-2), then ss' = ($<A_n \, w_{n+1}>$ cat-3), where $<A_n \, w_{n+1}>$ is derived from
A_n and w_{n+1} by SC (cf. 6.2.5), and cat-3 is derived from cat-1 and cat-2 by co_i.

6.3   The Derivational Structure of LA-Grammar

In LA-grammar a complete well-formed expression is derived in a sequence of
transitions from a start state to a final state.

6.3.1 Definition of the Set of Well-Formed Expressions

The set WE of *well-formed expressions* generated by an LA-grammar
is defined as follows:

1. If [rp_S cat-1] is a start state, and nw = (surf nw-cat) is in LX such
   that nw-cat = cat-1, then [rp_S nw] ε WE.

---

[13]I.e., a pair consisting of a sentence start and a next word.

[14]To give computational recursion a form that is not impredicative in the mathematical sense, Dana
Scott suggested the use of rule *names* in the rule packages.

2. If [rp$_i$ ss] ϵ WE, r$_j$ ϵ rp$_i$, nw ϵ LX, and the output of r$_j$ (ss nw) is [rp$_j$ ss'], then [rp$_j$ ss'] ϵ WE.
3. Nothing is in WE unless it so follows from (1) and (2).

WE is also called the reflexive-transitive closure of an LA-grammar.

Intuitively, an expression is regarded as well-formed if it can be continued into a complete expression. For example, [rp-2 (aaab (bbccc))] is a well-formed expression of the language $a^k b^k c^k$ defined below because it can be continued into the complete well-formed expression [rp-3 (aaabbbccc, ϵ)]. The set of complete well-formed expressions of a language is characterized by the final states of its grammar. Because [rp-3, ϵ] is the final state of $a^k b^k c^k$, all well-formed expressions of that language with rp-3 as their rule package and ϵ as their category are considered complete.

6.3.2 Definition of the Set of Complete Well-Formed Expressions

The set of *complete well-formed expressions* CWE $\subset$ WE is the set of pairs [rp$_i$ ss], where [rp$_i$ ss-cat] ϵ ST$_F$.

Corresponding to the sets WE and CWE we define the sets of surfaces and complete surfaces, respectively:

6.3.3 Definition of the Set of Surfaces

The set of "phrases" or *surfaces* S, S $\subset$ W$^+$, is
{s | s is the surface of we ϵ WE}.

6.3.4 Definition of the Set of Complete Surfaces

The set of "sentences" or *complete surfaces* CS, CS $\subset$ W$^+$, is
{s$_f$ | s$_f$ is the surface of cwe ϵ CWE}.

In addition to the start states ST$_S$ and final states ST$_F$, which are defined directly by the grammar (cf. clause 6 and 7 of 6.2.1), the output of the rules specifies a set of the rule states. The notion of a rule state has the following definition.

6.3.5 Definition of the Set of Rule States

The state associated with rule r$_i$ is called st$_i$ and defined as a pair [rp$_i$ cat-3], where rp$_i$ is the rule package of r$_i$ and cat-3 is the category specified in the output of r$_i$. The set of all rule states is called ST$_R$.

The derivation of a well-formed expression in LA-grammar may be described as sequence of transitions based on states, nw-intake, application sets, and application. These notions are defined as follows.

6.3.6 Definition of a State

A *state* is an element of the set ST$_S$ $\cup$ ST$_R$ $\cup$ ST$_F$.

Application sets are derived from states by means of the following function:

6.3.7 Definition of the nw-Intake Function

The function *nw-intake* takes a state st$_i$ ($0 \leq i < n$) of the form [rp$_i$ cat-1] and a nw ε LX of the form (surf cat-2), as input, and renders the application set [rp$_i$ (cat-1 cat-2)] as output.

6.3.8 Definition of an Application Set

An *application set* in LA-grammar is defined as a pair [rp$_i$ (cat-1 cat-2)] where rp$_i$ is a rule package and (cat-1 cat-2) is a pair of categories.

States are derived from application sets by means of the following function:

6.3.9 Definition of the Application Function

The function *application* takes an application set [rp$_i$ (cat-1 cat-2)] as input, applies each rule j ε rp$_i$ to (cat-1 cat-2), and renders a (possibly empty) set of states as output.

The interaction of states, nw-intake, applications sets, and application in a left-associative derivation is illustrated in the following schema:

6.3.10 The Recursion of a Left-Associative Derivation

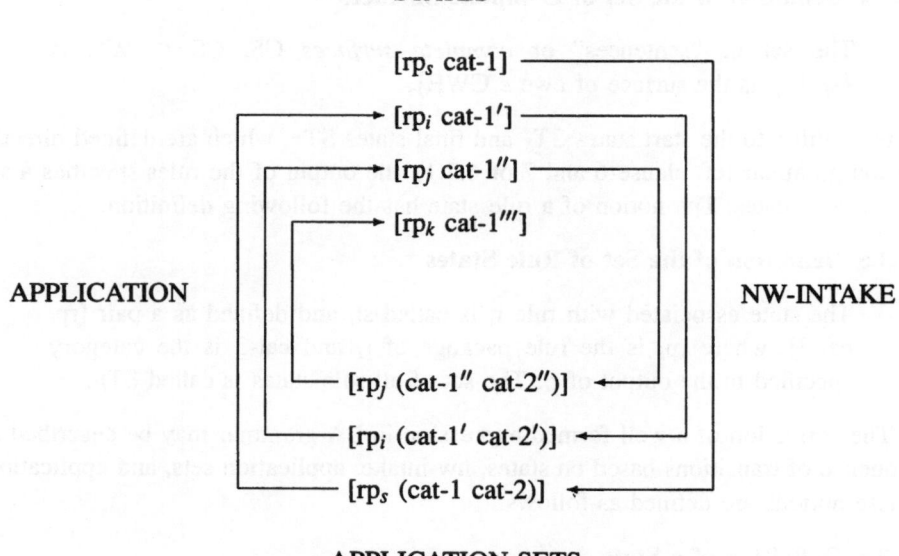

STATES

APPLICATION   NW-INTAKE

APPLICATION SETS

6.3.11 Definition of a Left-Associative Transition

A left-associative *transition* is a function from a state into a set of rule
states. A transition is a composite function, consisting of *nw-intake* and
application.

A left-associative transition can result in two different types of ambiguity, called
lexical ambiguity and syntactic ambiguity. Each reading of a lexically ambiguous
next word is represented by a category; if an nw has i readings nw-intake will
create i application sets. Syntactic ambiguity arises when, in a given application set,
more than one state is generated because more than one rule in the rule package
accepts the input pair. Since lexical ambiguity is associated with *nw-intake* and
syntactic ambiguity is associated with *application*, both kinds of ambiguity may
occur simultaneously in a transition.

6.4   A Notation for LA-Grammar

The definition of LA-grammar has been given in a very general abstract form. In the
approach advocated in this book, however, we have used only left-associative rules
that can be expressed by simple manipulations of sequences. These are formulated by
categorial operations co_i which specify the input categories and the output category
by means of *category expressions*.

Category expressions may contain **variables** for category segments (written as
seg1, seg2, etc.), and for sequences of category segments of length ≥ 0 (written as
X, Y, etc.). For example, if (X) is (bc), then (bXc) = (bbcc).

6.4.1 Definition of a Category Expression

A *category expression* is a list consisting of zero or more category
segments, zero or more segment variables, and zero or more segment-
sequence variables. The empty list is represented as ϵ.

Examples of category expressions are (*a*), (*a* X), (X), (*seg1 a* X), (X *a* Y), where
a is a category segment ε C. A category cat ε C*, is **compatible** with a category
expression CAT, if the structure of the category matches the pattern specified by the
expression. For example, the categories (*a*), (*aa*), and (*abc*) are compatible with the
category expression (*a* X).

We now define the subset relation, CAT $\subseteq$ CAT', between category expressions
to mean that every category compatible with CAT is compatible with CAT', and
similarly for $\subset, =, \neq, \not\subset,$ and $\not\subseteq$. A list of category segments (without any variables),
e.g., (a), (a a), or ϵ, is regarded as a category if it occurs as part of an analyzed
expression. Otherwise it is a category expression.

Left-associative rules are notated by expressions of the form [(ss nw) $\Rightarrow$ (rp$_i$ ss')],
where ss, ss' are expressions representing sentence starts ε (W$^+$ $\times$ C*), and nw is

an expression representing a "next word" ϵ ($W \times C^+$). Because surface composition SC is the same in all left-associative rules, it may be omitted in the definitions. This results in the following simplified notation of left-associative rules:

6.4.2 Notation of a Left-Associative Rule

The i-th rule of an LA-grammar has the form

r_i: [CAT-1 CAT-2] $\Rightarrow$ [rp_i CAT-3]

where CAT-1, CAT-2, and CAT-3 are the category expressions of ss, nw, and ss', respectively, and rp_i is the rule package of r_i.

If the categorial operation co_i cannot be expressed directly by the structure of the category expressions CAT-1, CAT-2, and CAT-3, a rule may be augmented with additional clauses which explain the category expressions and the relationships among them (see 4.1.2 and 7.5.1 as examples). The LA-grammars presented in this book use augmentations solely as abbreviatory devices which permit the collapsing of several rules without augmentations into a single rule.

Within a rule the categorial variables are bound. For example, in

r-1: [(X) (bc)] $\Rightarrow$ [{r-1, r-2} (bXc)]

the sequence of category segments referred to by X in CAT-1 and CAT-3 is the same. Note that r-1 has an output only if the next word matches the category (bc).

If the categorial operation of a rule does not express a function, the rule is not considered well-formed. For example, the rule "r-i: [(X)(Y)] $\Rightarrow$ [rp-i (Z)]" is not well-formed because its categorial operation does not express a function.

An LA-grammar is usually specified by (i) a lexicon LX, (ii) a set of start states ST_S, (iii) a sequence of rules, and (iv) a set of final states ST_F. Let us illustrate this general format of LA-grammars with a simple example of a formal language, namely the context-sensitive language $a^k b^k c^k$.

6.4.3 The Definition of $a^k b^k c^k$

LX $=_{def}$ {[a (bc)], [b (b)], [c (c)]}
ST_S $=_{def}$ {[{r-1, r-2} (bc)]}
r-1: [(X) (bc)] $\Rightarrow$ [{r-1, r-2} (bXc)],
r-2: [(bXc) (b)] $\Rightarrow$ [{r-2, r-3} (Xc)],
r-3: [(cX) (c)] $\Rightarrow$ [{r-3} (X)]
ST_F $=_{def}$ {[rp-3 ϵ]}.

In the specification of an LA-grammar like 6.4.3, the sets of word surfaces W and category segments C are implicitly characterized in the definition of LX: W $=_{def}$ {a, b, c} and C $=_{def}$ {b, c}. The sequences CO and RP, furthermore, are implicitly characterized in the definition of the rules r-1, r-2, and r-3.

The rule packages of the start states are specified by content (e.g., {r-1, r-2}) rather than by name because they are not called by any rule. The final states, on the other hand, are like rule states except that their category expressions are more restricted. (e.g., ϵ rather than (X)). Because the rule package(s) of final state(s) are related to rules, they are specified by name rather than content (e.g., rp-3 rather than {r-3}).

6.4.4 An Abstract Derivation of $a^k b^k c^k$ for k = 3

Input:	a	a	a	b	b	b	c	c	c

⇓ *lexical look-up* ⇓

r-1:	a	a	a	b	b	b	c	c	c
	(bc)	(bc)	(bc)	(b)	(b)	(b)	(c)	(c)	(c)

r-1:	aa	a	b	b	b	c	c	c
	(bbcc)	(bc)	(b)	(b)	(b)	(c)	(c)	(c)

r-2:	aaa	b	b	b	c	c	c
	(bbbccc)	(b)	(b)	(b)	(c)	(c)	(c)

r-2:	aaab	b	b	c	c	c
	(bbccc)	(b)	(b)	(c)	(c)	(c)

r-2:	aaabb	b	c	c	c
	(bccc)	(b)	(c)	(c)	(c)

r-3:	aaabbb	c	c	c
	(ccc)	(c)	(c)	(c)

r-3:	aaabbbc	c	c
	(cc)	(c)	(c)

r-3:	aaabbbcc	c
	(c)	(c)

aaabbbccc

ϵ

A well-formed string of length n is derived in n-1 left-associative combinations.

Strictly speaking, the surfaces of well-formed expressions of $a^k b^k c^k$ should be represented as, e.g, (*aaabbbccc*) rather than *aaabbbccc*. The parentheses surrounding sentence-start surfaces are omitted for simplicity. The parentheses are present in the representation of the categories, however, in order to maintain the distinction between categories, e.g., (*b*), and category segments, e.g., *b*. In LA-grammars of natural language, a sequence consisting of *a*, *b*, *c* is written as (*a b c*) rather than (*abc*) in order to permit use of category segments like *S3* consisting of more than one letter.

The combination rules of an LA-grammar are equally suitable for analysis and generation. The use of the combination rules of $a^k b^k c^k$ (cf. 6.4.3) in the analysis of input strings has been illustrated above. Next, consider the use of these rules in the generation of the well-formed string *abc* of $a^k b^k c^k$.

The start state ensures that the expression begins with an expression of category (bc), i.e., an *a*. The start rule package provides a choice between r-1 and r-2 for the next combination. Assume we pick r-2. Then the next word must be of category (b), i.e., it must be a *b*. The result of applying r-2 is *ab* of category (c). For the next combination, rp-2 gives us a choice between r-2 and r-3. Assume we try r-2 first. This attempt fails, because r-2 requires that cat-1 starts with a *b*. Next, we try r-3, which is applicable, because it requires that cat-1 starts with a *c*. r-3 requires that cat-2 is of category (c), i.e., the next word must be a *c*. The result of this combination is [rp-3 (abc, ϵ)], which is an element of CWE, the set of *complete well-formed expressions* of $a^k b^k c^k$.

6.5   On the Generative Power of LA-Grammar

Given the formal definition of LA-grammar and the left-associative algorithm, the following theorems may be proved:

6.5.1 Theorem 1

> LA-grammars (and the associated parsers and generators) accept and generate at most recursive languages.

Proof: Assume an input string of finite length *n*. Each word in the input string has a finite number of readings (> 0).

Combination step 1: The finite set of start states ST_S and all readings of the first word w_1 result in a finite set of well-formed expressions $WE_1 = \{(rp_S \text{ ss'}) \mid \text{ss' } \varepsilon$ $(W^+ \times C^+)\}$.[15]

Combination step n: Combination step k-1, k > 1, has produced a finite set of well-formed expressions $WE_k = \{(rp_i \text{ ss'}) \mid i \varepsilon \text{ n, ss' } \varepsilon (W^+ \times C^*)$, and the surface of each ss' has length k}. The next word w_{k+1} has a finite number of readings.

Therefore, the Cartesian product of all elements of WE_k and all readings of the current next word will be a finite set of pairs. Each pair is associated with a rule package containing a finite set of rules. Therefore, combination step k will produce only finitely many new sentence starts. The derivation of this finite set of new

---

[15]See 6.3.1, (1).

sentence starts is decidable because the categorial operations are defined to be total recursive functions.

$$Q.E.D.$$

Since all possible analyses are derived in finitely many steps for any given finite input, there is no halting problem in LA-grammar and associated parsers. Consequently, LA-grammars and LA-parsers generate and accept—at most—recursive languages. Since LA-grammars and LA-parsers are recursive, they satisfy condition 3 of the Criteria of Procedural Adequacy (cf. 2.4.1).

6.5.2 Theorem 2

LA-grammars (and the associated parsers and generators) accept and generate all recursive languages.

Proof:[16] Let L be a recursive language with the alphabet W. Because L is recursive, there is a total recursive function ϱ: $W^* \rightarrow \{0,1\}$, i.e., the characteristic function of L.

Let LAG^L be an LA-grammar defined as follows:
The set of word surfaces of LAG^L is W.
The set of category segments C $=_{def}$ W $\cup$ $\{0,1\}$.
For a, b ε W^+, (a (b)) ε LX if and only if a = b.

$LX =_{def} \{(a\ (a)),\ (b\ (b)),\ ...\}$
$ST_S =_{def} \{[\{r\text{-}1,\ r\text{-}2\}\ (seg1)]\}$
r-1: $[(X)(seg1)] \Rightarrow [\{r\text{-}1,\ r\text{-}2\}\ (X\ seg1)]$
r-2: $[(X)(seg1)] \Rightarrow [\emptyset\ \varrho(X\ seg1)]$
$ST_F =_{def} \{[rp\text{-}2\ (1)]\}$

After any given combination step, the rule package rp-1 offers two choices: application of r-1 to continue reading the input string, or application of r-2 to test whether the input read so far is a well-formed expression of L. In the latter case, the function ϱ is applied to the concatenation of the input categories, which are identical to the input surfaces. If the result of applying r-2 is [rp-2 (1)],[17] the input surface is accepted; if it is [rp-2 (0)], it is rejected.

Since the categorial operations of LAG^L can be any total recursive function, LAG^L may be based on ϱ, the characteristic function of L. Therefore, LAG^L accepts and generates any recursive language.

$$Q.E.D.$$

---

[16]This proof was provided by Dana Scott.
[17]I.e., if ϱ maps the category (X seg1), representing the surface, into the category (1).

This completes the proof that LA-grammar generates all (Theorem 2) and only (Theorem 1) recursive languages.

If we were to allow the categorial operations co_i to be any *partially recursive* function,[18] LA-grammar would generate precisely all the recursively enumerable languages; this could be proven similarly to Theorem 1 and Theorem 2. If we were to restrict the categorial operations to the *primitive-recursive* functions, we could show that LA-grammar generates exactly the primitive-recursive languages.

Theorem 2 makes use of the possibility of defining LA-grammars which code the recognition of strings completely into the last combination step; all other combination steps are assumed to be trivial, i.e., they consist only of reading the string. Despite the power of its categorial operations, LA-grammar still generates only the recursive languages. This is because of the completely regular derivation structure, which derives each reading of a well-formed string of length n in exactly $n-1$ steps (and derives only finitely many readings per input string).

Theorems 1 and 2 characterize the formalism of LA-grammar on the most general level. The next step is to investigate LA-grammars like the one defined in 6.4.3, where the categorial operations of each combination contribute to the overall structure. The following two questions will be discussed:

1. Which restrictions on the categorial operations of LA-grammars result in the regular, the context-free, and the context-sensitive languages, respectively. This issue is the topic of Section 7.1.

2. What is the computational complexity of LA-grammars which satisfy certain natural restrictions on their categorial operations, their control structure, and their lexical lookup? This question is investigated in Chapter 10.

---

[18]See the definition of categorial operations in 6.2.1, (4).

7. Language Hierarchies

Section 7.1 presents three theorems which relate types of LA-grammars to the recursive languages in the Chomsky hierarchy. Section 7.2 introduces a new hierarchy, which is more natural for LA-grammar. Section 7.3 explains the notions of nondeterminism, syntactic ambiguity, and lexical ambiguity. Section 7.4 discusses an example of a syntactically-ambiguous LA-grammar. Section 7.5 explains the properties of lexically-ambiguous LA-grammars.

7.1 LA-Grammars for Regular, CF, and CS Languages

In automata theory, formal languages are divided into type 0 or **recursively enumerable** languages; type 1 or **context-sensitive** languages; type 2 or **context-free** language; and type 3 or **regular** languages. Thereby, the context-sensitive languages are a subset of the recursively enumerable languages, the context-free languages are a subset of the context-sensitive languages, and the regular languages are a subset of the context-free languages. This hierarchy of formal languages is called the "Chomsky hierarchy."

Formal languages are characterized in two ways: (i) by the kind of formal automata which recognize them, and (ii) by the formal properties of their grammars. Recursively enumerable languages are recognized by the most general kind of formal automaton, a **Turing machine**. Context-sensitive languages are recognized by **linear-bounded automata**, a restricted form of a Turing machine. Context-free languages are recognized by **pushdown automata**. And the regular languages are recognized by **finite automata**, the most restricted of the formal automata.[1]

The differences betweeen these types of languages have been characterized grammatically by different kinds of **rewriting rules** of PS-grammars. A PS-grammar generates a context-free language (and is called a context-free grammar) if it uses only productions of the form $A \rightarrow \alpha$, where A is a variable and α is a string of terminal or non-terminal symbols.[2] A grammar generates a context-sensitive language (and is called a context-sensitive grammar) if its productions of the form $\alpha \rightarrow \beta$ obey the restriction that β is at least as long as α.[3] A grammar generates a regular language (and is called a regular or finite-state grammar) if it is right-linear or left-linear. A grammar is called right-linear if all productions are of the form $A \rightarrow wB$ or $A \rightarrow w$, where A and B are variables and w is a (possibly empty) string

---

[1] See Hopcroft and Ullman (1979) for further discussion.
[2] See Hopcroft and Ullman (1979), p. 79.
[3] See Hopcroft and Ullman (1979), p. 223.

of terminals. A grammar is called left-linear if all productions are of the form A $\rightarrow$ Bw or A $\rightarrow$ w.[4]

As in PS-grammar, we define the LA-grammars for regular, context-free, and context-sensitive languages by the different properties of their respective rules. The characteristic differences are defined by (i) the length of the sentence start category cat-1, and (ii) by restrictions on the categorial operations defined by left-associative rules. The following three theorems relate different types of LA-grammars to the recursive languages in the Chomsky hierarchy.

7.1.1 Theorem 3

Consider LA-grammars (and the associated parsers and generators) which satify the following restriction on the length of their input and output categories:

1. No category is longer than C, where C is a constant.

This class of LA-grammars accepts and generates all regular languages.

Proof: An LA-grammar is "finite state" if the category expressions specified in the rules are matched only by finitely many categories. The number of categories compatible with a category expression is infinite only if there is no restriction on the length of the categories.

That these restricted types of LA-grammar generate all regular languages follows because finite state automata are simulated by LA-grammars with "empty categorial operations" (cf. Section 8.2).

Q.E.D.

7.1.2 Theorem 4

Consider LA-grammars (and the associated parsers and generators) which satisfy the following restrictions on their categorial operations co_i:

1. co_i may look only at the first segment of cat-1.
2. cat-2 may consist of only one segment.
3. cat-3 equals cat-1 except for the initial segment.

This class of LA-grammars accepts and generates all context-free languages.

Proof: The restrictions on co_i correspond to the restrictions on pushdown automata for context-free languages.[5]In particular, the automata may look only at the top of the stack, represented in the grammar by cat-1, and the automata may only push or pop one element at a time from the stack (cf. 2, 3).

Q.E.D.

Because the LA-grammar formalism is non-deterministic, LA-grammars with categorial operations simulating pushdown automata accept all context-free languages. For example, consider the language WW^r, which is not accepted by any deterministic pushdown automaton.[6]

7.1.3 The LA-Grammar of the Context-Free Language WW^r

$LX =_{def} \{(a\ (a)),\ (b\ (b)),\ (c\ (c)),\ (d\ (d)),\ ...\}$
$ST_S =_{def} \{[\{r\text{-}1,\ r\text{-}2\}(seg1)]\}$
$r\text{-}1:\ [(X)(seg1)] \Rightarrow [\{r\text{-}1,\ r\text{-}2\}(seg1\ X)]$
$r\text{-}2:\ [(seg1\ X)(seg1)] \Rightarrow [\{r\text{-}2\}(X)]$
$ST_F =_{def} \{[rp\text{-}2\ \epsilon]\}$

This language consists of an arbitrarily long sequence of arbitrary letters (called W) followed by an inverse sequence. The LA-grammar 7.1.3 is context-free according to Theorem 4: the categorial operations look only at the beginning of the categories, and only add or remove one segment at a time. Consider the sample derivation 7.1.4.

7.1.4 Analysis of abccba in WW^r

```
*  (z a b c c b a)
;  1: Applying rules (RULE-1)
;  2: Applying rules (RULE-1 RULE-2)
;  3: Applying rules (RULE-1 RULE-2)
;  4: Applying rules (RULE-2)
;  4: Applying rules (RULE-1 RULE-2)
;  5: Applying rules (RULE-2)
;  5: Applying rules (RULE-1 RULE-2)
; Number of rule applications: 11.

2    *START-0
1
     (A) A
     (B) B
   *RULE-1
   2
     (B A) A B
     (C) C
   *RULE-1
   3
     (C B A) A B C
     (C) C
   *RULE-2
   4
     (B A) A B C C
     (B) B
   *RULE-2
```

---

[4]See Hopcroft and Ullman (1979), p. 217.
[5]Hopcroft & Ullman (1979), pp. 107 f.
[6]Hopcroft and Ullman (1979), p. 113.

```
    5
        (A) A B C C B
        (A) A
    *RULE-2
    6
        (NIL) A B C C B A


1   *START-0
    1
        (A) A
        (B) B
    *RULE-1
    2
        (B A) A B
        (C) C
    *RULE-1
    3
        (C B A) A B C
        (C) C
    *RULE-1
    4
        (C C B A) A B C C
        (B) B
    *RULE-1
    5
        (B C C B A) A B C C B
        (A) A
    *RULE-1
    6
        (A B C C B A) A B C C B A
```

LA-grammar characterizes WW^r as an ambiguous language. The first reading analyzes ABC as W, while the second reading analyzes ABCCBA as W. Only the first reading constitutes a complete expression of WW^r. The most complex derivations in WW^r involve inputs with an even number of equal letters. The worst case complexity of WW^r is $[(1/4 \cdot n^2) + (1/2 \cdot (n - 8))]$ rule applications — well below n^2.

The language WW, on the other hand, is a context-sensitive language. Its LA-grammar is given in 7.1.5.

7.1.5 The LA-Grammar of the Context-Sensitive Language WW

LX $=_{def}$ {(a (a)), (b (b)), (c (c)), (d (d)), ...}
ST$_S$ $=_{def}$ {[{r-1, r-2}(seg1)]}
r-1: [(X)(seg1)] $\Rightarrow$ [{r-1, r-2}(X seg1)]
r-2: [(seg1 X)(seg1)] $\Rightarrow$ [{r-2}(X)]
ST$_F$ $=_{def}$ {[rp-2 ϵ]}

This language consists of an arbitrarily long sequence of arbitrary letters (called W) followed by an identical sequence. The LA-grammar 7.1.5 is not context-free in the sense of Theorem 4: the categorial operation of r-1 adds a segment at the end of the sentence-start category, while the categorial operation of r-2 looks at the beginning of the sentence-start category. Consider a sample derivation.

7.1.6 Analysis of abcabc in WW with Active Rule Counter

```
*  (z a b c a b c)
;  1: Applying rules (RULE-1)
;  2: Applying rules (RULE-1 RULE-2)
;  3: Applying rules (RULE-1 RULE-2)
;  4: Applying rules (RULE-2)
;  4: Applying rules (RULE-1 RULE-2)
;  5: Applying rules (RULE-2)
;  5: Applying rules (RULE-1 RULE-2)
; Number of rule applications: 11.

2    *START-0
     1
         (A) A
         (B) B
     *RULE-1
     2
         (A B) A B
         (C) C
     *RULE-1
     3
         (A B C) A B C
         (A) A
     *RULE-2
     4
         (B C) A B C A
         (B) B
     *RULE-2
     5
         (C) A B C A B
         (C) C
     *RULE-2
     6
         (NIL) A B C A B C


1    *START-0
     1
         (A) A
         (B) B
     *RULE-1
     2
         (A B) A B
         (C) C
     *RULE-1
     3
         (A B C) A B C
         (A) A
     *RULE-1
     4
         (A B C A) A B C A
         (B) B
```

```
*RULE-1
5
   (A B C A B) A B C A B
   (C) C
*RULE-1
6
   (A B C A B C) A B C A B C
```

Even though WW^r is context-free and WW is context-sensitive, the definitions of the two grammars are almost identical. The only difference is in the output condition of the respective rules r-1: WW^r uses (seg1 X), while WW uses (X seg1). Furthermore, the two languages have exactly the same complexity, namely $[(1/4 \cdot n^2) + (1/2 \cdot (n - 8))]$ rule applications in the worst case. WW^r and WW illustrate that the distinction between context-free and context-sensitive languages has no relevance for complexity analysis in LA-grammar.

7.1.7 Theorem 5

Consider LA-grammars (and the associated parsers and generators) which satisfy the following restriction on the length of sentence-start categories cat-1 in the derivation of complete well-formed expressions:

1. In the derivation of any complete well-formed expression E, no sentence-start category of intermediate expressions is longer than $C \cdot n$, where n is the length of E and C is a constant.

This class of LA-grammars accepts and generates all context-sensitive languages.

Proof: The restriction on the length of cat-1 corresponds to the restrictions on linear-bounded automata for context-sensitive languages.[7]

$$Q.E.D.$$

For example, in the LA-grammar for the context-sensitive language $a^k b^k c^k$ — defined in 6.4.3—sentence-start categories in the first third of a well-formed input string have the length $2 \cdot k$; in the second third the category length decreases to length k; and in the last third, the category length decreases to 0. As another example, consider 7.2.5.

---

[7]Hopcroft & Ullman (1979), p. 225.

7.2   The Hierarchy of A-LAGs, B-LAGs, and C-LAGs

While the Chomsky hierarchy is clearly reflected in the formalism of LA-grammar,[8] it turns out to be irrelevant for specifying computational complexity in LA-grammar. A more natural way of dividing possible languages in LA-grammar is based on the properties of the categorial operations of the rules. The crucial formal property of a categorial operation—from a complexity point of view—is whether or not it has to search through indefinitely-long sentence-start categories.

7.2.1 Definition of the Class of C-LAGs

> The class of *constant* LA-grammars, or C-LAGs, consists of grammars where no categorial operation co_i looks at more than k segments in the sentence-start categories, for a finite constant k.[9] A language is called a C-language iff it is recognized by a C-LAG.

LA-grammars for regular and context-free languages are all C-LAGs because in regular languages the length of the sentence-start category is restricted by a finite constant (cf. Theorem 3, 7.1.1), and in context-free languages the categorial operation may only look at a finite number of segments at the beginning of the sentence-start category (cf. Theorem 4, 7.1.2). But the LA-grammars for many context-sensitive languages, e.g., $a^k b^k c^k$, $a^k b^k c^k d^k e^k$, WW, and WWW, are also C-LAGs.

Generally speaking, an LA-grammar is a C-LAG if its rules conform to the following schemas:

r_i: [(seg-1...seg-k X) CAT-2] $\Rightarrow$ [rp_i CAT-3]

r_i: [(X seg-1...seg-k) CAT-2] $\Rightarrow$ [rp_i CAT-3]

r_i: [(seg-1...seg-i X seg-i+1...seg-k) CAT-2] $\Rightarrow$ [rp_i CAT-3]

Thereby, CAT-3 may contain at most one sequence variable (e.g., X).

On the other hand, if an LA-grammar has rules of the form

r_i: [(X seg-1...seg-k Y) CAT-2] $\Rightarrow$ [rp_i CAT-3]

the grammar is not a constant LA-grammar. In non-constant LA-grammars CAT-3 may contain more than one sequence variable (e.g., X and Y).[10]

Non-constant LA-grammars are divided into the *B-LAGs* and *A-LAGs*.

---

[8]See Theorem 3 (7.1.1), Theorem 4 (7.1.2), and Theorem 5 (7.1.7) above.

[9]This finite constant will vary between different grammars.

[10]The definition of C-LAGs and B-LAGs benefitted from a discussion with Helmut Schwichtenberg.

7.2.2 Definition of the Class of B-LAGs

The class of *bounded* LA-grammars or B-LAGs consists of grammars where for any complete well-formed expression E the length of intermediate sentence-start categories is bounded by $C \cdot n$, where n is the length of E and C is a constant. A language is called a B-language if it is recognized by a B-LAG, but not by a C-LAG.

7.2.3 Definition of the Class of A-LAGs

The class of A-LAGs consists of *all* LA-grammars because there is no limit on the length of the categories, or on the number of category segments read by the categorial operations. A language is called an A-language if it is recognized by an A-LAG, but not by a B-LAG.

The three classes of LA-grammars defined above are related in the following hierarchy:

7.2.4 The Hierarchy of A-LAGs, B-LAGs, and C-LAGs

The class of A-LAGs recognizes all recursive languages, the class of B-LAGs recognizes all context-sensitive languages, and the class of C-LAGs recognizes most context-sensitive languages, all context-free languages, and all regular languages.

Let cs_c represent the context-sensitive languages recognized by C-LAGs and cs_b the context-sensitive languages recognized by B-LAGs. Then the conventional classes of regular (r), context-free (cf), context-sensitive (cs), recursive (rec), and recursively enumerable languages (r.e.) relate to the A-, B-, and C-languages as follows:

$$r \subset cf \subset cs_c \subseteq \mathbf{C} \subset cs_b \subseteq \mathbf{B} \subset \mathbf{A} = rec \subset r.e.$$

As an example of a B-language consider $a^k b^m c^{k \cdot m}$.

7.2.5 The B-LAG for $a^k b^m c^{k \cdot m}$

LX $=_{def}$ {(a (a)), (b (b)), (c (c))}
ST_S $=_{def}$ {[{r-1, r-2}(a)]}
r-1: [(X)(a)]   ⇒ [{r-1, r-2} (a X)]
r-2: [(X)(b)]   ⇒ [{r-3, r-4}(X \$ X)]
r-3: [(X \$ Y)(b)] ⇒ [{r-3, r-4}(Y X \$ Y)]
r-4: [(a X)(c)]   ⇒ [{r-4}(X)]
ST_F $=_{def}$ {[rp-4 (\$ Y)]}

This language consists of sentences like *abc, aabbbccccc, aaabbbccccccccc*, etc. Note that r-3 has a CAT-1 of the form (X $ Y). Each time a *b* is added, the categorial operation co_3 copies the category segments after the $ and adds them at the front of the ss-category;[11] the segments after the $ "remember" how many *a*'s were read at the beginning of the sentence. The CAT-3 of rule r-2 contains two variables for segment sequences, while the CAT-3 of rule r-3 contains three such variables.

$a^k b^m c^{k \cdot m}$ is an example of a B-language because no limit may be specified on the length of category Y in (X $ Y). The reason is, of course, that no limit exists for the number of initial *a*'s: the number of steps performed by co_3 is determined by the length of the initial *a* sequence.

The length of the intermediate categories of $a^k b^m c^{k \cdot m}$ is bounded by the length of the input expression (provided it is a complete well-formed expression of the language). For example, in the derivation of *aabbbccccc* the intermediate expression *aabbb* has the category (aa aa aa $ aa). Even though this category is longer than the surface of the intermediate expression in question, it is still shorter than the surface of the complete input expression.

7.2.6 Theorem 6

> The classes of A-languages, B-languages, and C-languages are each closed under union, concatenation, and Kleene closure.

Proof: Let L1 and L2 be two languages of the same class, generated by the LA-grammars LA-1 and LA-2. The **union** of L1 and L2 is generated by the grammar LA-U, which is constructed from LA-1 and LA-2 by (i) joining the LX-sets of LA-1 and LA-2; (ii) joining their respective ST_S sets; and (iii) joining the ST_F sets. LA-U uses the rules of LA-1 and LA-2 (with adjusted numbering).

The **concatenation** of L1 and L2 is generated by the grammar LA-C, which is constructed from LA-1 and LA-2 by (i) joining the LX-sets; (ii) writing a new rule r-c which combines the expressions of the ST_F set of LA-1 with the expressions of the ST_S set of LA-2; and (iii) adding r-c to all rule packages mentioned in ST_F of LA-1. In addition to r-c, LA-C uses the rules of LA-1 and LA-2 (with adjusted numbering).

The **Kleene closure** of L1 is generated by the grammar L-K, which is constructed from LA-1 by (i) writing a new rule r-c which combines the expressions of the ST_F set of L1 with the expressions of the ST_S set of L1; and (ii) adding r-c to all rule packages mentioned in ST_F of L1.

$$Q.E.D.$$

The closure properties described in Theorem 6 are "effective closure properties" (cf. Hopcroft and Ullman (1979), p. 58). If two LA-grammars are in different classes,

---

[11]The categorial operation of r-3 defines a *function* because the segment $ is introduced only once (by r-2).

then their union and concatenation results in an LA-grammar which belongs to the larger of the two classes. For example, if LA-1 is a C-LAG and LA-2 is a B-LAG, then the union and concatenation of LA-1 and LA-2 result in B-LAGs.

What are the main differences between the Chomsky hierarchy of regular, context-free, context-sensitive, and recursively enumerable languages, on the one hand, and the hierachy of C-, B-, and A-languages, on the other? The ABC-hierarchy does not recognize the regular languages as a separate class because all unambiguous C-LAGs are parsed in linear time.[12] Because it is not possible to parse faster than linear time, there is no reason (at least none related to complexity) for a separate treatment of the regular languages.

Furthermore, the ABC-hierarchy represents the recursive language class, which is not mentioned in the Chomsky hierarchy. The Chomsky hierarchy represents the class of the recursively enumerable languages, which is not mentioned in the ABC-hierarchy. The ABC-hierarchy does not contain recursively enumerable languages because LA-grammar recognizes only the recursive languages. This is also the reason why the recursive languages are represented in the ABC-hierarchy as the class of A-languages.

The context-sensitive languages are represented in both hierarchies; in the ABC-hierarchy the context-sensitive languages are called B-languages. That leaves the C-languages of the ABC-hierarchy, and the context-free languages of the Chomsky hierarchy. The latter are a proper subset of the C-languages. Which of these two different classes is the more natural one?

B-LAGs and C-LAGs are distinguished because of complexity analysis: the categorial operations of the C-LAGs are such that a rule application may be taken as the primitive operation of a computation, while this is not the case for the B-LAGs (cf. Section 10.1). The distinction between the context-free and the context-sensitive languages, on the other hand, is reflected in LA-grammar as a minor difference in the categorial operations: an LA-grammar is context-free iff the categorial operations work only on one end of the categories.

The distinction between context-free C-LAGs and context-sensitive C-LAGs is not justified by complexity theoretical properties (cf. the analysis WW^r and WW in 7.1.3 and 7.1.5). Here is another example illustrating the unnaturalness of the context-free language class from the viewpoint of LA-grammar; consider the context-free language $L_1 = \{a^i b^j c^k \mid k \geq i \text{ or } k \geq j\}$.

7.2.7 The PS-grammar for L_1

(1) S $\rightarrow$ AB	(7) B $\rightarrow$ ϵ
(2) S $\rightarrow$ C	(8) C $\rightarrow$ aCc
(3) A $\rightarrow$ aA	(9) C $\rightarrow$ aC

---

[12]For detailed discussion of finite automata see Section 8.2. The complexity result for unambiguous C-LAGs is given in Section 10.1.

(4) A → ϵ (10) C → D
(5) B → bBc   (11) D → bD
(6) B → bB   (12) D → ϵ

L_1 is an example of a context-free language which is not a DCFL—a deterministic context-free language (see Hopcroft and Ullman (1979), p. 245). An equivalent context-free formulation in LA-grammar is given in 7.2.8.

7.2.8 A "Context-Free" C-LAG for L_1

LX $=_{def}$ {(a (a)), (b (b)), (c (c))}
$ST_S =_{def}$ {[{r-1, r-4}(a)]}
r-1: [(X)(a)] ⇒ [{r-1, r-2} (a X)]
r-2: [(X)(b)] ⇒ [{r-2, r-3}(X)]
r-3: [(a X)(c)] ⇒ [{r-3, r-7}(X)]
r-4: [(X)(a)] ⇒ [{r-4, r-5} (X)]
r-5: [(X)(b)] ⇒ [{r-5, r-6}(b X)]
r-6: [(b X)(c)] ⇒ [{r-6, r-7}(X)]
r-7: [ϵ (c)] ⇒ [{r-7} ϵ]
$ST_F =_{def}$ {[rp-3 ϵ], [rp-6 ϵ], [rp-7 ϵ]}

This C-LAG is context-free because the categorial operations look only at the beginning of the categories. The language is generated by separating the $k \geq i$ part from the $k \geq j$ part, forming two parallel branches which originate in the set of start states. The $k \geq i$ part is handled by the rules r-1, r-2, r-3, and r-7. r-1 accumulates the a's, r-2 adds an arbitrary number of b's, r-3 adds as many c's as there were a's, and r-7 adds an arbitrary number of additional c's. The $k \geq j$ part is handled by the rules r-4, r-5, r-6, and r-7. r-4 adds an arbitrary number of a's, r-5 accumulates the b's, r-6 adds as many c's as there were b's, and r-7 adds an arbitrary number of additional c's.

A more efficient formulation may be achieved, however, if the categorial operations look at both ends of the categories. Consider the equivalent grammar defined in 7.2.9:

7.2.9 A Standard C-LAG for L_1

LX $=_{def}$ {(a (a)), (b (b)), (c (c))}
$ST_S =_{def}$ {[{r-1}(a)]}
r-1: [(X)(a)] ⇒ [{r-1, r-2} (a X)]
r-2: [(a X)(b)] ⇒ [{r-2, r-3, r-4}(X b)]
r-3: [(b X)(b)] ⇒ [{r-3, r-4, r-5} (b X)]
r-4: [(X b)(c)] ⇒ [{r-4, r-5} (X)]
r-5: [(X seg1)(c)] ⇒ [{r-5} ϵ], where seg1 ϵ {a, ϵ}
$ST_F =_{def}$ {[rp-4 ϵ], [rp-5 ϵ]}

r-1 accumulates the a's. r-2 adds the b's, each time subtracting an a at the beginning of the category and adding a b at the end. If there are more a's than b's, the input to r-4 is an expression with a category of a form such as (aabbbb). If there are more b's than a's, the input to r-3 is an expression with a category of the form (bbbbb), where the number of b's in the category equals the number of a's in the surface. Then r-3 can add arbitrarily many more b's without changing the category. Thus, the number of b's in the initial input to r-4 represents the shorter of the a and b sequences in the surface. r-4 adds c's until all b's in the category have been cancelled. Then r-5 may add any number of additional c's.

The C-LAG defined in 7.2.9 is not context-free because the categorial operation of r-2 works on both ends of the category, subtracting an a at the beginning and adding a b at the end. The grammar 7.2.9 is more efficient than the context-free formulation 7.2.8 because its derivations are based on a single branch.

Finally, compare the context-free languages and the class of C-languages according to their **subclasses**. One subclass of the context-free languages consists of the deterministic context-free languages. The DCFLs are defined by the fact that they are recognized by LR-grammars (cf. Hopcroft and Ullman (1979), pp. 233 f.). The class of DCFLs is of practical importance, because these languages are parsed by LR-parsers in linear time. This distinction is irrelevant in LA-grammar, however, because the LA-algorithm parses all unambiguous C-LAGs — including all unambiguous context-free languages and most unambiguous context-sensitive languages—in linear time.

On the other hand, there is a subclass of the C-LAGs, called the decidable C-LAGs, or D-LAGs[13]. The C-LAGs cover all context-free and most context-sensitive languages, while the D-LAGs cover most context-free and many context-sensitive languages. In other words, the inclusion of some context-sensitive languages characteristic of the C-LAGs reappears in the D-LAG subclass. In LA-grammar, no instances are known where the property of context-freeness plays an independently-motivated role in classifying weak generative capacity, or in determining computational complexity.

7.3   Ambiguity of Languages

Earley (1970) showed that the Earley algorithm recognizes **unambiguous** context-free grammars in $|G|^2 \cdot n^2$, but **ambiguous** context-free grammars in $|G|^2 \cdot n^3$ (where $|G|$ is the size of the grammar and n the length of the input string). Thus, computational complexity in PS-grammar depends not only on the class of the grammar, e.g., regular, context-free, or context-sensitive, but also on whether or not the grammar is ambiguous.

---

[13]The class of D-LAGs is defined in Section 9.2

It is similar in LA-grammar: computational complexity depends not only on whether the grammar is a C-LAG, B-LAG, or A-LAG, but also on whether or not the grammar is ambiguous. LA-grammar distinguishes three levels of ambiguity:

7.3.1 Three Levels of Ambiguity in LA-Grammar

1. unambiguous grammars
2. syntactically-ambiguous grammars
3. lexically-ambiguous grammars

We will show that unambiguous C-LAGs parse in n (linear time), syntactically-ambiguous C-LAGs parse in n^2 (square time), and lexically[14] ambiguous C-LAGs "packed parse" in n (linear time).

In preparation of the proofs given in Chapter 10, let us specify the formal properties defining deterministic, non-deterministic, unambiguous, syntactically-ambiguous and lexically-ambiguous LA-grammars.

7.3.2 Definition of Non-Deterministic LA-Grammars:

> An LA-grammar is non-deterministic iff (i) there is at least one rule package with more than one rule, and (ii) at each transition only one rule in the current rule package is applied, whereby the choice of the rule is at random.

The present implementation of LA-grammar is deterministic. That is, at each transition **all** rules in the current rule package are applied, in the order in which they appear in the package. In a parallel implementation, the rules in a rule package would be applied simultaneously. The notion of a non-deterministic LA-grammar is important for theoretical reasons.[15]

If the rule package(s) of an LA-grammar contain(s) more than one rule, the rules may be distinguished as to whether or not they accept the same input.

7.3.3 Three Types of Input Conditions

1. **Incompatible input conditions**: Two rules have incompatible input conditions if there exist no input pairs which are accepted by both rules.
2. **Compatible input conditions**: Two rules have compatible input conditions if there exists at least one input pair accepted by both rules, and there exists at least one input pair accepted by one rule, but not the other.

---

[14]Earley doesn't distinguish between syntactically- and lexically-ambiguous LAGs. His result of n^3 for "ambiguous" context-free grammars holds only for "packed parsing" (cf. Section 10.3).

[15]Cf. Hopcroft and Ullman (1979), Chapter 12. Berwick and Weinberg (1984), p. 149, call non-deterministic systems a "convenient mathematical fiction."

3. **Identical input conditions**: Two rules have identical input conditions if it holds for all input pairs that they are either accepted by both rules, or rejected by both rules.

7.3.4 Definition of Unambiguous LA-Grammars

An LA-grammar is unambiguous if and only if (i) it holds for all rule packages that their rules have **incompatible** input conditions, and (ii) there are no lexical ambiguities.

Examples of incompatible input conditions are [(a X)(b)] and [(c X)(b)], as well as [(a X)(b)] and [(a X)(c)].

7.3.5 Definition of Syntactically-Ambiguous LA-Grammars

An LA-grammar is syntactically ambiguous if and only if (i) it has at least one rule package containing at least two rules with **compatible** input conditions, and (ii) there are no lexical ambiguities.

For example, [(a X)(b)] and [(X a)(b)] represent compatible input conditions.

7.3.6 Definition of Lexically-Ambiguous LA-Grammars

An LA-grammar is lexically ambiguous if its lexicon contains at least two analyzed words with identical surfaces.

For example, the C-LAG lexicon of the language 3SAT, defined in 7.5.1, contains unambiguous words like (u1 (1)) and (u0 (0)), representing propositional constants with specific categories (truth values), and ambiguous words like (u (1)) and (u (0)), representing the propositional variable u, which takes both (1) and (0) as its categories. If we type an unambiguous word like u1, lexical look-up returns one analyzed word, i.e., (u1 (1)); if we type an ambiguous word like u, lexical look-up returns more than one analyzed word, i.e., (u (1)) and (u (0)).

Instead of treating the lexical ambiguity of, e.g., propositional variables by alternative lexical categorizations, it may be coded syntactically with rules which have **identical input conditions**. Assume, for example, that the propositional variable u is categorized unambiguously as (u ($)). Then ambiguous truth values may be introduced by the syntax, using rules like the following:

r-1: [(X) ($)] ⇒ [{r-i, r-j, ...} (X 1)]

r-2: [(X) ($)] ⇒ [{r-i, r-j, ...} (X 0)]

For reasons of perspicuity and modularity, lexical ambiguities should be handled by means of alternative lexical categorizations, and not by means of rules with identical input conditions. Therefore, LA-grammars using rules with identical input conditions and specific nw-categories (e.g., ($) rather than (seg1)) are not considered sound.

Having described the grammatical mechanisms for handling ambiguity let us turn to the structural properties of unambiguous, syntactically-ambiguous, and lexically-ambiguous languages. Because ambiguities increase the complexity of the analysis of a language, we need a clear criterion to distinguish between genuine ambiguities, which are a structural property of the language, and spurious ambiguities, which represent redundancies of a less than optimal grammar.

From a purely structural point of view, we call a language expression grammatically ambiguous if its surface belongs to two different syntactic (or lexical) classes. For example, *flying air planes* is an ambiguous surface, because the reading "to fly in air planes" is a singular noun phrase while the reading "air planes which fly" is a plural noun phrase. The class of singular noun phrases differs from the class of plural noun phrases because singular and plural nouns have different combinatorial properties.

This structural definition of ambiguity as a *surface-overlap* of two different grammatical classes must be clearly distinguished from alternative semantic readings of a word. For example, the word *bank* may be used to refer to a financial institution and to a place to sit on. But with either interpretation, *bank* belongs to the same grammatical class (singular nouns). Thus, it is not an instance of a grammatical ambiguity, and it should not be taken as grounds to produce two different syntactic derivations for the sentence *John went to the bank*. It is not that different readings of bank should not be treated at all, but that they should not be treated in the combinatorial part of the grammar, i.e., in the syntactic rules and the categorial classification of the lexicon.

The semantically-interpreted LA-grammar of English analyzes words as ordered triples, consisting of a surface, a category, and a list of one or more meanings, defined as frame-names. For example, the semantically-ambiguous noun *bank* is analyzed as the triple (bank (S-H) (BANK1 BANK2 BANK3)), where the first element is the surface, the second is the category, and the third is a list of semantic readings. BANK1 names a frame dominated by "money," BANK2 names a frame dominated by "sit," and BANK3 names a frame dominated by "river." The sentence *John went to the bank* is derived with one syntactic derivation and one semantic hierarchy containing the three fillers BANK1, BANK2, and BANK3 under the slot dominated by the frame PREPOSITIONAL-OBJECT. Which of these three fillers is the most likely interpretation is not determined in the syntactico-semantic derivation, but during pragmatic interpretation. In this way, semantic ambiguities of words do not affect the computational complexity of the combinatorial aspect of the grammar.

Similar considerations hold for different interpretations of *book by Mary* as "authored by" versus "located near." The category of the complex expression *book by Mary* is the same on either interpretation (i.e., a singular noun). Therefore we are not dealing with two different grammatical classes of complex expressions, and there is no possibility of a syntactic ambiguity. Furthermore, because the preposition *by* has the same syntactic category and the same syntactic function on either interpretation, it does not belong to two different classes of basic expressions, and consequently cannot be lexically ambiguous (in our structural sense), either.

What then is a spurious grammatical ambiguity? Because grammatical classes are defined by abstract properties, such as a particular syntactic category, it is possible to define two different classes which are nevertheless associated with the same set of surfaces. It is this total surface-overlap of two different classes which constitutes spurious grammatical ambiguities. In order for a surface to be genuinely ambiguous, the classes it belongs to must not only differ in their abstract property, e.g., category, but the classes must also differ concretely in their sets of associated surfaces. In order to avoid spurious ambiguities, different classes with total surface-overlap are ruled out in syntactic LA-analysis.

Most grammatical ambiguities proposed in the linguistic literature are genuine. For example, *flying air planes* arises in the surface-overlap of two surface-distinct grammatical classes.[16] The same is true for the lexical ambiguity of a word like *work*, which can be a noun or a verb. *Work* represents a genuine lexical ambiguity because not all present tense verb forms can function also as nouns (e.g., *admire*).

After this intuitive characterization of the distinction between genuine and spurious grammatical ambiguity, let us give a precise characterization of these notions within LA-grammar. Two well-formed expressions (cf. definition 6.3.1) wf_1 and wf_2 belong to the same class if they have the same rule package and the same category. If wf_1 and wf_2 belong to the same class they must have different surfaces, because otherwise they would be the same well-formed expression.

Let K1 and K2 represent the class of well-formed expressions characterized by the state [rp-i CAT-1] and [rp-j CAT-1'], where K1 and K2 differ at least in their respective rule packages i.e., rp-i versus rp-j.

7.3.7 Definition of Surface-Overlap

> Two different classes of language expressions, K1 and K2, have a surface-overlap iff there is at least one expression [rp-i (s1 cat-1)] in K1 and one expression [rp-j (s2 cat-1')] in K2, such that s1 = s2.

If the surface-overlap of two classes is partial (or if there is no surface-overlap at all), the two classes are called *surface-distinct*.

7.3.8 Definition of Surface-Distinctness

> Two classes of language expressions, K1 and K2, are called surface-distinct iff there is at least one expression [rp-i (s1 cat-1)] in K1 such that [rp-j (s1 cat-1')] does not occur in K2, and there is at least one

---

[16]E.g., *the house* belongs in the class of singular noun phrases, but not in the class plural noun phrases. Furthermore, *the houses* belongs in the class of plural noun phrases, but not in the class of singular noun phrases.

expression [rp-j (s2 cat-1')] in K2 such that [rp-i (s2 cat-1)] does not occur in K1.

Genuine ambiguities satisfy the Ambiguity Criterion:

7.3.9 Ambiguity Criterion

A surface is genuinely ambiguous if and only if it occurs in the **surface-overlap** of two **surface-distinct** classes of language expressions.

The ambiguity criterion 7.3.9 may be used to demonstrate that a language is, in fact, grammatically ambiguous. The first step is to find a surface associated with more than one grammatical class. The second step is to show that the classes in question are surface-distinct. The ambiguity criterion applies to syntactic and lexical ambiguities alike.

7.3.10 Definition of Syntactic Ambiguity

A surface is an instance of a genuine syntactic ambiguity if and only if it occurs in the surface-overlap of two surface-distinct classes of **complex expressions**.

7.3.11 Definition of Lexical Ambiguity

A surface is an instance of a genuine lexical ambiguity if and only if it occurs in the surface-overlap of two surface-distinct classes of **basic expressions**.

We emphasize again that this structural notion of a lexical ambiguity does not affect the handling of semantically ambiguous words like *bank*, except that it places their treatment outside the combinatorial machinery of the grammar. Instead of *lexical ambiguity* we could have used the terms "syntactic ambiguity of **basic** expressions," and instead of syntactic ambiguity we could have used the terms "syntactic ambiguity of **complex** expressions." The present terminology is justified by the fact that a lexical ambiguity arises because of alternative lexical look-up, and that a syntactic ambiguity arises because of alternative input-compatible syntactic rules.

7.4   Syntactically-Ambiguous LA-grammars

The C-LAG 6.4.3 for the unambiguous language $a^k b^k c^k$ is an unambiguous grammar in the sense of definition 7.3.4: all its rules have incompatible input conditions and there are no lexical ambiguities. Let us turn now to the language $a^n b^n c^m d^m \cup a^n b^m c^m d^n$, which has been called an *inherently ambiguous language* because there exist no unambiguous PS-grammars for it.[17]

---

[17]See Hopcroft and Ullman (1979), pp. 99 – 103, for a detailed discussion of this language within the PS-grammar paradigm.

7.4.1 The C-LAG for $a^nb^nc^md^m \cup a^nb^mc^md^n$

LX $=_{def}$ {(a (a)), (b (b)), (c (c)), (d (d))}
ST$_S$ $=_{def}$ {[{r-1, r-2, r-5} (a)]}
r-1: [(X) (a)] $\Rightarrow$ [{r-1, r-2, r-5} (a X)]
r-2: [(a X) (b)] $\Rightarrow$ [{r-2, r-3} (X)]
r-3: [(X) (c)] $\Rightarrow$ [{r-3, r-4} (c X)]
r-4: [(c X) (d)] $\Rightarrow$ [{r-4}(X)]
r-5: [(X) (b)] $\Rightarrow$ [{r-5, r-6} (b X)]
r-6: [(b X) (c)] $\Rightarrow$ [{r-6, r-7} (X)]
r-7: [(a X) (d)] $\Rightarrow$ [{r-7} (X)]
ST$_F$ $=_{def}$ {[rp-4 ϵ], [rp-7 ϵ]}

The rules characterize this language as context-free in the sense of Theorem 4 (7.1.2), and as a C-LAG (with $k = 1$) in the sense of definition 7.2.1. The grammar defined in 7.4.1 exhibits a syntactic ambiguity in the sense of definition 7.3.5: the rule package rp-1 calls the input-compatible rules r-2 and r-5, and the rule package rp-3 calls the input-compatible rules r-3 and r-4.

The syntactic ambiguity of $a^nb^nc^md^m \cup a^nb^mc^md^n$ is clearly reflected in the derivation of examples. Consider the sample derivation, with active rule counter, in 7.4.2:

7.4.2 Analysis of aabbbccddd in $a^nb^nc^md^m \cup a^nb^mc^md^n$:

```
* (z a a b b b c c d d d)
;   1: Applying rules (RULE-1 RULE-2 RULE-5)
;   2: Applying rules (RULE-1 RULE-2 RULE-5)
;   3: Applying rules (RULE-5 RULE-6)
;   3: Applying rules (RULE-2 RULE-3)
;   4: Applying rules (RULE-5 RULE-6)
;   4: Applying rules (RULE-2 RULE-3)
;   5: Applying rules (RULE-5 RULE-6)
;   6: Applying rules (RULE-6 RULE-7)
;   7: Applying rules (RULE-6 RULE-7)
;   8: Applying rules (RULE-6 RULE-7)
;   9: Applying rules (RULE-7)
; Number of rule applications: 23.

    *START-0
    1
        (A) A
        (A) A
    *RULE-1
    2
        (A A) A A
        (B) B
    *RULE-5
    3
        (B A A) A A B
        (B) B
    *RULE-5
    4
        (B B A A) A A B B
```

```
   (B) B
*RULE-5
5
   (B B B A A)  A A B B B
   (C) C
*RULE-6
6
   (B B A A)  A A B B B C
   (C) C
*RULE-6
7
   (B A A)  A A B B B C C
   (C) C
*RULE-6
8
   (A A)  A A B B B C C C
   (D) D
*RULE-7
9
   (A)  A A B B B C C C D
   (D) D
*RULE-7
10
   (NIL)  A A B B B C C C D D
```

Even though the output is unambiguous, the rule applications show that two different rule packages apply in the 3rd combination. This means that two of the three rules in the rule package of the 2nd combination accept the same input pair. The ambiguity is continued in the 4th combination, but resolved in the 5th.

The language is genuinely ambiguous because some strings have two derivations (those with equal numbers of a's, b's, c's, and d's), while all others have only one derivation. Thus, the ambiguity arises because of a surface-overlap of two surface-distinct classes, represented intuitively by $a^n b^n c^m d^m$ and $a^n b^m c^m d^n$. The derivation of an ambiguous expression of $a^n b^n c^m d^m \cup a^n b^m c^m d^n$ is illustrated in 7.4.3:

7.4.3 Analysis of aabbccdd in $a^n b^n c^m d^m \cup a^n b^m c^m d^n$:

```
*  (z a a b b c c d d)
;  1: Applying rules (RULE-1 RULE-2 RULE-5)
;  2: Applying rules (RULE-1 RULE-2 RULE-5)
;  3: Applying rules (RULE-5 RULE-6)
;  3: Applying rules (RULE-2 RULE-3)
;  4: Applying rules (RULE-5 RULE-6)
;  4: Applying rules (RULE-2 RULE-3)
;  5: Applying rules (RULE-6 RULE-7)
;  5: Applying rules (RULE-3 RULE-4)
;  6: Applying rules (RULE-6 RULE-7)
;  6: Applying rules (RULE-3 RULE-4)
;  7: Applying rules (RULE-7)
;  7: Applying rules (RULE-4)
; Number of rule applications: 24.

2     *START-0
   1
      (A) A
```

```
      (A)  A
*RULE-1
2
      (A A)  A A
      (B)  B
*RULE-2
3
      (A)  A A B
      (B)  B
*RULE-2
4
      (NIL)  A A B B
      (C)  C
*RULE-3
5
      (C)  A A B B C
      (C)  C
*RULE-3
6
      (C C)  A A B B C C
      (D)  D
*RULE-4
7
      (C)  A A B B C C D
      (D)  D
*RULE-4
8
      (NIL)  A A B B C C D D
```

1   *START-0
```
1
      (A)  A
      (A)  A
*RULE-1
2
      (A A)  A A
      (B)  B
*RULE-5
3
      (B A A)  A A B
      (B)  B
*RULE-5
4
      (B B A A)  A A B B
      (C)  C
*RULE-6
5
      (B A A)  A A B B C
      (C)  C
*RULE-6
6
      (A A)  A A B B C C
      (D)  D
*RULE-7
7
      (A)  A A B B C C D
```

```
    (D)  D
 *RULE-7
 8
    (NIL)  A  A  B  B  C  C  D  D
```

The formal analysis of this language in LA-grammar satisfies definition 7.3.10 of genuine syntactic ambiguity. For example, *aabb* belongs to two different classes, namely [rp-2 (X)] and [rp-5 (bX)]. So there is a surface-overlap. Yet [rp-2 (X)] and [rp-5 (bX)] are surface distinct classes because, e.g., *aabbb* belongs to the class [rp-5 (bX)], but not to [rp-2 (X)].

7.5   Lexically-Ambiguous LA-grammars

An example of a C-LAG for a lexically-ambiguous language is the grammar 7.5.1 for the language 3SAT. Well-formed expressions of 3SAT consist of logical conjunctions of complex propositions, which in turn consist of disjunctions of three negated or unnegated elementary propositions. For example, (*z or not y or not z*) and [(*z or not y or not z*) *and* (*y or z or u*)] are well-formed expressions of 3SAT. 3SAT is a lexically-ambiguous language because it contains propositional variables which are assumed to have two readings, represented by the categories (1) and (0). These categories are intuitively regarded as the truth-values *true* and *false*.

7.5.1 The Lexically-Ambiguous C-LAG for the Language 3SAT

$LX =_{def}$ {(u (1)), (u (0)), (x (1)), (x (0)), (y (1)), (y (0)), (z (1)), (z (0)),
    (u1 (1)), (u0 (0)), (x1 (1)), (x0 (0)), (y1 (1)), (y0 (0)), (z1 (1)),
    (z0 (0)), ([(L)), (] (R)), (not (NOT)), (and (AND)), (or (OR))}

$ST_S =_{def}$ {[{r-1} (L)]}

r-1: [(X L) (seg1)] $\Rightarrow$ [{r-2, r-6} (X L seg1)],
    where seg1 ε {0, 1, NOT}

r-2: [(X seg1) (OR)] $\Rightarrow$ [{r-3, r-4, r-6} (X seg1 OR)],
    where seg1 ε {0, 1}

r-3: [(X L seg1 OR) (seg2)] $\Rightarrow$ [{r-2, r-6} (X L seg1 OR seg2)],
    where seg2 ε {0, 1, NOT}

r-4: [(X L seg1 seg2 seg3 OR) (seg4)] $\Rightarrow$ [{r-5, r-6}
    (X L seg1 seg2 seg3 OR seg4)], where seg4 ε {0, 1, NOT}

r-5: [(seg1 X) (R)] $\Rightarrow$ [{r-7} (seg2)], where seg1 ε {0, 1, L};
    seg2 = 1 if 1 ε {X} and seg1 ε {L, 1}; otherwise seg2 = 0.

r-6: [(X NOT) (seg1)] $\Rightarrow$ [{r-2, r-5} (X seg2)],
    where seg1 ε {0, 1}; seg2 = 1 if seg1 = 0, otherwise seg2 = 0.

r-7: [(seg1 X) (AND)] $\Rightarrow$ [{r-8} (seg1 AND)],
    where seg1 ε {0, 1}

r-8: [(X AND) (L)] $\Rightarrow$ [{r-1} (X AND L)]

$ST_F =_{def}$ {[rp-5 (1)], [rp-5 (0)]}

The lexicon of 3SAT contains the propositional variables u, x, y, and z, which are ambiguous between the categories (1) and (0), and the propositional constants $u1$, $u0$, $x1$, $x0$, $y1$, $y0$, $z1$, and $z0$, which are not lexically ambiguous. Their truth-value corresponds to the second letter in their surface.[18] The rules of this grammar illustrate the fact that 3SAT is a context-free language, because all categorial operations work at the end of the categories.[19]

What is the complexity of this language? Under the most general interpretation there are no restrictions on the values of the propositional variables u, x, y, and z. With this kind of lexical look-up, a string containing p propositional variables with binary readings has exactly 2^p readings.

7.5.2 Derivation of [*x or not y or not z*] *and* [*y or z or u*]
(With unrestricted lexical look-up. The remaining 63 readings are omitted)

```
(z [ x or not y or not z ] and [ y or z or u ])
Real time:     1.30 s
Run time:      0.78 s

64    *START-0
   1
      (L) [
      (0) X
   *RULE-1
   2
      (L 0) [ X
      (OR) OR
   *RULE-2
   3
      (L 0 OR) [ X OR
      (NOT) NOT
   *RULE-3
   4
      (L 0 OR NOT) [ X OR NOT
      (0) Y
   *RULE-6
   5
      (L 0 OR 1) [ X OR NOT Y
      (OR) OR
   *RULE-2
   6
      (L 0 OR 1 OR) [ X OR NOT Y OR
      (NOT) NOT
   *RULE-4
   7
      (L 0 OR 1 OR NOT) [ X OR NOT Y OR NOT
      (0) Z
   *RULE-6
```

---

[18]The inclusion of at least one unambiguous propositional constant in the lexicon of 3SAT is necessary in order for the propositional variables to be *genuinely* lexically ambiguous in the sense of definition 7.3.11.

[19]Alternatively, the rules could have been defined to operate only at the *beginning* of the categories. But then the categories would be intuitively less transparent.

```
8
    (L 0 OR 1 OR 1) [ X OR NOT Y OR NOT Z
    (R) ]
*RULE-5
9
    (1.) [ X OR NOT Y OR NOT Z ]
    (AND) AND
*RULE-7
10
    (1 AND) [ X OR NOT Y OR NOT Z ] AND
    (L) [
*RULE-8
11
    (1 AND L) [ X OR NOT Y OR NOT Z ] AND [
    (0) Y
*RULE-1
12
    (1 AND L 0) [ X OR NOT Y OR NOT Z ] AND [ Y
    (OR) OR
*RULE-2
13
    (1 AND L 0 OR) [ X OR NOT Y OR NOT Z ] AND [ Y OR
    (0) Z
*RULE-3
14
    (1 AND L 0 OR 0) [ X OR NOT Y OR NOT Z ] AND [ Y OR Z
    (OR) OR
*RULE-2
15
    (1 AND L 0 OR 0 OR) [ X OR NOT Y OR NOT Z ] AND [ Y OR Z OR
    (0) U
*RULE-4
16
    (1 AND L 0 OR 0 OR 0) [ X OR NOT Y OR NOT Z ] AND [ Y OR Z OR U
    (R) ]
*RULE-5
17
    (0) [ X OR NOT Y OR NOT Z ] AND [ Y OR Z OR U ]
```

The grammar 7.5.1 generates 3SAT with all possible truth-value assignments for the propositional variables. A formula like [x or not y or not z] and [y or z or u] has 64 readings, because its truth-table distinguishes 64 (= 2^6) possible assignments.

A second, less general, type of lexical look-up requires a **consistent** value assignment for propositional variables throughout a formula. This requirement of consistency may be regarded as a form of **agreement**. It is not true for natural languages, however, that lexically-ambiguous words are always assigned consistent values. For example, *These people work a lot because they like their work* requires inconsistent value assignments to the lexically-ambiguous word *work*.

An even more restricted interpretation of 3SAT regards formulas as well-formed only if (i) the propositional variables have consistent value assignments and (ii) the formulas are true. This last case is known as the *Boolean satisfiability problem*.[20] If we restrict the grammar defined in 7.5.1 in this manner, the number of ambiguities is greatly reduced. For example, [*x or not y or not z*] *and* [*y or z or u*] has only 12 true readings with consistent lexical look-up, instead of the 64 readings for the unrestricted case.

---

[20]Hopcroft and Ullman, p. 325.

8. LA-Grammar and Automata

This chapter describes the relationship between LA-grammars and LA-parsers in comparison with other systems proposed in the literature. Section 8.1 characterizes the formal relationship between LA-grammar and associated LA-parsers and generators. Section 8.2 gives a formal account of the relation between LA-grammar and finite automata. Section 8.3 describes how LA-grammar differs from recursive-transition networks (RTNs) and augmented-transition networks (ATNs). Section 8.3 compares LA-grammars with Predictive Analyzers and Deterministic Parsers. Section 8.5 compares LA-grammars and Register Machines.

8.1 Input-Output Equivalence of Grammars and Parsers

Todays general parsing algorithms are based on the formalism of PS-grammar. Because the formalism of PS-grammar fails to be input-output equivalent with parsers, general parsing algorithms cannot apply the rules of PS-grammars directly. Instead they must reconstruct the grammatical analysis indirectly by means of *charts* or *tables*.

> All practical general parsing algorithms seem to be like Earley's algorithm in that they employ the tabular parsing method; they all construct *well-formed substring tables*. In chart parsing, such tables are called *charts*. The representation of one well-formed substring is called an "edge" in active chart parsing, a "state" in Earley's algorithm, a "dotted rule" in Graham's algorithm, and an "item" in Aho and Ullman.
>
> Tomita (1986), pp. 71 – 72.

However, conventional constituent-structure based grammars of natural language are not even written as pure PS-grammars, but use additional transformations, meta-rules, etc., to capture "linguistic generalizations". Therefore, if the grammar is to be parsed by means of a general parsing algorithm, it must be *preprocessed* into the PS-grammar format. The preprocessing of GPSG-grammars into the form of a context-free PS-grammar, for example, results in gigantic "object grammars" which may literally contain trillions of rules.[1]

A left-associative parser, on the other hand, is formally defined as an ordered pair (M_p, G), where M_p is a "motor"[2] and G is an LA-grammar. The motor applies the

---

[1]Barton et al., (1987), p. 189.
[2]Or "driver", in the terminology of LR-parsing. See Aho & Ullman (1979), pp. 197 f.

rules of the LA-grammar. The language analyzed by the LA-grammar may be any recursive language.

The motor action is abstractly characterized by the following algorithm:

8.1.1 The Algorithm of Left-Associative Parsers

Assume that the input is $(w_1 \ w_2 \ ...)$, where w_1 is the first word, w_2 is the second word, etc.

1. Set cc = $([rp_S \ w_1] \ w_2 \ ...)$, where cc is the current composition, and $[rp_S \ w_1]$ is an initial well-formed expression.

2. Suppose cc = $([rp \ A] \ w_i \ ...)$, where rp is the current rule package, A is an analysis of the input already processed, and w_i is the current next word. Pick a rule name from rp and apply the corresponding rule to $(A \ w_i)$. Generate new cc = $([rp' \ A'] \ w_{i+1} \ ...)$.

3. Go to (2).

Because left-associative parsers use the rules of LA-grammar directly, parsers and grammars are strongly input-output equivalent in the following sense:

8.1.2 I/O-Equivalence between a Grammar and its Parser

1. A grammar and its parser are input-equivalent if and only if both take unanalyzed strings as input.

2. A grammar and its parser are output-equivalent if and only if they derive the same syntactic analysis, using the same rules in the same derivation order, and assigning the same categories to intermediate expressions.

Because of this strong input-output equivalence between LA-grammar and LA-parsers (and LA-generators, see below), LA-grammars achieve absolutely type transparency.[3]

A left-associative generator, like a left-associative parser, is defined as an ordered pair $(M_g \ G)$, where M_g is a motor for generators, and G is a left-associative grammar. M_g uses a different algorithm than M_p, and that algorithm is abstractly characterized in 8.1.3.

8.1.3 The Algorithm of Left-Associative Generators

1. Pick a word w_1 from the lexicon LX with a category compatible with a start state $[rp_S \ cat\text{-}1] \ \epsilon \ ST_S$, and form $[rp_S \ w_1] \ \epsilon \ WE$.

2. Suppose $[rp \ A]$ is a well-formed expression. Pick a word w_n from LX and apply r_i, $i \ \epsilon \ rp$, to $(A \ w_n)$, generating $[rp' \ A']$.

3. Go to (2).

---

[3]Berwick & Weinberg (1984), p. 41.

Because left-associative generators use the rules of LA-grammar directly, generators and grammars are strongly input-output equivalent in the following sense:

8.1.4 I/O-Equivalence between a Grammar and its Generator

1. A grammar and its generator are input-equivalent if and only if both take (sequences of words from) a lexicon as input.

2. A grammar and its generator are output-equivalent if and only if they generate the same set of well-formed expressions, deriving each expression with the same rules in the same derivation order, and assigning the same categories to intermediate expressions.

A parser (cf. example 8.1.6) and a generator (cf. example 8.1.7) which work for any LA-grammar have been implemented in LISP.

8.1.5 Lemma 1

The set of expressions accepted by an LA-grammar is exactly the set of expressions generated by it.

Proof: For any expression E of length $k + 1$, $E \; \varepsilon \; W^+$, if it is accepted by the rule sequence R_k of length k, E is also generated by R_k, and *vice versa*. Consider combination step $i + 1$, $i < k$, involving the left-associative composition of the well-formed expression $[rp_m \; E_i]$, $E_i \; \varepsilon \; (W^+ \times C^*)$, and the next word $w_{i+1} \; \varepsilon \; (W^+ \times C^+)$. The combination step is grammatical if and only if there is at least one rule r_p in rp_m which accepts the categories of E_i and w_{i+1}. If E is being *analyzed*, w_{i+1} is provided by lexical look-up. If E is being *generated*, w_{i+1} is chosen from the lexicon L. In either case, the rule $r_p \; \varepsilon \; rp_m$ serves to check the categorial compatibility of E_i and w_{i+1}, and if r_p is defined for the input, it will derive $[rp_p \; E_{i+1}]$.

$$Q.E.D.$$

As an illustration of the relationship between an LA-grammar and its parser, consider the following NEWCAT derivation of *aaabbbccc* using the grammar for $a^k b^k c^k$ defined in 6.4.3.

8.1.6 Sample Derivation of aaabbbccc with Active Rule Counter[4]

```
*  (z a a a b b b c c c)
;   1: Applying rules (RULE-1 RULE-2)
;   2: Applying rules (RULE-1 RULE-2)
;   3: Applying rules (RULE-1 RULE-2)
;   4: Applying rules (RULE-2 RULE-3)
;   5: Applying rules (RULE-2 RULE-3)
;   6: Applying rules (RULE-2 RULE-3)
```

---

[4]The rule counter is part of the testing environment of LA-grammar, and was written with the help of Todd Kaufmann of Carnegie Mellon University.

```
;  7: Applying rules (RULE-3)
;  8: Applying rules (RULE-3)
; Number of rule applications: 14.

    *START-0
    1
        (B C) A
        (B C) A
    *RULE-1
    2
        (B B C C) A A
        (B C) A
    *RULE-1
    3
        (B B B C C C) A A A
        (B) B
    *RULE-2
    4
        (B B C C C) A A A B
        (B) B
    *RULE-2
    5
        (B C C C) A A A B B
        (B) B
    *RULE-2
    6
        (C C C) A A A B B B
        (C) C
    *RULE-3
    7
        (C C) A A A B B B C
        (C) C
    *RULE-3
    8
        (C) A A A B B B C C
        (C) C
    *RULE-3
    9
        (NIL) A A A B B B C C C
```

The rule applications specify (i) the number of the combination step, e.g.,
"; 3:", and (ii) the rule package(s) active at this combination step, e.g., "(RULE-1
RULE-2)". The number of rules fired in a combination step is the sum of all rules in
the rule packages associated with this combination step. Because $a^k b^k c^k$ is an unambiguous language, each combination step has only one rule package. In ambiguous
derivations, at least one combination step number occurs more than once, which
means that more than one rule package is fired in the combination (see example
7.4.2).

The rule applications in 8.1.6 show that the first $2k$ combination steps involve
two applications each, whereas the remaining $k - 1$ combination steps involve only
one rule application. The LA-grammar defined in 6.4.3 parses well-formed strings
of length n in exactly $[4/3n + 1/3(n - 1)]$ rule applications. That is, $a^k b^k c^k$ is parsed
in linear time. Furthermore, a parallel implementation of the LA-grammar for $a^k b^k c^k$

with two processors would parse with time complexity of $(n - 1)$.[5]

The relationship between the abstract derivation 6.4.4 and the NEWCAT analysis 8.1.6 satifies the notion of input-output equivalence between a grammar and its parser as defined in 8.1.2. That is, the parser derives the same syntactic analysis as the abstract grammar, using the same rules in the same derivation order and assigning the same categories to intermediate expressions.

In LA-parsers, the algorithm 8.1.1 is implemented as a bottom-up, breadth-first procedure. At each left-associative combination step, the parser forms the Cartesian product of all readings of the sentence start and the next word. Then the rules in the rule package of each sentence start are applied to the pair consisting of the sentence-start reading and a reading of the next word. LA-parsers derive all possible readings of a sentence start word-by-word in a parallel, breadth-first manner. Because the combinations of LA-grammars (and parsers) always take a sentence start and a next word as input, they employ a standard look-ahead of 1.

As an illustration of the relation between an LA-grammar and its generator, consider the following NEWCAT derivation of well-formed expressions up to length 12 using the grammar for $a^k b^k c^k$ defined in 6.4.3.[6]

8.1.7 Generating the Representative Sample of $a^k b^k c^k$

```
* (gram-gen 3 '(a b c))

Parses of length 2:
 A B
   2      (C)
 A A
   1      (B B C C)

Parses of length 3:
 A B C
   2 3    (NIL)
 A A B
   1 2    (B C C)
 A A A
   1 1    (B B B C C C)

Parses of length 4:
 A A B B
   1 2 2    (C C)
 A A A B
   1 1 2    (B B C C C)
 A A A A
   1 1 1    (B B B B C C C C)

Parses of length 5:
 A A B B C
   1 2 2 3    (C)
 A A A B B
```

---

[5]For further discussion of LA-grammar complexity see Chapter 10.

[6]This generator for LA-grammar was implemented by Todd Kaufmann.

```
   1 1 2 2    (B C C C)
A A A A B
   1 1 1 2    (B B B C C C)
Parses of length 6:
A A B B C C
   1 2 2 3 3    (NIL)
A A A B B B
   1 1 2 2 2    (C C C)
A A A A B B
   1 1 1 2 2    (B B C C C C)
Parses of length 7:
A A A B B B C
   1 1 2 2 2 3    (C C)
A A A A B B B
   1 1 1 2 2 2    (B C C C C)
Parses of length 8:
A A A B B B C C
   1 1 2 2 2 3 3    (C)
A A A A B B B B
   1 1 1 2 2 2 2    (C C C C)
Parses of length 9:
A A A B B B C C C
   1 1 2 2 2 3 3 3    (NIL)
A A A A B B B B C
   1 1 1 2 2 2 2 3    (C C C)
Parses of length 10:
A A A A B B B B C C
   1 1 1 2 2 2 2 3 3    (C C)
Parses of length 11:
A A A A B B B B C C C
   1 1 1 2 2 2 2 3 3 3    (C)
Parses of length 12:
A A A A B B B B C C C C
   1 1 1 2 2 2 2 3 3 3 3    (NIL)
```

After loading the same grammar as used for parsing, the function 'gram-gen' is called with two arguments: the "recursion factor" of the grammar, and a list of the words to be used.[7] The output is a systematic generation, starting with well-formed expressions of length 2. Each derivation consists of a surface, a sequence of rules, and a result category. As an example of a single derivation, consider 8.1.8.

8.1.8 A Complete Well-Formed Expression in $a^k b^k c^k$

```
A A A B B B C C C
   1 1 2 2 2 3 3 3    (NIL)
```

---

[7]In another version, 'gram-gen' is called with the maximal surface length rather than the recursion factor.

The surface and the rule sequence are lined up so that it is apparent which word was added by which rule. Derivation 8.1.8 characterizes a complete well-formed expression because it represents the rule state (rp-3 ϵ), which is element of the set of complete well-formed expressions of the C-LAG for $a^k b^k c^k$ defined in 6.4.3.

The recursion factor specifies how often the increasing recursions of the grammar have to be applied in order to arrive at a "representative sample". During the generation of longer and longer expressions, the system keeps track of increasing recursions, and stops the recursion as soon as the number specified by the recursion factor has been reached. Once the increasing recursions have been stopped, the generation terminates "naturally" after a finite number of steps. The theory for generating representative samples for C-LAGs is explained in Sections 9.2 and 9.3.

The generator produces all well-formed expressions of a certain length (and not just the complete well-formed expression). That's because expressions of length $n+1$ are derived from expressions of length n. Because complete well-formed expressions are formally characterized by the grammar (in the set ST_F), printing of incomplete well-formed expressions may be suppressed.

The relationship between the generation 8.1.8, the sample derivation 8.1.6, and the abstract derivation 6.4.4 satisfies the notion of input-output equivalence between generators, parsers, and grammars defined in 8.1.2 and 8.1.4. The generator derives the same syntactic analysis as the grammar and the parser (though in a slightly different format). It uses the same rules in the same derivation order, and assigns the same categories to intermediate expressions.

8.2   Simulating Finite Automata in LA-grammar

Some of the earliest and most widespread parsing formalisms for natural language are recursive-transition networks (RTNs) and augmented-transition networks (ATNs).[8] Because RTNs and ATNs are extensions of finite automata (FAs), let us begin with an analysis of the relationship between LA-grammar and finite automata.

A finite automaton is formally defined as 5-tuple $(Q, \sum, \delta, q_0, F)$, where Q is a finite set of *states*, $\sum$ is a finite input *alphabet*, q_0 in Q is the *initial* state, $F \subseteq Q$ is the set of *final* states, and δ is the *transition function* mapping $Q \times \sum$ to Q. That is, $\delta(q, a)$ is a state for each q and input symbol a.[9]

For both FAs and LA-grammars, input strings are read from left to right, word by word. But adding a word in FAs results in a direct move from one state q_k to another state q_l, where states are basic structures. A transition from q_k to q_l by way of adding word W may be written as $\delta(q_k, W) = q_l$.

In LA-grammars, on the other hand, states are defined as pairs consisting of a rule package and a (resulting sentence start) category, e.g., [rp$_i$ cat-1]. A transition

---

[8]Woods (1970).
[9]After Hopcroft & Ullman (1979), p. 17.

consists of two steps: (i) the addition of a next word to a state, resulting in the intermediate structure of an application set, e.g., [rp_i (cat-1 cat-2)], and (ii) an application of the rules in rp_i to the input pair represented by (cat-1 cat-2), resulting in a new set of states.

The crucial difference between LA-grammars and FAs resides in the derivation of resulting sentence starts. Without the sentence-start category, an LA-grammar state would be equivalent to an FA state, because the rule package rp_i of rule r_i is merely an explicit statement of all transitions possible after the successful application of r_i. Furthermore, without the sentence-start category, it would be impossible to define the categorial operations of the left-associative rules. Thus, there would be no intermediate stage of an application set, and transitions would go directly from a primitive state (rule package) to another primitive state via addition of a next word.[10]

Because FA states and transitions are special cases of LA-grammar states and transitions, we may directly simulate FAs in LA-grammar without changing the basic formalism of LA-grammar. This simulation is based on the use of empty categorial operations, defined as follows:

8.2.1 Definition of an Empty Categorial Operation

A categorial operation co_i is called an *empty categorial operation* if it maps an empty sentence-start category and a next-word category into an empty resulting-sentence-start category:

$$co_i: [\epsilon \text{ cat-2}] \Rightarrow [\epsilon]$$

The associated rule has the form:

$$r_i: [\epsilon \text{ cat-2}] \Rightarrow [rp_i \ \epsilon]$$

LA-grammars using only empty categorial operations simulate FAs in that (i) their states [$rp_i \ \epsilon$] are primitive, i.e., they consist solely in a set of connections to other states (represented explicitly by the rule packages); and (ii) their transitions consist of adding a next word to a primitive state, resulting in the activation of a new rule package (i.e., a new primitive state).

Let us illustrate this point with the regular language consisting of expressions of even numbers of zeros and even numbers of ones, e.g., 00, 11, 1010, 101000, 11010001, henceforth called E01.[11]

---

[10]Even though LA-grammar did not evolve from FAs, it may be regarded formally as an extension of FAs. But it constitutes by no means the first formal extension of standard FAs. Rabin and Scott (1959) investigated the decision properties of two-way, two-tape FAs.

[11]See Hopcroft and Ullman (1970), pp. 16 – 21 for a detailed discussion of this language.

8.2.2 FA Definition of the Regular Language E01

The set of states $Q =_{def} \{q_0, q_1, q_2, q_3\}$
The set of letters (or words) $=_{def} \{0, 1\}$
The set of final states $=_{def} \{q_0\}$
The transition function δ:

  (1): $\delta(q_0, 0) = q_2$
  (2): $\delta(q_0, 1) = q_1$
  (3): $\delta(q_1, 0) = q_3$
  (4): $\delta(q_1, 1) = q_0$
  (5): $\delta(q_2, 0) = q_0$
  (6): $\delta(q_2, 1) = q_3$
  (7): $\delta(q_3, 0) = q_1$
  (8): $\delta(q_3, 1) = q_2$

In order to simulate an FA in an LA-grammar, the FA has to be translated into the LA-formalism. This translation is accomplished in two steps.

8.2.3 Systematic Translation of FAs into LA-grammars

  1. Copy the left side of the FA equations characterizing δ, e.g., $(q_0, 1)$, into rules with empty categorial operations and still unspecified rule packages, e.g., r-2: $[\epsilon\ (1)] \Rightarrow [RP\ \epsilon]$.
  2. For the right side of the equations, e.g., q_1, find the left-hand sides with the same state names, e.g., $\delta(q_1, 0)$ and $\delta(q_1, 1)$, collect the corresponding rule names into a set, e.g, $\{r\text{-}3, r\text{-}4\}$, and add these sets to the LA-rules in question, e.g., as the rule package of r-2.

The LA-grammar which directly simulates the FA defined in 8.2.2 translates the eight FA transitions into eight LA rules, and represents the four FA states as four pairs of equivalent rule packages.

8.2.4 The LA-Grammar Simulating the FA Defined in 8.2.2

$LX =_{def} \{(0\ (0)), (1\ (1))\}$
$ST_0 =_{def} \{[\{r\text{-}1, r\text{-}2\}\ \epsilon]\}$
r-1: $[\epsilon\ (0)] \Rightarrow [\{r\text{-}5, r\text{-}6\}\ \epsilon]$
r-2: $[\epsilon\ (1)] \Rightarrow [\{r\text{-}3, r\text{-}4\}\ \epsilon]$
r-3: $[\epsilon\ (0)] \Rightarrow [\{r\text{-}7, r\text{-}8\}\ \epsilon]$
r-4: $[\epsilon\ (1)] \Rightarrow [\{r\text{-}1, r\text{-}2\}\ \epsilon]$
r-5: $[\epsilon\ (0)] \Rightarrow [\{r\text{-}1, r\text{-}2\}\ \epsilon]$
r-6: $[\epsilon\ (1)] \Rightarrow [\{r\text{-}7, r\text{-}8\}\ \epsilon]$
r-7: $[\epsilon\ (0)] \Rightarrow [\{r\text{-}3, r\text{-}4\}\ \epsilon]$
r-8: $[\epsilon\ (1)] \Rightarrow [\{r\text{-}5, r\text{-}6\}\ \epsilon]$
$ST_F =_{def} \{[rp\text{-}1\ \epsilon], [rp\text{-}2\ \epsilon]\}$

The LA simulation of the FA analysis of E01 is non-deterministic: each rule application permits two possible transitions, represented by two rules in the rule package. Which transition is chosen is determined by the next word. Technically speaking, the LA-grammar 8.2.4 defines eight rule states (one for each rule). But because the resulting sentence-start category is always ϵ, these eight rule states are constituted by four pairs of equivalent rule packages, which correspond to the four states of the FA 8.2.2.

8.2.5 The Correlation of FA States in 8.2.2 and LA Rule Packages in 8.2.4

$q_2 = \{r\text{-}5, r\text{-}6\}$ (used by r-1 and r-8)
$q_1 = \{r\text{-}3, r\text{-}4\}$ (used by r-2 and r-7)
$q_3 = \{r\text{-}7, r\text{-}8\}$ (used by r-3 and r-6)
$q_0 = \{r\text{-}1, r\text{-}2\}$ (used by r-4 and r-5)

As an illustration of the LA simulation 8.2.4 of a finite automaton, consider the following derivation:

8.2.6 Derivation of 11010001 with the LA-grammar 8.2.4[12]

```
* (z $ I I O I O O O I)
Real time:      0.00 s
Run time:       0.00 s

    *START-0
    1
        (NIL) $
        (1) 1
    *RULE-2
    2
        (NIL) $ 1
        (1) 1
    *RULE-4
    3
        (NIL) $ 1 1
        (0) 0
    *RULE-1
    4
        (NIL) $ 1 1 0
        (1) 1
    *RULE-6
    5
        (NIL) $ 1 1 0 1
        (0) 0
    *RULE-7
    6
        (NIL) $ 1 1 0 1 0
        (0) 0
    *RULE-3
    7
```

---

[12]The implementation of 8.2.4 uses the symbol $ to indicate the empty sentence start.

```
    (NIL) $ 1 1 0 1 0 0
    (0) 0
*RULE-7
8
    (NIL) $ 1 1 0 1 0 0 0
    (1) 1
*RULE-4
9
    (NIL) $ 1 1 0 1 0 0 0 1
```

Although the use of empty categorial operations allows systematic simulation of any finite automaton as an LA-grammar, the resulting LA-grammars are far from optimal. As an alternative definition of E01, using an LA-grammar with non-empty categorial operations, consider 8.2.7.

8.2.7 The LA-Grammar for the Regular Language E01

LX $=_{def}$ {(0 (0)), (1 (1))}
ST$_S$ $=_{def}$ {[{r-1} ϵ]}
r-1: [(seg1)(seg1)] $\Rightarrow$ [{r-2} ϵ]
r-2: [ϵ (seg1)] $\Rightarrow$ [{r-1, r-3} (seg1)]
r-3: [(seg1)(seg2)] $\Rightarrow$ [{r-4} (seg1 seg2)]
r-4: [(seg1 seg2)(seg2)] $\Rightarrow$ [{r-1, r-3} (seg1)]
ST$_F$ $=_{def}$ {[rp-1 ϵ]}

In the interpretation of this grammar, we assume that (i) seg1 and seg 2 have the values 0 or 1; (ii) within a rule, seg1 and seg2 have different values; and (iii) the segments in a complex category are unordered, i.e., (seg1 seg2) = (seg2 seg1). We make these assumptions in order to arrive at the most general statement of the grammar.

The transition network representing the control structure of this LA-grammar has the following form:

8.2.8 The Control Structure of LA-Grammar Defined in 8.2.7

Left-associative transition networks (LANs) represent the rule states in terms of the rule packages, omitting the output-category expression. Because the categorial operations are handled rule internally, there are no nw category labels on the arcs.

The start rule package rp$_S$ of the LA-grammar defined in 8.2.7 is identical to the rule package rp$_1$, and therefore has been omitted.

The states provided by the rules r-2 and r-4 are equivalent in the sense that both permit transitions to rules r-1 and r-3. But they are kept distinct in the representation 8.2.8 of the transition network, because rp-2 can be accessed from rp-1, while rp-4 cannot; furthermore, rp-4 can be accessed from rp-3, while rp-2 cannot.

The LA-grammar 8.2.7 for E01 is illustrated in the following sample derivation:

8.2.9 Derivation of 11010001

```
(z I I O I O O O I)
Real time:      0.00 s
Run time:       0.00 s

    *START-0
    1
        (1) 1
        (1) 1
    *RULE-1
    2
        (NIL) 1 1
        (0) 0
    *RULE-2
    3
        (0) 1 1 0
        (1) 1
    *RULE-3
    4
        (0 1) 1 1 0 1
        (0) 0
    *RULE-4
    5
        (1) 1 1 0 1 0
        (0) 0
    *RULE-3
    6
        (1 0) 1 1 0 1 0 0
        (0) 0
    *RULE-4
    7
        (1) 1 1 0 1 0 0 0
        (1) 1
    *RULE-1
    8
        (NIL) 1 1 0 1 0 0 0 1
```

The power of LA-grammar derives from (i) dividing an FA state into a rule package and a sentence-start category, and (ii) dividing an FA transition into the derivation of an application set and the evaluation of the application set. The pivotal entity, which is missing in finite automata, is the resulting sentence start.

8.3   The LAG Control Structure Compared with RTNs

Well-known extensions of finite-state automata are recursive-transition networks or RTNs.[13] While finite-state automata allow only terminal symbols (i.e., words or word categories) as transition labels, RTNs allow terminal symbols as well as state names, representing sub-networks. This raises the generative power of RTNs: FAs recognize only the regular languages, while RTNs recognize the context-free languages. Further extensions are augmented-transition networks or ATNs. ATNs go beyond RTNs by specifying conditions on the transitions.[14] This raises the generative power of ATNs to the level of Turing machines: ATNs recognize the recursively enumerable languages, and are therefore not guaranteed to halt.

What is the difference between conventional transition networks—such as FAs, RTNs, and ATNs on the one hand—and the control structure of LA-grammar on the other? In conventional networks, the "roles" of transitions are the names of **categories** or the names of **subnetworks**, while in left-associative networks (LANs) (e.g., 8.3.2 below) the "roles" are represented by the names of **left-associative rules**. LA-grammar uses rules as transition labels, because left-associative rules are of a strictly binary structure, taking a sentence start and a next word as input. Conventional transition networks do not use rules as transition labels, because the structure of the rewriting rules (even binary ones) is represented by **several transitions**.

For example, the rule

NP → Det + {Adj} + Noun

is represented in a conventional RTN as the following sub-network:

8.3.1 Representation of a Rewriting Rule in an RTN

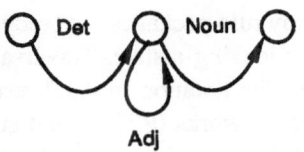

A transition network like 8.3.1 represents a cut through a non-binary tree. The **constituent structure** generated by the phrase-structure rules is reflected in RTNs and ATNs by a system with levels where several networks are embedded in each other. Consider, for example, the composition of *Peter gave Fido* and *the*. After finding the article *the*, an RTN would push into a lower NP network, continue there until the NP is completed, and pop up to insert the whole NP into the higher network.

---

[13]Woods (1970).
[14]Another extension of context-free grammars are "attribute grammars" (Knuth 1969).

Conventional transition networks are not left-associative because (i) they represent rules which cover several transitions in the network, and (ii) they permit the embedding of sub-networks into higher networks. LA-grammar, on the other hand, is left-associative, because its rules always cover a single transition. A left-associative transition always adds a next word to a sentence start, whether the next word is a complete basic constituent, the beginning of a complex constituent, or the continuation of a complex constituent.

Whereas conventional transition networks represent the **content** of a PS-grammar's rewriting rules (in terms of several transitions which have category or sub-network labels), LANs represent only the **control structure** of the LA-grammar. The control structure is defined by the rule packages associated with the rules. The actual transitions, on the other hand, are defined by the **categorial operations** of the rules. For example, the category of *Peter gave Fido the* is such that only DET+NOUN and DET+ADJ in the current rule package are applicable.[15] For the category of *Peter gave Fido cookies*, on the other hand, only rules like CMPLT or START-RELCL are applicable.

As a simple example of a LAN consider 8.3.2—which represents the control structure of $a^k b^k c^k$ as defined in 6.4.3.

8.3.2 The Control Structure of an LA-Grammar (Preliminary Notation)

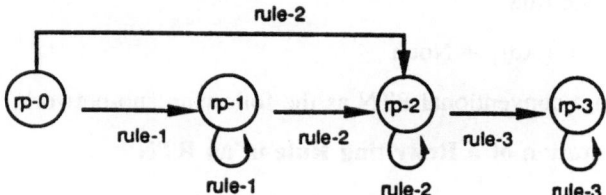

The states are represented by rule packages, whereby the content of a rule package corresponds to the set of arcs leaving a state. Traversal of an arc represents the application of a particular rule. The notation in 8.3.2 resembles traditional finite-state networks, recursive-transition networks (RTNs), and augmented-transition networks (ATNs) in that the "roles" of the transitions are indicated at the respective arcs. But 8.3.2 differs from conventional transition networks because the "roles" are represented by the names of left-associative rules, and not by terminal symbols (words or word categories) or sub-network names.

The left-associative control structure of 8.3.2 is redundant because the rule package at the end of an arc, e.g., rp-2, has a name directly related to the label of the arc, e.g, rule-2. In other words, left-associative networks have a special formal property: arcs with the same label always go into the same state. We may therefore represent the content of a LAN solely by its states. This leads to the following alternative

---

[15]Cf. history section 3 of 3.2.2.

representation of a left-associative control structure.

8.3.3 The Control Structure of an LA-Grammar (Final Notation)

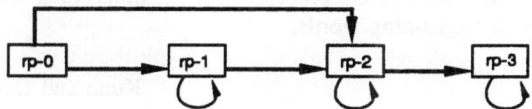

8.3.2 and 8.3.3 are equivalent. But the notation of 8.3.3 is simpler, especially for the complex control structures of natural language (cf. 4.1.3).

LA-parsers handle complex structures of natural language, such as center-embedding,[16] solely with LA-grammar rules, while conventional systems treat such structures by using special parsing procedures involving stacks and queues. The completely regular and simple parsing algorithm of NEWCAT is possible because (i) the categories of LA-grammar are defined as sequences which serve the function of stacks and queues, and (ii) each rule of LA-grammar specifies the set of rules to be applied next.

In summary, the representation of LANs á la 8.3.3 differs from conventional networks (including finite-state networks) in that (i) "roles" are represented in LANs by rule names; (ii) "states" are represented in LANs by the successful application of a rule; (iii) categories are handled only rule-internally in LANs; and (iv) rules in LANs handle only single transitions, consisting of the left-associative composition of a sentence start and a next word. Finally, LANs differ from RTNs and ATNs in that (i) LANs do not contain any sub-networks, and (ii) LANs do not contain "jumps".

8.4   Predictive Analyzers and Deterministic Parsers

This section compares LA-grammar and LA-parsing with two more parsing systems proposed in the literature, namely the "Multiple Path Syntactic Analyzer" by Kuno and Oettinger (1963), and the "Deterministic Parser" by Marcus (1980, 1978). These systems resemble the very early work in computational language analysis, which did not separate the linguistic analysis (the grammar) from the computer program. Rather, natural language is described by automata theoretic notions like *push-down stores*, *look-ahead*, *backtracking*, *well-formed substring table*, etc.

One of these early traditions was the "predictive analyzer" designed by Rhodes (1959), Alt and Rhodes (1961), Oettinger (1961), and Sherry (1961), which

---

[16]See Hausser (1986), Section 4.3., for the analysis of center-embedded relative clauses in German.

aims at obtaining a single most probable description of the structure of an input sentence in a single left-to-right scan through the sentence. The computer program uses a storage area called the *prediction pool*. At any intermediate point in the analysis of the sentence, the prediction pool contains a single set of *predictions*, generated by the processing of the preceeding words, that may be fulfilled by the remaining words.

Kuno and Oettinger (1963)

Kuno and Oettinger go on to say that the use of a single prediction pool makes the handling of several readings "inordinately difficult". In order to handle ambiguous sentences, they extended the predictive analyzer into a "Multiple Path Syntactic Analyzer" by differentiating the prediction pool into a set of subpools. The predictions are formulated in a grammar table, defined as a "rectangular array". Prediction pools are generated by rules whose subrules generate the subpools. Multiple analyses come about by following these subpools in a depth-first manner, with subsequent backtracking.

8.4.1 A Rule in the Multiple Path Syntactic Analyzer

G(sentence, PRN)

This rule is interpreted as "A sentence may begin with a pronoun".

8.4.2 The Subrules of G(sentence, PRN)[17]

g_1 = | PERIOD | PREDICATE (as in "/ They / go / .")

g_2 = | PERIOD | PREDICATE | ADJECTIVE CLAUSE (as in "We / who are ready to die / salute you /.")

g_3 = | PERIOD | PREDICATE | COMMA | ADJECTIVE PHRASE | COMMA (as in "/ They / , / knowing the truth / , /came to the right conclusion / .")

g_4 = | PERIOD | PREDICATE | COMMA | SUBJECT PHRASE | COMMA (as in "We/ , / the people of the United States/ , / love peace /.")

g_5 = | PERIOD | PREDICATE | SUBJECT PHRASE | AND-OR (as in "/They / and / John / came /.")

g_6 = | SENTENCE | COMMA | PARTICIPLE (as in "/They / having done the right thing / , / we can trust them.")

g_7 = | SENTENCE | COMMA | PARTICIPLE | SUBJECT PHRASE | AND-OR (as in "/They / and / John / having done the right thing / , / we can trust them.")

g_8 = | SENTENCE | COMMA | PARTICIPLE | COMMA | SUBJECT PHRASE | COMMA (as in "/They / , / the Russians / , / having said no/ , / we took a decisive step.")

---

[17]Quoted from Kuno and Oettinger (1963).

Because the predictions are defined as a push-down store, and because the top of a push-down store is conventionally interpreted as the *right-hand end* of a list, the predictions must be read from right to left. Thus, the prediction of g_1 is that there is first a PREDICATE and then a PERIOD.

The idea of encoding "predictions" resembles the theory of possible continuations intuitively. But beyond that, the Multiple Path Syntactic Analyzer and LA-grammar are different. In particular, the subrules in 8.4.2 are not left-associative, because they mention whole constituents (e.g., ADJECTIVE PHRASE, SUBJECT PHRASE) rather than single-word continuations. Thus, the grammatical analysis of the Multiple Path Syntactic Analyzer is more closely related to the transition network of an RTN, with its subnetworks representing constituents, than to the strictly left-associative procedure of combining a sentence start with a next word.

Furthermore, LA-grammar is not just a parsing algorithm, but a completely general mathematical theory for the recursive languages. In its formalism, it clearly reflects the regular, the context-free, and the context-sensitive languages. Parsing and generation do not constitute a separate theory in LA-grammar. Rather, parsers and generators are extremely simple algorithms which "apply the grammar".

Next, let us turn to the "Deterministic Parser" by Marcus (1978, 1980). Whereas the predictive analyzer originated from computer programs for natural language processing (and never attained the status of a linguistic theory), the deterministic parser originated in the inverse direction as an attempt to show that certain claims by Chomsky about language universals make sense computationally. Thus, we must distinguish between certain computational assumptions by Marcus, and the linguistic theory he tries to model.

Regarding the computational assumptions there is some agreement and some disagreement between Marcus' approach and LA-grammar. Agreement exists regarding the assumption that grammatical structures should not be changed during the course of the derivation, that the system should reflect "expections", that the system should be data-driven,[18] and that backtracking should be rejected. Furthermore, there is a resemblance between the use of "rule packets" by Marcus and "rule packages" in LA-grammar, though this similarity is superficial because Marcus uses rule packets solely for the sake of efficiency, while LA-grammar uses the rule packages to define the *control structure* of LA-grammar.[19]

Differences, on the other hand, include the use of look-ahead by Marcus: LA-grammar never looks further than the next word. Furthermore, Marcus' look-ahead is implemented as a buffer for **constituents** of arbitrary complexity, rather than next words. Finally, Marcus rejects "pseudoparallelism"—and presumably parallelism as well— because his system never produces complete sentences with more than one

---

[18]Though Marcus' system is only partly data driven. See Marcus 1980, p. 14.

[19]The modified version of Marcus' parser presented in Berwick (1985) does without rule packets.

reading. LA-grammar, on the other hand, generates genuine syntactic ambiguities[20] and would be particularily suitable for a parallel implementation (cf. Section 4.1).

There remains the linguistic aspect of Marcus' system, which is perched on Chomsky's "trace theory". As an example of a trace-theoretic analysis consider 8.4.3.

8.4.3

(1a) What did John give to Sue?

(1b) What did John give *t* to Sue?

(1c) John gave *what* to Sue?

The "deep structure" of the sentence is (1c). The output of Marcus' parser is an "annotated" surface structure like (1b).

Quoting from Marcus (1978, p. 239), "One use of a trace is to indicate the underlying position of the wh-head of a question or relative clause. Thus, the structure built by the parser for (1a) would include the trace shown in (1b), with the trace's binding shown by the line under the sentence. The position of the trace indicates that (1a) has an underlying structure analogous to the overt surface structure of (1c)."

The basic fact of the matter is that the direct object of *give* is *what* in (1a). This may also be indicated without the non-linear contortions of trace theory. Consider the hierarchical analysis in 8.4.4, which obtains an equivalent result on the basis of a strictly time-linear derivation.

8.4.4 *What did John give to Sue?*

```
* (z What did John give to Sue ?)

*** Lex Lookup
Real time:     0.00 s
Run time:      0.00 s

*** Parse Timings
Real time:     1.70 s
Run time:      1.66 s

    Linear Analysis:

    *START_0
    1
        (W-H) WHAT
        (N DO V) DID
    *MAIN&W+AUX_11
    2
        (N DO WT VI) WHAT DID
        (NH) JOHN
    *FVERB+NOM_10
    3
        (DO WT VI) WHAT DID JOHN
```

---

[20]Cf. 3.4.4, 3.4.5, 10.4.2, 10.4.3.

```
      (NOM A TO V) GIVE
   *OBJ+VERB_12
   4
      (A TO* VI) WHAT DID JOHN GIVE
      (ADP NP) TO
   *FVERB+MAIN_4
   5
      (NP VI) WHAT DID JOHN GIVE TO
      (NH) SUE
   *PREP+NP_5
   6
      (VI) WHAT DID JOHN GIVE TO SUE
      (VI INTERROG) ?
   *CMPLT_13
   7
      (INTERROG) WHAT DID JOHN GIVE TO SUE ?
```

```
Hierarchical Analysis:

(PROPOSITION-7_10_18
 (MOOD (INTERROGATIVE-7_10_18))
 (PROP-CONTENT
  ((SENT-2_10_18
    (TOP ((NP-1_10_18 (W-PRO (WHAT-1_10_18)))))
    (AUX (DO-2_10_18))
    (SUBJ ((NP-3_10_18 (NAME (JOHN-3_10_18)))))
    (PREDICATE
     ((NFV-4_10_18
       (INF (GIVE-4_10_18))
       (DIR-OBJ ("NP-1_10_18"))
       (PREPOSITIONAL_OBJ
        ((PREP-5_10_18
          (PREPOSITION (TO-5_10_18))
          (PREPOSITIONAL-ARG ((NP-6_10_18 (NAME (SUE-6_10_18)))))))))))))))))))
```

The node dominating the topicalized *what* is NP-1_10_18. The grammatical role of this noun phrase as the direct object of the verb is indicated by quoting this node in the direct-object slot of the verb frame.

Another example analyzed by Marcus is 8.4.5.

8.4.5

(2a) The meeting was scheduled for Wednesday.

(2b) The meeting was scheduled *t* for Wednesday.

(2c) ▽ scheduled a meeting for Wednesday.

According to Marcus (1978, p. 239) "Another use of trace is to indicate the underlying position of the surface subject of a passivized clause. For example, (2a) will be parsed into a structure that includes a trace as shown as (2b); this trace indicates that the subject of the passive clause has the underlying position shown in (2c). The symbol '▽' signifies the fact that the subject position of (2c) is filled by an

NP that dominates no lexical structure. (Following Chomsky, I assume that a passive sentence in fact has *no underlying subject*, that an agentive 'by NP' prepositional phrase originates as such in the underlying structure.)" (emphasis by Marcus).

The LA-grammar analysis of this example captures the grammatical facts alternatively by means of a "phrasal passive". The expectation of an optional agent phrase is visible in history section 4 in 8.4.6 of the linear analysis (cf. the BY segment in the category):

```
(BY V) THE MEETING WAS SCHEDULED
```

Regarding the agent phrase in passives, the present version of LA-grammar takes the option of not displaying anything (rather than displaying a dummy agent) in the frame-theoretic semantics if no agent is specified in the surface.

8.4.6 *The meeting was scheduled for Wednesday.*

```
* (z The meeting was scheduled for Wednesday \.)

*** Lex Lookup
Real time:    0.02 s
Run time:     0.02 s

*** Parse Timings
Real time:    1.18 s
Run time:     1.14 s

   Linear Analysis:

   *START_0
   1
      (GQ) THE
      (S-H) MEETING
   *DET+NOUN_2
   2
      (S) THE MEETING
      (S3 B V) WAS
   *NOM+FVERB_3
   3
      (B V) THE MEETING WAS
      (HV A) SCHEDULED
   *ADD-VERB_6
   4
      (BY V) THE MEETING WAS SCHEDULED
      (ADP NP) FOR
   *ADD-ADP_14
   5
      (NP BY V) THE MEETING WAS SCHEDULED FOR
      (N-H) WEDNESDAY
   *PREP+NP_5
   6
      (BY V) THE MEETING WAS SCHEDULED FOR WEDNESDAY
      (V DECL) .
   *CMPLT_13
   7
      (DECL) THE MEETING WAS SCHEDULED FOR WEDNESDAY .
```

```
Hierarchical Analysis:

(PROPOSITION-7_8_19
 (MOOD (DECLARATIVE-7_8_19))
 (PROP-CONTENT
  ((SENT-3_8_19
    (SUBJ
     ((NP-1_8_19 (REF (THE-1_8_19 SG-1_8_19)) (NOUN ((MEETING-2_8_19))))))
    (AUX (BE-3_8_19))
    (PASSIVE-PREDICATE
     ((NFV-4_8_19
       (PAST-PART (SCHEDULE-4_8_19))
       (ADVERB
        ((PREP-5_8_19
          (PREPOSITION (FOR-5_8_19))
          (PREPOSITIONAL-ARG
           ((NP-6_8_19 (NAME (WEDNESDAY-6_8_19))))))))))))))))
```

Next consider 8.4.7, which displays the third example of Marcus (1978).

8.4.7

(3a) John was believed to be happy.

(3b) John was believed [$_S$ t to be happy].

"The trace in (3c)" writes Marcus, " indicates that the phrase 'to be happy', which the brackets show is really an embedded clause, has an underlying subject which is identical with the surface subject of the matrix S, the clause that dominates the embedded complement. Note that what is conceptually the underlying subject of the embedded clause has been passivized into subject position of the matrix S, a phenomenon commonly called 'raising'."

LA-grammar has no constituent structure, and consequently no raising. The only task during the linear derivation of the hierarchical semantics is to indicate the proper grammatical relationships. Note that in the hierarchical analysis of 8.4.8 the NP-frame of the subject is quoted as the subject of the infinitive.

8.4.8 *John was believed to be happy.*

```
* (z John was believed to be happy \.)

*** Lex Lookup
Real time:    0.00 s
Run time:     0.00 s

*** Parse Timings
Real time:    1.66 s
Run time:     1.64 s

   Linear Analysis:

   *START_0
```

```
1
    (NH) JOHN
    (S3 B V) WAS
*NOM+FVERB_3
2
    (B V) JOHN WAS
    (HV INF&N) BELIEVED
*ADD-VERB_6
3
    (INF&N V) JOHN WAS BELIEVED
    (ADP NP) TO
*START-INF_7
4
    (INF V) JOHN WAS BELIEVED TO
    (M B) BE
*ADD-VERB_6
5
    (B V) JOHN WAS BELIEVED TO BE
    (ADJ) HAPPY
*ADD-VERB_6
6
    (V) JOHN WAS BELIEVED TO BE HAPPY
    (V DECL) .
*CMPLT_13
7
    (DECL) JOHN WAS BELIEVED TO BE HAPPY .
```

```
Hierarchical Analysis:

(PROPOSITION-7_9_20
 (MOOD (DECLARATIVE-7_9_20))
 (PROP-CONTENT
  ((SENT-2_9_20
    (SUBJ ((NP-1_9_20 (NAME (JOHN-1_9_20)))))
    (AUX (BE-2_9_20))
    (PASSIVE-PREDICATE
     ((NFV-3_9_20
       (PAST-PART (BELIEVE-3_9_20))
       (DIR-OBJ
        ((COMP-4_9_20
          (COMP (TO-4_9_20))
          (INF
           ((NFV-5_9_20
             (INF (BE-5_9_20))
             (SUBJ ("NP-1_9_20"))
             (PREDICATE
              ((ADJ-6_9_20 (ADJECTIVE (HAPPY-6_9_20)))))))))))))))))))))))))
```

Finally consider Marcus' argument that grammars having difficulties with garden path sentences are psychologically more realistic than grammars which do not. This argument is is not convincing because it is by no means clear that the possible delay in the interpretation of garden path sentences is caused by the syntactic analysis.

It is certain that the pragmatic interpretation of sentences occurs simultaneously with the syntactico-semantic analysis. The hearer does not wait to the end of the sentence before determining the referents of noun phrases, establishing semantic relations, etc. If the syntactico-semantic analysis is ambiguous (as in the case of a garden path sentence), all readings must coexist during the parse because there may be a possible continuation which is compatible with only one of the readings (see the example analyzed in 3.4.4 and 3.4.5).

The pragmatics, on the other hand, may immediately hypothesize a most likely reading (of the input read so far), which is used as the default in the pragmatic interpretation of the remainder of the sentence. It seems much more plausible to explain the delay in the interpretation of garden path sentences because of a revision in the *pragmatic interpretation*, rather than an alleged inability of the grammar to parse these perfectly normal and common syntactic structures.

In summary, Marcus' parser is neither a general purpose parsing algorithm like Earley's, nor a general theory of formal and natural languages. Instead, linguistic arguments and computational methods are closely intertwined, as illustrated by formulations like "The ability to drop the trace into the buffer is at the heart of the arguments presented here." (Marcus 1978, p. 245). More generally, the "Multiple Path Syntactic Analyzer" and the "Deterministic Parser" differ from LA-grammar in that they compute their predictions on the level of constituents, while LA-grammar computes possible continuations for next words.

8.5   LA-Grammar and Register Machines

This section[21] investigates whether arbitrary LA-grammars can be simulated by register machines, and whether arbitrary register machines can be simulated by LA-grammars. In other words, is there a general procedure which translates an arbitrary LA-grammar into an equivalent register machine, and vice versa? This question is not only of general interest, but also constitutes the background for the definition of a large subclass of C-LAGs for which many questions are decidable, such as $L(G) = \emptyset$, $L(G)$ is ambiguous, $L(G^1) \subset L(G^2)$, and $L(G^1) = L(G^2)$. This class of decidable C-LAGs, called D-LAGs, is defined in Section 9.2.

A register machine is a simple mathematical model of a computer, like a finite automaton or a Turing machine. Register machines are equivalent to Turing machines. In particular, they (i) accept all recursively enumerable languages, and (ii) provide a concise notion of an *effective procedure*. But the formal structure of register machines is considered more convenient for mathematical proofs than that of Turing machines. According to Ebbinghaus, Flum, and Thomas (1984, pp. 150 f), register machines may be described as follows.

A register machine consists of (i) a *register program* and (ii) an unlimited number of *registers*, where individual registers can store expressions of arbitrary length. For

---

[21]This section resulted from several discussions with Helmut Schwichtenberg.

different initial register contents, a register machine performs different computations (using the same program). A register containing only the empty string is called an "empty register".

A program, defined over a fixed alphabet $A = \{a_0, ..., a_0\}$, consists of instructions, where each instruction begins with a natural number L—its *label*. There are only five kinds of instructions.

8.5.1 Instruction Types of a Register Machine

1. L; $R_i = R_i + a_j$.
   (Add a_j to expression in register R_i. Go to next line.)

2. L; $R_i = R_i - a_j$.
   (If the expression in register R_i ends in a_j, subtract a_j from register R_i; otherwise leave R_i unchanged. Go to next line.)

3. L; If $R_i = \emptyset$, then L' else L_0 or L_1 ... or L_r.
   (If register R_i is empty, go to line L'; if the expression in R_i ends with a_0 (resp. a_1, ..., a_r) go to line L_0 (resp. L_1, ..., L_r).)

4. L; PRINT.
   (Print expression stored in register R_0. Go to next line.)

5. L; HALT.

8.5.2 Definition of a Register Machine Program

A *register program* is a finite sequence $\alpha_0, ..., \alpha_k$ of instructions of the form (1) through (5) in 8.5.1. A register program has the following properties:

1. α_i has label i ($i = 0, ..., k$).
2. In an instruction of the form (3) in 8.5.1 the labels L', L_0, ..., L_r are $\leq k$.
3. Only α_k is a halt-instruction.

For an example of a register program, consider 8.5.3.

8.5.3 Program M of a Register Machine

$A = \{1\}$
0; If $R_1 = \emptyset$, then 4 else 1.
1; $R_1 = R_1 - 1$.
2; $R_0 = R_0 + 1$.
3; If $R_1 = \emptyset$, then 4 else 1.
4; PRINT.
5; HALT.

Let $\{M\}^n$ represent an n-place function, defined on $x_0, ..., x_{n-1}$ in the first n registers, and for empty auxiliary registers R_n, R_{n+1}, etc. If $\{M\}^n$ halts for initially empty auxiliary registers and y in register R_0, we say

$$\{M\}^n (x_0, ..., x_{n-1}) \simeq y$$

For example, the program defined in 8.5.3 computes the 2-place function $(x + y)$, whereby

$$\{M\}^2 (3,4) \simeq 7$$

The values of the arguments x and y are represented by the content of the registers R_0 and R_1 before the start of the computation, while the operator "+" is coded into the program.

The following properties hold for register programs: .

8.5.4 General Properties of Register Machines

1. There is no general procedure for determining, with a given program and a given initial configuration of registers, whether the computation will halt. In the case of small programs like 8.5.3, one is often able from experience to decide this question, but there are register programs of several thousand lines where this is impossible.

2. If a register machine implements an n-place total function (where $n > 0$) in such a way that the arguments of the function are represented by the first n registers of the machine, and the auxiliary registers R_n, R_{n+1}, etc., are empty at the beginning of the computation, then the register machine will halt after finitely many steps. Such register machines may be called n-total register machines. n-total register machines constitute a proper subset of all register machines, so that all members of this subset are known to halt when started on empty auxiliary registers.

3. If a register machine implements a total n-place function so that the n arguments of the function are represented by the first n registers, and some or all of the auxiliary registers R_n, R_{n+1}, etc., are initially non-empty, nothing can be said about the behavior of the program. In particular, we cannot say whether the machine will halt for such computations.

4. Any register program using more than two registers can be simulated by an equivalent register program using only two registers.

Like Turing machines, register machines may be used to prove a number of interesting undecidability results. Consider, for example, the question of whether an arbitrary register machine program halts on empty initial registers. Let T be a recursive function such that T(M,y) holds iff M is a program for a register machine and y is a terminating computation of M starting with empty registers. Assume that $\exists y T(M,y)$ is recursive. If this holds, then

(i) $\exists y T(S(M,M),y)$

is also recursive, where $S(M,x)$ is a modification of M, such that $S(M,x)$ initially puts x into the first register of the machine, and then computes the same way as M. Note that .

(ii) $T(S(M,M),y) \Leftrightarrow T(M,M,y)$

where $T(M,x,y)$ holds if M is a program for a register machine, and y is a terminating computation of M starting with x in the first register, whereby all other registers are empty.

But if $\exists y T(S(M,M),y)$ is recursive, then so is

(iii) $\neg \exists y T(S(M,M),y)$

Because $\neg \exists y T(S(M,M),y)$ is recursive, a register machine M_0 exists which enumerates all M with the property $\neg \exists y T(S(M,M),y)$. In other words, M_0 with M in its first register terminates if and only if $\neg \exists y T(S(M,M),y)$ holds. That is, for all M,

(iv) $\exists y T(M_0,M,y) \Leftrightarrow \neg \exists y T(S(M,M),y)$

Because of (ii), we obtain a contradiction by substituting M_0 for M in (iv). Therefore, it is undecidable whether arbitrary register machines stop on empty initial registers.

Let $L(M)$ be the "language" accepted by a register machine, i.e.,

$$L(M) =_{def} \{x \mid \exists y\ T(M,x,y)\}$$

In other words, the language L accepted by a register machine M consists of expressions x, so that there is a terminating computation y for x in the first register. Using methods similar to those above, we can see that for this notion of a language accepted by a register machine M it is undecidable whether $L(M) = \emptyset$. Furthermore, if we consider two arbitrary register machines M^1 and M^2, it is undecidable whether $L(M^1) \subset L(M^2)$, and whether $L(M^1) = L(M^2)$.

What are the implications here for LA-grammar? The diagonalization argument is basically a construction $M_0(M)$, where a register machine M_0 halts if another register machine M does not halt, and where M is coded into the first register of M_0. Register machines may fail to halt because register machines accept all recursively enumerable languages. LA-grammar, on the other hand, accepts only the recursive languages (Theorem 1, 6.5.1). This means that LA-grammars are guaranteed to halt for any finite input. Therefore, the diagonalization argument cannot be reconstructed in this specific form[22] in LA-grammar.

The next question is whether the properties of register machines can be exported to LA-grammars by way of simulations. A general simulation cannot work, because

---

[22]Of course, one may use properties other than "halting" to construct diagonalization arguments in LA-grammar. See Cantor's diagonalization lemma in Shoenfield (1967), p. 131.

LA-grammars specify a finite set of start states. A given register machine, on the other hand, is defined for infinitely many configurations of computation-initial register contents. Thus, there is no notion of register machine simulation in LA-grammar which preserves the languages generated.

That leaves the possibility of a specialized simulation. Consider the following construction[23] limited to register machines with two empty registers. These machines are simulated by C-LAGs with categories of the form (11111$1111), where the numbers to the left of '$' represent the content of the left register, and the numbers to the right represent the content of the right register, and the next line is specified in the rule package. Only rules with the categorial operation coding the test instruction (cf. clause 3 of 8.5.1) have rule packages containing more than one rule.

Each instruction of a register program is translated into a left-associative rule. The input strings of the C-LAG are sequences of the same letter, whereby each letter represents a step performed by the register machine. A C-LAG simulating a 2-register machine with empty initial registers would look as follows:

$LX =_{def} \{(a\ (1))\}$

$ST_S =_{def} \{[\{r\text{-}1\}(1)]\}$

r-1: $[(1)(1)] \Rightarrow [\{r\text{-}2\ \}(\$)]$

r-2: $[(\$)(1)] \Rightarrow [\{r\text{-}3\}(1\$)]$

etc.

It holds for this specialized simulation that the C-LAG accepts an input string of length n iff the machine halts after n steps in a computation which began with empty registers.

The diagonalization proof described above shows that, for arbitrary (two) register machines with empty initial registers, it is undecidable whether they halt. Consequently, it is undecidable for C-LAGs G simulating such register machines whether or not $L(G) = \emptyset$. Thus, it is not possible to arrive at general decidability results for the whole class of C-LAGs.

The next chapter investigates for which kinds of C-LAGs G^1 and G^2 it is decidable whether or not $L(G^1) = \emptyset$, $L(G^1)$ is ambiguous, $L(G^1) \subset L(G^2)$, and $L(G^1) = L(G^2)$. We shall also show for which classes of C-LAGs these questions are not decidable, and why.

---

[23] Provided by Helmut Schwichtenberg.

9. Decidability and Efficiency

Section 9.1 describes a method for recognizing grammatical recursions in LA-grammar. Section 9.2 defines the procedure for constructing finite "representative samples" for a large subclass of the C-LAGs, called D-LAGs. Section 9.3 extends this method to the simultaneous construction of representative samples for two D-LAGs. Representative samples provide the basis for deciding, in the case of arbitrary D-LAGs G^1, G^2, whether $L(G^1) = \emptyset$, whether $L(G^1)$ is ambiguous, whether $L(G^1) \subset L(G^2)$, and whether $L(G^1) = L(G^2)$. Section 9.4 discusses methods for avoiding redundancies and other inefficiencies. Section 9.5 shows how these methods can be used to the handle ambiguities.

9.1 Recognition of Grammatical Recursion

For the empirical work of a linguist it is essential to know whether two grammars generate the same language, and whether the language generated by one grammar is a subset of the language generated by another. For example, if grammar G^{n+1} was designed to be a more efficient version of grammar G^n, then $L(G^{n+1})$ should be equal to $L(G^n)$. The same goes for the case of up-scaling: If G^{n+1} is an improved version of G^n where data coverage is concerned, $L(G^n)$ should be a subset of $L(G^{n+1})$; i.e., the new version of the grammar should cover the same linguistic constructions as the old.

In PS-grammar it is not possible to decide, in the case of arbitary context-free grammars G^1 and G^2, whether $L(G^1)$ is ambiguous[1], whether $L(G^1) \cap L(G^2) = \emptyset$, whether $L(G^1) \subset L(G^2)$, and whether $L(G^1) = L(G^2)$. This is true also for all systems based on PS-grammar, such as Transformational Grammar, GB, LFG, and GPSG. The only reason for claiming, e.g., that two grammars within the PS-grammar paradigm are equivalent is "experience".

The undecidability of the issues at hand is directly related to the undecidability of **Post's Correspondence Problem** (PCP), defined as follows:[2]

9.1.1 Post's Correspondence Problem

An instance of *Post's Correspondence Problem over alphabet* Σ is a finite set of pairs in $\Sigma^+ \times \Sigma^+$ (i.e., a set of pairs of non-empty strings over Σ). The problem is to determine if there exists a finite sequence

---

[1]Hopcroft and Ullman (1979), p. 200, Theorem 8.9.
[2]Quoted after Aho and Ullman (1972), pp. 32,3.

of (not necessarily distinct) pairs $(x_1 \ y_1)$, $(x_2 \ y_2)$, ..., $(x_m \ y_m)$, such that
$x_1, x_2, ..., x_m = y_1, y_2, ..., y_m$

The relationship between the PCP and PS-grammar ambiguity is as follows: An ambiguous PS-grammar may be regarded as the union of two PS-grammars G^1 and G^2, so that the languages generated by these grammars overlap. The first element in the pairs defined in 9.1.1— e.g., x_k— may be regarded as a substring generated by a grammar G^1. The second— e.g., y_k—may be regarded as a substring generated by a grammar G^2. If, for a sequence of substrings $x_1, x_2, ..., x_m$ generated by G^1, one could find an equivalent sequence of substrings generated by G^2, then G^2 would have been shown to generate that expression, too. But because the PCP is known to be undecidable, ambiguity of context-free PS-grammars is also undecidable. The undecidability of the other questions is shown with similar reductions to the PCP.

Where decidability is concerned, LA-grammar differs from PS-grammar. That's because the output of LA-grammar is much more structured than that of PS-grammar and related systems. In contrast to the irregular trees produced by PS-grammar, LA-grammar systematically generates longer and longer sentence starts. Furthermore, while the PCP is defined for unanalyzed sequences of terminal symbols, LA-grammar generates well-formed expressions, consisting of a rule package, a surface, and a category (cf. 6.3.1 and 6.3.2). The technique for deciding the properties of LA-grammars is based on inspecting systematically generated sample derivations, not on analyzing the grammar rules.

The crucial problem for proving decidability in LA-grammar is to determine how often grammatical recursions have to be applied in order for the set of completions to be a "representative sample". We shall see that such a "recursion factor" exists for the class of C-LAGs. Those C-LAGs where the process of systematic derivation, controlled by a grammar-dependent recursion factor, results in finite sets of representative samples are called D-LAGs ("Decidable C-LAGs").

The D-LAGs cover most context-free and context-sensitive languages. The D-LAGs are a *proper* subset of the C-LAGs because in some C-LAGs the systematic derivation of examples may produce a structural constellation where the recursion factor does not function. For any given C-LAG it may be decided whether it is a D-LAG or not. If a C-LAG is not a D-LAG, then the indicated questions (ambiguity, inclusion, equivalence) are not decidable.

The first step in deriving the set of abstract sentence types generated by an LA-grammar is construction of an abstract lexicon ALX from the lexicon LX of the LA-grammar in question. In ALX each lexical category is represented by a unique surface.

9.1.2 Definition of an Abstract Lexicon or ALX

If LX is the lexicon of a given LA-grammar G, then an *abstract lexicon* of G is constructed by forming abstract analyzed words (k cat$_i$), where cat$_i$ is a lexical category characterizing a non-empty class of word forms, and k is a symbol (e.g., a letter or a number) representing the class of word forms uniquely, for each lexical category in LX.

For example, if LX $=_{def}$ {[a (x)], [b (x)], [c (y)], [d (y)]}, then {[1 (x)], [2 (y)]} would be a corresponding ALX.

Note that lexical ambiguities are not possible in an ALX. For example, the lexicon LX $=_{def}$ {[a (x)], [b (x)], [c (y)], [d (y)], [a (y)]} contains the lexically ambiguous form *a* with the readings [a (x)] and [a (y)]. In a corresponding ALX, such as {[1 (x)], [2 (y)]}, this lexical ambiguity disappears. The reason is that lexical ambiguities arise as a surface overlap of different lexical classes (cf. Section 7.3). In an ALX no surface overlap is possible because all lexical classes are unit sets.

Using an abstract lexicon ALX, we begin the generation of abstract sentence types by applying all rules of the start state ST_S to all pairs in ALX × ALX. The result is a finite number of well-formed expressions with abstract surfaces of length 2.

9.1.3 Abstract Derivations of Length 2

If [rp-k ((xy) cat-i)] is a well-formed expression with the abstract two-word surface xy, then the corresponding *abstract derivation* has the following form:

$$xy$$
$$k \ cat\text{-}i$$

The set of all abstract derivations ad_2 of length 2 is called AD_2.

In the set AD_2 we distinguish those elements which can be continued, and those which cannot (because a final state has been reached). The set AD_3 is derived from the set AD_2 as follows: For each ad_2, apply the rules of the rule package (e.g., rp-k) to all elements of ss_2 × ALX, where ss_2 (e.g., ((xy) cat-i)) is the abstract sentence start inherent in ad_2. In this manner, AD_{n+1} may be derived recursively from AD_n, where AD_{n+1} contains elements with surfaces of length n+1.

The systematic derivation of AD-sets with elements having longer and longer surfaces is like the systematic derivation of corresponding well-formed expressions, with one exception: The elements of an AD-set contain a record of the sequence of rule applications, and correlate the rule sequence directly to the abstract surface it generated. The correlated sequences of abstract word surfaces and rule applications is required in order to recognize grammatical **recursions**. Compare the following examples of abstract derivations:

9.1.4 Apparent and Real Recursion in four Abstract Derivations

(i)   [xvxvx
        12345 cat-h

(ii)   [xvxvx
        12323 cat-i

(iii)   [xvxvx]a[xv
        123456712 cat-j

(iv)   [xvxvx]a[xvxvx]a[
        12345671234567 cat-k

The abstract derivations (i) and (ii) of 9.1.4 have the same surface. This surface exhibits a repetition of a subsequence (vx), suggesting the possibility of a grammatical recursion. But whether there really is a grammatical recursion can only be determined by looking at the surface and the rules simultaneously. The rules in example (i) show that the surface in question was generated by a sequence of rules without any recursion. Such an analysis is appropriate if the goal is to generate a specific symbol sequence—as in the language 3SAT,[3] where disjuncts must have exactly three propositions.[4]

But if an arbitrary number of disjuncts is permitted, then such a surface must be generated by a grammatical recursion. Example (ii) is an instance of a true grammatical recursion in LA-grammar because the repetition of subsequences on the surface level is mirrored by a repetition of subsequences at the level of the rules. Because further repetitions (additional loops through the recursion) will likely result in "more of the same", we are interested in the question of when a recursion may be stopped for the purposes of generative testing.

An abstract derivation is considered an instance of a grammatical recursion only if the repeating subsequences on the surface, as well as of the rule level, are **contiguous**. In example (iii) the repeating surface subsequences '[xv' are not contiguous. Thus one cannot yet tell whether it is an instance of a true grammatical recursion. Example (iv) illustrates how the derivation of longer and longer AD-sets will eventually result in a true recursion.

9.1.5 Definition of a Grammatical Recursion

An abstract derivation exhibits a grammatical recursion if and only if

1. the surface exhibits two or more identical subsequences which are directly adjacent,
2. the rule sequence exhibits two or more identical subsequences which correspond to the surface, and
3. each instance of the recursion affects the sentence-start category in a regular way.

How sentence-start categories are affected by a recursion depends on the type of the recursion. LA-grammar distinguishes between (i) constant, (ii) increasing, (iii) decreasing, and (iv) simultaneously increasing and decreasing grammatical recursions.

Here is how the algorithm recognizes and types recursions: Assume the generator has derived a string of length n, and is in the process of adding the n+1st word—e.g., A—by means of a certain rule, e.g. 1.

```
.......ABCABC A
.......123123 1 (cat)
```

---

[3]Cf. 7.5.1.

[4]In 9.1.4, x may be interpreted as a propositional variable, v as logical "or", and a as logical "and".

Before adding this derivation to the AD-set, the algorithm checks whether rule 1 had two predecessors. If so, it checks whether the (abstract) surfaces added by the occurrences of rule 1 are all the same. If so, it checks whether the rule sequences and the surface sequences between the occurrences of rule 1 are identical. If all these conditions are satisfied, a recursion has been recognized. Finally, the recursion is typed by comparing the categories of the expression in question with its shorter predecessors consisting of surface A and rule 1.

Let us call the three categories involved in the typing of a recursion cat_1, cat_2, and cat_3, where cat_3 is the category of the expression being tested, while cat_2 and cat_1 are the categories of the "recursion predecessors". If the three categories are identical, the recursion is constant. If cat_1 is shorter than cat_2, and cat_2 is shorter than cat_3, and the categories differ by one fixed sequence of segments (occurring either at the beginning or the end of the categories), the recursion is increasing. If cat_1 is longer than cat_2, and cat_2 is longer than cat_3, and the categories differ by a fixed sequence of segments, the recursion is decreasing.

That leaves the simultaneously increasing and decreasing recursions, of which there are three kinds, called i=d-recursions, i<d-recursions, and i>d-recursions. In i=d-recursions the increase and the decrease are of equal length; if cat_1, cat_2, and cat_3 are of equal length, but different, the recursion is of type i=d. In i<d-recursions, the increase is smaller than the decrease; if cat_1 is shorter than cat_2, and cat_2 is shorter than cat_3, and the categories differ by a fixed set of sequences of segments, the recursion is of type i<d. Finally, in i>d-recursions the increase is larger than the decrease; if cat_1 is longer than cat_2, and cat_2 is longer than cat_3, and the categories differ by a fixed set of sequences of segments, the recursion is of type i>d.

In summary, grammatical recursions are not determined by looking at the grammatical rules, but by looking at **derivations** which are generated systematically, starting with surface length 2. These derivations have a structure which specifies which word was added by which rule, and which provides the complete content of the sentence-start category. It is because of this derivational structure, which is unique to LA-grammar, that grammatical recursions can (i) be recognized by the simultaneous repetition of subsequences on the surface and the rule level, and (ii) be typed (as in constant versus increasing recursions) via the variation of the sentence-start categories. The recognition and typing of recursions is a straightforward, simple algorithm, and is implemented in the generator described in Section 8.1 (see example 8.1.7).

9.2   The Recursion Factor of C-LAGs

Once a grammatical recursion has been recognized in an AD-set, it can be tested by deriving abstract derivations exhibiting additional repetitions of the relevant subsequences. In this way, a grammatical recursion can be "applied" a certain number of times in the context of generative testing of an LA-grammar.

As surfaces get longer and longer, some elements of the AD-set will reach a final state while all remaining elements will eventually exhibit at least one instance of grammatical recursion. This is because the number of rules in LA-grammars is finite, while the surface of the AD-set members may grow indefinitely. Thus, from a certain point on AD_n and AD_{n+100}, for example, will differ only in terms of the number of recursive repetitions exhibited by their members. The question is how many recursions have to be tested to make sure that this point has been reached, and that all genuine sentence types of the grammar have been generated.

For generative testing, constant recursions have to be applied only twice, i.e., often enough to be recognized at all. Clearly, if the sentence-start category remains constant, the recursion can occur arbitrarily many times, but at the same time no new grammatical states will be reached.[5]

The number of decreasing recursions, on the other hand, depends on the length of the sentence-start category at the beginning of the loop. Thus, decreasing recursions are guaranteed to terminate on their own, and neither require nor permit any external limit on the number of their applications.

Now consider the increasing recursions. If, in an increasing recursion, $n+1$ applications always render the same set of possible continuations as n applications, then two applications of the recursion are sufficient to represent all possible sentence types connected with it. The critical factor in generative testing involves increasing recursions where $n+1$ applications lead to a different set of possible continuations than n applications. Consider the following example:

9.2.1 The C-LAG $G^{r=C}$, Requiring a Fixed Number of Recursions = C

$LX =_{def}$ {(a (a)), (b (b)), (c (c))}
$ST_S =_{def}$ {[{r-1, r-2} (a)]}
r-1: [(X)(a)] $\Rightarrow$ [{r-1, r-2, r-3} (a X)]
r-2: [(a a a a a)(c)] $\Rightarrow$ [$\emptyset$ ϵ]]
r-3: [(a X)(b)] $\Rightarrow$ [{r-3} (X)]
$ST_F =_{def}$ {[rp-2 ϵ] [rp-3 ϵ]}

This grammar generates the language $a^k b^k$, plus the string *aaaaac*, iff five *a*'s have been accumulated in the surface. Thus, four applications of the r-1 recursion lead to a different set of possible continuations than three applications. Consider the related AD-sets.

---

[5]Constant recursions are distinct from simultaneously increasing and decreasing recursions.

9.2.2 Derivation of AD-sets for 9.2.1 (Up to Length 6)

ab
  3 ϵ

aa   aab   aabb
 1 (aa)   13 (a)   133 ϵ

         aaa   aaab   aaabb   aaabbb
        11 (aaa)   113 (aa)   1133 (a)   11333 ϵ

                  aaaa   aaaab   aaaabb
                  111 (aaaa)   1113 (aaa)   11133 (aa)

                            aaaaa   aaaaab
                            1111 (aaaaa)   11113 (aaaa)

                                      aaaaac
                                    11112 ϵ

                                    aaaaaa
                                    11111 (aaaaaa)

In 9.2.2, *ab*, *aabb*, *aaabbb*, and *aaaaac* cannot be continued. (Also, they happen to be final states of the grammar defined in 9.2.1.) Regarding the remaining "active" elements in the AD-set, we would like to systematically stop those grammatical recursions which result only in "more of the same" (e.g., *aaaaaa*). The goal is to terminate the derivation of longer and longer AD-sets as soon as all grammatical states have been reached.

9.2.3 Stopping a Recursion in an AD-set Derivation

> If an abstract derivation of an AD_n-set is an instance of a grammatical recursion, then the recursion may be *stopped*; i.e., the recursion in question is not applied the next time it would be possible.

Like the recognition and typing of recursions, the stopping of recursions after a certain number of applications has been implemented in the generator illustrated in 8.1.7 and 9.2.12.

The stopping of recursions may result in *second-order recursions*, as illustrated in 9.2.4.

9.2.4 Example of a Second Order Recursion

```
...  ABCABC DFGDFG ABCABC DFGDFG A
...  123123 456456 123123 456456 1
```

The derivation in 9.2.4 is the result of stopping the ABC-recursion after the second time, entering the DFG-recursion, stopping that after the second time, getting back into the ABC-recursion, and repeating the sequence. Such a second order recursion may go on indefinitely. But second order recursions are also recognized by the algorithm, and may also be stopped.

If we stop grammatical recursions as soon as they are recognized, we would not get to generate the sentence type represented by *aaaaac* in the AD-set 9.2.2. Can we tell from the rule system how many increasing recursions[6] are needed to ensure that all sentence types generated by the grammar are exemplified in the AD-set?

Because the categorial operations of a C-LAG look only at a finite number of segments, any additional applications of an increasing recursion beyond this constant are not recognizable by the rules. Thus, as a first approximation, we conclude that recursions should be tried k times, where k is the maximum number of segments specified by the categorial operations of the grammar. In this way generation of the sentence type represented by *aaaaac* in 9.2.2 would be guaranteed.

But there is one further possibility, exemplified by the following C-LAG.

9.2.5 The C-LAG $G^{r > C}$ Requiring a Fixed Number of Recursions $> C$

LX $=_{def}$ {(a (a)), (b (b)), (c (c))}
$ST_S =_{def}$ {[{r-1, r-2} (a)]}
r-1: [(X)(a)] $\Rightarrow$ [{r-1, r-2, r-6} (a X)]
r-2: [(a X)(b)] $\Rightarrow$ [{r-3} (X)]
r-3: [(a X)(b)] $\Rightarrow$ [{r-4} (X)]
r-4: [(a X)(b)] $\Rightarrow$ [{r-5} (X)]
r-5: [(a a a a a)(c)] $\Rightarrow$ [{$\emptyset$ ϵ]]
r-6: [(a X)(b)] $\Rightarrow$ [{r-6} (X)]
$ST_F =_{def}$ {[rp-5 ϵ] [rp-6 ϵ]}

This grammar generates the language $a^k b^k$ plus the expression *aaaaaaaaabbbc*. Derivation of this expression requires seven applications of rule r-1, which is more than the characteristic constant of this grammar. (The maximal number of segments looked at by the categorial operations is five.) This is because r-2 feeds into the "rule chute" consisting of r-2, r-3, r-4, and r-5. Once r-2 has been applied, the only

---

[6] Abstract derivations such as 9.2.2 indicate, by the sentence-start categories, whether a recursion is constant, decreasing, or increasing. For example, the derivations of *aa*, *aaa*, and *aaaa* are instances of an increasing recursion, because the sentence-start categories increase by an *a* each time an *a* is added to the surface. Similarly, the derivations *aaab*, *aaabb*, and *aaabbb* are instances of a decreasing recursion, because the sentence-start categories decrease by an *a* each time a *b* is added to the surface.

possibility is r-3, then r-4, and then r-5. The rules r-2, r-3, and r-4 cancel segments of the kind looked at by r-5.

A sequence of rules r-1, r-2, r-3, etc., is called a rule chute if the only possible successor of r-1 is r-2, the only possible successor of r-2 is r-3, etc. One property of a rule chute is that it requires a new rule for each continuation. Thus, if a grammar has n rules, the maximum length of a rule chute affecting the number of increasing recursions to be tested is $n-2$. That's because there must be a recursive rule preceding the rule chute, and a "big foot" rule checking for a specific number of segments after the rule chute has been applied.

The following principle provides a summary of the above considerations on the number of applications of recursions:

9.2.6 The Maximal Recursion Principle of Generative Testing

> The AD-set of C-LAG contains at least one representative of each sentence type generated by the grammar if constant recursions are applied twice, if increasing recursions are applied $k + (n - 2)$, and if decreasing recursions are applied as often as possible.

The grammar-dependent constant $k + (n - 2)$ of the Maximal Recursion Principle[7] is called the "recursion factor" of the C-LAG.

The derivation of AD-sets, based on the Maximal Recursion Principle, is intended to result in a "representative sample" of the expressions generated by the grammar in question, in the sense that all grammatical states of the grammar—and all possible sentence types—are exemplified. The elements of an AD-set are still tokens. In order to turn an AD-set into a set of sentence types, different tokens belonging to the same sentence type have to be collapsed under some suitable notation. Although such a move is possible (and perhaps desirable for theoretical reasons), it is not essential for our present goal of deciding whether or not the language generated by a C-LAG is ambiguous.

That leaves the simultaneously increasing and decreasing recursions, which are not covered by the Maximal Recursion Principle.

In i=d-recursions, the number of segments added is the same as the number of segments removed, as in the sequence of categories (aaaa), (aaab), (aabb), (abbb), (bbbb). Here the recursion factor defined in 9.2.6 will suffice to insure that no possible continuations are omitted.

In i<d-recursions the increase is smaller than the decrease, as in (aaaa), (aab), (bb). These are regarded as decreasing recursions. The recursion will find a natural end when the decrease is completed. Because the decreases are larger than the increases, the process will terminate on its own.

---

[7]Whereby K is the maximal number of segments mentioned by any categorial operation of the grammar, and n is the number of grammar rules.

In i>d-recursions, finally, the increase is greater than the decrease. Consider the following sequence of categories, where the lengths of the left and right "halves" of each category are indicated by numbers.

(2.0)	(0.4)	(8.0)
(1.2)	(2.3)	(7.2)
(0.4)	(4.2)	(6.4)
	(6.1)	(5.6)
	(8.0)	(4.8)
		(3.10) etc.

The recursion in the left-most column is decreasing in the front end of the category, but increasing in the rear end. If we treat the recursion as increasing, we may not reach the point where the decreasing recursion has reached its natural end, and a new grammatical state is entered. But if we treat the recursion as decreasing, the rear end of the category is built up to length 10.

When the new grammatical state is entered (after the completion of a decreasing recursion), the rear end of the category may be used for the decreasing part of an i>d-recursion. Thus the dilemma arises again—as indicated in the middle column: Either we treat the recursion as increasing, in which case the recursion factor may prevent us from entering a legitimate grammatical state; or we treat the recursion as decreasing, in which case an even bigger buffer is created on the other end of the category, which may be used by the next i>d-recursion (cf. right column).

As an example of a C-LAG which—due to an i>d-recursion—is not susceptible to the process of generating a representative sample, consider the grammar for the language $ab2ab4ab$. Well-formed expressions of $ab2ab4ab$ consist of an arbitrary number of a's, followed by an equal number of b's, followed by the double number of a's and b's, followed by the double number again, etc.

9.2.7 The C-LAG "ab2ab4ab" with i>d-Recursion

$LX =_{def} \{(a \ (a)), (b \ (b))\}$

$ST_S =_{def} \{[\{r\text{-}1\} \ (a)]\}$

r-1: $[(X)(a)] \Rightarrow [\{r\text{-}1, r\text{-}2\} \ (a \ X)]$

r-2: $[(a \ X)(b)] \Rightarrow [\{r\text{-}2, r\text{-}3\} \ (X \ b \ b)]$

r-3: $[(b \ X)(a)] \Rightarrow [\{r\text{-}3, r\text{-}2\} \ (X \ a)]$

$ST_F =_{def} \{[rp\text{-}2 \ (b \ X)]\}$

The reason why $ab2ab4ab$ is not susceptible to the algorithm for stopping recursions is apparent from the the following sample derivation:

9.2.8 Derivation of $3a3b6a6b12a$ in ab2ab4ab

```
AAABBBAAAAAABBBBBBAAAAAAAAAAAA
11222333333322222233333333333333    (AAAAAAAAAAAAAAAAAAAAAAAA)
```

There is no problem in recognizing the i>d-recursion of rule r-2. But what should be done once it is recognized? If we treat the i>d-recursion of rule r-2 as a decreasing recursion, the algorithm will step from a decreasing recursion of length n to a decreasing recursion of length $2n$, etc. The problem is that these second order recursions cannot be recognized, because the length of the rule sequences is never the same in 9.2.8. Yet if we treat rule r-2 as an increasing recursion, the recursion factor of the C-LAG for *ab2ab4ab*, which happens to be two, will stop the derivation process before the next grammatical state (rule r-3) has been reached.

The C-LAG 9.2.7 is a reasonable grammar for a reasonable context-sensitive language. Because there are no input-compatible rules in the same rule package, the grammar is known to be unambiguous (cf. 7.3.5). Therefore, the grammar parses in linear time (Theorem 12, 10.1.2). It is just that the present algorithm for deriving representative samples cannot recognize the kind of recursions exhibited by this type of grammar.

It is tempting to consider ways to extend the algorithm so that it will also handle grammars like 9.2.7.[8] But because the class of C-LAGs covers all context-free languages, and because the context-free languages are undecidable for ambiguity, inclusion, and equivalence (due to the Post Correspondence Problem), it is not possible that the algorithm can be extended to cover all C-LAGs. Furthermore, the simulation by C-LAGs of register machines with two initially empty registers, (described in Section 8.5), also shows that decidability for the whole class of C-LAGs cannot be achieved.

The difficulty with i>d-recursions does not interfere with the systematic derivation of AD-sets for arbitrary C-LAGs. As long as no i>d-recursion has occurred, the Maximal Recursion Principle guarantees that all grammatical states (possible for the current length of the sample) are reached. This process continues until either the derivation process terminates naturally (because of cessation of increasing recursions), or an i>d-recursion is found. In the former case, the resulting AD-set is a representative sample; in the latter case, the process is aborted. Thus, the derivation of AD-sets, controlled by a recursion factor, always terminates for arbitrary C-LAGs.

9.2.9 Definition of a Representative Sample of a C-LAG

> An AD-set of a C-LAG is a *representative sample* of the expressions generated by the grammar, if and only if the AD-set was generated in accordance with the Maximal Recursion Principle such that the process terminated "naturally" (because no i>d-recursion was encountered).

---

[8] An obvious possibility of checking for second order i>d-recursions is based on looking for regular increases in the length of the rule sequence.

9.2.10 Definition of the Class of D-LAGs

A C-LAG is called a *decidable* C-LAG, or D-LAG, iff a representative sample may be generated for it.

Because it may be decided for arbitrary C-LAGs whether or not they generate a representative sample, the class of D-LAGs is decidable.

The crucial point of the representative sample is that there are no structural properties of the language which do not show up in at least one of its derivations. For example, if there are no ambiguous derivations in a representative sample with a certain maximal surface length, there will be no ambiguous derivations in any AD-set with longer surfaces. In other words, the language has been shown to be unambiguous. Similarly, if there is no complete derivation in a representative sample of a certain length, there will be no complete derivation in any AD-set with longer surfaces. In other words, the language has been shown to be empty.

9.2.11 Theorem 7

It is decidable for an arbitrary D-LAG G whether L(G) is ambiguous.

Proof: Given the maximal recursion principle, a "representative sample" of the grammar may be derived in finitely many steps. The grammar is syntactically ambiguous iff the representative sample contains at least two complete derivations with the same surface.

Because the presence of lexical ambiguity may be read directly off the lexical definitions, it is decidable whether or not a D-LAG is ambiguous in general.

Q.E.D.

The ability to decide for each member of a large class of context-free and context-sensitive languages whether it's ambiguous is important for complexity analysis. For example, Earley's (1970) result of $|G|^2 \cdot n^2$ for unambiguous context-free PS-grammars is not fully applicable, because it cannot be decided for an arbitrary context-free PS-grammar whether it is ambiguous. The only way a context-free PS-grammar can be known to be unambiguous is through "experience". For any unfamiliar context-free PS-grammar, one must rely on Earley's general result, which is $|G|^2 \cdot n^3$.

As an example of a representative sample for an ambiguous language, consider 9.2.12. Because the LA-grammar (defined in 7.4.1) has seven rules, and because the categorial operations look (at most) at one segment, the recursion factor of this grammar is six. However, because the grammar does not contain any "big foot" rules or "rule chutes", a recursion factor of two would be sufficient for generating a representative sample. The resulting ambiguities are marked in 9.2.12 with "!!" (cf. parses of lengths 4, 8, and 12). To conserve space, the following representative sample of $a^n b^n c^m d^m \cup a^n b^m c^m d^n$ is derived with recursion factor three rather than six.

9.2.12 Derivation of a Representative Sample for $a^n b^n c^m d^m \cup a^n b^m c^m d^n$

```
* (gram-gen 3 '(a b c d))

Parses of length 2:
 A B
    5    (B A)
 A B
    2    (NIL)
 A A
    1    (A A)

Parses of length 3:
 B B C
    5 6    (B)
 B B B
    5 5    (B B B)
 A B C
    5 6    (A)
 A B B
    5 5    (B B A)
 A B C
    2 3    (C)
 A A B
    1 5    (B A A)
 A A B
    1 2    (A)
 A A A
    1 1    (A A A)

Parses of length 4:
 B B C C
    5 6 6    (NIL)
 B B B C
    5 5 6    (B B)
 B B B B
    5 5 5    (B B B B)
 A B C D                    !!
    5 6 7    (NIL)
 A B B C
    5 5 6    (B A)
 A B B B
    5 5 5    (B B B A)
 A B C D                    !!
    2 3 4    (NIL)
 A B C C
    2 3 3    (C C)
 A A B C
    1 5 6    (A A)
 A A B B
    1 5 5    (B B A A)
 A A B B
    1 2 2    (NIL)
 A A A B
    1 1 5    (B A A A)
 A A A B
    1 1 2    (A A)
 A A A A
```

```
      1 1 1    (A A A A)

Parses of length 5:
 B B B C C
   5 5 6 6    (B)
 B B B B C
   5 5 5 6    (B B B)
 A B B C C
   5 5 6 6    (A)
 A B B B C
   5 5 5 6    (B B A)
 A B C C D
   2 3 3 4    (C)
 A B C C C
   2 3 3 3    (C C C)
 A A B C D
   1 5 6 7    (A)
 A A B B C
   1 5 5 6    (B A A)
 A A B B B
   1 5 5 5    (B B B A A)
 A A B B C
   1 2 2 3    (C)
 A A A B C
   1 1 5 6    (A A A)
 A A A B B
   1 1 5 5    (B B A A A)
 A A A B B
   1 1 2 2    (A)
 A A A A B
   1 1 1 5    (B A A A A)
 A A A A B
   1 1 1 2    (A A A)

Parses of length 6:
 B B B C C C
   5 5 6 6 6    (NIL)
 B B B B C C
   5 5 5 6 6    (B B)
 A B B C C D
   5 5 6 6 7    (NIL)
 A B B B C C
   5 5 5 6 6    (B A)
 A B C C D D
   2 3 3 4 4    (NIL)
 A B C C C D
   2 3 3 3 4    (C C)
 A A B C D D
   1 5 6 7 7    (NIL)
 A A B B C C
   1 5 5 6 6    (A A)
 A A B B B C
   1 5 5 5 6    (B B A A)
 A A B B C D
   1 2 2 3 4    (NIL)
 A A B B C C
   1 2 2 3 3    (C C)
```

```
A A A B C D
1 1 5 6 7    (A A)
A A A B B C
1 1 5 5 6    (B A A A)
A A A B B B
1 1 5 5 5    (B B B A A A)
A A A B B B
1 1 2 2 2    (NIL)
A A A A B C
1 1 1 5 6    (A A A)
A A A A B B
1 1 1 5 5    (B B A A A A)
A A A A B B
1 1 1 2 2    (A A)
```

Parses of length 7:
```
B B B B C C C
5 5 5 6 6 6    (B)
A B B B C C C
5 5 5 6 6 6    (A)
A B C C C D D
2 3 3 3 4 4    (C)
A A B B C C D
1 5 5 6 6 7    (A)
A A B B B C C
1 5 5 5 6 6    (B A A)
A A B B C C D
1 2 2 3 3 4    (C)
A A B B C C C
1 2 2 3 3 3    (C C C)
A A A B C D D
1 1 5 6 7 7    (A)
A A A B B C C
1 1 5 5 6 6    (A A A)
A A A B B B C
1 1 5 5 5 6    (B B A A A)
A A A B B B C
1 1 2 2 2 3    (C)
A A A A B C D
1 1 1 5 6 7    (A A A)
A A A A B B C
1 1 1 5 5 6    (B A A A A)
A A A A B B B
1 1 1 5 5 5    (B B B A A A A)
A A A A B B B
1 1 1 2 2 2    (A)
```

Parses of length 8:
```
B B B B C C C C
5 5 5 6 6 6 6    (NIL)
A B B B C C C D
5 5 5 6 6 6 7    (NIL)
A B C C C D D D
2 3 3 3 4 4 4    (NIL)
A A B B C C D D                    !!
1 5 5 6 6 7 7    (NIL)
A A B B B C C C
```

```
  1 5 5 5 6 6 6      (A A)
A A B B C C D D                      !!
  1 2 2 3 3 4 4      (NIL)
A A B B C C C D
  1 2 2 3 3 3 4      (C C)
A A A B C D D D
  1 1 5 6 7 7 7      (NIL)
A A A B B C C D
  1 1 5 5 6 6 7      (A A)
A A A B B B C C
  1 1 5 5 5 6 6      (B A A A)
A A A B B B C D
  1 1 2 2 2 3 4      (NIL)
A A A B B B C C
  1 1 2 2 2 3 3      (C C)
A A A A B C D D
  1 1 1 5 6 7 7      (A A)
A A A A B B C C
  1 1 1 5 5 6 6      (A A A A)
A A A A B B B C
  1 1 1 5 5 5 6      (B B A A A A)
A A A A B B B B
  1 1 1 2 2 2 2      (NIL)

Parses of length 9:
A A B B B C C C D
  1 5 5 5 6 6 6 7      (A)
A A B B C C C D D
  1 2 2 3 3 3 4 4      (C)
A A A B B C C D D
  1 1 5 5 6 6 7 7      (A)
A A A B B B C C C
  1 1 5 5 5 6 6 6      (A A A)
A A A B B B C C D
  1 1 2 2 2 3 3 4      (C)
A A A B B B C C C
  1 1 2 2 2 3 3 3      (C C C)
A A A A B C D D D
  1 1 1 5 6 7 7 7      (A)
A A A A B B C C D
  1 1 1 5 5 6 6 7      (A A A)
A A A A B B B C C
  1 1 1 5 5 5 6 6      (B A A A A)
A A A A B B B B C
  1 1 1 2 2 2 2 3      (C)

Parses of length 10:
A A B B B C C C D D
  1 5 5 5 6 6 6 7 7      (NIL)
A A B B C C C D D D
  1 2 2 3 3 3 4 4 4      (NIL)
A A A B B C C D D D
  1 1 5 5 6 6 7 7 7      (NIL)
A A A B B B C C C D
  1 1 5 5 5 6 6 6 7      (A A)
A A A B B B C C D D
  1 1 2 2 2 3 3 4 4      (NIL)
```

```
A A A B B B C C C D
 1 1 2 2 2 3 3 3 4    (C C)
A A A A B C D D D D
 1 1 1 5 6 7 7 7 7    (NIL)
A A A A B B C C D D
 1 1 1 5 5 6 6 7 7    (A A)
A A A A B B B C C C
 1 1 1 5 5 5 6 6 6    (A A A A)
A A A A B B B B C D
 1 1 1 2 2 2 2 3 4    (NIL)
A A A A B B B B C C
 1 1 1 2 2 2 2 3 3    (C C)
```

Parses of length 11:
```
A A A B B B C C C D D
 1 1 5 5 5 6 6 6 7 7    (A)
A A A B B B C C C D D
 1 1 2 2 2 3 3 3 4 4    (C)
A A A A B B C C D D D
 1 1 1 5 5 6 6 7 7 7    (A)
A A A A B B B C C C D
 1 1 1 5 5 5 6 6 6 7    (A A A)
A A A A B B B B C C D
 1 1 1 2 2 2 2 3 3 4    (C)
A A A A B B B B C C C
 1 1 1 2 2 2 2 3 3 3    (C C C)
```

Parses of length 12:
```
A A A B B B C C C D D D            !!
 1 1 5 5 5 6 6 6 7 7 7    (NIL)
A A A B B B C C C D D D            !!
 1 1 2 2 2 3 3 3 4 4 4    (NIL)
A A A A B B C C D D D D
 1 1 1 5 5 6 6 7 7 7 7    (NIL)
A A A A B B B C C C D D
 1 1 1 5 5 5 6 6 6 7 7    (A A)
A A A A B B B B C C D D
 1 1 1 2 2 2 2 3 3 4 4    (NIL)
A A A A B B B B C C C D
 1 1 1 2 2 2 2 3 3 3 4    (C C)
```

Parses of length 13:
```
A A A A B B B C C C D D D
 1 1 1 5 5 5 6 6 6 7 7 7    (A)
A A A A B B B B C C C D D
 1 1 1 2 2 2 2 3 3 3 4 4    (C)
```

Parses of length 14:
```
A A A A B B B C C C D D D D
 1 1 1 5 5 5 6 6 6 7 7 7 7    (NIL)
A A A A B B B B C C C D D D
 1 1 1 2 2 2 2 3 3 3 4 4 4    (NIL)
```

Next we turn to the problem of deciding whether L(G) is empty, for a given grammar G. This question is undecidable for arbitrary context-sensitive languages.[9] But for context-sensitive languages which are recognized by D-LAGs the following theorem holds.

9.2.13 Theorem 8

It is decidable for an arbitrary D-LAG G whether $L(G) = \emptyset$.

Proof: Given the maximal recursion principle, a "representative sample" of the grammar may be derived in finitely many steps. The language generated by the grammar is non-empty, iff the representative sample contains at least one complete well-formed expression.

Q.E.D.

An example illustrating the decidability of emptiness for are large class of C-LAGs is the representative sample 8.1.7, which generates well-formed expressions of context-sensitive $a^k b^k c^k$ with a recursion factor of three.

Finally consider why the decidability question was raised only for the class of C-LAGs. Although non-constant LA-grammars pose no problem for the recognition and typing of recursions, they fail to provide a categorially motivated recursion factor. Thus, non-constant LA-grammar permit construction of AD-sets, but because of the absence of a recursion factor there is no well-motivated limit.

Consider, for example, the A-LAG defined in Theorem 2. The set of well-formed expressions of length 2 generated by this grammar consists of the expressions [rp-1 ((aa) (aa))], [rp-1 ((ab) (ab))], ... , and [rp-2 ((aa) (0))], [rp-2 ((ab) (0))] ... . If there is at least one well-formed expression of the form [rp-2 ((..) (1))], we know L(G) is non-empty. But if well-formed expressions of length 2 do not contain any complete expressions, we must generate well-formed expressions of length 3, etc. There is no way to determine when this process should be stopped.

In summary, C-LAGs which are not D-LAGs are undecidable because their recursion factor does not function, while non-constant LA-grammars are undecidable because no recursion factor is known.

9.3   Equivalence of C-LAGs

In this section we turn to decidability questions involving two grammars. In PS-grammar it is not possible to decide for arbitrary context-free grammars G^1 and G^2 whether the associated languages $L(G^1)$ and $L(G^2)$ are equivalent, or whether $L(G^1)$ is a subset of $L(G^2)$[10]. The reason again is that the question may be reduced to Post's Correspondence Problem.

---

[9]Hopcroft and Ullman (1979), p. 281.
[10]Hopcroft and Ullman (1979), p. 203, Theorem 8.11.

In LA-grammar, on the other hand, the proof of whether or not $L(G^1) \subset L(G^2)$, for any two D-LAGs with homomorphic lexica, is based on the fact that a D-LAG generates only a finite number of sentence types. Furthermore, these sentence types can be systematically generated for any D-LAG. The subset relationship between two D-LAGs G^1 and G^2 is proven by showing that the sentence types of G^1 are a subset of the sentence types of G^2. This requires the simultaneous generation of AD-sets for the two grammars.

The generation of AD-sets for two grammars is based on two abstract lexica.[11] In order for two D-LAGs to be comparable, their lexica must be homomorphic.

9.3.1 Definition of Homomorphic Lexica

Let LX^1 and LX^2 be two lexica, so that LX^1 is constructed from the sets W_1 and C_1, and LX^2 is constructed from the sets W_2 and C_2. Then LX^2 is *homomorphic* with LX^1 if and only if

1. $W_1 \subseteq W_2$
2. For any two surfaces w_p and $w_q \epsilon W_1$, if they occur in analyzed words with the same category in LX^1, then they also occur in analyzed words with the same category in LX^2.

For example, if

$LX^1 =_{def} \{[a\ (x)], [b\ (x)], [d\ (y)]\}$, and

$LX^2 =_{def} \{[a\ (p)], [b\ (p)], [c\ (p)], [d\ (q)], [e\ (q)]\}$,

then LX^2 is homomorphic with LX^1, but not vice versa. Two lexica LX^1 and LX^2 are **isomorphic**, if LX^1 is homomorphic with LX^2, and LX^2 is homomorphic with LX^1. Isomorphic lexica have the same set of surfaces, and their categorial analyses partition the set of surfaces in the same way.

From two homomorphic lexica, two abstract lexica ALX^1 and ALX^2 are constructed in such a way that ALX^1 and ALX^2 use the same abstract symbols for the representation of equivalent surface.

9.3.2 Definition of the Abstract Junction of Homomorphic Lexica

If LX^2 is homomorphic with LX^1, then the *abstract junction* of LX^1 and LX^2 is constructed by forming abstract analyzed words (k cat_i^1) and (k cat_j^2), where k is a symbol (e.g., a letter or a number) representing the set of surface expressions W_i^1 ($\subseteq W_j^2$) uniquely, for each lexical category of LX^1.

For example, if

$LX^1 =_{def} \{[a\ (x)], [b\ (x)], [d\ (y)]\}$, and

---

[11]However, if the set of word forms characterized by a lexical category is a unit set, for all lexical categories, no abstract lexica need to be constructed.

$LX^2 =_{def} \{[a\ (p)],\ [b\ (p)],\ [c\ (p)],\ [d\ (q)],\ [e\ (q)]\}$,
then an abstract junction of these two lexica is
$\{[1\ (x)],\ [1\ (p)],\ [2\ (y)],\ [2\ (q)]\}$.

9.3.3 Definition of Abstract Lexica Pairs

> If $AJ^{1,2}$ is an abstract junction derived from LX^1 and LX^2, then an abstract lexicon ALX^1, corresponding to LX^1, is the set of all abstract words in $AJ^{1,2}$ with LX^1 categories, and an abstract lexicon ALX^2 is the set of abstract words in $AJ^{1,2}$ with LX^2 categories.

The point of the abstract junction is not only to turn sets of word forms into abstract words, but to ensure that corresponding sets in the two abstract lexica get the same abstract surface. If LX^1 is part of the grammar G^1, and LX^2 is part of the grammar G^2, then we may use ALX^1 and ALX^2 to derive abstract expressions in G^1 and G^2. For example, if *11212* is an abstract expression derivable in G^1 as well as G^2, then we know that the corresponding set of real G^1 surfaces is a subset of the corresponding set of real G^2 surfaces. Because isomorphic lexica are also homomorphic, an abstract junction may be constructed for isomorphic lexica as well.

Next we turn to the simultaneous generation of complex expressions in G^1 and G^2.

9.3.4 Definition of a Common Surface Matrix or csm

> If G^1 and G^2 are two LA-grammars with homomorphic lexica, and ad^1 and ad^2 are abstract derivations of G^1 and G^2, respectively, such that ad^1 and ad^2 have identical surfaces, then ad^1 and ad^2 are joined into a csm by writing the second line of ad^2 directly under the second line of ad^1.

For example, if ad^1 and ad^2 are defined as (i) and (ii),

> (i)   abcdef
>   12345 cat-i

> (ii)   abcdef
>   43234 cat-j

respectively, then the resulting csm has this form:

> (iii) abcdef
>   12345 cat-i
>   43234 cat-j

A csm represents two well-formed expressions with the same surface, generated by two different grammars. The first level of a csm represents the surface, the second level represents the derivational history and analysis of the first grammar, and the third level represents the derivational history and analysis of the second grammar.

Just as the AD_{n+1}-set (containing abstract derivations with surfaces of length $n+1$) may be derived systematically from the AD_n-set of a grammar, a CSM_{n+1}-set of a pair of grammars may be derived systematically from a CSM_n-set. In fact, for the purpose of a systematic derivation of CSM-sets with elements having longer and longer surfaces, a csm may be regarded as a joint representation of two abstract derivations which happen to have the same surface, and are generated by two different grammars.

For example, if the AD_n-set of G^1 contains two abstract derivations with the surface x (x is ambiguous), and the AD_n-set of G^2 contains three abstract derivations with the surface x, then the corresponding CSM_n-set will contain six csm with the surface x. CSM-sets contain the **product** of ambiguous abstract derivations with the same surface. This is to ensure that all instances of *simultaneous completion* and *simultaneous recursion* are represented in the CSM-sets. As soon as a simultaneous completion or recursion has been found, all *related* common surface matrices are eliminated from the CSM-set.

The notions of "related csm", "simultaneous completion", and "simultaneous recursion" are defined as follows.

9.3.5 Definition of Related Common Surface Matrices

Two csm are *related* iff they (i) have the same surface and (ii) have the same second-level (G^1) analysis.

9.3.6 Definition of Simultaneous Completion

A csm is an instance of a *simultaneous completion* iff the second-level rule number and category constitute a final state of G^1, and the third-level rule number and category constitute a final state of G^2.

9.3.7 Definition of Simultaneous Recursion

A csm is an instance of a *simultaneous recursion* if the two abstract derivations it represents are instances of recursions of the same kind (e.g., constant, increasing, decreasing), affecting the same surface subsequences.

9.3.8 Theorem 9

If G^1 and G^2 are D-LAGs using homomorphic lexica LX^1 and LX^2, then it is decidable whether $L(G^1) \subset L(G^2)$.

Proof: **Step 1:** Apply all rules in ST^1_S to all pairs in $ALX^1 \times ALX^1$, resulting in the set of well-formed expressions W^1_2 with surfaces of length 2. Apply all rules in ST^2_S to all pairs in $ALX^2 \times ALX^2$, resulting in the set of well-formed expressions W^2_2, likewise with surfaces of length 2. Because ALX^1, ST^1_S, ALX^2, and ST^2_S are finite, W^1_2 and W^2_2 are finite.

If the set of surfaces of W_2^1 is not a subset of the set of surfaces of W_2^2, and if the set of complete surfaces of W_2^1 is not a subset of the set of complete surfaces of W_2^2, the proof completed: it has been shown that $L(G^1)$ is not a subset of $L(G^2)$. Otherwise, the set of common surface matrices of length 2 (CSM_2-set) is constructed.

Reduction of the set CSM_2: All items related to instances of a simultaneous completion are removed from csm_2.

Step i+1: Given the finite sets W_i^1 and W_i^2, construct W_{i+1}^1 and W_{i+1}^2, using ALX^1 and ALX^2, respectively.

If the set of surfaces of W_{i+1}^1 is not a subset of the set of surfaces of W_{i+1}^2, and if the set of complete surfaces of W_{i+1}^1 is not a subset of the set of complete surfaces of W_{i+1}^2, the is proof complete: it has been shown that $L(G^1)$ is not a subset of $L(G^2)$. Otherwise, the set of common surface matrices of length i+1 (CSM_{i+1}-set) is constructed from the CSM_i-set.

Reduction of the set CSM_{i+1}: All instances of two constant simultaneous recursions, and $k+(n-2)$ increasing simultaneous recursions are stopped. Furthermore, all items related to simultaneous recursions or completions are removed from CSM_{i+1}.

Because both G^1 and G^2 have only a finite number of rules, this process of deriving CSM-sets with longer and longer surfaces must terminate, either because there are G^1-expressions not derivable in G^2 (in which case $L(G^1)$ is not a subset of $L(G^2)$), or because the current CSM-set is empty (in which case $L(G^1) \subset L(G^2)$).

Q.E.D.

Following is an example of two grammars G^1 and G^1 such that $L(G^1) \subset L(G^1)$:

9.3.9 An Example of $L(G^1) \subset L(G^2)$

Definition of G^1:

$LX^1 =_{def} \{(a\ (a)),\ (b\ (b))\}$
$ST_S^1 =_{def} \{[\{r\text{-}1,\ r\text{-}2\}\ (a)]\}$
r-1: $[(X)(a)] \Rightarrow [\{r\text{-}1,\ r\text{-}2\}\ (a\ X)]$
r-2: $[(a\ X)(b)] \Rightarrow [\{r\text{-}2\}\ (X)]$
$ST_F^1 =_{def} \{[rp\text{-}2\ \epsilon]\}$

Definition of G^2:

$LX^2 =_{def} \{(a\ (a)),\ (b\ (b)),\ (c\ (c))\}$
$ST_S^2 =_{def} \{[\{r\text{-}1\}(seg1)]\}$
r-1: $[(X)(seg1)] \Rightarrow [\{r\text{-}1\}(X)]$
$ST_F^2 =_{def} \{[rp\text{-}1\ (X)]\}$

G^1 generates the familiar context-free language $a^k b^k$ (cf. 10.2.3), while G^2 generates a regular language consisting of arbitrary sequences of a, b, and c. The recursion factor of G^1 is 1 (the categorial operations of G^1 specify, at most, 1 segment, plus 2 (the number of rules) minus 2). Thus, increasing simultaneous recursions may be stopped as soon as they are recognized (i.e., after two applications).

The lexicon LX^2 is homomorphic with LX^1. Furthermore, there is no need to construct abstract lexica ALX^1 and ALX^2, because the word classes characterized by lexical categories are unit sets. Consider the CSM-sets of G^1 and G^2 up to length 5.

CSM_2:	CSM_3:	CSM_4:	CSM_5:	CSM_6:
ab				
2 ϵ				
1 (a)				
aa	aab	aabb		
1 (aa)	12 (a)	122 ϵ		
1 (a)	11 (a)	111 (a)		
	aaa	aaab	aaabb	aaabbb
	1ĭ (aaa)	112 (aa)	1122 (a)	11222 ϵ
	11 (a)	111 (a)	1111 (a)	11111 (a)

ab and *aabb* are not continued, because they are instances of simultaneous completion. *aaa* is stopped, because it is an instance of a simultaneous recursion which satisfies the recursion factor. The non-recursive G^1 continuation of *aaa* is *aaab*, which leads to a simultaneous completion in CSM_6. Because the only member of CSM_6 is a simultaneous completion, CSM_7 is empty, which proves that $L(G^1) \subset L(G^2)$.

9.3.10 Theorem 10

If G^1 and G^2 are D-LAGs using isomorphic lexica LX^1 and LX^2, then it is decidable whether $L(G^1) = L(G^2)$.

Proof: $L(G^1) = L(G^2)$ iff $L(G^1) \subset L(G^2)$ and $L(G^2) \subset L(G^1)$.

Q.E.D.

Following is an example of two grammars G^1 and G^2 where $L(G^1) = L(G^1)$:

9.3.11 An Example of $L(G^1) = L(G^2)$

Definition of G^1:

$LX^1 =_{def} \{(a\ (bc)),\ (b\ (b)),\ (c\ (c))\}$

$ST^1_S =_{def} \{[\{r\text{-}1,\ r\text{-}2\}\ (bc)]\}$

r-1: $[(X)\ (bc)] \Rightarrow [\{r\text{-}1,\ r\text{-}2\}\ (bXc)]$

r-2: $[(bXc)\ (b)] \Rightarrow [\{r\text{-}2,\ r\text{-}3\}\ (Xc)]$

r-3: $[(cX)\ (c)] \Rightarrow [\{r\text{-}3\}\ (X)]$

$ST_F =_{def} \{[rp\text{-}3\ \epsilon]\}.$

Definition of G^2:

$LX^2 =_{def} \{(a\ (a)),\ (b\ (b)),\ (c\ (c))\}$

$ST^2_S =_{def} \{[\{r\text{-}1,\ r\text{-}2\}\ (a)]\}$

r-1: $[(X)(a)] \Rightarrow [\{r\text{-}1,\ r\text{-}2\}\ (aX)]$

r-2: $[(aX)(b)] \Rightarrow [\{r\text{-}2,\ r\text{-}3\}\ (Xb)]$

r-3: $[(bX)(c)] \Rightarrow [\{r\text{-}3,\ r\text{-}4\}\ (X)]$

$ST^2_F =_{def} \{[rp\text{-}3\ \epsilon]\}$

G^1 and G^2 both generate the familiar context-sensitive language $a^k b^k c^k$, whereby G^1 is the formulation of 6.4.3 and G^2 is written in analogy to the grammar defined in 10.2.8. The recursion factor of G^1 is 3 (the categorial operations of G^1 specify at most 2 segments, plus 3 (the number of rules) minus 2). This recursion factor is more than required to generate a representative sample of G^1 (2 would be sufficient). But the point of the recursion factor is to set a finite limit on the number of increasing recursions which **guarantees** generation of a representative sample set.

Even though the lexica LX^1 and LX^2 are different, they are isomorphic. Also, there is no need to construct abstract lexica ALX^1 and ALX^2, because the word classes characterized by lexical categories are unit sets. Consider the CSM-sets of G^1 and G^2 up to length 6:

CSM₂:	CSM₃:	CSM₄:	CSM₅:	CSM₆:
ab	abc			
2 (c)	23 ε			
2 (b)	23 ε			
aa	aab	aabb	aabbc	aabbcc
(bbcc)	12 (bcc)	122 (cc)	1223 (c)	12233 ε
(aa)	12 (ab)	122 (bb)	1223 (b)	12233 ε
	aaa	aaab	aaabb	aaabbb
	11 (bbbccc)	112 (bbccc)	1122 (bccc)	11222 (ccc)
	11 (aaa)	112 (aab)	1122 (abb)	11222 (bbb)
		aaaa	aaaab	aaaabb
		11Ĭ (bbbbcccc)	1112 (bbbcccc)	11122 (bbcccc)
		111 (aaaa)	1112 (aaab)	11122 (aabb)

abc and *aabbcc* are not continued because they are instances of simultaneous completions. The r-1 recursion of G^1 is stopped after the third application (in accordance with the recursion factor of G^1), resulting in *aaaa*. All continuations of *aaaab* will eventually terminate, resulting in simultaneous completions and an empty CSM_{13}-set. Thus, $L(G^1) \subset L(G^2)$. The equivalence of the two grammars may be shown by proving that $L(G^2) \subset L(G^1)$. This may be demonstrated by constructing another CSM-set.

Finally, consider the question of whether the technique of proving the subset and the equality relationship for a large class of context-free and context-sensitive languages can be used for PS-grammars as well. Because PS-grammars have a different derivational structure, the method of deriving longer and longer sentence starts cannot be applied directly in PS-grammar. There remains the possibility of translating PS-grammars into C-LAGs, and proving the properties in question indirectly by way of the weakly equivalent C-LAGs.

However, this approach requires that there is a general algorithm for translating PS-grammars into LA-grammars. No such algorithm has been found. Furthermore, experience writing LA-grammars for languages described originally as PS-grammars (cf. Section 10.2) has shown that the construction of the LA-grammar is never based on the PS-grammar for the language, but proceeds from the language directly. Thus, it is unlikely that such an algorithm exists.

9.4   Improving Efficiency

General purpose parsers, such as the Earley algorithm and the CYK algorithm, give complexity results for the whole class of context-free grammars. Whether a given grammar belonging to this class is efficiently designed does not influence the complexity result, except that the **size** of the grammar (number of rules) is reflected in the complexity formula.

In LA-grammar, on the other hand, the size of the grammar does not affect the computational complexity.[12] But the design of the grammar makes a great difference for the resulting complexity behavior. Thus, while the whole class of unambiguous C-LAGs is known to parse in linear time, a well-designed grammar may parse in *2(n-1)*, while a badly designed grammar of the same language may parse in *10(n-1)*. Furthermore, the badly designed grammar may be half the size of its well-designed counterpart.

The following sections describe three sources of inefficiency in LA-grammar. LA-grammars which avoid these inefficiencies are called *sound* LA-grammars. A first step in the definition of sound LA-grammars is the Redundancy Constraint.

---

[12]Also, LA-grammars happen to be very small. The LA-grammar generating the 421 sample sentences of English listed in Appendix C has a size of 25K (without the frame semantics).

9.4.1 The Redundancy Constraint

An LA-grammar is non-redundant only if it holds for all rule packages rp_k that

1. they contain only the names of rules with a CAT-1 which is compatible with the output category CAT-3 of r_k, and
2. they do not contain rules with "vacuous" CAT-2 expressions, i.e., categorial expressions which are never matched by any actual lexical categories.

The redundancy constraint prevents inefficiencies of a very simple kind, similar to the *useless symbols* in PS-grammar.[13] It is obvious that satisfaction of the redundancy constraint does not result in a loss of generative power.

The second step in the design of sound LA-grammar concerns the purpose of different types of recursions. Increasing recursions are used to keep a **record** of certain occurrences. Decreasing recursions are used to generate occurrences which **correspond** to certain other occurrences. Increasing rules should be used only if there are corresponding decreasing rules which are applied later in the derivation. If there is no need to keep a record of occurrences, constant recursions are appropriate.

Increasing and decreasing recursions, simultaneously increasing and decreasing recursions, and constant recursions may not be mixed freely if they are input-compatible. Assume, for example, that the recursively increasing rule r_k has built up the category (aaaaX). If r_k could call another recursively increasing rule r_j which is input-compatible and extends the category (aaaaX) into (aaaaXaa) then the count would be confused in case X is empty. Note that *non-compatible* recursively increasing rules are permitted. For example, nothing prevents extending (aaaaX) into (bbbaaaaX) or (aaaaXbbb).[14]

Or consider a sentence start with the category (aaaaX). If a recursively decreasing rule r_k could call an input-compatible increasing rule r_j before the category is reduced to (X), this would result in a confusion of the count: (aaaaX) could be reduced to (aaX) and then increased again to (aaaaaaX).

9.4.2 The Counter Constraint

1. An increasing recursion must be followed by related decreasing rules.[15] The decreasing rules may either be a decreasing recursion, or simultaneously decreasing and increasing recursion, or a rule chute, or a combination of a rule chute and recursion. In complete well-formed expressions, segments introduced by an increasing recursion must all be cancelled.

---

[13]Cf. Hopcroft and Ullman, 1970, p. 88, Lemma 4.1.

[14]This is the case in the grammar defined in 7.4.1.

[15]The decreasing rules are *related* to the increasing recursion in the sense that they cancel the category segments introduced by the increasing recursion.

2. An increasing recursion may not directly call an input-compatible increasing recursion, an simultaneously increasing and decreasing recursion, or a constant recursion. If an increasing recursion R1 is followed by an input-compatible simultaneously decreasing and increasing recursion R2, R1 may call R2 only via a "marker rule" which separates the segments introduced by R1 from those introduced by R2.

3. A decreasing recursion, or simultaneously decreasing and increasing recursion, may not directly call an input-compatible decreasing or constant recursion. If a decreasing recursion is followed by another input-compatible decreasing recursion, the segments to be cancelled by the first recursion must be separated from those of the second recursion by a categorial marker. The first decreasing recursion may only call the second decreasing recursion by way of a "fix-point rule", which requires the categorial marker in a specific position in order to apply.

4. A constant recursion may not call an input-compatible increasing or decreasing recursion.

The counter constraint 9.4.2 does not reduce the generative capacity of an LA-grammar. Violations of the Counter Constraint result in grammars where increasing and decreasing recursions fail to produce the intended correspondences. If no correspondences are required, constant recursions are appropriate. Thus, for any LA-grammar violating the Counter Constraint, we may define an equivalent one, using constant recursions. Furthermore, violations of the Counter Constraint are easily recognizable, by inspecting the structure of the rules of the grammar, the systematic derivation of AD-sets, or the parsing of examples.

As an example illustrating the Counter Constraint, consider the following definitions of C-LAGs for the language WWW, appropriately called W3.GOOD and W3.BAD, respectively. Because W3.BAD violates the Counter Constraint, it fails to produce the intended output. For the actual output of W3.BAD, an alternative grammar satisfying the Counter Constraint is defined.

9.4.3 The C-LAG W3.GOOD for Context-Sensitive WWW

$LX =_{def}$ {(a (a)), (b (b)), (c (c)), (d (d)), ...}
$ST_S =_{def}$ {[{r-1 r-2} (seg1)]}
r-1: [(X)(seg1)] $\Rightarrow$ [{r-1, r-2} (X seg1)]
r-2: [(seg1 X)(seg1)] $\Rightarrow$ [{r-3, r-4} (X $ seg1)]
r-3: [(seg1 X)(seg1)] $\Rightarrow$ [{r-3, r-4} (X seg1)]
r-4: [($ seg1 X)(seg1)] $\Rightarrow$ [{r-5} (X $)]
r-5: [(seg1 X)(seg1)] $\Rightarrow$ [{r-5} (X)]
$ST_F =_{def}$ {[rp-4 ($)]}

In W3.GOOD, an increasing recursion (r-1) is followed by a simultaneously decreasing and increasing recursion (r-3), which is followed by a decreasing recursion (r-5). W3.GOOD satisfies clause 2 of the counter constraint because the segments introduced by the initial recursion are separated from the segments introduced by the simultaneously decreasing and increasing rule r-3 by the marker rule r-2, which introduces the marker $. W3.GOOD satisfies clause 3 of the Counter Constraint because the simultaneously decreasing and increasing recursion of r-3 calls the decreasing recursion of r-5 by way of the fix-point rule r-4, which requires the marker $ introduced by r-2 in the initial position. W3.GOOD satisfies clause 1 of the Counter Constraint because the increasing recursion (r-1) is followed by decreasing rules (r-2, r-3) which cancel all segments introduced by the initial recursion. Furthermore, all segments introduced by the simultaneously decreasing and increasing recursion (r-3) are cancelled by the decreasing rules r-4 and r-5.

Now let's consider the alternative grammar, W3.BAD.

9.4.4 The C-LAG W3.BAD for Context-Sensitive WWW

$LX =_{def}$ {(a (a)), (b (b)), (c (c)), (d (d)), ...}
$ST_S =_{def}$ {[{r-1 r-2} (seg1)]}
r-1: [(X)(seg1)] $\Rightarrow$ [{r-1, r-2} (X seg1)]
r-2: [(seg1 X)(seg1)] $\Rightarrow$ [{r-2, r-3} (X seg1)]
r-3: [(seg1 X)(seg1)] $\Rightarrow$ [{r-3} (X)]
$ST_F =_{def}$ {[rp-3 ϵ])}

In W3.BAD, the increasing recursion of r-1 directly calls the simultaneously decreasing and increasing recursion r-2, violating clause 2 of the Counter Constraint. r-2 moves initial category segments to the final position. Without a categorial marker indicating the end of the increasing recursion, this process can go on indefinitely in the worst case, i.e., in the case where W consists of a sequence of equal letters. Furthermore, if W consists of different letters, e.g., *abc*, the second as well as the third occurrence of *abc* in the string *abc abc abc* will be accepted by r-2, resulting in considerable overgeneration. In fact, W3.BAD accepts an arbitrary number ≥ 3 of W, e.g., *abc abc abc abc*.... This language is properly generated by the C-LAG defined in 9.4.5, which satisfies the counter constraint.

9.4.5 The C-LAG for the Context-Sensitive Language $W^{k \geq 3}$

$LX =_{def}$ {(a (a)), (b (b)), (c (c)), (d (d)), ...}
$ST_S =_{def}$ {[{r-1 r-2} (seg1)]}
r-1: [(X)(seg1)] $\Rightarrow$ [{r-1, r-2} (X seg1)]
r-2: [(seg1 X)(seg1)] $\Rightarrow$ [{r-3} (X $ seg1)]
r-3: [(seg1 X)(seg1)] $\Rightarrow$ [{r-3 r-4} (X)]
r-4: [($ seg1 X)(seg1)] $\Rightarrow$ [{r-5} (X $ seg1)]
r-5: [(seg1 X)(seg1)] $\Rightarrow$ [{r-5 r-4} (X)]
$ST_F =_{def}$ {[rp-5 ($ X)] }

The recursion consisting of r-4 and r-5 is a constant recursion in that the sentence-start category is the same at the start of each new application of the recursion. All segments introduced by the increasing recursion r-1 are cancelled in complete well-formed expressions of $W^{k\geq3}$; the segments remaining in the final category ($ X) are copies made by r-4 and r-5.

The grammars for W3.GOOD, W3.BAD and $W^{k\geq3}$ are D-LAGs. Therefore, our argument may be supported by the derivation of representative samples, which explicitly display the types of expressions generated by each grammar.

9.5   Sound LA-Grammars

A particularly costly source of inefficiency are spurious ambiguities (cf. Section 7.3). LA-grammar distinguishes four types of syntactic ambiguity, based on the binary features ± *local* and ± *recursive*. In a local ambiguity only one branch reaches a final state, whereas in a non-local ambiguity two or more branches reach a final state. A syntactic ambiguity is called recursive if it arises inside a recursive loop, and non-recursive otherwise.

A local non-recursive ambiguity is exemplified by the derivation 7.4.2, while a non-local non-recursive ambiguity is exemplified by the derivation 7.4.3. Furthermore, derivation 7.1.6 is an instance of a local recursive ambiguity, while derivation 10.4.2 is an instance of a global recursive ambiguity. Adapting[16] the notation of "abstract derivations" (cf. 9.2.2) to the task of describing ambiguities, instances of different types of ambiguity may be characterized as follows:

9.5.1 A Local Non-Recursive Ambiguity in $a^nb^nc^md^m \cup a^nb^mc^md^n$

```
              bbbbcccddd
              2222333444
      aaaa
       111
              bbbcccdddd
              5556667777
```

After reading *aaaa*, the analysis splits into two branches. 9.5.1 characterizes a local ambiguity, because the two branches have different surfaces. If the input string has the form *aaaabbbc*, the upper branch is discarded; if it has the form *aaaabbbb* the lower. The ambiguity is non-recursive because rule r-1 (which causes the ambiguity by calling the input-compatible rules r-2 and r-5) is not called again after the split.

---

[16]The abstract derivations 9.5.1, 9.5.2, etc., omit the sentence-start categories, and indicate the ambiguity "split" by a common initial branch.

9.5.2 A Non-Local Non-Recursive Ambiguity in $a^nb^nc^md^m \cup a^nb^mc^md^n$

```
        bbbbccccdddd
        222233334444
 aaaa
  111
        bbbbccccdddd
        555566667777
```

The ambiguity characterized in 9.5.2 is non-local because both branches reach a final state.

9.5.3 A Local Recursive Ambiguity in WW

```
        abc abc
        11 222
            abc abc abc
            111 222 222
                abc abc abc abc
                111 222 222 222
                    abc abc abc ...
                    111 222 222
                        abc abc ...
                        111 222
                            abc ...
                            111
```

This ambiguity is local because only [rp-1 ϵ] characterizes a final state in WW. It is recursive because rule r-1 (which causes the ambiguity by calling the input-compatible rules r-1 and r-2) is called again after (or rather *in*) the split.[17]

Of the possible types of ambiguity in LA-grammar, only the recursive ambiguities are of any concern to complexity analysis. Consider the branching structure of WW.

9.5.4 The Branching Structure of WW

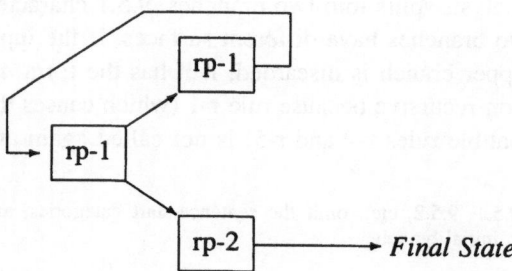

The worst case complexity of WW is known to be well below n^2 (cf. 7.1.5 f). The reason for the surprisingly good complexity is that of the two input-compatible rules responsible for the ambiguity only one (namely r-1) reenters the recursion.

Is this structural feature merely an idiosyncratic property of WW, or is it an instance of a general principle in LA-grammar? As an abstract example of an ambiguity with double recursion, consider 9.5.5:

9.5.5 An Ambiguity with a Double Recursion

```
        cda b ...
        234 1
     ab
     1
        cda b ...
        567 1
```

Here we have two recursive loops, characterized by the rule sequences *1234* and *1567*.

Are ambiguities with a double recursion necessary from the viewpoint of generating capacity? If the two recursions are of the same kind (e.g., both are increasing), one of them may be eliminated, and the ambiguity-split postponed until after the recursion has been exited. If they are of different kinds, on the other hand, the structure of 9.5.5 results in a confusion of the count: one recursion may take the decreasing branch, the next may take the increasing branch, etc. But if the different branches of the ambiguity are not characterized by different well-defined counter properties (because of the confusion of the count), then there is no empirical reason to introduce the ambiguity in the first place.

These purely generative considerations leading to the rejection of ambiguities with double recursions are complemented by the earlier discussion of well-defined syntactic ambiguities (cf. Section 7.3). The use of two different input-compatible rules (rather than one rule) must be motivated by valid grammatical distinctions, such as different continuation properties of the different branches. But if the different branches introduced by a rule with an ambiguous rule package may both return recursively to this rule, then the grammatical distinction supposedly motivating the branching cannot be valid.

As a case in point, consider the "ambiguity" between postnominal and adverbial readings of adverbs. If the two interpretations are implemented as different syntactic readings, the result is an exponential number of readings. This is illustrated schematically in 9.5.6.

---

[17]The derivational structure of a non-local recursive ambiguity is described in 10.4.3.

9.5.6 Example of a Spurious ambiguity with Double Recursion

                                                        in the garden.
                                                        postnominal

                                    behind the tree
                                    postnominal

                                                        in the garden.
                                                        adverbial

                on the table
                postnominal

                                                        in the garden.
                                                        postnominal

                                    behind the tree
                                    adverbial

                                                        in the garden.
                                                        adverbial

John ate the apple

                                                        in the garden.
                                                        postnominal

                                    behind the tree
                                    postnominal

                                                        in the garden.
                                                        adverbial

                on the table
                adverbial

                                                        in the garden.
                                                        postnominal

                                    behind the tree
                                    adverbial

                                                        in the garden.
                                                        adverbial

The only way such an exponential ambiguity can be analyzed in polynomial time is by packed parsing (cf. Section 10.3 below). But there is no reason to treat the phenomenon in question as a syntactic ambiguity. On the contrary, because the postnominal and the adverbial interpretations of prepositional clauses do not constitute two surface-distinct classes, 9.5.6 violates the Ambiguity Criterion 7.3.9. Instead of generating a doubly recursive ambiguity and packing it, we treat this sentence as syntactically unambiguous, but code the possible "readings" into the semantic representation, where they may cause a *pragmatic ambiguity*.

9.5.7 The ECAT Analysis of Postnominal/Adverbial Modifiers

* (z John ate the apple on the table behind the tree in the garden \.)

```
*** Lex Lookup
Real time:   0.16 s
Run time:    0.02 s

*** Parse Timings
Real time:   3.36 s
Run time:    2.16 s

    Linear Analysis:

    *START_0
    1
        (NH) JOHN
        (N A V) ATE
    *NOM+FVERB_3
    2
        (A V) JOHN ATE
        (GQ) THE
    *FVERB+MAIN_4
    3
        (GQ V) JOHN ATE THE
        (S-H) APPLE
    *DET+NOUN_2
    4
        (V) JOHN ATE THE APPLE
        (ADP NP) ON
    *ADD-ADP_14
    5
        (NP V) JOHN ATE THE APPLE ON
        (GQ) THE
    *PREP+NP_5
    6
        (GQ V) JOHN ATE THE APPLE ON THE
        (S-H) TABLE
    *DET+NOUN_2
    7
        (V) JOHN ATE THE APPLE ON THE TABLE
        (ADP NP) BEHIND
    *ADD-ADP_14
    8
        (NP V) JOHN ATE THE APPLE ON THE TABLE BEHIND
        (GQ) THE
    *PREP+NP_5
    9
        (GQ V) JOHN ATE THE APPLE ON THE TABLE BEHIND THE
        (S-H) TREE
    *DET+NOUN_2
    10
        (V) JOHN ATE THE APPLE ON THE TABLE BEHIND THE TREE
        (ADP NP) IN
    *ADD-ADP_14
    11
        (NP V) JOHN ATE THE APPLE ON THE TABLE BEHIND THE TREE IN
        (GQ) THE
```

```
*PREP+NP_5
12
    (GQ V) JOHN ATE THE APPLE ON THE TABLE BEHIND THE TREE IN THE
    (SH) GARDEN
*DET+NOUN_2
13
    (V) JOHN ATE THE APPLE ON THE TABLE BEHIND THE TREE IN THE GARDEN
    (V DECL)  .
*CMPLT_13
14
    (DECL) JOHN ATE THE APPLE ON THE TABLE BEHIND THE TREE IN THE GARDEN
```

```
Hierarchical Analysis:

(PROPOSITION-14_17_1
 (MOOD (DECLARATIVE-14_17_1))
 (PROP-CONTENT
  ((SENT-2_17_1
    (SUBJ ((NP-1_17_1 (NAME (JOHN-1_17_1)))))
    (VERB (EAT-2_17_1))
    (DIR-OBJ
     ((NP-3_17_1
       (REF (THE-3_17_1 SG-4_17_1))
       (NOUN ((APPLE-4_17_1)))
       (PNM
        ((PREP-5_17_1
          (PREPOSITION (ON-5_17_1))
          (PREPOSITIONAL-ARG
           ((NP-6_17_1
             (REF (THE-6_17_1 SG-7_17_1))
             (NOUN ((TABLE-7_17_1)))
             (PNM
              ((PREP-8_17_1
                (PREPOSITION (BEHIND-8_17_1))
                (PREPOSITIONAL-ARG
                 ((NP-9_17_1
                   ((THE-9_17_1 SG-10_17_1))
                   (NOUN ((TREE-10_17_1)))
                   (PNM
                    ((PREP-11_17_1
                      (PREPOSITION (IN-11_17_1))
                      (PREPOSITIONAL-ARG
                       ((NP-12_17_1
                         (REF (THE-12_17_1 SG-13_17_1))
                         (NOUN ((GARDEN-13_17_1))))))))))))))))))))))))
    (ADVERB ("PREP-5_17_1" "PREP-8_17_1" "PREP-11_17_1"))))))
```

The semantic representation specifies the six (2 · 3) possible positions of the three prepositional phrases. This technique, called **semantic doubling**, is so far unique to LA-grammar.

Semantic doubling results in something like a packed representation (cf. Section 10.3). From the representation in 9.5.7 a separate display of the six different possible "readings" may be constructed. But a more practical solution is definition of a pragmatic interpretation function which selects the right interpretation (or interpretations) relative to an utterance context directly from the "packed" representation.

Semantic doubling differs from packed parsing in that the syntactic derivation is completely unambiguous. There is not a single instance of fusion in the derivation of 9.5.7. Instead, the alternative possibilities indicated in the semantic representation are the result of a double interpretation of the syntactic combination.

Because ambiguities with double recursions are descriptively superfluous, methodologically self-defeating, and complexity-theoretically a nightmare, they are not permitted in sound LA-grammars. The possible count confusions arising from ambiguities with double recursion are not covered by the counter constraint, however, because the call of the second recursion occurs *in the middle* of the first. Thus, it does not hold in 9.5.5 (as one example) that an increasing recursion calls another increasing recursion. In addition to the Counter Constraint, sound LA-grammars must obey the Single Return Principle.

9.5.8 The Single Return Principle (SRP)

> If a syntactic ambiguity arises inside a recursion, then only one of the branches resulting from the ambiguity may feed back into the recursion.

The SRP results in a welcome reduction of the maximal number of syntactic ambiguities in sound LA-grammars.

9.5.9 Lemma 2

> LA-grammars satisfying the SRP have—at most—$(C \cdot n)$ readings.

Proof: Assume that G is an LA-grammar satisfying the SRP with one rule introducing a recursive ambiguity. For any derivation in G, the number of readings increases by at most one at each combination step. Thus the highest number of readings of an input string of length n is n. Each additional rule in G introducing a recursive ambiguity will contribute no more than n additional readings. The number of rules is constant in a grammar. Therefore, recursive ambiguities obeying the SRP increase the number of readings only by a constant factor C times n.

$$Q.E.D.$$

The three restrictions on sound LA-grammars proposed in Section 9.4 and the present section are summarized in the following definition:

9.5.10 Definition of a Sound LA-Grammar
An LA-grammar G is *sound* if and only if

1. G obeys the Redundancy Constraint (RC, cf. 9.4.1),
2. G obeys the counter constraint (CC, cf. 9.4.2), and
3. G obeys the Single Return Principle (SR, cf. 9.5.8).

9.5.11 Theorem 11

For any LA-grammar which is not sound, there is an equivalent sound
LA-grammar.

Proof: Sound LA-grammars are defined by the Redundancy Constraint, the Counter
Constraint, and the Single Return Principle. Because these restrictions do not decrease the generative capacity of LA-grammar, there is a sound LA-grammar for
any unsound one.

Q.E.D.

For any given D-LAG, violations of the RC, CC and SRP may be determined systematically by inspecting the finite representative sample of the grammar, the rules
of the grammar, and parses of examples. Using standard techniques, any located
violations of the RC, CC, and SRP may be eliminated. Equivalence of the resulting
sound D-LAG and its unsound predecessor may be proven in accordance with Theorem 10 (9.3.10). On the other hand, for LA-grammars which are not D-LAGs the
RC, CC and SRP serve as general guidelines for the construction of well-designed,
efficient systems.

10. Computational Complexity Results

Section 10.1 defines the primitive operation of C-LAGs and proves that unambiguous C-LAGs parse in linear time. Section 10.2 presents complexity results of LA-grammar for a number of context-free languages in comparison to Earley's algorithm. Section 10.3 discusses the method of "packing" an exponential number of readings. Section 10.4 proves that sound syntactically ambiguous C-LAGs parse in n^2. Section 10.5 investigates different types of lexical ambiguity.

10.1 Complexity of Unambiguous C-LAGs

The first step in the analysis of computational efficiency of a new algorithm is the choice of the **primitive operation**. Consider how Earley specified and motivated his choice of a primitive operation for the Earley algorithm:

> Griffiths and Petrick...have expressed their algorithms as sets of nondeterministic rewriting rules for a Turing-machine-like device. Each application of one of these is a primitive operation. We have chosen as our primitive operation the act of adding a state to a state set (or attempting to add one which is already there). We feel that this is comparable to their primitive operation because both are in some sense the most complex operation performed by the algorithm whose complexity is independent of the size of the grammar or the input string.

> Earley (1970), p. 100.

Earley is able to use the act of adding, or attempting to add, a state to a state set as his primitive operation. That is because even though "for some grammars the number of states in a state set can grow indefinitely with the length of the string being recognized"[1], the operation of testing whether or not a state has already been added to the state set is handled in such a way that the size of the search space is independent of the length of the string under analysis.[2] This is possible because of a structured build-up of the state set. The efficiency of the Earley algorithm derives directly from the fact that the presence of a state in a state set can be checked in an amount of time which is independent of the size of the state set.

What is the most natural definition of a primitive operation in LA-grammar? The most complex operation, whose complexity is independent of the size of the grammar

---

[1]Earley (1970), p. 98.
[2]See Earley (1970), p. 97, (3).

or the input string, is the application of a rule to a given ss-nw pair. However, rule applications may be taken as the primitive operations of LA-grammar only if categorial operations do not have to search through indefinitely long sentence-start categories. This condition is satisfied by the class of C-LAGs defined in 7.2.1.

10.1.1 The Primitive Operation of C-LAGs

> In C-LAGs the *primitive operation* is defined as the application of a rule to a given ss-nw pair.

B-LAGs are not necessarily slower than C-LAGs. It is just that their complexity analysis cannot use rule applications as their primitive operations, because the categorial operations may have to look at an indefinite number of CAT-1 segments. Since C-LAGs cover all context-free languages as well as many context-sensitive languages, our discussion of C-LAG complexity is considerably more general than the traditional discussion of context-free PS-grammar complexity.

Whether or not a given LA-grammar is a C-LAG is obvious from the structure of the rules. Furthermore, the exact complexity of a given input string is provided automatically by the rule counter during a parse. In addition, based on the grammar and the complexity measures of inputs, it is often possible to find a "closed form expression" which characterizes the complexity of the grammar for arbitrary n. Thus, the C-LAG 6.4.3 for $a^k b^k c^k$ was determined to parse in $[4/3n + 1/3(n-1)]$, the C-LAGs 7.1.3 for WW^r and 7.1.5 for WW were determined to parse in $[(1/4 \cdot n^2) + (1/2 \cdot (n-8))]$, etc.

Beyond the complexity analysis of individual grammars, however, we would like to arrive at general results for whole classes of languages. The first such general result is presented in Theorem 7.

10.1.2 Theorem 12

> Unambiguous C-LAGs are parsed in $C \cdot n$, where C is a small constant representing the maximal number rules in a rule package, and n is the length of the input.

Proof: An LA-grammar is unambiguous iff (i) it holds for all rule packages that their rules have incompatible input conditions, and (ii) there are no lexical ambiguities (7.3.5). Therefore, each combination step results in, at most, one continuation. Thus the number of elementary operations at any transition is equal to the number of rules in the current rule package.

$$Q.E.D.$$

This result is considerably better than that of Earley (1970). Earley's algorithm parses unambiguous context-free languages in $|G|^2 \cdot n^2$, where $|G|$ is the size of the context-free grammar, and n is the length of the input string.

First, the complexity of the Earley's algorithm, as well as any other conventional parsing algorithm, depends heavily on the size $|G|$ of the grammar,[3] whereas LA-grammar complexity is independent of the size of the grammar. Second, regarding the length of the input n, LA-grammar parses C-LAGs in linear time n, whereas the Earley algorithm parses context-free grammars in square time n^2. And third, C-LAGs cover not only all context-free languages but also a large portion of the context-sensitive languages (including "hard" context-sensitive languages, c.f. 10.2.8), while the Earley algorithm, as well as all other conventional general purpose parsers such as CYK, parse only the context-free languages, or a mere subset of the context-free languages (e.g., LR-parsers).

10.2   Empirical Results

To get a feeling for the relationship between PS-grammars and equivalent LA-grammars, and for their respective behaviors in terms of efficiency, let us consider the formal languages described in Earley (1970), namely ab^k, a^kb, a^kb^k, ab^kcd^m, Propositional Calculus, GRE, and NSE. We describe each language by (i) an LA-grammar, (ii) the PS-grammar provided by Earley (1970), and (iii) the complexity results for LA-grammar, the Earley algorithm, and—if available—the BU (bottom-up), SBU (specialized bottom-up), TD (top-down), and STD (specialized top-down) algorithms as evaluated by Griffiths and Petrick (1965). The LA-grammars are presented in canonical form, consisting of (i) a lexicon LX, (ii) a set of start states ST_S, (iii) a set of rules, called r-0, r-1, etc., and (iv) a set of final states ST_F. Note that Earley formulated the PS-grammars for ab^k, a^kb, etc., so that exponents like k must usually be interpreted as > 0.

10.2.1   The Regular Language ab^k

1. Formulation in LA-grammar:

   $LX =_{def} \{(a\ (a)), (b\ (b))\}$
   $ST_S =_{def} \{[\{r\text{-}1\}\ (a)]\}$
   r-1: $[(seg1)(b)] \Rightarrow [\{r\text{-}1\}\ (b)]$
   $ST_F =_{def} \{[rp\text{-}1\ (b)]\}$

2. Formulation in PS-grammar:

   (1) $S \rightarrow Ab$
   (2) $A \rightarrow a$
   (3) $A \rightarrow Ab$

---

[3]Barton, Berwick, and Ristad (1987) say on p. 250: "Crucially, grammar size affects recognition time in all known CFG recognition algorithms. For GPSG , this corresponds to the set of admissible local trees, and this set is astronomical...".

3. Complexity (Number of operations per input of length n):

> Early: [4n + 7]
> TD: [1/2 · (n² + 7n +2)]
> STD: [1/2 · (n² + 7n +2)]
> BU: [9n + 5]
> SBU: [9n + 5]
> LAG: [n-1]

A string of length n is derived in $n - 1$ steps by the LAG defined in 10.2.1 above because the sole rule package contains only a single rule. Thus, after each combination step only one rule can be applied to the next ss-nw pair.

10.2.2 The Regular Language $a^k b$

1. Formulation in LA-grammar:

> $LX =_{def} \{(a\ (a)),\ (b\ (b))\}$
> $ST_S =_{def} \{[\{r\text{-}1,\ r\text{-}2\}\ (a)]\}$
> r-1: $[(a)(a)] \Rightarrow [\{r\text{-}1,\ r\text{-}2\}\ (a)]$
> r-2: $[(a)(b)] \Rightarrow [\emptyset\ (b)]$
> $ST_F =_{def} \{[rp\text{-}2\ (b)]\}$

2. Formulation in PS-grammar:

> (1) S → aB
> (2) B → aB
> (3) B → b

3. Complexity (Number of operations per input of length n):

> Early: [4n + 4]
> TD: [3n + 2]
> STD: [2n + 2]
> BU: [(11 · n²) + 7]
> SBU: [4n + 4]
> LAG: [2(n - 1)]

The LAG defined in 10.2.2 derives a string of length n in $2(n - 1)$ steps, because at each combination two rules are being tried on the next ss-nw pair.

10.2.3 The Context-Free Language $a^k b^k$

1. Formulation in LA-grammar:

LX $=_{def}$ {(a (a)), (b (b))}

$ST_S =_{def}$ {[{r-1, r-2} (a)]}

r-1: [(X)(a)] $\Rightarrow$ [{r-1, r-2} (a X)]

r-2: [(a X)(b)] $\Rightarrow$ [{r-2} (X)]

$ST_F =_{def}$ {[rp-2 ϵ]}

2. Formulation in PS-grammar:

(1) S $\rightarrow$ aSb

(2) S $\rightarrow$ ab

3. Complexity (Number of operations per input of length n):

Early: [6n + 4]

TD: [5n - 1]

STD: [5n - 1]

BU: [11 · 2^{n-1}]

SBU: [6n]

LAG: [(n-1) + 1/2n]

In the first half of the input string, two rules (i.e., r-1 and r-2) are applied after each combination. This amounts to $(n - 1)$ operations. In the second half of the input string, only one rule (i.e., r-2) is applied after each combination, amounting to an additional $(1/2n)$ steps.

10.2.4 The Regular Language $ab^k cd^m$

1. Formulation in LA-grammar:

LX $=_{def}$ {(a (a)), (b (b)), (c (c)), (d (d))}

$ST_S =_{def}$ {[{r-1}(a)]}

r-1: [(a)(b)] $\Rightarrow$ [{r-2, r-3,} (b)]

r-2: [(b)(b)] $\Rightarrow$ [{r-2, r-3} (b)],

r-3: [(b)(c)] $\Rightarrow$ [{r-4} (d)],

r-4: [(d)(d)] $\Rightarrow$ [{r-4} (d)]

$ST_F =_{def}$ {[rp-3 (d)], [rp-4 (d)]}

2. Formulation in PS-grammar:

(1) S $\rightarrow$ AB   (4) B $\rightarrow$ bc

(2) A $\rightarrow$ a   (5) B $\rightarrow$ bB

(3) A $\rightarrow$ Ab   (6) B $\rightarrow$ Bd

3. Complexity (Number of operations per input of length n):

Early: $[18n + 8]$

TD: $[2^{n+6}]$

STD: $[2^{n+2}]$

BU: $[2^{n+5}]$

SBU: $[1/3 \cdot (n^2 + (21 \cdot n^2) + 46n + 15)]$

LAG: $[1 + 2k + m]$, which is less than $[2 (n-1)]$.

For the languages Propositional Calculus, NSE and GRE, neither Petrick and Griffiths (1965) nor Earley (1970) provide "closed-form expressions" for their complexity results. Instead, Earley (1970) gives the number of operations for specific sentences of the languages. In the case of propositional calculus grammar and NSE, Earley (1970) provides data for the PA,[4]SBU, and the Earley algorithm. In the case of GRE, he provides data for the SBU and the Earley algorithm only.

10.2.5 The Context-Free Language Propositional Calculus

1. Formulation in LA-grammar:

LX = {(p (T)), (q (T)), (r (T)), (p' (T)), (q' (T)), (r' (T)), (and (BIN)),
        (or (BIN)), (impl (BIN)), (not (NEG)), ([(L)), (] (R))}

$ST_S =_{def}$ {[{r-1, r-2} (seg1)]}, where seg1 ε {L, T, NEG}

r-1: [(X NEG)(seg2)] $\Rightarrow$ [{r-1, r-2, r-3} (X seg2)],
      where seg2 ε {L, T}

r-2: [(X L)(seg1)] $\Rightarrow$ [{r-1, r-2, r-3} (X L seg1)],
      where seg1 ε {L, T, NEG}

r-3: [(X T)(BIN)] $\Rightarrow$ [{r-4} (X BIN)]

r-4: [(X BIN)(seg1)] $\Rightarrow$ [{r-1, r-2, r-3, r-5} (X seg1)],
      where seg ε {L, T, NEG}

r-5: [(X L T)(R)] $\Rightarrow$ [{r-3 r-5} (X T)]

$ST_F =_{def}$ {[rp-0 (T)], [rp-4 (T)], [rp-5 (T)]}

2. Formulation in PS-grammar:

(1) F → C	(9) L → L'
(2) F → S	(10) L → p
(3) F → P	(11) L → q
(4) F → U	(12) L → r
(5) C → U impl U	(13) S → U or S
(6) U → (F)	(14) S → U or U
(7) U → not U	(15) P → U and P
(8) U → L	(16) P → U and U

3. Complexity (Number of operations per input of length n):

Sentence	Length	PA	SBU	Earley	LAG
p	1	14	18	28	1
(p and q)	5	89	56	68	11
(p' and q) or r or p or q'	13	232	185	148	24
p impl ((q impl not (r' or (p and q))) impl (q' or r))	26	712	277	277	57
not (not p' and (q or r) and p')	17	1955	223	141	32
((p and q) or (q and r) or (r and p')) impl not ((p' or q') and (r' or p))	38	2040	562	399	84

10.2.6 The Regular Language GRE

1. Formulation in LA-grammar:

$LX =_{def}$ {(a (a)), (b (b)), (e (e)), (d (d))}

$ST_S =_{def}$ {[{r-1, r-2}(seg1)]}

r-1: [(seg1)(seg2)] $\Rightarrow$ [∅ (a)],

where seg1 = a and seg2 = b, or seg1 = e and seg2 = a.

r-2: [(e)(d)] $\Rightarrow$ [{r-3} (d)]

r-3: [(d)(e)] $\Rightarrow$ [{r-2, r-4} (e)]

r-4: [(e)(a)] $\Rightarrow$ [{r-5} (b)]

r-5: [(b)(b)] $\Rightarrow$ [{r-5} (b)]

$ST_F =_{def}$ {[rp-1 (a)], [rp-4 (b)], [rp-5 (b)]}

2. Formulation in PS-grammar:

(1) X → a   (4) Y → e

(2) X → Xb   (5) Y → YdY

(3) X → Ya

3. Complexity (Number of operations per input of length n):

Sentence	Length	PA	SBU	Earley	LAG
ededea	6	35	52	33	8
ededeab[4]	10	75	92	45	12
ededeab[10]	16	99	152	63	18
ededeab[200]	206	859	2052	663	208

---

[4]PA refers to the "predictive analyzer", a modified top-down algorithm described in Griffiths and Petrick (1965).

$(ed)^4eabb$	12	617	526	79	16
$(ed)^7eabb$	18	24352	16336	194	25
$(ed)^8eabb$	20	86139	54660	251	28

The worst case for this LAG is the sequence "eded...", which requires $3/2n$ steps.

10.2.7 The Regular Language NSE

1. Formulation in LA-grammar:

$$LX =_{def} \{(a\ (a)),\ (b\ (b)),\ (c\ (c)),\ (d\ (d))\}$$
$$ST_S =_{def} \{[\{r\text{-}1,\ r\text{-}2,\ r\text{-}3\}\ (a)]\}$$
r-1: $[(a)(d)] \Rightarrow [\{r\text{-}3,\ r\text{-}4\}\ (d)]$
r-2: $[(a)(b)] \Rightarrow [\{r\text{-}5,\ r\text{-}6\}\ (b)]$
r-3: $[(d)(d)] \Rightarrow [\{r\text{-}3,\ r\text{-}4\}\ (d)]$
r-4: $[(d)(b)] \Rightarrow [\{r\text{-}5\}\ (b)]$
r-5: $[(b)(c)] \Rightarrow [\{r\text{-}6,\ r\text{-}7\}\ (c)]$
r-6: $[(c)(d)] \Rightarrow [\{r\text{-}3,\ r\text{-}4\}\ (d)]$
r-7: $[(c)(b)] \Rightarrow [\{r\text{-}5\}\ (b)]$
$$ST_F =_{def} \{[rp\text{-}2\ (b)],\ [rp\text{-}4\ (b)],\ [rp\text{-}7\ (b)]\}$$

2. Formulation in PS-grammar:

(1) S → AB   (5) B → DB
(2) A → a   (6) C → c
(3) A → SC   (7) D → d
(4) B → b

3. Complexity (Number of operations per input of length n):

Sentence	Length	SBU	Earley	LAG
$adbcddb$	7	43	44	13
$ad^3bcbcd^3bcd^4b$	18	111	108	34
$adbcd^2bcd^5bcd^3b$	19	117	114	37
$ad^{18}b$	20	120	123	39
$a(bd)^3d^2(bcd)^2dbcd^4b$	24	150	141	46
$a(bcd)^2dbcd^3bcb$	16	100	95	32

Because none of the LA-rules have rule packages containing more than two rules, this LA-grammar parses in less than $2(n-1)$ steps (linear time).

The analysis of the language NSE completes the comparison of grammars for the languages described by Earley (1970). In each of the above comparisons the LAG-algorithm turned out to be by far the fastest. Furthermore, the LAG-algorithm parses a much larger class of languages than the Earley algorithm.

Let us illustrate this last point once more by defining an LA-grammar for the context-sensitive language $a^k b^k c^k d^k e^k$. In the context of grammar formalisms close to PS-grammar, such as Tree Adjoining Grammars (Vijay-Shanker, Weir, and Joshi (1987)), and Head Grammars (Pollard (1984)), $a^k b^k c^k d^k e^k$ is regarded a "hard" context-sensitive language, in contrast to $a^k b^k c^k$, which is considered "mildly context-sensitive" (Joshi, Vijay-Shanker, and Weir (forthcoming)).

10.2.8 The "Hard" Context-Sensitive Language $a^k b^k c^k d^k e^k$

$LX =_{def} \{(a\ (a)), (b\ (b)), (c\ (c)), (d\ (d)), (e(e))\}$
$ST_S =_{def} \{[\{r\text{-}1, r\text{-}2\}(a)]\}$
r-1: $[(X)(a)] \Rightarrow [\{r\text{-}1, r\text{-}2\}\ (aX)]$
r-2: $[(aX)(b)] \Rightarrow [\{r\text{-}2, r\text{-}3\}\ (Xb)]$
r-3: $[(bX)(c)] \Rightarrow [\{r\text{-}3, r\text{-}4\}\ (Xc)]$
r-4: $[(cX)(d)] \Rightarrow [\{r\text{-}4, r\text{-}5\}\ (Xd)]$
r-5: $[(dX)(e)] \Rightarrow [\{r\text{-}5\}\ (X)]$
$ST_F =_{def} \{[rp\text{-}5\ \epsilon]\}$

This grammar for $a^k b^k c^k d^k e^k$ is clearly an unambiguous C-LAG (K = 1). And, like all unambiguous C-LAGs, it parses in linear time.

10.2.9 Sample Derivation of aabbccddee with Active Rule Counter

```
* (z a a b b c c d d e e)
;  1: Applying rules (RULE-1 RULE-2)
;  2: Applying rules (RULE-1 RULE-2)
;  3: Applying rules (RULE-2 RULE-3)
;  4: Applying rules (RULE-2 RULE-3)
;  5: Applying rules (RULE-3 RULE-4)
;  6: Applying rules (RULE-3 RULE-4)
;  7: Applying rules (RULE-4 RULE-5)
;  8: Applying rules (RULE-4 RULE-5)
;  9: Applying rules (RULE-5)
; Number of rule applications: 17.

   *START-0
   1
       (A)  A
       (A)  A
   *RULE-1
   2
       (A A)  A A
       (B)  B
   *RULE-2
   3
       (A B)  A A B
       (B)  B
```

```
*RULE-2
4
    (B B)  A A B B
    (C) C
*RULE-3
5
    (B C)  A A B B C
    (C) C
*RULE-3
6
    (C C)  A A B B C C
    (D) D
*RULE-4
7
    (C D)  A A B B C C D
    (D) D
*RULE-4
8
    (D D)  A A B B C C D D
    (E) E
*RULE-5
9
    (D)  A A B B C C D D E
    (E) E
*RULE-5
10
    NIL A A B B C C D D E E
```

The exact C-LAG complexity of $a^k b^k c^k d^k e^k$ is $[8k+(k-1)]$, which is below $2(n-1)$. In LA-grammar, it does not matter whether a language consists of three equally long same-letter sequences (e.g., $a^k b^k c^k$), five such sequences (e.g., $a^k b^k c^k d^k e^k$), or a thousand such sequences. In each case, the grammar will parse below $2(n-1)$.

10.3   Packing vs. Restricting Ambiguities

Next, we turn to the complexity analysis of ambiguous C-LAGs. Ambiguous grammars may generate an exponential number of readings (e.g., 7.5.2). To print an exponential number of analyses requires exponential time. Exponential time complexity is computationally intractable.[5] Does this mean that the computational analysis of certain ambiguous grammars is computationally intractable? Earley's algorithm[6] handles ambiguous context-free grammars in n^3. How is it possible to analyze a language with 2^n readings in n^3 steps?

Let us consider an example. The phrase-structure formulation presented in 10.3.1 is a simplified version of 3SAT (cf. 7.5.1), called 2SAT. 2SAT is like 3SAT, except that the disjunctions consist of two rather than three disjuncts.

---

[5]See Barton, Berwick, and Ristad(1987), p. 9, Figure 1.1, for a comparison of polynomial and exponential time complexity.

[6]Earley (1970).

10.3.1 PS-grammar for 2SAT

(1) S → C1   (8) S → C0
(2) C1 → C1 and C1   (9) C0 → C0 and C0
                                   (10) C0 → C0 and C1
                                   (11) C0 → C1 and C0
(3) C1 → D1   (12) C0 → D0
(4) D1 → (1 or 1)   (13) D0 → (0 or 0)
(5) D1 → (1 or 0)
(6) D1 → (0 or 1)
(7) 1 → x   (14) 0 → x

The grammar defined in 10.3.1 assumes unrestricted lexical look-up (cf. Section 7.5), for which reason only one propositional variable (x) is needed. For any well-formed formula of 2SAT, the grammar 10.3.1 provides all possible truth-table assignments as readings. For example, the formula [(x or x) and (x or x)] has 16 (= 2^4) readings. Two of these readings are represented in 10.3.2 as phrase-structure trees.

10.3.2 Two Readings of (x or x) and (x or x)

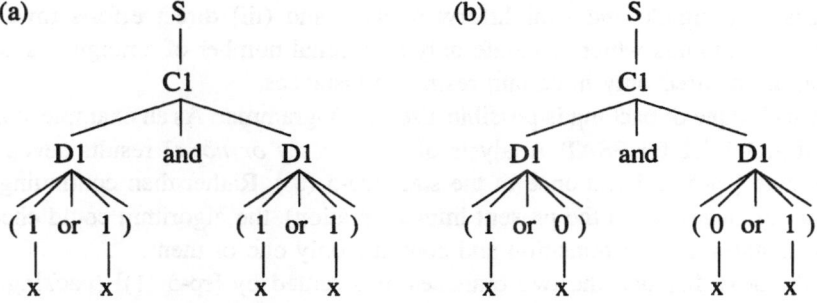

Earley's algorithm can recognize expressions generated by a grammar like 2SAT in n^3 steps, because the different readings of ambiguous constituents are fused as soon as the algorithm arrives at equivalent dominating nodes. For example, the assignments to the first disjunction in the two readings of 10.3.2 are different. But as soon as the algorithm has reduced the respective disjunctions to the D1 nodes they are not distinguished any more. This fusion of readings occurs because "states" (or items) are added to a "state set" only if they are not already a member (Earley (1970), p. 97).

Earley's algorithm has been called both—an n^3 **recognizer**[7] and an n^3 **parser**.[8]

---

[7]An algorithm is called a "recognizer" for a language if it can decide for any expression whether it is a well-formed expression of that language. An algorithm is called a "parser" for a language if it provides an analysis (e.g., tree structure) for each reading of a well-formed expression of the language. Although parsers are recognizers, the converse does not apply.

[8]Hopcroft and Ullman (1979), p. 145, call the Earley algorithm "the most practical, general, context

Earley's algorithm is not an n^3 parser for ambiguous languages, because printing an exponential number of analyses requires exponential time. But Earley's algorithm is more than just a recognizer, because it may produce a "packed forest" which analyzes the different readings of an ambiguous sentence in compact form: The fusion of readings during the recognition process may be displayed in the form of fused trees. In short, Earley's algorithm is a **packed parser** (of complexity n^3) for ambiguous languages.[9]

A packed parser must provide for a mapping from the packed representations into a set of individual analyses, which is not a trivial problem. For example, Tomita (1986) shows that Earley's packed representation permits derivation of readings which are not generated by the grammar. Furthermore, the concept of packing may be pushed *ad absurdum* by defining the "ultimate packed parser":[10] For any input string, the ultimate packed parser returns an ordered pair, consisting of the input string and the rules of the grammar. From this trivial "packed representation", analyses of all the different readings may be derived.

Nevertheless, if a representation of all readings of an exponentially ambiguous language is required, packed representations are the only possibility. But the analysis of ambiguous languages should (i) clearly distinguish between packed parsers and parsers proper, (ii) insure that packed representation may be mapped into individual analyses in a simple and straightforward way, and (iii) direct efforts toward the design of grammars which generate only a minimal number of ambiguities, so that packing is required only in certain restricted instances.

The technique of packing is possible also in LA-grammar. As an example, consider the C-LAG 7.5.1 for 3SAT. Analysis of [*x or not y or not z*] results seven times in the state [rp-5 (1)] and once in the state [rp-5 (0)]. Rather than continuing eight separate branches (as in the present implementation), the algorithm could check for identical states at each transition and continue only one of them.

At the next disjunct, the two branches represented by [rp-5 (1)] (packing seven "true" analyses of the first disjunct) and [rp-5 (0)] will each split again, eventually resulting in seven "true" analyses and one "false" analysis of the [rp-5 (1)] branch, and eight "false" analyses of the [rp-5 (0)] branch. The seven "true" analyses, represented again by the state [rp-5 (1)], and the nine "false" analyses, represented by the [rp-5 (0)], may again be fused, bringing the number of branches back down to two.

In other words, the first disjunct results in eight readings, which are reduced to two

---

[9]The traditional distinction between "all reading" parsers and "single reading" parsers misses the point in the case of an algorithm like Earley's. The algorithm is characterized by the fact that it (i) performs a **complete** search of the grammatical structure, and (ii) systematically **fuses** analyses during that search. The notion of a "single-reading" parser implies that only a single reading is being derived. It is misleading to call an n^3 packed parser an n^3 "single reading" parser just because an exponential number of readings in a packed representation cannot be individually printed out in polynomial time.

[10]This possibility was mentioned by Professor Masaru Tomita.

branches. Each of these results in eight readings (totalling 16), which are reduced to two, etc. Because the number of branches vacillates systematically between two and sixteen, C-LAG recognition of 3SAT is only of linear complexity: No derivation requires more than $C \cdot n$ rule applications, for some constant C.

Furthermore, there is an obvious way to "LA-pack" the display of the parallel branches: Rather than printing one history section per transition, between two and sixteen history sections are printed out per transition. This is done in a horizontal manner, displaying the history sections representing different readings side by side. A suitable numbering indicates which history sections representing composition n+1 were derived from which history sections of composition n. Mapping this type of LA-packed representation into the usual sequence of different readings (cf. 7.5.2) is straightforward.

When is this LA-packing method possible? Consider a syntactically ambiguous C-LAG where the only ambiguous rule package is rp-1, where rp-1 contains two input-compatible rules. The number of readings can grow exponentially in this grammar only if both branches feed back into r-1, split up again, feed back into r-1, split up again, etc. This situation is illustrated in 10.3.3:

10.3.3 Two Branches Returning to the Same Potential Split

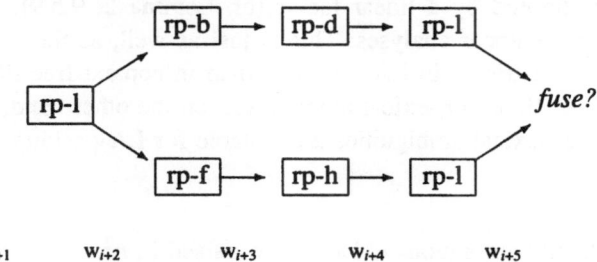

If we could fuse the branches each time before they go into rp-1, the number of parallel readings would be two at most (in LA-packed parsing). It is not generally possible, however, to fuse two branches if they permit equivalent splits, because the conditions for fission are easier to satisfy than the conditions for fusion. In order for two branches to undergo equivalent splits, they must represent equivalent category *expressions*, while in order for two branches to be fused, they must have identical *categories*.[11]

As an alternative to packing, we have investigated whether grammars should really generate ambiguities of the kind illustrated in 10.3.3. The Single Return Principle

---

[11]See 6.2.2. and 6.4.1. Because PS-grammar uses primitive categories, there is no distinction between category expressions and categories. In LA-grammar, on the other hand, the categorial operations are defined by category expressions, whereas equivalence of state tokens is defined by identical categories (cf. 6.3.6 f.). Thus, while the technique of "packing" may be used in LA-grammar to recognize ambiguous languages, its application is more restricted than in PS-grammar.

(9.5.8) prohibits syntactic ambiguities like 10.3.3. Thus, in sound LA-grammars, the need for packing is limited to lexical ambiguities, for which LA-packing is possible.

10.4   Complexity of Syntactically Ambiguous C-LAGs

Because LA-grammar distinguishes between *syntactic* and *lexical* ambiguities, the complexity of ambiguous C-LAGs is analyzed in two steps. Section 10.4 describes the complexity of sound syntactically ambiguous C-LAGs. Section 10.5 describes the complexity of lexically ambiguous C-LAGs.

Given that ambiguous grammars may generate an exponential number of readings, there are only two known methods for achieving polynomial complexity results. One method accepts an exponential number of readings, and arrives at polynomial complexity by means of "packed parsing". This is the approach of Earley (1970), Tomita (1986),[12] and others. The other method provides a principle for systematically restricting the number of readings generated by the grammar. The second approach is exemplified by the Single Return Principle described in Section 9.5.

LA-grammar uses both methods. In sound C-LAGs, syntactic ambiguities are restricted by means of the Single Return Principle (SRP). Because the number of syntactic analyses is limited by a linear factor (cf. Lemma 2, 9.5.9), there is no need for LA-packing the linear analyses. This is just as well, as the possibility of packing is much more restricted in LA-grammar than in context-free PS-grammar, as explained in Section 10.3. For lexical ambiguities, on the other hand, the SRP is not applicable. Instead, lexical ambiguities are suitable for LA-packing.

10.4.1 Theorem 13

Sound syntactically ambiguous C-LAGs are parsed in n^2.

Proof: Assume that G is an LA-grammar satisfying the SRP with one rule introducing a recursive ambiguity. For any derivation in G, the number of readings increases by, at most, one at each combination step (cf. Lemma 2, 9.5.9). Thus, the highest possible number of operations in deriving an input string of length n is $\sum_{i=1}^{i=(n-1)} i$, which is equivalent to $[1/2((n-1)\cdot n)]$, which is well below n^2. Because the number of rules is constant, additional rules introducing recursive ambiguities increase the number of readings only by a constant factor.

Q.E.D.

---

[12]Tomita (1986) (i) extends LR-parsing to the whole class of context-free languages, (ii) devises a packing method based on *graph structured stacks*, and (iii) shows that this system is faster than Earley's algorithm for certain "natural" context-free grammars. The improvement in speed is due to the precompilation of the grammar characteristic of LR-parsing.

Since for any syntactically ambiguous C-LAG there exists a weakly equivalent *sound* C-LAG (Theorem 11, 9.5.11), any syntactically ambiguous C-language can be parsed in n^2.

The argument culminating in Theorem 13 may be summarized as follows. In traditional language analysis, there are two reasons for treating a construction as syntactically ambiguous: (i) strings which could otherwise not be generated or would be generated less efficiently (syntactic ambiguity), and (ii) treatment of certain semantic intuitions (semantic ambiguity).

Examples of syntactic ambiguity are the grammars for the formal languages $a^n b^n c^m d^m \cup a^n b^m c^m d^n$ (cf. 7.4.1), WW (cf. 7.1.5), and WW^R (cf. 7.1.3). Here the Single Return Principle (9.5.8) is clearly appropriate: if the only purpose of the ambiguity is the generation of certain surface strings, then one loop is enough.

A potential example of a syntactically treated semantic ambiguity, on the other hand, is the distinction between an adverbial and a postnominal interpretation of prepositional phrases in English. Here the question arises whether a syntactic ambiguity is really necessary for expressing the semantic alternative in question. In LA-grammar the answer is "no".

Given that the semantic ambiguity in question may result in an exponential number of readings, the best result that can be achieved in exponential time is a "packed" representation. In traditional PS-grammar based systems, packed representations come about by **fusing** different branches of the syntactic derivation. But in LA-grammar we have available a new, even more efficient technique, namely the method of **semantic doubling**.

The result of semantic doubling looks like a packed representation, but it does not result from fusing syntactic ambiguities. Since the semantic intuitions in question can be expressed without concomitant syntactic ambiguities, the Single Return Principle is appropriate for semantic ambiguities as well. Since the Single Return Principle does not result in a decrease of generative power, there exists a weakly equivalent sound LA-grammar for any LA-grammar violating the Single Return Principle.

A natural language example exhibiting a syntactic ambiguity (treated in terms of four alternative readings) and a semantic ambiguity (treated in terms of semantic doubling) is 10.4.2.

10.4.2 *The bone was given to the dog by the man by the woman by the child.*

```
*  (z The bone was given to the dog by the man by the woman by the child \.)

4    Linear Analysis:

   *START_0
   1
      (GQ) THE
      (S-H) BONE
   *DET+NOUN_2
   2
      (S) THE BONE
      (S3 B V) WAS
```

```
*NOM+FVERB_3
3
    (B V) THE BONE WAS
    (HV A TO) GIVEN
*ADD-VERB_6
4
    (TO BY V) THE BONE WAS GIVEN
    (ADP NP) TO
*FVERB+MAIN_4
5
    (NP BY V) THE BONE WAS GIVEN TO
    (GQ) THE
*PREP+NP_5
6
    (GQ BY V) THE BONE WAS GIVEN TO THE
    (S-H) DOG
*DET+NOUN_2
7
    (BY V) THE BONE WAS GIVEN TO THE DOG
    (ADP NP) BY
*FVERB+MAIN_4
8
    (NP V) THE BONE WAS GIVEN TO THE DOG BY
    (GQ) THE
*PREP+NP_5
9
    (GQ V) THE BONE WAS GIVEN TO THE DOG BY THE
    (SH) MAN
*DET+NOUN_2
10
    (V) THE BONE WAS GIVEN TO THE DOG BY THE MAN
    (ADP NP) BY
*ADD-ADP_14
11
    (NP V) THE BONE WAS GIVEN TO THE DOG BY THE MAN BY
    (GQ) THE
*PREP+NP_5
12
    (GQ V) THE BONE WAS GIVEN TO THE DOG BY THE MAN BY THE
    (SH) WOMAN
*DET+NOUN_2
13
    (V) THE BONE WAS GIVEN TO THE DOG BY THE MAN BY THE WOMAN
    (ADP NP) BY
*ADD-ADP_14
14
    (NP V) THE BONE WAS GIVEN TO THE DOG BY THE MAN BY THE WOMAN BY
    (GQ) THE
*PREP+NP_5
15
    (GQ V) THE BONE WAS GIVEN TO THE DOG BY THE MAN BY THE WOMAN BY THE
    (SH) CHILD
*DET+NOUN_2
16
    (V) THE BONE WAS GIVEN TO THE DOG BY THE MAN BY THE WOMAN BY THE CHILD
    (V DECL) .
*CMPLT_13
17
    (DECL) THE BONE WAS GIVEN TO THE DOG BY THE MAN BY THE WOMAN BY THE CHILD
```

Hierarchical Analysis:

```
(PROPOSITION-17_49_1
 (MOOD (DECLARATIVE-17_49_1))
 (PROP-CONTENT
  ((SENT-3_49_1
    (SUBJ
     ((NP-1_49_1 (REF (THE-1_49_1 SG-2_49_1)) (NOUN ((BONE-2_49_1))))))
    (AUX (BE-3_49_1))
    (PASSIVE-PREDICATE
     ((NFV-4_49_1
       (PAST-PART (GIVE-4_49_1))
       (PREPOSITIONAL_OBJ
        ((PREP-5_49_1
          (PREPOSITION (TO-5_49_1))
          (PREPOSITIONAL-ARG
           ((NP-6_49_1 (REF (THE-6_49_1 SG-7_49_1)) (NOUN ((DOG-7_49_1)))))
          ))))
       (AGENT-PHRASE
        ((PREP-8_49_1
          (PREPOSITION (BY-8_49_1))
          (PREPOSITIONAL-ARG
           ((NP-9_49_1
             (REF (THE-9_49_1 SG-10_49_1))
             (NOUN ((MAN-10_49_1)))
             (PNM
              ((PREP-11_49_1
                (PREPOSITION (BY-11_49_1))
                (PREPOSITIONAL-ARG
                 ((NP-12_49_1
                   (REF (THE-12_49_1 SG-13_49_1))
                   (NOUN ((WOMAN-13_49_1)))
                   (PNM
                    ((PREP-14_49_1
                      (PREPOSITION (BY-14_49_1))
                      (PREPOSITIONAL-ARG
                       ((NP-15_49_1
                         (REF (THE-15_49_1 SG-16_49_1))
                         (NOUN ((CHILD-16_49_1)))))))))))))))))))
    (ADVERB ("PREP-11_49_1" "PREP-14_49_1"))))))
```

3   Linear Analysis:

```
    *START_0
    1
        (GQ) THE
        (S-H) BONE
    *DET+NOUN_2
    2
        (S) THE BONE
        (S3 B V) WAS
    *NOM+FVERB_3
    3
        (B V) THE BONE WAS
        (HV A TO) GIVEN
    *ADD-VERB_6
    4
        (TO BY V) THE BONE WAS GIVEN
```

```
        (ADP NP) TO
    *FVERB+MAIN_4
    5
        (NP BY V) THE BONE WAS GIVEN TO
        (GQ) THE
    *PREP+NP_5
    6
        (GQ BY V) THE BONE WAS GIVEN TO THE
        (S-H) DOG
    *DET+NOUN_2
    7
        (BY V) THE BONE WAS GIVEN TO THE DOG
        (ADP NP) BY
    *ADD-ADP_14
    8
        (NP BY V) THE BONE WAS GIVEN TO THE DOG BY
        (GQ) THE
    *PREP+NP_5
    9
        (GQ BY V) THE BONE WAS GIVEN TO THE DOG BY THE
        (SH) MAN
    *DET+NOUN_2
    10
        (BY V) THE BONE WAS GIVEN TO THE DOG BY THE MAN
        (ADP NP) BY
    *FVERB+MAIN_4
    11
        (NP V) THE BONE WAS GIVEN TO THE DOG BY THE MAN BY
        (GQ) THE
    *PREP+NP_5
    12
        (GQ V) THE BONE WAS GIVEN TO THE DOG BY THE MAN BY THE
        (SH) WOMAN
    *DET+NOUN_2
    13
        (V) THE BONE WAS GIVEN TO THE DOG BY THE MAN BY THE WOMAN
        (ADP NP) BY
    *ADD-ADP_14
    14
        (NP V) THE BONE WAS GIVEN TO THE DOG BY THE MAN BY THE WOMAN BY
        (GQ) THE
    *PREP+NP_5
    15
        (GQ V) THE BONE WAS GIVEN TO THE DOG BY THE MAN BY THE WOMAN BY THE
        (SH) CHILD
    *DET+NOUN_2
    16
        (V) THE BONE WAS GIVEN TO THE DOG BY THE MAN BY THE WOMAN BY THE CHILD
        (V DECL) .
    *CMPLT_13
    17
        (DECL) THE BONE WAS GIVEN TO THE DOG BY THE MAN BY THE WOMAN BY THE CHILD


Hierarchical Analysis:

(PROPOSITION-17_48_1
 (MOOD (DECLARATIVE-17_48_1))
 (PROP-CONTENT
  ((SENT-3_48_1
```

```
(SUBJ
 ((NP-1_48_1 (REF (THE-1_48_1 SG-2_48_1)) (NOUN ((BONE-2_48_1)))))))
(AUX (BE-3_48_1))
(PASSIVE-PREDICATE
 ((NFV-4_48_1
   (PAST-PART (GIVE-4_48_1))
   (PREPOSITIONAL_OBJ
    ((PREP-5_48_1
      (PREPOSITION (TO-5_48_1))
      (PREPOSITIONAL-ARG
       ((NP-6_48_1
         (REF (THE-6_48_1 SG-7_48_1))
         (NOUN ((DOG-7_48_1)))
         (PNM
          ((PREP-8_48_1
            (PREPOSITION (BY-8_48_1))
            (PREPOSITIONAL-ARG
             ((NP-9_48_1
               (REF (THE-9_48_1 SG-10_48_1))
               (NOUN ((MAN-10_48_1)))))))))))))))
   (ADVERB ("PREP-8_48_1"))
   (AGENT-PHRASE
    ((PREP-11_48_1
      (PREPOSITION (BY-11_48_1))
      (PREPOSITIONAL-ARG
       ((NP-12_48_1
         (REF (THE-12_48_1 SG-13_48_1))
         (NOUN ((WOMAN-13_48_1)))
         (PNM
          ((PREP-14_48_1
            (PREPOSITION (BY-14_48_1))
            (PREPOSITIONAL-ARG
             ((NP-15_48_1
               (REF (THE-15_48_1 SG-16_48_1))
               (NOUN ((CHILD-16_48_1)))))))))))))))
(ADVERB ("PREP-14_48_1"))))))))
```

2   Linear Analysis:

```
*START_0
1
   (GQ) THE
   (S-H) BONE
*DET+NOUN_2
2
   (S) THE BONE
   (S3 B V) WAS
*NOM+FVERB_3
3
   (B V) THE BONE WAS
   (HV A TO) GIVEN
*ADD-VERB_6
4
   (TO BY V) THE BONE WAS GIVEN
   (ADP NP) TO
*FVERB+MAIN_4
5
   (NP BY V) THE BONE WAS GIVEN TO
   (GQ) THE
```

```
*PREP+NP_5
6
    (GQ BY V) THE BONE WAS GIVEN TO THE
    (S-H) DOG
*DET+NOUN_2
7
    (BY V) THE BONE WAS GIVEN TO THE DOG
    (ADP NP) BY
*ADD-ADP_14
8
    (NP BY V) THE BONE WAS GIVEN TO THE DOG BY
    (GQ) THE
*PREP+NP_5
9
    (GQ BY V) THE BONE WAS GIVEN TO THE DOG BY THE
    (SH) MAN
*DET+NOUN_2
10
    (BY V) THE BONE WAS GIVEN TO THE DOG BY THE MAN
    (ADP NP) BY
*ADD-ADP_14
11
    (NP BY V) THE BONE WAS GIVEN TO THE DOG BY THE MAN BY
    (GQ) THE
*PREP+NP_5
12
    (GQ BY V) THE BONE WAS GIVEN TO THE DOG BY THE MAN BY THE
    (SH) WOMAN
*DET+NOUN_2
13
    (BY V) THE BONE WAS GIVEN TO THE DOG BY THE MAN BY THE WOMAN
    (ADP NP) BY
*FVERB+MAIN_4
14
    (NP V) THE BONE WAS GIVEN TO THE DOG BY THE MAN BY THE WOMAN BY
    (GQ) THE
*PREP+NP_5
15
    (GQ V) THE BONE WAS GIVEN TO THE DOG BY THE MAN BY THE WOMAN BY THE
    (SH) CHILD
*DET+NOUN_2
16
    (V) THE BONE WAS GIVEN TO THE DOG BY THE MAN BY THE WOMAN BY THE CHILD
    (V DECL) .
*CMPLT_13
17
    (DECL) THE BONE WAS GIVEN TO THE DOG BY THE MAN BY THE WOMAN BY THE CHILD
```

Hierarchical Analysis:

```
(PROPOSITION-17_47_1
  (MOOD (DECLARATIVE-17_47_1))
  (PROP-CONTENT
   ((SENT-3_47_1
     (SUBJ
      ((NP-1_47_1 (REF (THE-1_47_1 SG-2_47_1)) (NOUN ((BONE-2_47_1)))))))
     (AUX (BE-3_47_1))
     (PASSIVE-PREDICATE
      ((NFV-4_47_1
```

```
(PAST-PART (GIVE-4_47_1))
(PREPOSITIONAL_OBJ
 ((PREP-5_47_1
   (PREPOSITION (TO-5_47_1))
   (PREPOSITIONAL-ARG
    ((NP-6_47_1
      (REF (THE-6_47_1 SG-7_47_1))
      (NOUN ((DOG-7_47_1)))
      (PNM
       ((PREP-8_47_1
         (PREPOSITION (BY-8_47_1))
         (PREPOSITIONAL-ARG
          ((NP-9_47_1
            (REF (THE-9_47_1 SG-10_47_1))
            (NOUN ((MAN-10_47_1)))
            (PNM
             ((PREP-11_47_1
               (PREPOSITION (BY-11_47_1))
               (PREPOSITIONAL-ARG
                ((NP-12_47_1
                  (REF (THE-12_47_1 SG-13_47_1))
                  (NOUN ((WOMAN-13_47_1))))))))))))))))))))))))
(ADVERB ("PREP-8_47_1" "PREP-11_47_1"))
(AGENT-PHRASE
 ((PREP-14_47_1
   (PREPOSITION (BY-14_47_1))
   (PREPOSITIONAL-ARG
    ((NP-15_47_1
      (REF (THE-15_47_1 SG-16_47_1))
      (NOUN ((CHILD-16_47_1))))))))))))))))))))
```

1   Linear Analysis:

```
*START_0
1
    (GQ) THE
    (S-H) BONE
*DET+NOUN_2
2
    (S) THE BONE
    (S3 B V) WAS
*NOM+FVERB_3
3
    (B V) THE BONE WAS
    (HV A TO) GIVEN
*ADD-VERB_6
4
    (TO BY V) THE BONE WAS GIVEN
    (ADP NP) TO
*FVERB+MAIN_4
5
    (NP BY V) THE BONE WAS GIVEN TO
    (GQ) THE
*PREP+NP_5
6
    (GQ BY V) THE BONE WAS GIVEN TO THE
    (S-H) DOG
*DET+NOUN_2
7
```

```
    (BY V) THE BONE WAS GIVEN TO THE DOG
    (ADP NP) BY
*ADD-ADP_14
8
    (NP BY V) THE BONE WAS GIVEN TO THE DOG BY
    (GQ) THE
*PREP+NP_5
9
    (GQ BY V) THE BONE WAS GIVEN TO THE DOG BY THE
    (SH) MAN
*DET+NOUN_2
10
    (BY V) THE BONE WAS GIVEN TO THE DOG BY THE MAN
    (ADP NP) BY
*ADD-ADP_14
11
    (NP BY V) THE BONE WAS GIVEN TO THE DOG BY THE MAN BY
    (GQ) THE
*PREP+NP_5
12
    (GQ BY V) THE BONE WAS GIVEN TO THE DOG BY THE MAN BY THE
    (SH) WOMAN
*DET+NOUN_2
13
    (BY V) THE BONE WAS GIVEN TO THE DOG BY THE MAN BY THE WOMAN
    (ADP NP) BY
*ADD-ADP_14
14
    (NP BY V) THE BONE WAS GIVEN TO THE DOG BY THE MAN BY THE WOMAN BY
    (GQ) THE
*PREP+NP_5
15
    (GQ BY V) THE BONE WAS GIVEN TO THE DOG BY THE MAN BY THE WOMAN BY THE
    (SH) CHILD
*DET+NOUN_2
16
    (BY V) THE BONE WAS GIVEN TO THE DOG BY THE MAN BY THE WOMAN BY THE CHILD
    (V DECL) .
*CMPLT_13
17
    (DECL) THE BONE WAS GIVEN TO THE DOG BY THE MAN BY THE WOMAN BY THE CHILD


Hierarchical Analysis:

(PROPOSITION-17_46_1
 (MOOD (DECLARATIVE-17_46_1))
 (PROP-CONTENT
  ((SENT-3_46_1
    (SUBJ
     ((NP-1_46_1 (REF (THE-1_46_1 SG-2_46_1)) (NOUN ((BONE-2_46_1)))))))
    (AUX (BE-3_46_1))
    (PASSIVE-PREDICATE
     ((NFV-4_46_1
       (PAST-PART (GIVE-4_46_1))
       (PREPOSITIONAL_OBJ
        ((PREP-5_46_1
          (PREPOSITION (TO-5_46_1))
          (PREPOSITIONAL-ARG
           ((NP-6_46_1
```

```
                 (REF (THE-6_46_1 SG-7_46_1))
                 (NOUN ((DOG-7_46_1)))
                 (PNM
                  ((PREP-8_46_1
                    (PREPOSITION (BY-8_46_1))
                    (PREPOSITIONAL-ARG
                     ((NP-9_46_1
                       (REF (THE-9_46_1 SG-10_46_1))
                       (NOUN ((MAN-10_46_1)))
                       (PNM
                        ((PREP-11_46_1
                          (PREPOSITION (BY-11_46_1))
                          (PREPOSITIONAL-ARG
                           ((NP-12_46_1
                             (REF (THE-12_46_1 SG-13_46_1))
                             (NOUN ((WOMAN-13_46_1)))
                             (PNM
                              ((PREP-14_46_1
                                (PREPOSITION (BY-14_46_1))
                                (PREPOSITIONAL-ARG
                                 ((NP-15_46_1
                                   (REF (THE-15_46_1 SG-16_46_1))
                                   (NOUN ((CHILD-16_46_1)))))))))))))))))))))))))
      ))))
           (ADVERB ("PREP-8_46_1" "PREP-11_46_1" "PREP-14_46_1")))))))))))
```

The four readings of 10.4.2 represent the following distinctions.

10.4.3 Ambiguity Structure of 10.4.2

The bone was given to the dog   by the man   by the woman   by the child
                                   agent   *pnm/adverb*   *pnm/adverb*

                                  by the man   by the woman   by the child
                                  pnm/adverb   *agent*   *pnm/adverb*

                                  by the man   by the woman   by the child
                                  pnm/adverb   *pnm/adverb*   *agent*

                                  by the man   by the woman   by the child
                                  pnm/adverb   *pnm/adverb*   *pnm/adverb*

As 10.4.3 shows, analysis 10.4.2 satisfies the Single Return Principle: The split between an *agent*-reading and a *pnm/adverb*-reading is never repeated in a given branch.

If the distinction between the postnominal (pnm) and the adverbial interpretation of the prepositional phrases were treated as a syntactic ambiguity, then the sentence in question would have a total of twenty readings. These twenty different possible interpretations of the sentence analyzed in 10.4.2 are represented in "packed"—or rather "doubled"—form in the hierarchical analyses of the four readings.

10.5   Complexity of Lexically Ambiguous C-LAGs

Next, we turn to the complexity analysis of lexical ambiguity. In natural language,
we find non-local lexical ambiguities which can be packed, and local ambiguities
which cannot.

10.5.1 A Non-Local Lexical Ambiguity

```
* (w-eval "sheep")
(("SHEEP" (S-H) SHEEP)
 ("SHEEP" (P-H) SHEEP))

* (z the sheep grazed)

2    Linear Analysis:

    *START_0
    1
        (GQ) THE
        (P-H) SHEEP
    *DET+NOUN_2
    2
        (P) THE SHEEP
        (N V) GRAZED
    *NOM+FVERB_3
    3
        (V) THE SHEEP GRAZED

Hierarchical Analysis:

(SENT-3_5_4
  (SUBJ ((NP-1_5_4 (REF (THE-1_5_4 PL-2_5_4))
                   (NOUN ((SHEEP-2_5_4))))))
  (VERB (GRAZE-3_5_4)))


1    Linear Analysis:

    *START_0
    1
        (GQ) THE
        (S-H) SHEEP
    *DET+NOUN_2
    2
        (S) THE SHEEP
        (N V) GRAZED
    *NOM+FVERB_3
    3
        (V) THE SHEEP GRAZED

Hierarchical Analysis:

(SENT-3_4_4
  (SUBJ ((NP-1_4_4 (REF (THE-1_4_4 SG-2_4_4))
                   (NOUN ((SHEEP-2_4_4))))))
  (VERB (GRAZE-3_4_4)))
```

The lexical analysis (cf. (*w-eval "sheep"*) in 10.5.1) characterizes *sheep* as lexically ambiguous between a singular noun denoting a non-human, represented by the category (S-H), and a plural noun denoting a non-human, represented by the category (P-H). In combination with general quantifiers like *the*, the ambiguity is preserved. If the resulting ambiguous noun phrase *the sheep* is combined with a verb form which has no agreement restriction with respect to the nominative—like *grazed* (in contrast to *grazes*)—the ambiguity is preserved. Thus, *the sheep grazed* has two separate derivations in 10.5.1.

The resulting categories, however, are the same for each derivation: They are both (V). Therefore, the two derivations may be fused (packed) at this point. A sentence like *The sheep grazed peacefully on the green meadow, when suddenly...* has an ambiguous beginning, but in a packed parser the continuation after *the sheep grazed* is a single branch. In this sense, 10.5.1 is—at least theoretically— an example of a lexical ambiguity in natural language which is suitable for packing.

Next, consider a local lexical ambiguity in natural language:

10.5.2 A Local Lexical Ambiguity

```
* (w-eval "work")
(("WORK" (NOM V) WORK)
 ("WORK" (S-H) WORK))

* (z the work)

    Linear Analysis:

    *START_0
    1
        (GQ) THE
        (S-H) WORK
    *DET+NOUN_2
    2
        (S) THE WORK

Hierarchical Analysis:

(NP-1_2_5 (REF (THE-1_2_5 SG-2_2_5))
          (NOUN ((WORK-2_2_5))))


* (z they work)

Linear Analysis:

    *START_0
    1
        (P3) THEY
        (NOM V) WORK
    *NOM+FVERB_3
    2
        (V) THEY WORK
```

Hierarchical Analysis:

```
(SENT-2_2_6 (SUBJ ((NP-1_2_6 (PRO ((THEY-1_2_6))))))
            (VERB (WORK-2_2_6)))
```

The lexical analysis (cf. (*w-eval "work"*) in 10.5.2) characterizes *work* as lexically ambiguous between a finite verb with a nominative valency, represented by the category (NOM V), and a singular noun denoting a non-human, represented by the category (S-H). In combination with the general quantifier *the*, only the second reading survives. In combination with the plural noun phrase *they*, only the first reading survives. In other words, 10.5.2 is an example of a local lexical ambiguity where packing is neither possible nor necessary.

Whether or not a potential lexical ambiguity in a natural language results in serious inefficiency is largely up to the linguist. For example, if the traditional notion of a grammatical paradigm is applied to languages with a reduced morphology, the resulting lexical categorization can lead to a tremendous number of readings, sometimes even causing the parser to grind to a halt (stack overflow).[13] But such lexical ambiguities may be eliminated in line with the principle of surface compositionality. The alternative analysis constitutes not only a much more efficient grammar, but also a far superior linguistic analysis.

As a case in point consider nouns of English, which can be used with and without quantifiers, in both the singular and the plural. For example, in *John drank the beer*, the singular noun *beer* is a count noun used with a determiner, but in *John drank beer*, the same noun is used as a mass noun without a determiner. Similarly, in *John knows these beers*, the plural noun *beers* is used as a count noun with a determiner, but in *John knows beers*, the same noun is used without a determiner as a "bare plural". Does this mean that the singular and the plural of the noun should each be lexically ambiguous?

First, an analysis based on lexical ambiguity would be inefficient because each time the parser encounters a noun it has to check two lexical readings rather than one. Second, such an analysis would fail to explain why natural language finds it convenient to systematically use nouns in these alternative ways. An analysis which accounts for the alternative interpretations without a lexical ambiguity, results not only in a faster grammar, but at a more intelligent linguistic explanation.

In the following LA-grammar derivations, the use of *beer* as a singular count noun and as a singular mass noun is based one single lexical analysis of the noun *beer*; it is categorized as (S-H), i.e., as a singular noun (S) denoting a non-human entity (-H). The count/mass noun distinction is based solely on different combinatorics. Count nouns are defined by the fact that they take a determiner, while mass nouns are defined by the fact that they (i) are singular and (ii) do not take a determiner.

---

[13]This has been shown in detail for the analysis of German determiners, nouns, and adjectives in Hausser (1986), pp. 61 f.

10.5.3 *BEER* as a Singular Count Noun

```
* (z John drank the beer \.)

*** Lex Lookup
Real time:  · 0.08 s
Run time:     0.00 s

*** Parse Timings
Real time:    0.88 s
Run time:     0.66 s

    Linear Analysis:

    *START_0
    1
        (NH) JOHN
        (N A V) DRANK
    *NOM+FVERB_3
    2
        (A V) JOHN DRANK
        (GQ) THE
    *FVERB+MAIN_4
    3
        (GQ V) JOHN DRANK THE
        (S-H) BEER
    *DET+NOUN_2
    4
        (V) JOHN DRANK THE BEER
        (V DECL) .
    *CMPLT_13
    5
        (DECL) JOHN DRANK THE BEER .

Hierarchical Analysis:

(PROPOSITION-5_5_1
 (MOOD (DECLARATIVE-5_5_1))
 (PROP-CONTENT
  ((SENT-2_5_1
    (SUBJ ((NP-1_5_1 (NAME (JOHN-1_5_1)))))
    (VERB (DRINK-2_5_1))
    (DIR-OBJ ((NP-3_5_1 (REF (THE-3_5_1 SG-4_5_1))
                        (NOUN ((BEER-4_5_1)))))))))))
```

In this derivation, the article *the* is added by the rule FVERB+MAIN, and the noun *beer* by the rule DET+NOUN. The grammatical number SG-4 is determined from the category (S-H) of the noun and added under the determiner node, called REF (for "reference type").

10.5.4 *BEER* as a Mass Noun

```
* (z John drank beer \.)

*** Lex Lookup
Real time:    0.02 s
```

```
Run time:      0.02 s

*** Parse Timings
Real time:     0.64 s
Run time:      0.64 s

    Linear Analysis:

    *START_0
    1
        (NH) JOHN
        (N A V) DRANK
    *NOM+FVERB_3
    2
        (A V) JOHN DRANK
        (S-H) BEER
    *FVERB+MAIN_4
    3
        (V) JOHN DRANK BEER
        (V DECL) .
    *CMPLT_13
    4
        (DECL) JOHN DRANK BEER .

Hierarchical Analysis:

(PROPOSITION-4_4_2
  (MOOD (DECLARATIVE-4_4_2))
  (PROP-CONTENT
   ((SENT-2_4_2
     (SUBJ ((NP-1_4_2 (NAME (JOHN-1_4_2)))))
     (VERB (DRINK-2_4_2))
     (DIR-OBJ ((NP-3_4_2 (REF (MASS-NOUN-3_4_2))
                          (NOUN ((BEER-3_4_2)))))))))))
```

In this derivation, the singular noun *beer* is added directly by the rule FVERB+MAIN. This triggers the frame-theoretic analysis of the noun phrase as a MASS-NOUN. According to this analysis, the mass noun property is a kind of use which can be chosen for any noun. It is sometimes difficult to find a natural mass noun interpretation. This is not a syntactic phenomenon, but due to properties of the objects referred to by the nouns.

Next, consider the distinction between plural count nouns and bare plurals. In LA-grammar, both uses of a plural noun like *beers* are based on a single lexical analysis (P-H), i.e., as a plural noun (P) denoting a non-human entity (-H). Again, the count/bare-plural noun distinction is reduced to different combinatorics. Count nouns take a determiner, while bare plurals are defined by the fact that they (i) are plural and (ii) do not take a determiner.

10.5.5 *BEERS* as a Plural Count Noun

```
* (z John likes these beers \.)

*** Lex Lookup
```

```
Real time:     0.00 s
Run time:      0.00 s

*** Parse Timings
Real time:     1.06 s
Run time:    ` 1.00 s

    Linear Analysis:

    *START_0
    1
        (NH) JOHN
        (S3 SC V) LIKES
    *NOM+FVERB_3
    2
        (SC V) JOHN LIKES
        (PQ) THESE
    *FVERB+MAIN_4
    3
        (PQ V) JOHN LIKES THESE
        (P-H) BEERS
    *DET+NOUN_2
    4
        (V) JOHN LIKES THESE BEERS
        (V DECL) .
    *CMPLT_13
    5
        (DECL) JOHN LIKES THESE BEERS .

Hierarchical Analysis:

(PROPOSITION-5_7_3
 (MOOD (DECLARATIVE-5_7_3))
 (PROP-CONTENT
  ((SENT-2_7_3
    (SUBJ ((NP-1_7_3 (NAME (JOHN-1_7_3)))))
    (VERB (LIKE-2_7_3))
    (DIR-OBJ
     ((NP-3_7_3 (REF (THESE-3_7_3 PL-4_7_3))
                (NOUN ((BEER-4_7_3)))))))))))
```

This derivation resembles 10.5.3 in that the article *these* is added by the rule FVERB+MAIN, and the plural noun *beers* by the rule DET+NOUN. Again, the grammatical number PL-4 is determined from the category (P-H) of the noun and added under the determiner node REF.

10.5.6 *BEERS* as a Bare Plural

```
* (z John likes beers \.)

*** Lex Lookup
Real time:     0.00 s
Run time:      0.00 s

*** Parse Timings
Real time:     0.66 s
```

```
Run time:      0.66 s

    Linear Analysis:

    *START_0
    1
        (NH)  JOHN
        (S3 SC V)  LIKES
    *NOM+FVERB_3
    2
        (SC V)  JOHN LIKES
        (P-H)  BEERS
    *FVERB+MAIN_4
    3
        (V)  JOHN LIKES BEERS
        (V DECL)  .
    *CMPLT_13
    4
        (DECL)  JOHN LIKES BEERS .

Hierarchical Analysis:

(PROPOSITION-4_4_4
 (MOOD (DECLARATIVE-4_4_4))
 (PROP-CONTENT
  ((SENT-2_4_4
    (SUBJ ((NP-1_4_4 (NAME (JOHN-1_4_4)))))
    (VERB (LIKE-2_4_4))
    (DIR-OBJ ((NP-3_4_4 (REF (BARE-PLURAL-3_4_4))
                        (NOUN ((BEER-3_4_4)))))))))))
```

In this derivation, the plural noun *beers* is added directly by the rule FVERB+MAIN, which triggers the frame-theoretic analysis of the noun phrase as a BARE-PLURAL.

The analyses 10.5.3 through 10.5.6 are completely unambiguous. Thus, a combinatorially-based analysis as in 10.5.3 through 10.5.6 does not amount to changing a lexical ambiguity into a syntactic one, but results in the absence of ambiguity. This technique not only offers computational efficiency, but makes sense also linguistically. It explains a frequent construction of English in terms of **economy** (i.e., the use of the same word in different constructions for different purposes).

Positing large-scale lexical ambiguities in the linguistic analysis of natural language amounts to saying that natural language creates needless confusion. This is a self-defeating viewpoint for a linguist. Given that natural languages evolved—and continue to evolve—naturally, the linguistic analysis should proceed on the assumption that the structures found in natural language are the "fittest", i.e., they strike a natural balance between economy, redundancy (for safeguarding the message), and expressiveness.

LA-grammars for natural language systematically use the technique of avoiding lexical ambiguity by making use of alternative syntactic combinatorics. For example, the use of the preposition *by* in agent phrases and in postnominal/adverbial phrases is based on an unambiguous lexical analysis (cf. the four different readings of example

10.4.2). This is also the case with *to*, which may be used as a preposition (cf. 10.4.2), and as a subordinating conjunction to indicate the beginning of an infinitive phrase (cf. 8.4.8 and B.3.1). There is no lexical ambiguity; both constructions are instances of alternative uses of the same word in different constructions for different purposes.

In summary, we found the following three cases of potential lexical ambiguity in natural language:

1. genuine non-local lexical ambiguity based on instances of morphological decay or other isolated, historically founded cases of homonymy (cf. 10.5.1).

2. genuine lexical ambiguity which is local because the diverse categorization of the different readings ensures immediate disambiguation (cf. 10.5.2).

3. lexical ambiguities which are spurious because the phenomenon is really an instance of different syntactic uses of a word or a word class in different constructions (cf. 10.5.3 through 10.5.6).

Based on the linguistic study of agreement morphology and syntactic combinatorics, systematic lexical ambiguities may be avoided in the analysis of natural language. Thus, there is no complexity theoretic necessity for lexical packing in natural language parsing. Furthermore, while it is theoretically possible to combine LA-packing and the technique of semantic doubling, it is a non-trivial implementation task. Therefore, LA-packing is not implemented for lexically ambiguous grammars of natural language.

But for theoretical reasons, we are interested in systematic lexical ambiguities of *formal* languages. Consider, for example, the definition of LOGCAT, a left-associative grammar for propositional calculus with semantic interpretation. The lexical ambiguity arises because the categories of propositions are defined as their truth-value. We distinguish propositions like $p1$ and $p0$, which have definite truth-values (namely 1 and 0 respectively), from propositional variables like p, which can have either 1 or 0 as their categories. Only the latter kind of propositions introduce ambiguities.

10.5.7 The Definition of LOGCAT

LX $=_{def}$ {[p1, (1)], [p0, (0)], [p, (1)], [p, (0)], [[(L)], [] (R)],
        [not (NEG)], [and (CON)], [or (DIS)], [impl (IMP)], [= (EQ)]}
ST$_S$ $=_{def}$ {[[{r-1}(L)]]}
r-1: [(X L)(seg1)] $\Rightarrow$ [{r-1, r-2, r-3} (X L seg1)]
    where seg1 ε {0, 1, L, NEG}.
r-2: [(X seg1)(seg2)] $\Rightarrow$ [{r-3} (X seg1 seg2)]
    where seg1 ε {0, 1} and seg2 ε {CON, DIS, IMP, EQ}
r-3: [(X seg1)(seg2)] $\Rightarrow$ [{r-1, r-4, r-5} (X seg1 seg2)]
    where seg1 ε {CON, DIS, IMP, EQ, NEG} and seg2 ε {0, 1, L}
r-4: [(X L seg1 seg2 seg3)(R)] $\Rightarrow$ [{r-2, r-4, r-5} (X seg4)]

where seg1,seg3 ε $\{0, 1\}$, seg2 ε $\{$CON, DIS, IMP, EQ$\}$ and
    if seg2 = CON, then seg4 = 1 iff seg1 = 1 and seg3 = 1,
    if seg2 = DIS, then seg4 = 0 iff seg1 = 0 and seg3 = 0,
    if seg2 = IMP, then seg4 = 0 iff seg1 = 1 and seg3 = 0, and
    if seg2 = EQ, then seg4 = 1 iff seg1 = seg3.
r-5: [(X L NEG seg1)(R)] $\Rightarrow$ [$\{$r-2, r-4, r-5$\}$ (X seg2)]
    where seg-1, seg-2 ε $\{0, 1\}$ and iff seg1 = 1, then seg2 = 0.
$ST_F =_{def}$ $\{$[rp-4 (0)], [rp-4 (1)], [rp-5 (0)], [rp-5 (1)]$\}$

LOGCAT differs from 3SAT defined in 7.5.1 in that LOGCAT permits left-branching structures like [((*p and q*) *or p*) *and* (*not q*)] and right-branching structures like [*p and* (*q or* (*p and* (*not q*)))], while 3SAT allows only "flat" structures in the normal form ([*x or y or z*] *and* [*x or not y or z*] *and* ...). LOGCAT is a more general formulation of propositional calculus; it permits the derivation of asymmetric hierarchies which exhibit different complexity and LA-packing behavior in ambiguous formulas.

In unambiguous formulas different bracketing structures result in identical timings. For example, both ((*p and q*) *impl r*)) and (*p and* (*q impl r*)) parse in equal time, provided both formulas are unambiguous. This observation corresponds to the fact that for lexically unambiguous formulas LOGCAT is a single continuation grammar which parses all input in linear time, irrespective of its structure.

However, in LOGCAT derivations with ambiguous proposition variables we observe that left-branching formulas like (((*p and q*) *or r*) *and s*) parse consistently a little faster than right-branching formulas of equal length, e.g., (*p and* (*q or* (*r and s*))). The reason is that the left-branching structure has an initial sequence of left-parentheses, which is derived as a single reading, while the right-branching structure has a final sequence of right parentheses, which is derived with the maximal number of readings.

Next consider the LA-packed parse behavior of LOGCAT. It turns out that systematically ambiguous left-branching formulas like (((*p and q*) *impl r*) *or s*) LA-packed parse in linear time, while right branching formulas like (*p and* (*q impl* (*r or s*))) LA-packed parse in exponential time. This is because the grammar defined in 10.5.7 doesn't evaluate a partial formula like (*p and* (. Instead it waits until all the embedded formulas have been evaluated.

As an example consider 10.5.8, which represents the first reading of a derivation in non-packed format. For reasons of generality, we assume unrestricted value assignment to the propositional variables. That is, different occurrences of the same variable may have different truth values.

10.5.8 A Right Branching LOGCAT Derivation

```
*  (z [ p and [ q and [ p and q ] ] ])

16     *START-0
   1
```

```
    (L)  [
    (O)  P
 *RULE-1
 2
    (L 0)  [ P
    (CON)· AND
 *RULE-2
 3
    (L 0 CON)  [ P AND
    (L)  [
 *RULE-3
 4
    (L 0 CON·L)  [ P AND [
    (0)  Q
 *RULE-1
 5
    (L 0 CON L 0)  [ P AND [ Q
    (CON)  AND
 *RULE-2
 6
    (L 0 CON L 0 CON)  [ P AND [ Q AND
    (L)  [
 *RULE-3
 7
    (L 0 CON L 0 CON L)  [ P AND [ Q AND [
    (0)  P
 *RULE-1
 8
    (L 0 CON L 0 CON L 0)  [ P AND [ Q AND [ P
    (CON)  AND
 *RULE-2
 9
    (L 0 CON L 0 CON L 0 CON)  [ P AND [ Q AND [ P AND
    (0)  Q
 *RULE-3
 10
    (L 0 CON L 0 CON L 0 CON 0)  [ P AND [ Q AND [ P AND Q
    (R)  ]
 *RULE-4
 11
    (L 0 CON L 0 CON 0)  [ P AND [ Q AND [ P AND Q ]
    (R)  ]
 *RULE-4
 12
    (L 0 CON 0)  [ P AND [ Q AND [ P AND Q ] ]
    (R)  ]
 *RULE-4
 13
    (0)  [ P AND [ Q AND [ P AND Q ] ] ]
```

The categories in 10.5.8 not only grow longer until the right parentheses appear, they are also different in the different readings, because they code the different value assignments. Since these long, different categories represent different states, the LOGCAT analyses of right-branching structures cannot be LA-packed. Even though LOGCAT is descriptively adequate, it fails to sufficiently utilize the linear structure of the formulas.

What should be concluded from this observations? Is the asymmetric LA-packing behavior of left-branching and right-branching structures in LOGCAT a general property of LA-grammar, or is it just that LOGCAT is not well designed for the purpose of LA-packed parsing? As a first clue consider how Earley's algorithm can packed parse a systematically ambiguous right-branching formula in n^3: The Earley algorithm fuses different readings of a right-branching structure like $[p \ and \ [$ by interpreting the grammar rules as top-down predictions on the possible values of the embedded formula.

This simultaneous top-down and bottom-up analysis characteristic of the Earley algorithm can be simulated in LA-grammar. We simply introduce "loaded left parentheses" ([(L1)) and ([(L0)). The first reading of '[' with the category L1 assumes that the embedded formula is true, while the second reading with the category L0 assumes that the embedded formula is false. Thus, the initial part of a right-branching formula, e.g., $[p \ and \ [$ has the following analyses.

10.5.9 * (z [p and [)

```
4     *START-0
    1
         (L)  [
         (0)  P
    *RULE-1
    2
         (L 0)  [ P
         (CON)  AND
    *RULE-2
    3
         (L 0 CON)  [ P AND
         (L0)  [
    *RULE-3
    4
         (L0 L0)  [ P AND [


3     *START-0
    1
         (L)  [
         (0)  P
    *RULE-1
    2
         (L 0)  [ P
         (CON)  AND
    *RULE-2
    3
         (L 0 CON)  [ P AND
         (L1)  [
    *RULE-3
    4
         (L0 L1)  [ P AND [


2     *START-0
```

```
1
    (L) [
    (1) P
*RULE-1
2
    (L 1) · [ P
    (CON) AND
*RULE-2
3
    (L 1 CON) [ P AND
    (L0) [
*RULE-3
4
    (L0 L0) [ P AND [


1    *START-0
1
    (L) [
    (1) P
*RULE-1
2
    (L 1) [ P ·
    (CON) AND
*RULE-2
3
    (L 1 CON) [ P AND
    (L1) [
*RULE-3
4
    (L1 L1) [ P AND [
```

The derivation in 10.5.9 exhibits a technique called **anticipating split**, which is widely used in LA-grammar. For example, the garden path sentence analyzed in 3.4.4 and 3.4.5, as well as the unbounded dependencies in B.4.1 use anticipating splits. Anticipating splits are a general method for avoiding back-tracking in favor of a complete computation of possible continuations with subsequent disambiguation. The derivation in 10.5.9 produces twice as many readings as the corresponding LOGCAT derivation, but the overall behavior of this new LA-grammar of interpreted propositional calculus, called NEWLOG, is much more efficient in LA-packed parsing than LOGCAT, which doesn't use anticipating splits.

NEWLOG LA-packed parses both left-branching and right-branching formulas with an exponential number of readings in linear time. Even though the categories grow in length (because the number of left parentheses must be coded to insure proper match with right parentheses), the formulas can be systematically LA-packed because each formula has at most two loaded left parentheses (all other left parentheses are of category "L"). Consider the first reading of a right- and left-branching formula of propositional calculus (in non-packed format).

10.5.10 A Right- and Left-Branching NEWLOG Derivation

```
(z [ p and [ q or [ [ [ p impl q ] and q ] = [ not p ] ] ] ])
```

```
64    *START-0
      1
         (L)  [
         (0)  P
      *RULE-1
      2
         (L 0)  [ P
         (CON)  AND
      *RULE-2
      3
         (L 0 CON)  [ P AND
         (L0)  [
      *RULE-3
      4
         (L0 L0)  [ P AND [
         (0)  Q
      *RULE-1
      5
         (L0 L0 0)  [ P AND [ Q
         (DIS)  OR
      *RULE-2
      6
         (L0 L0 0 DIS)  [ P AND [ Q OR
         (L0)  [
      *RULE-3
      7
         (L0 L L0)  [ P AND [ Q OR [
         (L)  [
      *RULE-1
      8
         (L0 L L0 L)  [ P AND [ Q OR [ [
         (L)  [
      *RULE-1
      9
         (L0 L L0 L L)  [ P AND [ Q OR [ [ [
         (0)  P
      *RULE-1
      10
         (L0 L L0 L L 0)  [ P AND [ Q OR [ [ [ P
         (IMP)  IMPL
      *RULE-2
      11
         (L0 L L0 L L 0 IMP)  [ P AND [ Q OR [ [ [ P IMPL
         (0)  Q
      *RULE-3
      12
         (L0 L L0 L L 1)  [ P AND [ Q OR [ [ [ P IMPL Q
         (R)  ]
      *RULE-4
      13
         (L0 L L0 L 1)  [ P AND [ Q OR [ [ [ P IMPL Q ]
         (CON)  AND
      *RULE-2
      14
         (L0 L L0 L 1 CON)  [ P AND [ Q OR [ [ [ P IMPL Q ] AND
         (0)  Q
```

```
*RULE-3
15
   (L0 L L0 L 0) [ P AND [ Q OR [ [ [ P IMPL Q ] AND Q
   (R) ]
*RULE-4
16
   (L0 L L0 0) [ P AND [ Q OR [ [ [ P IMPL Q ] AND Q ]
   (EQ) =
*RULE-2
17
   (L0 L L0 0 EQ) [ P AND [ Q OR [ [ [ P IMPL Q ] AND Q ] =
   (L1) [
*RULE-3
18
   (L0 L L L1) [ P AND [ Q OR [ [ [ P IMPL Q ] AND Q ] = [
   (NEG) NOT
 *RULE-5
19
   (L0 L L L1 NEG) [ P AND [ Q OR [ [ [ P IMPL Q ] AND Q ] = [ NOT
   (0) P
*RULE-6
20
   (L0 L L L1 1) [ P AND [ Q OR [ [ [ P IMPL Q ] AND Q ] = [ NOT P
   (R) ]
*RULE-7
21
   (L0 L L) [ P AND [ Q OR [ [ [ P IMPL Q ] AND Q ] = [ NOT P ]
   (R) ]
*RULE-4
22
   (L0 L) [ P AND [ Q OR [ [ [ P IMPL Q ] AND Q ] = [ NOT P ] ]
   (R) ]
*RULE-4
23
   (L0) [ P AND [ Q OR [ [ [ P IMPL Q ] AND Q ] = [ NOT P ] ] ]
   (R) ]
*RULE-4
24
   (0) [ P AND [ Q OR [ [ [ P IMPL Q ] AND Q ] = [ NOT P ] ] ] ]
```

NEWLOG is defined as follows:

10.5.11 The Definition of NEWLOG

$LX =_{def}$ {[p1, (1)], [p0, (0)], [p, (1)], [p, (0)], [[(L)], [[(L1)], [[(L0)],
        [ ] (R)], [not (NEG)], [and (CON)], [or (DIS)], [impl (IMP)], [= (EQ)]}

$ST_S =_{def}$ {[[{r-1}(L)]]}

r-1: [(X seg1)(seg2)] $\Rightarrow$ [{r-1, r-2, r-3, r-5, r-6} (X seg1 seg2)]
    where seg1 ε {L, L1, L0}, seg2 ε {0, 1, L, neg}, and
    if seg1 ε {L1, L0} and X $\neq \emptyset$, then seg2 ε {0, 1, L}

r-2: [(X seg0 seg1)(seg2)] $\Rightarrow$ [{r-3} (X seg0 seg1 seg2)] where seg0 ε {L, L0, L1}, seg1 ε {0, 1}, and seg2 ε {CON, DIS, IMP, EQ}

r-3: [(X seg0 seg1 seg2 seg3)(seg4)] $\Rightarrow$ [{r-1, r-4, r-5} (X seg5 seg6 seg7)]
   where seg3 ε {CON, DIS, IMP, EQ}, seg4 ε {0, 1, L1, L0}, and
   if seg3 = CON, then
      if seg1 = L1, then seg2 = 1 and seg4 ε {1, L1}, and val = 1;
      if seg1 = L0, then seg2 = 0 or seg4 ε {0, L0}, and val = 0;
      if seg1 = L,
         if seg2 = 1 and seg4 ε {1, L1}, then val = 1, else val = 0;
   if seg3 = DIS, then
      if seg1 = L0, then seg2 = 0 and seg4 ε {0, L0}, and val = 0;
      if seg1 = L1, then seg2 = 1 or seg4 ε {1, L1}, and val = 1;
      if seg1 = L,
         if seg2 = 0 and seg4 ε {0, L0}, then val = 0, else val = 1;
   if seg3 = IMP,
      if seg1 = L0, then seg2 = 1 and seg4 ε {0, L0}, and val = 0;
      if seg1 = L1, then seg2 = 0 or seg4 ε {1, L1}, and val = 1;
      if seg1 = L,
         if seg2 = 0 or seg4 ε {1, L1}, then val = 1, else val = 0;
   if seg3 = EQ,
      if seg1 = L1, then seg2 = 1 and seg4 ε {1, L1},
         or seg2 = 0 and seg4 ε {0, L0}, and val = 1;
      if seg1 = L0, then seg2 = 0 and seg4 ε {1, L1},
         or seg2 = 1 and seg4 ε {0, L0}, and val = 0;
      if seg1 = L and seg2 = 1, seg4 ε {1, L1},
         or seg2 = 0, seg4 ε {0, L0}, then val = 1, else val = 0;
   if seg4 ε {L1, L0},
      if seg1 ε {L1, L0}, then seg6 = seg4, and
         if seg0 ε {L1, L0}, seg5 = L, else seg5 = seg0,
      if seg1 = L,
         if val = 1, then seg5 = L1, and seg 6 = seg7 = ϵ.
         if val = 0, then seg5 = L0, and seg 6 = seg7 = ϵ.
   if seg4 ε {1, 0}, seg5 = seg0, seg6 = val, and seg7 = ϵ.

r-4: [(X seg1 seg2)(R)] $\Rightarrow$ [{r-2, r-4, r-5} (X seg3)]
   where if seg2 ε {0, 1}, then seg1 ε {L, L1, L0}, 1else seg2 ε {L, L1, L0};
      if seg2 = 1, then seg3 = 1,
      if seg2 = 0, then seg3 = 0,
      if seg2 ε {L1, L0, L},
         if seg1 $\neq \emptyset$ then if seg2 = L1, seg3 = 1, else seg3 = 0
      else seg3 = seg1

r-5: [(X seg1)(NEG)] ⇒ [{r-6} (X seg1 NEG)]
    where seg-1 ε {L, L0, L1}.

r-6: [(X seg1 NEG)(seg2)] ⇒ [{r-7} (X seg3)]
    where seg-2 ε {1, 0, L1, L0}, and
        if seg-2 = 1, then seg3 = 0,
        if seg-2 = 0, then seg3 = 1,
        if seg-2 = L1, then seg3 = L0,
        if seg-2 = L0, then seg3 = L1.

r-7: [(X seg1 seg2)(R)] ⇒ [{r-2, r-4, r-5} (X seg3)]
    if seg-1 = L1, then seg2 = 1 and seg3 = ε,
    if seg-1 = L0, then seg2 = 0, and seg3 = ε,
    if seg-1 = L, then
        if seg2 = 1, seg3 = 0,
        if seg2 = 0, seg3 = 1.

$ST_F =_{def}$ {[rp-4 (0)], [rp-4 (1)]}

In NEWLOG, the simulation of a top-down analysis by means of anticipating splits is used only for right-branching structures with systematic lexical ambiguities.

In the case of the language of propositional calculus, the transition from LOGCAT to NEWLOG is merely an exercise, motivated by the desire to achieve the same linear LA-packing behavior for left- and right-branching formulas. Since propositional calculus is an artificial language, this exercise taught us noting about the linear coding method of natural languages; it only illustrated the powerful coding possibilities of LA-grammar. The analogous procedure in the analysis of a natural language, however, would not only result in a more efficient grammar, but would help to explain the structures of natural language in terms of their characteristic linear coding.

The structure of propositional calculus is such that a right-associative analysis, parsing from right to left, would be no less efficient than a left-associative analysis. The reason is that propositional calculus did not evolve naturally in time-linear speech, but was designed to directly reflect a logical hierarchy. In natural language analysis, on the other hand, a right-associative grammar would fail to utilize any of the structural support of a naturally evolved syntax.

Because right-associative grammar, like left-associative grammar, is input-output compatible with parsers and generators, a well-designed right-associative analysis of a natural language fragment would presumably still be more efficient than traditional parsers based on constituent structure. But unlike a left-associative grammar, a right-associative grammar is not input-output compatible with the speaker-hearer; thus, it would fail to explain the structures of natural language in terms of their use, and remain a *par force* exercise, doomed to fail in the long run to achieve a complete and transparent description of natural language.

10.5.12 Theorem 14

For any lexically ambiguous C-language there exists a C-LAG which LA-packed parses it in linear time.

Proof: In the case of the non-systematic lexical ambiguities one may choose a linguistic analysis which ensures linear parsing (cf. 10.5.1—10.5.6). Systematic lexical ambiguities, on the other hand, LA-packed parse in linear time if the structure of the language is either flat (as in the normal-form propositional calculus 3SAT) or left-branching. In the case of right-branching structures with systematic lexical ambiguity, finally, a top-down analysis may be simulated systematically in terms of anticipating splits such that the derivations are suitable for linear LA-packing.

$$Q.E.D.$$

In summary, for unambiguous C-LAGs our complexity result (Theorem 12, 10.1.2) is better than any existing general purpose parser, e.g., the Earley algorithm or the CYK parser, because (i) unambiguous C-LAGs are parsed in linear time, (ii) the complexity is independent of the size of the grammar, and (iii) the class of C-languages is much larger than the class of context-free languages. For ambiguous C-LAGs, on the other hand, our result differs from conventional general purpose parsers: while Earley's algorithm will packed parse any grammar in the context-free format in $|G|^2 \cdot n^3$, ambiguous C-grammars can be of arbitrary complexity; but we know for any C-language that there **exists** a C-LAG (Theorem 11, 9.5.11) which will parse it in n^2 (Theorem 13, 10.4.1), or LA-packed parse it in linear time (Theorem 14, 10.5.12).

The result for ambiguous C-LAGs is in agreement with a research philosophy according to which a computationally efficient formulation of the grammar is an important part of the linguistic analysis. Complexity considerations (based on a time-linear derivation order) are regarded as essential for arriving at descriptions which are not only preferable from an efficiency viewpoint, but are actually better as linguistic analyses.

Instead of writing grammars which are motivated solely by the comparatively recent tradition of phrase/constituent-structure analysis, and then looking for parsers which will parse them as fast as possible, LA-grammars are written to make the best of a psychologically well-motivated derivation order. In natural language analysis, complexity considerations lead directly to a better understanding of why natural languages have their characteristic morphology and word order. Such an analysis of natural language, however, is meaningful only if it is based on the actual derivation order of language use.

Part III

Logic and Communication

11. Principles of Pragmatics

After the formal definition of LA-grammar as a syntactic rule system in Part II, we return now to the topic briefly touched upon in Section 2.2 and Chapter 5, namely the functioning of natural language in communication. A theory of communication is especially important for our theory of grammar, because we explain the structure of natural language solely by the function of the signs in communication, and without any recourse to structures which are supposed to be "innate" and/or "universal."

Describing the structure of natural-language signs, and explaining how these signs are used to transmit information, are different tasks. But there is clearly a connection between these two aspects of analysis, because the structure of the sign must be suitable for use, and the functioning of the use must be explained in part by the structure of the sign.

The general theory of pragmatics (or language use) developed in the present chapter is based on the assumption that the central task of pragmatics is the correct positioning of the sign relative to the interpretation context. The primary fix-point of this positioning procedure is the Space-Time-Agent-Recipient point of origin of the sign, or STAR-point for short. A secondary positioning is based on the linear structure of natural-language signs.

Section 11.1 gives a conceptual analysis of the reference mechanisms underlying the use of *symbols*, *icons*, and *indices*. Section 11.2 presents the First Principle of Pragmatics, and explains how the theory of literal meaning and its use differs from the theory of Grice. Section 11.3 uses a postcard to illustrate the principles of reference by examining of the correct positioning of each word in relation to the interpretation context. Section 11.4 applies this theory of pragmatics to different types of signs. Section 11.5, finally, explains the principles of non-literal use.

11.1 Peirce and the Theory of Signs

The most basic topic of a theory of communication is the structure of the different kinds of signs. Building on concepts pioneered by Charles S. Peirce (1839 – 1814),[1] we can distinguish four kinds of referring objects, namely *symbols*, *icons*, *indices*, and *pictures*. Of these, only symbols, icons, and indices are "signs." Furthermore, only symbols, icons, and pictures are "representations." In other words, indices are signs without being representations, pictures are representations without being signs,

---

[1]"The research begun by Peirce has not been followed up and this is a great pity. A better understanding of the complex processes of meaning in language...could be expected...from progress in the analysis of symbols." Beneviste (1971), p. 11.

while symbols and icons are both signs and representations.

11.1.1 Four Kinds of Referring Objects

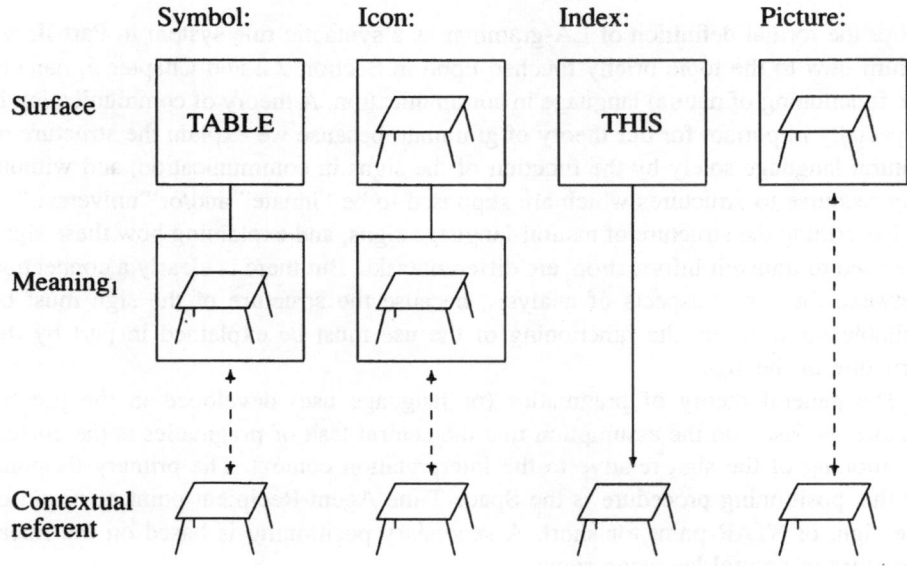

Of the four types of referring objects, two have an intermediate level of literal meaning (henceforth meaning₁), namely symbols and icons, and two have a similarity relation between surface and referent, namely icons and pictures.

Our analysis of symbols, indices and icons differs from Peirce's original definitions: "A symbol is a sign which would lose the character which renders it a sign if there were no interpretant. Such is any utterance of speech which signifies what it does only by virtue of its being understood to have signification." (Peirce (1940), p. 104). In the same vein, an index is defined by Peirce as a sign which would lose the character which renders it a sign as soon as the object it is pointing at is removed. And an icon is defined by Peirce as a sign which retains its character as a sign even if there is no object to refer to, and no interpretant.

In short, Peirce distinguishes between symbols, indices, and icons in terms of whether or not there has to be an interpretant, and whether or not there has to be a referent, in order for the respective types of signs to retain their character. Our definitions, on the other hand, distinguish between types of signs independently of the interpretant and the referent. As indicated in 11.1.2 below, the distinctions are based instead on (i) whether or not there is a similarity between the surface of the sign and its referent, and (ii) whether or not there is an intermediate meaning₁ level.

11.1.2 Surface Iconicity and Underlying Iconicity

	Symbol	Icon	Index	Picture
Similarity between Surface and Referent	−	+	−	+
Intermediate meaning$_1$ level	+	+	−	−

The disadvantage of Peirce's original definitions is the dependence on a referent and an interpretant. Our reinterpretation explains the functioning of different types of signs by means of their internal structure instead. This results in a theory of signs which explains transmission of information on a level of abstraction which is suitable for describing natural-language communication by people as well as computers (robots).

Let us turn now to the use of different signs by the speaker-hearer. We distinguish two types of reference mechanisms. The first is called the **iconic reference mechanism** and is based on a similarity between (a part of) the sign and the referent. This reference mechanism is used by pictures, icons, and symbols, and has the basic function of content transfer. The second reference mechanism is called the **indexical reference mechanism** and has the basic function of positioning the sign relative to the interpretation context. While indexical reference is contained to a large extent in the placement of the sign in time and space, it is controlled further by special words which have little iconic content, but are equipped with characteristic pointers. Such words include the pronouns *here*, *now*, or *he*.[2]

Returning to iconic reference, consider the reference mechanism of a picture. A picture is not a sign but, like a window, a representation of "context." But in contrast to a window looking out on, e.g., the Statue of Liberty, a picture of this statue may be said to "refer" if the viewer recognizes what is depicted and establishes a relationship between the picture and the real thing. This ability to recognize similarity and to establish a relationship between representations of objects and the objects themselves is taken as the basis of iconic reference.[3]

Icons differ from pictures in that they are conventionalized signs which, like symbols, may be used non-literally. The surface of the icon for non-smoking[4] has the literal meaning *no burning cigarette*, but this meaning is used to prohibit any

---

[2]*He* is partly iconic because of the restriction to male gender and because it is singular.

[3]The ability to recognize representations, and to establish a relationship between the representation and what it represents, seems to be limited to the visual and the auditory medium. Something may smell like something else (remind us of an earlier smelling experience), but smells are not used to represent something. Similar considerations hold for the other non-audio-visual sensations.

[4]I.e., the circle, crossed by a diagonal bar, containing a cigarette with a curly line at the tip, representing smoke.

kind of open fire. The prevention of pipe smoking by the literal meaning *no burning cigarette* is an example of a non-literal use of the non-smoking sign. A drawing or photograph of an extinguished cigarette, on the other hand, does not convey speaker meanings in terms of use relative to a context, but is rather a representation of a possible or actual context.[5]

Symbols differ from icons in that the surface of symbols is **demotivated**: the relationship between the symbol surface and the literal meaning is determined by convention (Saussure's "arbitraire de signe"), whereas in an icon the surface and the literal meaning are **isomorphic**. The reference mechanism of symbols and icons is the same, however. Both refer on the basis of a similarity relation between the meaning₁ and the contextual referent.

Symbols originated from icons through a gradual process of demotivation,[6] i.e., simplifying the surface resulted in a clear distinction between the surface and the associated literal meaning. That symbols retain iconic literal meanings can be deduced from the fact that symbols may be used to refer to new referents. Why can we use the word "table" to spontaneously refer to an orange crate, but not to a baseball bat? Because there is a similarity relation between the meaning₁ of *table* and an orange crate, which is absent in the case of a baseball bat.

The literal meanings of symbols and icons are **concepts** which originated via abstraction from sets of internal tokens of referents. The crucial step in the creation of language is the attachment of some of these concepts to signs (surfaces). In the case of icons, the concept itself (or salient parts of the concept) is used as the surface. This is the same as saying that in icons the meaning₁ and the surface are isomorphic.

Indices and pictures have in common that there is no intermediate meaning₁ level. But while pictures refer iconically via their surface, indices refer indexically via their characteristic pointer. For example, the pronoun *I* has a characteristic pointer which refers to the speaker, while the pronoun *you* has a characteristic pointer referring to the intended recipient. Similar pointers may be described for pronouns like *here*, *now*, etc.

A common characteristic of indices and symbols is that there is no similarity between their surface and their referents. But while indices can refer to any kind of object as long as the object is in "pointing reach," a symbol can only refer to

---

[5]The fact that a photograph of an extinguished cigarette positioned in, e.g., the waiting room of a hospital, may be interpreted iconically supports our view of a gradual transition from pictures to icons.

[6]"Prototypical *icon* and *symbol* are two extreme points on a scale that represents *degrees of abstraction* or *generalization*." Givon (1985), p. 192. Please note that Givon's historical derivation of the letter 'A' from "the pictorial representation of the Hebrew '*lf*—'bull', 'cattle' " (op. cit., pp. 193 – 5) differs from our correlation of symbols and icons insofar as in the case of the letter 'A' the abstraction process does not retain the original meaning. Thus, Givon's example does not illustrate a demotivation of the relation between an iconic meaning and its isomorphic (iconic) surface, but changes of a surface with concomitant loss of the original meaning.

objects compatible with the symbol's meaning$_1$.

The literal meaning of symbols is defined in a **minimal** way. Consider for example the term "Trahtenbrot theorem." The literal meaning of this term is simply "theorem related to Trahtenbrot," where "Trahtenbrot" is paraphrased as "person with the name Trahtenbrot," and "theorem" as "proposition that is not self-evident but that can be proved from accepted premises." From a technical point of view, we may assume that these paraphrases are implemented as frames, whereby the notions of the paraphrases are defined by their position in systematic semantic hierarchies (is-a hierarchy, has-parts hierarchy, is-part-of hierarchy). The definition of meaning in these hierarchies is not circular, because elementary meanings are defined outside the hierarchies, in terms of elementary perceptions, experiences, episodes, etc.

The point is that the biography of the person named Trahtenbrot or the mathematical content of the theorem in question is **not** part of the literal meaning of the term "Trahtenbrot theorem." What the term "means" for different people beyond its literal meaning is entirely a matter of the content of their respective context files.

11.2   Meaning, Use, and Grice's Intentions

Our basic approach to literal meaning and its use is summarized in the following principle:[7]

11.2.1 The First Principle of Pragmatics

$$\text{Use of} \boxed{\begin{array}{c}\text{surface}\\\text{meaning}_1\end{array}} \text{relative to a context} = \text{meaning}_2$$

Consider the notions used in 11.2.1. The context is defined as a representation of what the speaker-hearer perceives and believes at the time of the interpretation of the utterance (or a relevant subset thereof). A context may be formally constructed in a model-theoretic manner or as a database. The construction of the context is a speaker-hearer internal procedure.

The meaning$_1$ of an expression is defined as a representation of the literal meaning of the surface expression.[8] Like the context, a meaning$_1$ may be formally constructed as a minimal set-theoretic model or a minimal database. However, in order to facilitate the speaker-hearer internal matching procedure of meaning$_1$ and context, both structures should be defined on the basis of the same formalism.

---

[7]First proposed in Hausser (1978). For further discussion see Hausser (1979b,c, 1981, 1983, 1984b).

[8]The meaning$_1$ of a symbol is an iconic representation, the meaning$_1$ of an index is a characteristic pointer, and the meaning$_1$ of a complex natural language sign is a complex structure consisting of icons and pointers.

The assumption that the world around us is "full of meanings" is as widespread as it is false. Living beings recognize their environment by means of their perceptive capabilities and their ability to interpret this input on the basis of **concepts**. Thus, meanings are concepts in the interpreting agent, not properties of the surrounding environment.

Grice (1957) presents spots on the skin, as referred to in the sentence *These spots mean measles* as an example of "natural meaning." Grice's spots may be 'a sign of measles', but they are not a sign in the strict sense because they are not part of a language. And the spots may 'mean measles', but they are neither the literal meaning of a sign, nor the speaker meaning of an utterance. A completely different matter is the **sentence** *These spots mean measles*. This is a sign and has a meaning. We note in particular that the verb *to mean* can be used metaphorically in the sense of *to be caused by*.

As an example of "non-natural meaning," Grice presents the ring of a bell which is used conventionally to indicate *The bus is full*. But this example is misleading. The bus bell is not really a sign of a language, but a **signal**, like a red lamp indicating low oil pressure. One problem with signals which the speech community has in its "repertoire" is that signals cannot be freely combined, because they do not constitute a general purpose language. Instead, each signal is part of a closed system. While the symbols of a language refer via their (iconic) literal meanings to an open range of objects, signals do not really refer, but are a fixed part of their respective system.

Our notions of the literal meaning of an expression (meaning$_1$) and of the speaker meaning of an utterance (meaning$_2$) in 11.2.1 differ substantially from the similar notions used by Grice (1957, 1968). Grice proposes an "intentional account" based on the following definition.

11.2.2 Grice's Intentional Meaning Definition

Definiendum: U meant something by uttering x.

Definiens: For some audience a, U intends his utterance of x to produce in A some effect (response) E, by means of A's recognition of that intention.

While our theory takes an iconically- and indexically-defined literal meaning of sentences as basic, and while it defines the utterance meaning as the use of the literal meaning, Grice goes in the opposite direction. He takes the utterance meaning as basic, and defines sentence meaning as conventionalized use. According to Grice, the meaning of an utterance like *I know the way* is a **token** of the sentence meaning *I know the way*, defined as a **type**. The distinction between utterance meaning and sentence meaning is intended to explain the ontogenesis of sentence meanings (types) from utterance meanings (tokens).[9]

---

[9]The type-token distinction was introduced by Peirce.

Once sentence meanings are conventionally established, the hearer is able to discern the speaker's intention because the speaker "habitually" intends his utterance to have a certain effect. But in order to establish the type, the tokens have to work before the type is established. How can this transition from "speaker meaning" to "utterance meaning" to "sentence meaning" be accomplished initially?

Imagine a group of cavemen without a language, trying to communicate. They may well get simple meanings across, by pointing at things (indexical reference) and by making gestures and noises resembling the characteristic aspects of the referent (iconic reference). But if they were just sitting there, making sounds and expecting their communication partner to recognize their intention, they would fail to make themselves understood.[10]

The basic problem of a meaning definition based on intentions is that it requires the prior establishment of social conventions (i.e., sentence types). In contrast, a meaning definition based on indices and icons does not require a prior establishment of social conventions, but depends solely on the individual's ability to follow pointing gestures and to recognize similarities.[11]

Therefore, indexically- and iconically-defined literal meanings of signs are better suited to explain the interpretation of language than an undefined notion of speaker intentions. Rather than using intentions as the founding notion of the meaning definition, our approach assumes that the intentions of the speaker may be **deduced** from the literal meaning of the sign and its relationship to the utterance context.

Because utterance tokens are defined by Grice as instances of a particular sentence type, it is clear that this notion of utterance meaning does not extend to non-standard (non-literal) uses of a particular sentence type. For non-literal uses Grice (1975) proposes another apparatus, namely the theory of conventional implicatures. The theory of conventional implicatures defines a literal use as "context-independent" and a non-literal use as "context-dependent."

In contrast, our approach takes an indexically- and iconically-defined sentence meaning (meaning$_1$) as basic, and defines the speaker meaning in terms of using the meaning$_1$ relative to a contextual substructure. Thus, literal as well as non-literal uses are context-dependent in our theory.

We do not say "meaning is use," but rather "use of the literal meaning (meaning$_1$) relative to a context is the speaker meaning (meaning$_2$)." The use potential of a sign is not determined by its surface, but by its literal meaning. The literal meaning of symbols is not a convention, but an icon. As shown in Section 11.1, conventions serve only to establish the relation between the symbol surface and its icon.

---

[10]In this connection see the chapter on "Urschöpfung" in Paul (1920), pp. 174 f. "Wir haben gesehen, dass in der Sprache nichts usuell werden kann, was nicht *spontan* von verschiedenen Individuen geschaffen wird." (op. cit., p. 177, emphasis by R.H.)

[11]"In the psychological theory of sign language, two forms of gesture are usually distinguished, the indicative and the imitative" Cassirer (1923), p. 53, quoted from the English translation. The basic distinction between iconic and indexical reference may be traced back at least to Aristotle.

11.3   The Principles of Reference

How does the theory of signs presented in Section 11.1 relate to everyday communication by the speaker-hearer? Let us further explore the pragmatics of natural-language interpretation on the basis of a concrete example.

On a hot day in February, the hearer Heather is sitting on a beach in New Zealand, reading a postcard. The backside shows a photograph of the Statue of Liberty, while the frontside reads as follows (omitting the address):

New York, December 1, 1987

Dear Heather,

Your dog is doing fine. The weather is very cold. In the morning he played in the snow. Then he ate a bone. Right now I am sitting in the kitchen. Fido is here, too. The fuzzball hissed at him again. We miss you.

Love,

Spencer

The postcard is a concrete object, exhibiting signs and a picture. It was mailed in New York (spatial location) on December 1, 1987, (temporal location) by Spencer (agent) to Heather (intended recipient). We call these aspects of the origin of the sign (postcard) its **space-time-agent-recipient point** of origin, or **STAR-point**. Furthermore, let us call the interpretation of a sign at a spatio-temporal location by an agent an **interpretation-STA** of a sign.

Once the sign is sent off, the STAR-point is fixed.[12] The interpretation-STAs, on the other hand, are completely open-ended. If the postcard gets lost in the mail, there is no interpretation-STA at all. But there may also be an unlimited number of interpretation-STAs during the existence of a sign: a sign may be interpreted by anyone coming into contact with it. This fact is exemplified by an unintended audience. Spencer's postcard, for example, was intended for Heather, but was also read by Heather's curious landlady.

All interpreted signs have a STAR-point and an interpretation-STA. In a person talking to himself, STAR-point and interpretation-STA are identical. In oral communication, the temporal location of STAR-point and interpretation-STA are (practically) identical, but spatial location and agents are distinct. In the case of the postcard, the long journey from New York to New Zealand insures that the

---

[12]In oral communication, time and space in the STAR-point are unique contiguous intervals. But the STAR-point of signs may also consist of more than one location and time, such as a letter started on Monday in New York, continued on Tuesday in Washington, and finished on Wednesday in Philadelphia. Furthermore, the agent in a STAR-point may be a set of persons, such as a letter written by a committee, and the intended recipient may be a set of hearers.

spatio-temporal aspects of STAR-point and interpretation-STA of the card are well apart.

The most basic fix-point in the interpretation of natural-language signs is their **STAR-point**. For example, Heather does not protest that the weather is really quite hot, because she knows from the date line that the card originated in New York. We summarize this observation as follows:

11.3.1 The Second Principle of Pragmatics (Global Positioning)

> The primary anchoring (or positioning) of the sign relative to the interpretation context is determined by the STAR-point of the sign.

This principle replaces the model-theoretic practice of interpretation relative to a **neutral** index by an interpretation relative to **origin** of the sign.[13]

Before we turn to the more complicated aspects of reference let us consider the general mechanism of interpretating an isolated sentence. Consider *"The weather is very cold"*. In Spencer's postcard, this is a complex sign without any indexical words or overt reference to the previous text. Heather incorporates the meaning$_1$ representation denoted by the sentence into her context, attaching it to the node "New York on December 1, 1987, as reported by Spencer." This node is located in the general spatio-temporal framework of Heather's episodic context.[14] Note that Heather does not have to be familiar with the precise state of Spencer's context at the time of the card writing. The iconic structure of the meaning$_1$, and the origin of the sign suffice for Heather's correct interpretation. In short, Heather interprets the sentence by filing the meaning$_1$ at her internal representation of the sign's STAR-point.

The STAR-point of a sign provides the outermost fix-point of its pragmatic interpretation. But signs of natural language are usually complex, and we must arrive at a pragmatic interpretation of each of the parts of a complex sign. As an example of a complex sign consider the text on Spencer's card. It consists of a number of sentences, each containing a number of words. The sequence of sentences in the text, and the sequence of words in the sentences constitutes the basic structure of the complex sign.

Just as a change of the sequence of words in a sentence would change the meaning of the sentence, a change of the sequence of sentences would alter the meaning of the text. Permutations of the parts of a sign may result in ill-formed signs with garbled meanings, well-formed signs with non-equivalent meanings, or well-formed

---

[13]See Chapters 12 and 13 for a discussion of model-theoretic semantics. A <-constr,-sense> approach like standard model theory treats meanings as external entities which are regarded as independent of the speaker. If a speaker (hearer) is defined at all, it is only for the purpose of interpreting first (second) person pronouns. A <-constr,-sense> approach does not attempt to base the pragmatic interpretation of signs on their point of origin.

[14]The fix-point of this framework is Heather's "here and now," i.e., what Heather takes to be her spatio-temporal location at each moment.

signs with equivalent meanings. The latter are called paraphrases. A permutation resulting in an equivalent meaning may be regarded as a change of meaning insofar as it constitutes a change in the structure of the meaning.

The speaker is free to sequence the coding of information in any order he likes, as long as the order makes sense in terms of his or her priorities and in terms of the internal structure of the information described. Spencer, for example, chose to depict a sequence of events in a way that mirrors their temporal order: *In the morning he played in the snow. Then he ate a bone.* If we permute the two sentences, there is no sensible interpretation of *then*. Alternatively, Spencer could have chosen to describe the sequence of events as follows: *Fido ate a bone this morning. Before that he played in snow.* The second ordering has the effect of making the event involving the bone more prominent. Again, if we permute the order of the latter pair of sentences, there is no sensible interpretation of *before that*.

The sequencing of words in a sentence is partially restricted by the syntactic structure of the natural language in question, e.g., basic subject-verb-object (SVO) versus basic subject-object-verb (SOV) order. But apart from this, natural languages provide many alternative syntactic means to sequence the signs. Consider for example a temporal sequence of three events E-1, E-2, and E-3. There are six possible orders of E-1, E-2, and E-3. All six orders may be used as surface orders expressing the same temporal sequence E-1 < E-2 < E-3.

1. First E-1. Then E-2. Then E-3.

2. E-1. Then E-3. But between E-1 and E-3, E-2.

3. E-2. Before that, E-1. And after E-2, E-3.

4. E-2. After that E-3. But before E-2, E-1.

5. E-3. Before that E-2. And before that E-1.

6. E-3. Before that E-1. But between E-1 and E-3, E-2.

Of the six possible surface sequences given above, only the first is an example of **syntactic iconicity** in the sense of Givon (1985) and Haiman (1985b), who call natural-language constructions "iconic" if the surface order of the sign reflects a structural aspect of the subject matter depicted.[15]

Note, however, that syntactic iconicity is an optional property of the surface of the sign. This important fact is clearly illustrated by the examples 2 – 6 above, which are do not exhibit syntactic iconicity. Our notion of *meaning icons*, on the other hand, refers not to the surface, but to underlying meaning structures which are attached to the surface of certain signs. Underlying meaning icons are a necessary part of iconically referring signs,—including symbolic (or "non-iconic") signs.

---

[15]According to T. Givon's (1985) *iconicity meta-principle*, "All other things being equal, a coded experience is easier to *store, retrieve* and *communicate* if the code is maximally isomorphic to the experience" (op. cit., p. 189).

Syntactic iconicity can occur only if the matter described has a natural sequential structure. But there are many instances where no sequential structure is present. Consider for example the following two texts.

1. John wants to watch football. But Mary wants to see a movie.

2. Mary wants to see a movie. But John wants to watch football.

Both texts describe the same facts using different surface orders reflecting different speaker viewpoints. Because the facts depicted are not sequential, neither of the texts is iconic in the syntactic sense of Givon (1985) and Haiman (1985b) .

The crucial point in the interpretation of a text is not an occasional instance of syntactic iconicity, but that the text is inherently sequential. The order of sentences in a text must not be disturbed because it codes the structure of the underlying icon. For example, the sequence *But Mary wants to see a movie. John wants to watch football.* is ill-formed, because there is no sensible interpretation of the word *but*.[16]

The syntactic operators *but, then, before, after*, etc., **mediate** between the surface sequence and the inherent structure of the matter (e.g., events) described. The relationship between the chosen surface order and the inherent structure of the matter described motivates the choice of the syntactic operators. Without the linear surface order, the syntactic operators cannot perform their function. Sentences or texts which exhibit syntactic iconicity are a special case of this general sequencing procedure in that they code the complex meaning icon by means of a surface which happens to resemble the sequential structure of the matter described.

The interpretation of syntactic operators is only one concrete instance illustrating that the mechanism of pragmatic interpretation is founded on the **linear sequence** of complex signs.[17] The fundamental role of the inherently linear structure of natural language is demonstrated in general by the fact that the hearer understands the beginning of a sentence without knowing how it is going to be continued, and that the speaker can decide in midstream how to continue a sentence.[18]

Let us summarize these observations as follows:

11.3.2 The Third Principle of Pragmatics (Sign-Internal Sequencing)

In natural language, the pragmatic interpretation of the parts of a complex sign is based on the linear sequence of the parts of the sign.

Note that the interpretation of the parts of a sign, described by the Third Principle, presupposes the Second Principle. The first step of the interpretation is locating

---

[16]These kinds of pragmatic phenomena are called *cohesion* by Halliday and Hasan (1976), and *connectedness* by Van Dijk (1977).

[17]Another concrete example is the interpretation of pronouns on the basis of a "stack structure" in Grosz and Sidner (1986), which makes crucial use of the linear order of the text.

[18]We have shown in Part I that the surface order constitutes the backbone not only of the pragmatic interpretation of natural language, but also of syntactic and semantic analysis.

the STAR-point of the complex sign (Second Principle: global positioning). The next step is concerned with relating each sentence of the text, and each word of a sentence, to the interpretation context. The reference of basic signs depends in part on whether they are symbols or indices. But the local reference of each basic sign must be integrated into an overall interpretation strategy. According to 11.3.2, the basic structure to which all local reference procedures refer is the linear sequence of the complex sign.

Let us turn next to the interpretation of specific words. We begin with a discussion of indexicals, such as the word *here* on Spencer's card. Heather doesn't protest that Fido really isn't *here*, because she knows that this indexical word refers to Spencer's kitchen. This interpretation is more specific than the dateline (New York). It is based on the internal structure of the text on the card, which we view as a sequence of symbol-icons and index-pointers. If the card read *I am sitting in my living room* (rather than the kitchen), the indexical *here* would refer to a different location.

11.3.3 The Fourth Principle of Pragmatics (Indexical Reference)

> Indexical words in a sign perform a secondary anchoring in the interpretation context, which is based on the pointer characteristic of each indexical.

While the Second and Third Principle are concerned with aspects of the pragmatic interpretation of a complex sign, the Fourth Principle deals with the pragmatic interpretation of (one type of) elementary signs. In addition to the characteristic pointer of an indexical, its reference depends on its local position in the sign (Third Principle), and the global position of the sign in terms of the sign's STAR-point (Second Principle). Thus, the Fourth Principle is subordinate to the Third and Second Principle.

The Fourth Principle replaces the handling of indexicals in model theory[19] by a pointing mechanism. For example, the pronoun *I* has a pointer to the speaker. Similarly, the pronoun *you* points at the intended recipient.[20] The interpretation of indexicals depends on (i) the STAR-point of the sign; (ii) the place of the word in the sign (consider, for example, direct speech in a novel or a play); and (iii) the particular pointer characteristic of the indexical in question.

Indexicals do not function primarily as abbreviatory devices, but help to position and anchor the sign relative to the interpretation context. The referent of an indexical follows from the overall positioning of the sign. The task of pragmatics is not to

---

[19]I.e. the "coordinates approach" of Montague (1974), Lewis (1972), and others, which defines different kinds of indexicals in terms of additional parameters. See Section 12.2 for further discussion.

[20]Note that the recipient is distinct from the 'hearer'. Heather's landlady is a 'hearer' when she curiously reads the card to Heather. But the landlady wouldn't protest that she doesn't read dog, because she knows that she is not the intended recipient. In other words, the interpretation of second-person pronouns does **not** depend on the interpretation-STA (which would violate the Second Principle 11.3.1), but solely on the STAR-point.

assign referents to indexicals, but to state the principles and strategies for the correct positioning of signs relative to the interpretation subcontext.

The pointer of an indexical may be modified (and made more specific) (i) by additional iconic meaning properties which are part of the word meaning, and (ii) by words which serve as grammatical arguments. This is exemplified by the expression *your dog* on Spencer's card, which is a composite sign consisting of the indexical *your* and the symbol *dog*. The word *your* has a complex meaning, which may be paraphrased as "object(s) related to intended recipient(s)." In other words, the meaning of *your* consists of (i) an indexical pointer, (ii) an iconic part depicting the "possessor relation" (in a very general sense), and (iii) an open slot (variable) for the noun.[21]

Based on the meaning properties of *your* just described, and the fact that the STAR-point of the sign names her as the intended recipient, Heather is able to deduce that the first two words of the text on the card refer to something related to her. But how does she understand that the object in question is her dog, and not her cat or car? According to our analysis of different types of signs in Section 11.1, the reference mechanism of symbols is based on a matching relation between the literal meaning of the word and a corresponding structure in the internal context.

11.3.4 The Fifth Principle of Pragmatics (Symbolic Reference)

> Symbols refer on the basis of a similarity between their meaning$_1$ icon and the corresponding contextual structures.

The Fifth Principle replaces the handling of reference in model theory[22] by a more general mechanism involving pattern matching. This new method is computationally tractable, and explains why we can use symbols to refer spontaneously to objects seen for the first time.[23]

11.4 Successful Communication

The transmission of information, illustrated in the previous section with the example of a postcard, may be summarized as follows. The act of writing the card almost automatically defines the STAR-point of the resulting sign. The only aspects of the STAR-point decided by Spencer are (i) to produce a sign at all, and (ii) the choice of the intended recipient (e.g., Heather). The content of the card is a complex datastructure depicting certain aspects of Spencer's context. This datastructure is encoded in a linear sequence of symbol-icons and index-pointers.

---

[21] For a detailed analysis of pronouns, covering both their indexical and their anaphoric use, in terms of characteristic pointers called "context-variables," see Hausser (1979a,b), as well as Section 4.5.

[22] I.e. in terms of metalanguage definitions of the model structure (e.g., Montague (1974). See Chapter 12 for a detailed discussion.

[23] This is demonstrated on an elementary level by the color reader described in Section 12.3 below.

The interpretation of the postcard by Heather consists in recreating Spencer's meaning$_1$ representations from the surface of the text, and translating their anchoring in Spencer's context into **corresponding** anchorings in Heather's context. The most basic step of this translation consists in transforming Spencer's automatically given "here and now" into "Spencer's here and now at spatio-temporal location New York, December 1, 1987," as reconstructed by Heather from the STAR-point of the sign. Note that the subject matter of the sign, e.g., Heather's dog Fido, is stored automatically at the right location in Heather's context (i.e., Heather's "Fido-file"), because the interpretation is based on matching the meaning$_1$ of the sign with corresponding structures in the context.

Our theory of pragmatic interpretation is founded on the assumption that every sign has a STAR-point. This assumption differs markedly from model-theoretic approaches to meaning, which take an external representation of mathematical truth as their basic viewpoint, and add speakers and hearers only as an afterthought (by means of additional index parameters). Just as speakers cannot produce a sign without a STAR-point, hearers cannot interpret a sign without a hypothesis about its STAR-point, because without such a hypothesis the hearer cannot relate the meaning$_1$ structure of the sign to a specific location in her or his context.

While every sign has a STAR-point, the STAR-point need not be explicitly encoded in the sign. Furthermore, the interpretation of signs depends on knowledge of the STAR-point in various degrees. In a *Keep off the grass* sign, for example, the spatial aspect of the STAR-point is implicit in the location of the sign: it refers to grass in the sign's general location. The time and agent of the STAR-point, furthermore, are not indicated explicitly or implicitly, and are irrelevant for the interpretation. The intended recipient, finally, is implicit in the location of the sign: it is addressed to anybody standing close enough to read the sign.

Novels, books on mathematics, historical treatises, etc., may be interpreted reasonably accurately without knowledge of their real STAR-point. The authors of such books work hard to formulate their complex signs in such a way that they establish their own internal interpretation space. In "nonpersonal texts" like newspapers and books, the reader ('hearer') may simply use an auxiliary STAR-point, like "that grey book I found on my table," and base any subsequent pragmatic interpretation on the linear structure of the text alone.

Some novels use a fictional STAR-point, e.g., *I was born in the year 1492 in a small village in Yorkshire*. The reader has no trouble distinguishing between the internal structure of the story, and the origin of the sign as a piece of 20th Century fiction. For the enjoyment of the novel, an auxiliary STAR-point, like that "cheap paperback with the gaudy cover recommended by x" is sufficient. But for a deeper understanding, knowledge of the real STAR-point, including the author, intended audience, time, and place are crucial.

A related aspect of pragmatic interpretation is how the hearer views the author of a text. The same information given by different persons may carry quite different weight, depending on how the hearer relates to these persons. Similarly, it is important to know whether a news story appeared in the New York Times, for example, or the National Enquirer. The hearer's evaluation of purpose and trustworthiness of a sign is based on evaluation of the STAR-point agent. Thus, what is considered truth is, in the last analysis, a matter of trust. A similar conclusion may be drawn from Putnam's (1975) infamous "twin earth" example, where the definition of words like *water* is assigned to the "experts" or scientific authorities.

The pragmatic interpretation of a text deals mainly with the correct positioning of the sign relative to the hearer's context, based on the STAR-point of the sign. In more technical terms we view this process of positioning the sign as **activating** a specific substructure of the hearer's context. A meaning$_1$ icon positioned relative to a well-defined contextual substructure can be interpreted by the hearer in two ways: (i) it may be used to relate to objects already existing in the contextual substructure, or (ii) it may be used to incorporate additional objects or relations.

In other words, pragmatic interpretation by the hearer is defined in terms of **unifying** the literal meaning of the sign with the appropriate contextual substructure of the hearer. The speaker, on the other hand, communicates by **extracting** salient features of a subcontext and encoding them into a linear sequence of symbol-icons and index-pointers. Communication is successful if the speaker's process of creating the sign on the basis of extraction and the hearer's process of decoding the sign on the basis of unification result in subcontexts in the speaker and the hearer which are equivalent.

Even though the interpretation of a sign is a complicated process, we should remember that the whole interpretation process is based on only two fundamental reference mechanisms, namely iconic reference (content transfer) and indexical reference (correct positioning). The iconic and the indexical reference mechanism are the basis of the human ability to refer by means of natural language to objects which are not seen by the communicating agents. This ability is known in psychology as **displaced reference**.

Most animals are assumed to be incapable of displaced reference, with the notable exception of bees. How do worker bees tell their colleagues about abundant sources of nectar which may be several hundred meters away from the hive?

The language of the bees[24] consists in two distinct "dances."[25]

1. **round dance**: "If the food is to be found less than 80 meters away [the worker bee] performs a *round dance*, running around rapidly in a circle, first to the left, then to the right. ...The smell of the blossoms still remaining on the dancer gives the further information how the food source smells."

2. **tail-wagging dance**: "If...the food source is a good distance away, then the *tail-wagging dance* gives additional information about the exact location of

[24]Von Frisch, (1946).
[25]Quoted from Lindauer (1961), pp. 33,4.

the newly-discovered goal. ...The direction of the tail-wagging run conveys the direction of the goal, while the rhythm of the dance—that is, the number of these tail-wagging runs per unit of time—communicates the distance."

We can explain this form of communication in terms of iconic reference and indexical reference. The iconic component in both dances is the food sample carried by the worker bee. The indexical component, on the other hand, consists in the absence versus presence of a specified direction. If no direction is specified (round dance), the food source can be found by circling the hive within an 80-meter radius. Otherwise (tail-wagging dance), the bee flies in the specified direction from the hive. In both cases, the referent is determined iconically by matching the memorized smell of the sample with a corresponding smell found during the flight.

But there are crucial differences between the language of the bees and human languages. The pollen samples are not signs for something, but part of the thing itself. The bee does not match an abstract meaning concept with an internal context, but a sense impression (sample smell received from dancing co-worker) with another sense impression (external pollen source). Consequently, the bee uses neither literal meanings nor an internal context. The language of the bees is based on a much simpler reference procedure than human languages, but the basic principles for achieving displaced reference are similar.

As another example[26] of animal communication consider a thirteen year old cat named Omo, whose left front leg had to be amputated eight years ago after a gun shot wound. Because of this, Omo is unable to properly clean his left ear by himself. Recently Omo was joined by another, younger cat, whose help Omo enlisted as follows: He quickly licked the other cats ear a few times and then presented is own left ear. It didn't take long for the other cat to understand what Omo meant.

This example doesn't involve displaced reference, but it is interesting because it shows that the creative use of communicative behavior is not limited to humans. Since three-legged cats occur very rarely, we cannot explain Omo's communication in terms of innate or conventionalized behavior. We do, however, observe a clearly defined combination of an iconic component (licking of the other cats ear) and an indexical component (presentation of the ear requested to be licked).

Omo's initial ear licking has the status of an iconic **gesture** which plays a similar role as the pollen sample in the language of the bees. Omo's communication is more abstract and creative than the fixed language of the bees, however. The inference intended by Omo and correctly executed by the other cat, based on the juxtaposition of an iconic and an indexical gesture, makes perfect sense from a human point of view. Assuming that cats do not have a language (in the sense of a fixed system of external signs), we may conclude from this example that the pragmatic inferencing on which language interpretation is based exists prior to the evolution of language.

---

[26]Provided by Dr. M.W. Schlicht of Altpölla in Austria.

11.5   Non-Literal Uses

Let us turn now to a secondary aspect of pragmatic interpretation, which concerns the interaction between the positioned sign and the associated context structure, namely the distinction between literal use, vague use, metaphoric use, ironic use, and mentioning. The analysis of different uses presupposes that the sign has already been positioned relative to the proper subcontext in question.

A word like *dog*, for example, refers **literally** relative to a contextual substructure, if the context (i) contains an object[27] corresponding directly to the icon of *dog* or (ii) if the icon is used directly to add such an object to the context. But expressions in natural language are often used non-literally. As an example, consider the interpretation of the phrase *the fuzzball* on Spencer's postcard. What is the process leading to the correct interpretation that this metaphor refers to a precocious feline in the neighborhood?

When Heather gets to the sentence in question, she has already activated a well-defined contextual substructure, containing her memories of Fido, Spencer, and their living conditions in New York. While previous symbols refer successfully because they either relate to existing contextual structures (New York, dog, kitchen) or permit a straightforward extension of the context (weather, cold), the icon *the fuzzball*, in its literal interpretation, finds neither a counterpart in the subcontext nor does it lend itself to a sensible extension of the subcontext. After all, fuzzy balls are classified as inanimate objects, and as such incapable of hissing.

The fact that no natural referent is to be found, or to be added, for the icon "fuzzball," leads Heather to look for a non-literal interpretation. This procedure involves the tentative insertion of the "non-literal" icon into the subcontext. Then a local search is conducted to find the most likely counterpart already in existence or to be constructed. Assuming that Heather is familiar with the animal in question, she will add the information "has hissed at Fido"[28] to the existing node. Otherwise Heather will add the information to a newly created node, e.g., "that furry cat mentioned by Spencer."

The search procedures characteristic of different non-literal uses may be organized along the following hierarchy:[29]

---

[27]We view such "contextual objects" and the corresponding icons as **frame-structures**. For further discussion see Section 2.3.

[28]With a proper listing of the origin of the information

[29]First proposed in Hausser (1984b).

11.5.1 The Hierarchy of Language Uses

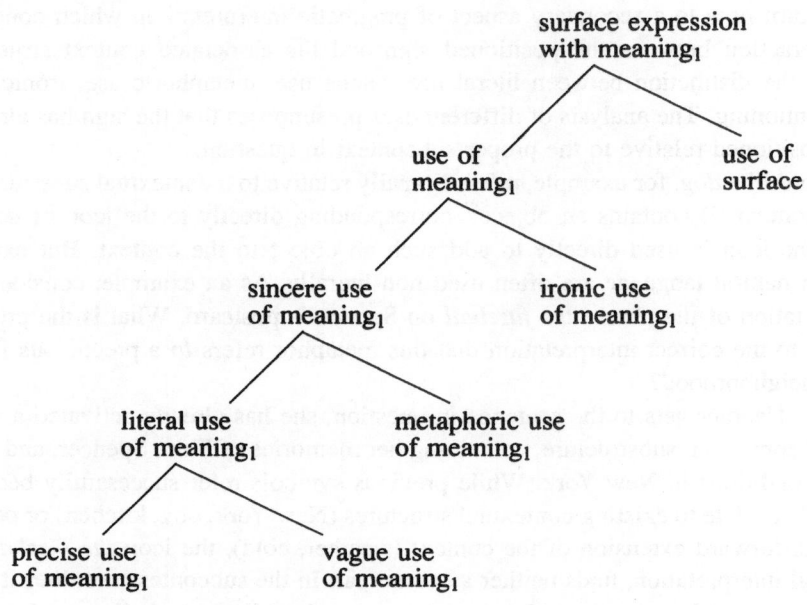

Why do people use language non-literally? Let us look at non-literal uses of meaning$_1$ from the viewpoint of the speaker. To have a language means that a small subset of the concepts is attached to a finite number of words. Thus, some of the concepts serve two functions: (i) They serve in the construction of the internal context like all the other concepts, and (ii) they serve as literal meanings of the language. The speaker's problem of expressing her or his feelings, of describing observations, etc., consists in finding the right meanings$_1$ to accurately depict the subcontext to be described.

The speaker is like a craftsman with the task of depicting a subtle landscape in a mosaic consisting of tiles with only five colors. Just as colors on the tiles are a subset of the colors of the landscape, the literal meanings of a language are a subset of the concepts of the context. The important property common to the tile colors and the literal meaning of words is that

1. they are attached to small external objects (tiles, words) which can be easily manipulated and combined into complex structures, while the landscape and the subcontext are an immovable given, and

2. they impose a simplification on the most elementary level of representation by making available only a comparatively limited set of color or concept values.

The comparison between a text and a mosaic must, of course, be understood *cum grano salis*. On the one hand, a mosaic is like a picture (cf. Section 11.1) in that there is no intermediate level of literal meaning. On the other, the craftsman is like a speaker in that he uses tiles, which, like words of a natural language, are given in advance and in a limited variety. He uses these to encode highly differentiated internal structures (perception, subcontext) as best he can. The "syntax" of the mosaic are the constraints of two-dimensional geometry, and the tiles are like icons in that their meanings (colors) are isomorphic with the surfaces.

After laying out the general structure of the landscape, the craftsman can use his limited range of tiles in several basic ways. Given a particular spot in the mosaic, he can pick a tile with a color closest to the corresponding spot in the landscape. If the color of this tile and the spot in the landscape are the same for all practical purposes, he uses the tile in a precise literal manner, according to the hierarchy of language uses 11.5.1. If they correspond only roughly, he uses the tile in a vague literal manner.

But given the inherent limitations in his set of tiles, the craftsman will not get far in the attempt to depict the whole landscape literally in his mosaic. There are just too many colors in the landscape for which there are no corresponding tiles. Thus, the craftsman has to use his tiles creatively.[30] Given the dark green of the fir trees, for example, he might prefer to represent them with the blue tiles rather than the green ones. The reason is that the blue tiles have a particular hue (second-order property) present also in the color of the fir trees, but lacking in the green tiles. The choice of the blue tiles to represent the color of the fir trees would be an instance of metaphoric use. According to hierarchy of language uses 11.5.1 this would be a non-literal, but sincere use.

After a while, the craftsman may not find any of the tiles suitable for a spot in his mosaic, or he might be fed up with trying to find something fitting, or he might just think that the mosaic needs a bit of livening up. Being a good craftsman, he will not pick just a random tile, but choose one that establishes an obvious contrast to what one would expect at this particular point in the mosaic. This may be classified as an instance of ironic use.

There remains the case of "mentioning," i.e., the use of the **surface** of a symbol rather than its meaning, as in *'Cicero' has six letters*.[31] Because we interpret the tiles as icons, they do not exhibit a difference between surface and meaning. Therefore, the mosaic example does not provide us with an analog for illustrating this particular use.

---

[30]W. Chafe (1979) reports a controlled experiment where different subjects describe a short movie scene. Their search for the right words is documented beautifully.

[31]This rather uncommon kind of use is central to Quine's attempt to explain intensional contexts within a nominalistic approach. In contrast to Frege's proposal to use a "sense" as a non-extensional denotation, Quine prefers to use the surface of the sign instead. Since the surface of signs is concretely given anyway, Quine hopes to arrive at a more parsimonious ontology than Frege, who postulates a separate level of "senses." See Quine (1960), Kaplan (1969).

Our analysis of non-literal uses presupposes that the sign is already firmly anchored in the subcontext. Thus, the hearer's search for alternative referents is based on a well-defined (and limited) subject matter. Furthermore, non-literal uses in general, and metaphor in particular, are not merely a rhetorical device—used as an ornament that could be replaced by equivalent literal terms if the speaker chose to do so (Aristotle's substitution theory).

As illustrated by the mosaic example, non-literal uses fill a genuine need to overcome the inherent limitations of a finite set of word meanings. This position on metaphor is perhaps closest to Black's (1979) "interaction theory."[32] Assuming that non-literal uses are a normal and necessary part of natural-language communication, nothing prevents their use for rhetorical purposes, even if a literal formulation is available. Non-literal uses serve both rhetorical purposes, such as style, brevity, etc., and a profound need to expand the expressive power of the language.

Since the possible uses of an expression in varying contexts are not explicitly specified morphologically, an inappropriate use interpretation may be construed quite easily (either in jokes or in philosophical paradoxes). But usually we have no difficulty in determining the appropriate interpretation. Furthermore, it is precisely the freedom of use which allows for the flexibility and expressive power inherent in natural language (utterances). The creativity of natural language resides not in the recursive nature of certain syntactic constructions (*pace* Chomsky),[33] but in the various ways an expression (and its iconic meaning) may be used relative to specific contexts.

One assumption of the iconic approach to literal meaning is that the icons are as simple and as minimalistic as possible. Their function is to activate the proper structures in the subcontext. If Heather has never heard about the "fuzzball" before, her context-file concerning this cat will contain no more and no less than the little specified on Spencer's postcard.

A second assumption is that the possible uses of a word or sentence can never be enumerated (just like the possible uses of a screwdriver). The reason is that the possible uses of a word depend on the possible contexts, and the store of new and surprising contexts will never be exhausted. Therefore, the possible uses of a word or

---

[32]Lakoff and Johnson (1980) adopt a Gricean approach and fail to recognize the crucial role of literal meaning in the interpretation of metaphoric uses. On page 12, they present the example *Please sit in the apple juice seat* and continue: "In isolation this sentence has no meaning at all, since the expression 'apple juice seat' is not a conventional way of referring to any kind of object." Yet without a literal meaning there is no way to explain why the seat referred to happens to be the one with the apple juice setting.

[33]The "conventional argument for the creativity of natural language is overly strained: who has actually heard of a 500 word sentence? In contrast, anyone who studies generation has available a far more reasonable and commonsense account of creativity, namely that one continually uses new utterances because one is continually faced with new situations." (McDonald et al., 1987, p. 163) But what is a "new utterance"? Tokens are always distinct from each other; therefore each utterance is new by definition. What is used are the expressions; relative to different contexts, uses of the same expression result in different speaker meanings.

sentence must be described in terms of the possible **interaction** of two well-defined mental structures, the literal meaning of the sign and the interpretation context. The possible interaction between these two structures is based on a number of simple, straightforward principles and strategies, which have been described in this chapter.

12. Meaning, Truth and Ontology

This chapter relates our approach to semantics and pragmatics described in the previous chapter to traditional theories of philosophical logic and model theory. This discussion is relevant for two reasons. Logical semantics in general, and predicate calculus in particular, have become the main paradigm for analyzing meaning in natural language. At the same time, predicate calculus plays an important role in Artificial Intelligence, including automatic theorem proving, rule based deductions, and planning. Therefore, this chapter may be read as an investigation of the ontological assumptions of model-theoretic semantics, and as a study of the "epistemological problems" of Artificial Intelligence (in the sense of McCarthy (1977)).

Section 12.1 explains Tarski's truth condition, which is the foundation of model-theoretic semantics. Section 12.2 presents a number of well-known limitations of this approach in the area of "propositional attitudes" and other aspects involving the speaker-hearer. Section 12.3 proposes a different approach to meaning and truth, based on the construction of a simple robot, called a color reader. This leads to a distinction between theories which choose to describe meaning as a relation between the external sign and its 'real' referent, called -constr approach, and theories which aim at a reconstruction of the meaning relation inside a robot, called a +constr approach. Section 12.4 introduces another binary feature, namely the distinction between extensional (-sense) and intensional (+sense) approaches to meaning within referential semantics. Section 12.5 summarizes these considerations by establishing four basic approaches to the definition of meaning, all of which have been advocated in the literature. It is shown that only a <+constr, +sense> approach to meaning is suitable for the construction of an NLC-robot.

12.1 Tarski's Truth Definition

Referential semantics is based on the idea that knowing the meaning of a sentence may be equated with knowing under what circumstances the sentence would be true. This influential theory of meaning and truth culminates in formal model theory.

The strategy of analyzing natural language formally by constructing larger and larger "fragments" with an explicit syntax and associated model-theoretic semantics—pioneered by Montague—has been justly regarded as a major advance over generative grammars without an explicitly defined semantics. But the basic question of whether Montague's approach can be extended to cover all of natural language is still open. What is the role of logic in the analysis of meaning?

On the one hand, model theory is a theory of truth. It aims to characterize all true sentences of a certain object language (normally a logical language), based on the meanings of the sentences and the meanings of their metalanguage translations. On the other hand, model theory is a theory of meaning. The meaning of a sentence is formally described in terms of its truth conditions.

If meanings were simply defined in terms of truth and truth defined in terms of meanings, the enterprise of model-theoretic semantics would be circular. Fortunately, the situation is more differentiated. Model-theoretic truth is defined in terms of a few basic meanings, constituted by clear logical concepts such as "set," "function," etc. The meanings analyzed in terms of model-theoretic truth, on the other hand, are natural-language meanings. Thus, one may look at natural-language analysis in terms of model-theory as a method of reducing natural-language meanings to well-understood logical constructs.

A large part of logic has been concerned with the construction of formal deductive systems. These systems consist of a list of basic expressions and of a set formation rules which generate the set of all well-formed complex expressions (the reflexive transitive closure). A subset of the well-formed expressions of the system is the set of true sentences, which consists of (a) the **axioms** of the system and (b) the **theorems**, i.e., sentences which can be derived from the axioms by means of inference rules. The derivation of a sentence from the axioms is called a **proof**. A logical system is called uninterpreted (or purely syntactic) if the derivation of proofs is based solely on **substitution** and **modus ponens**.

However, there are deductive systems where it is not possible to prove for each well-formed sentence A that either A is a theorem or not-A is a theorem by means of the syntactic method. That is, the set PR of provable sentences or theorems is **incomplete** for these systems. One goal of Tarski's definition of truth is to provide a **semantic** method for proving the completeness of some deductive systems which are incomplete in the sense of a syntactic characterization of true sentences.

According to Tarski, the notion of "x is a true sentence" is contained in the following schema:

12.1.1   x is a true sentence if and only if p.

Thereby x is a metalanguage name of a sentence in the object-language and p is a metalanguage translation of the object-language sentence. As an example of this schema, Tarski presents the sentence

12.1.2   *'It is snowing'* is a true sentence if and only if it is snowing.

The purpose of such a truth definition is to determine for each object-language sentence like "It is snowing" whether it is true or false.

One aspect of Tarski's formal proposal is the recursive definition of the truth condition in order to handle non-finite languages. A second aspect is the requirement that for any given p (cf. 12.1.1) we need an explicit criterion as to when that p is actually true. After all, the goal is to decide for each x whether it is true or false.

And the decision of whether x is a true sentence depends on the decision of whether p is true or not. Schema 12.1.1 is vacuous as long as there are no explicit criteria as to when the metalanguage sentences hold or do not hold.

This becomes quite clear when we look at the details of the concrete example, namely the calculus of classes, for which Tarski provides a formal definition of truth in accordance with 12.1.1. Tarski **constructs** a metalanguage (rather than presupposing it), and requires specifically (i) that all the signs and expressions of the metalanguage are explicitly enumerated, and (ii) that each sign and expression of the metalanguage has a clear meaning (op.cit., p. 172).

In the case of the calculus of classes, the requirement that the meaning of the metalanguage expressions be clear is not problematic. The expressions used are "not," "and," "for some," "is included in," "is identical with," "is an element of," "individual," "class," "relation," etc. These expressions have a clear meaning insofar as they refer to mathematical objects and set-theoretic operations.

A second group of expressions in the metalanguage comprises the names of object-language sentences, the truth value of which is to be determined. These expressions are called "structural descriptive names." The meaning of the object language expressions is no less clear than that of the metalanguage mentioned above, because the object-language expressions refer to the same well-established mathematical objects and operations. Tarski illustrates the intended relation between the calculus of classes, i.e., the object-language, and the constructed metalanguage, as follows:

12.1.3 Metalanguage and Object-Language in the Calculus of Classes

structural descriptive name   *translation of object-language sentence*

'$((ng\frown in)\frown v_1)\frown v_2$' is true if and only if <u>a is not included in b</u>.

NIx_ix_n
object-language sentence

12.1.3 is a proper instance of the T-condition: the meaning of the "structural descriptive name" of the object-language sentence is paraphrased in the metalanguage in terms of expressions which have a clear meaning in the context of the calculus of classes.

Once the relationship between the metalanguage and the object language is established in this manner, the main thrust of Tarski's proposal is the **recursive definition** of truth in order to account for the infinite number of sentences in the language of the calculus of classes. Tarski achieved this goal by introducing the notion of **satisfaction** into the metalanguage. The metalanguage expression "satisfaction" has a clear meaning in that it is explicitly defined in terms of other expressions already available, such as sequence, sentential function, etc. Based on the notion of satisfaction,

Tarski arrives at the following notion of truth for the calculus of classes:

12.1.4 Tarski's Truth-Definition for the Calculus of Classes

x is a true sentence—in symbols x ε Tr—if and only if x ε S and every finite sequence of classes satisfies x.

On the basis of this construction Tarski is able to prove the completeness of the calculus of classes.

12.2   Model Theory and Natural Language

Originally, Tarski's model-theoretic approach was intended to model the relationship between certain formalized languages of mathematical and scientific theories, and their formally-represented objects. Thus, the theory was not concerned with phenomena characteristic of natural language, such as spontaneous reference, metaphor, or even the analysis of meaning. The theory dealt only with a characterization of true sentences, and presupposed the meanings of the words, which referred to well-defined mathematical or other abstract entities.

Given this mathematical background, model theory naturally interprets the model structure as a representation of reality. It assumes, furthermore, that (i) meaning is defined as a **direct** relation between the expressions and their referents, and (ii) the meaning relation is an **external** relation; that is, both the language symbol and its referent are "out there in the world."

But then standard model theory was expanded to handle phenomena characteristic of natural language, such as indexicals, propositional attitudes, non-declarative sentence moods, and vagueness. These expansions, based on the original ontological foundations, raised numerous bewildering problems, all of which may be derived from the question: Where does the speaker-hearer fit within standard model theory?

If the model structure is interpreted as a representation of reality, then the speaker(s) can only be defined as **part of the model structure** (if they are taken into account at all). But what about cases where the speaker enters the model-theoretic interpretation of language—such as in the interpretation of indexicals?

The standard proposal to extend model-theoretic semantics to treat such indexicals as personal pronouns (like *I*, *you*, *we*), adverbs of time and space (like *here* and *now*), etc., studiously avoid any specifics on the "speaker-hearer question." This is exemplified by the "coordinates approach" (Montague, Lewis), in which the meaning of such pronouns as *I* and *you* is specified arbitrarily by the additional model-theoretic parameters S (for speaker) and H (for hearer). Thus, a sentence like *I am hungry* is interpreted relative to a model structure @, a space/time point (i,j), and furthermore relative to a speaker s (s ε S).

This treatment of indexicals is squarely within the original ontology of model-theoretic semantics. But what is the theoretical nature of reference in these systems? The coordinates approach does nothing more than **assign** referents to context-dependent expressions. This assignment is by definition, and therefore arbitrary. Consequently, there is no natural way to treat contextual interrelationships among indexicals in the coordinates approach. Such interrelations are constituted by the fact that, e.g., *I* means *you* in the ears of the hearer, while in the mind of the speaker *I* means *I*; and conversely, *you* means *I* in the ears of the hearer, but *you* means *you* in the mind of the speaker.

A second problem stemming from treating the speaker-hearer as part of the model structure is the analysis of non-literal uses, such as irony, metaphor, etc. Since there is only one notion of meaning (if any), defined as a direct relation between expressions and the model-theoretic reality, the only way to treat such non-literal uses is by postulating syntactico-semantic ambiguities. But logically analyzing the ironic use of *That's really nice weather* as *The weather is not so nice* amounts to extending *ad absurdum* the notion of a syntactic ambiguity; i.e., an ambiguity caused by the syntactic structure of the surface expression, as in *Flying airplanes can be dangerous* (Chomsky (1965)), or *They don't know how good meat tastes*.

A third problem characteristic of standard model theory is the treatment of propositional attitudes. For example, the sentence *John believes that Cicero denounced Catiline* implies that *John believes that Tully denounced Catiline* only if the sentence *John believes that Cicero is Tully* is true. This means that in order to treat this inference adequately, the model structure must describe not only the objectively-given real and possible worlds, but also the subjective belief-worlds of all the speakers and hearers it contains.[1] Since a model-theoretic simulation of the external reality is already way out of reach, the additional modeling of all speaker's and hearer's beliefs necessitated by a treatment of propositional attitudes may perhaps be accepted with equanimity.

A fourth problem is the treatment of vagueness in standard model theory. One proceeds by assuming the vagueness of natural-language concepts, treated in terms of different degrees of truth (or absence of a truth value), and then constructing systems which assign to a complex sentence a fuzzy truth-value, computed from the fuzzy truth-values of the parts (and similarly, in systems which use a third or undefined truth-value). This amounts to the same trivialization of reference as the treatment of indexicals (*I, you, this, now*) in terms of additional model-theoretic parameters. In both cases, the emphasis is on the compositional aspect (i.e., on what happens if a word has a certain indexical interpretation or if a word has a certain vague extension). But the crucial question of how indexical or vague words obtain their particular value is treated as a matter of definition.[2]

And finally, consider possible treatments of non-logical meanings in standard model theory. The words "red," "green," and "blue" have the same syntactic cat-

---

[1]For an alternative solution see Hausser (1979b), pp. 39ff and Section 7.

[2]For an alternative solution see Sections 14.4 and 14.5.

egories and behave alike semantically in that they denote functions with the same domain-range structure (same semantic type). But what about the meaning difference between these words? Could it be treated in terms of Tarskian truth conditions?

As examples of an effective and an ineffective instance of Tarski's truth definition, consider 12.2.1 and 12.2.2.

12.2.1 Example of an Effective Truth Condition

$(A \ \& \ B)^{@,i,j,g}$ is true if and only if $A^{@,i,j,g}$ is true and $B^{@,i,j,g}$ is true.[3]

12.2.1 shows the intriguing relationship between meaning and truth underlying model-theoretic semantics. The truth conditions of a complex expression, $(A \ \& \ B)$, are defined in terms of the truth-values of its parts A and B, and in terms of the metalanguage expressions "if and only if," "and," and "is true." The meaning of "and" in the metalanguage has a clear meaning in that its intended interpretion is set-theoretic conjunction. Similar mathematical interpretations may be given to other expressions in the metalanguage. Since A and B are variables for sentences, the central part of $(A \ \& \ B)$ is $\&$. Thus, 12.2.1 may be regarded as a definition of the meaning of $\&$ in terms of its truth conditions. At the same time, 12.2.1 contributes to the overall truth definition of the language (propositional calculus). The characterization of the meaning of $\&$ in 12.2.1 is effective because the values of the sentence variables A and B are restricted to 1 (true) and 0 (false).

12.2.2 Example of an Ineffective Truth Condition

$red(x)^{@,i,j,g}$ is true if and only if $g(x)$ is red.

While 12.2.2 is clearly an instance of Tarski's schema 12.1.1, and resembles definition 12.2.1, it does not provide an effective meaning analysis of the word *red*. It simply replaces the elementary object language expression "red" with an elementary metalanguage expression 'red'. 12.2.2 is vacuous as long as there are no clear criteria as to when the metalanguage word 'red' is actually true of an object. Without an additional theory of colors, 12.2.2 violates Tarski's condition that each sign of the metalanguage definition must have a clear meaning.

If non-logical meaning aspects cannot be characterized in terms of direct meta-language definitions, what other possibilities remain? The only one that comes to mind are restrictions on the model structure by means of **meaning postulates**, a method introduced by Carnap and further explored by Montague.

---

[3]This definition follows the style of Montague (1974), PTQ. @,i,j,g is the "index" relative to which the object language expressions denote. @ represents a model structure defined as a quintuple $\langle A,I,J,\leq,F \rangle$, where A is a set of individuals, I is a set of possible worlds, J is a set of moments of time, $\leq$ is a linear order on J, and F is a denotation function. i in the index represents a particular possible world, i ε I, j represents a particular moment of time, j ε J, and g is a variable assignment function. Tarski's truth definition in terms of satisfaction is reconstructed by Montague as 'true for all possible variable assignments g'. See 15.5.1 for the explicit definition of the logic system presumed here.

A meaning postulate may specify that for all logically possible interpretations, and for all x, if x is red, then x is not blue, not green, etc. While such restrictions on the possible model structures constitute a structural refinement in the meaning analysis of the non-logical constants in question, they do not amount to a criterion for deciding whether or not some x is in fact red. For example, if we asked someone who didn't know the English color words to get the red book in the other room, and explained to him, that red was different from green and blue, he would not be able to fetch the right book. Thus, the meaning postulate method fails to characterize non-logical meaning differences between constants of equal type.[4]

12.3   A Simple Robot: the Color Reader

According to the mathematically inspired ontology of Montague and related systems, the model structure represents the world, and the speaker-hearers are part of the model structure. The ultimate purpose of these kinds of systems is a characterization of "truth." An approach which aims at modelling the external reality is called a Paradigm I approach.[5] If a Paradigm I system takes the speaker-hearer into account at all, the speaker-hearer is defined as part of the model structure.

The purpose of natural-language processing, on the other hand, is to model the communicative behavior of speakers and hearers. Communication may be viewed as sharing and extending speaker-hearer internal models of beliefs (which may or may not reflect the external "real" world). An approach which aims at modelling the information processing of the speaker-hearer is called a Paradigm II approach. Paradigm II systems do not attempt to model the external reality, but rather presuppose it. If model theory is used in a Paradigm II system, the model is treated as part of the speaker-hearer, and not the other way around.[6]

Let us clarify the difference between a Paradigm I and a Paradigm II approach with a thought experiment - the construction of a color reader. A color reader is a robot that moves around a simple environment containing boxes of different colors. The task of the robot is to look at each box and name its color. Confronted with the red box, for example, the robot would say "This is red". What would be required to build such a color reader?

First of all, it would have to have artificial vision. The robot would distinguish different colors by measuring the electro-magnetic frequency of its input (leaving aside questions of color intensity and brightness). The representation of these measurements inside the robot constitutes a relevant part of its internal **context**.

---

[4]The attempt to define meanings solely in terms of system internal **oppositions** originated with Saussure. This structuralist goal was carried on by Carnap in *Der Logische Aufbau der Welt*. Goodman's (1951) critique of this work showed conclusively that a meaning analysis based solely on oppositions is not capabable of unique identification.

[5]Hausser (1981).

In order to classify a given color measurement, the robot would need a set of color words, each consisting of a surface form and a concept. The word *red*, for example, consists of the surface, i.e., the orthographical representation "red," and the concept of red, whereby the latter is basically a **sample** of this color. This sample may be implemented abstractly as a specific interval of the electromagnetic spectrum or, equivalently, as a little red card. The robot recognizes colors by matching its color concepts with color readings of the context.

It remains to **articulate** the observation of the robot. Here we may simply assume that the robot has a tape containing a small set of appropriate sentences, and that a certain internal color classification triggers the appropriate portion of the tape.

The action of the color reader is shown schematically in 12.3.1.

12.3.1 Schematic Representation of the Color Reader

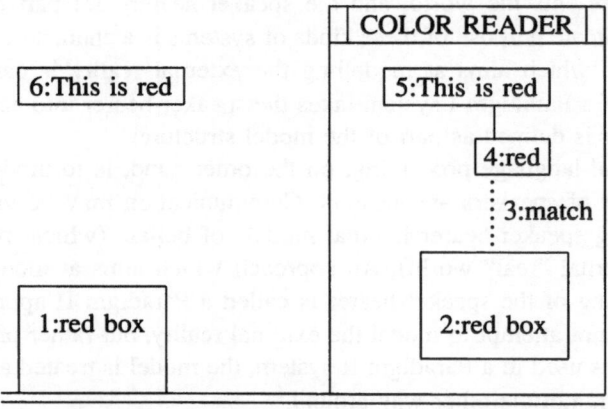

In 12.3.1 the contextual measurement falls into a certain interval, which happens to match best with the concept *red*. This triggers the appropriate sentence.

To extend the color reader from a speaker to a speaker-hearer we refine the basic design as follows: (i) Add a symbol recognition facility which allows the robot to recognize a small set of sentences of the form *Is this X?*, where X is a variable for a color word. (ii) Add a facility which permits the person interacting with the robot to control its "attention" by zooming in on particular boxes. (iii) Expand the set of phrases it can utter by *Yes* and *No*.

For example, if we direct the attention of the robot to a blue box, and ask "Is this red?", the color reader creates an internal representation of the sentence and an internal representation of the box in question. Then it compares the concept

---

[6]See Hausser (1979a,b, 1981) for further discussion.

associated with "red" and the color reading of the box, determines a mismatch, and triggers the utterance *No*.

The system described above is based on three basic matching procedures.

12.3.2 The Three Basic Matching Procedures

1. **context recognition/manipulation**: a match between external context[7] (1) and internal context-representation (2). Such a match may be achieved by building an internal copy of the external context (recognition), or by adjusting the external environment to the internal context (manipulation). Manipulation requires a robot to have goals as well as means to influence its environment. A robot with "hands" may match the external context to the internal context by building a certain structure corresponding to its internal blueprint. And a robot with locomotion may match the external context to the internal context by moving to a position which corresponds to a specified spot on its internal map.

2. **token recognition/verbalization**: a match between the external token of the symbol (6) and the internal symbol representation (5). Such a match may be achieved by building an internal copy of the external symbol token (recognition), or by producing an external copy of the internal symbol representation (verbalization).

3. **pragmatic interpretation of symbols**: a match between the internal concept (4) and the internal context representation (2). If the system is in the **hearer mode**, pragmatic interpretation consists of finding or building structures in the internal context which match the internal concepts associated with the input symbol. If the system is in the **speaker mode**, pragmatic interpretation consists of finding language concepts which match the structures in the internal context.

The design of the color reader is simple and straightforward. Given favorable conditions, a schoolboy could build one in a matter of days. There are no immediate puzzles or paradoxes, and while we could enter here into a discussion of "homunculi" (Dennett (1978)) or "mentalese" (Fodor (1975, 1981)), there is no immediate need for that. At present, the main point is that our color reader will actually work. It may be primitive, but it is capable of genuine color classification: the robot can classify boxes it has never seen before.

It is tempting to go further into the technical details of improving and actually building such a color reader. But the main purpose of our color reader is to introduce some basic distinctions in the area of meaning analysis.

The construction of the color reader supports a distinction between the actual "external" referent (1) and its "internal" counterpart (2), i.e., the contextual representation of the external referent inside the robot, based on perception. The robot

---

[7]The numbers represent the corresponding components in diagram 12.3.1.

also supports a distinction between the "external" language symbol (6) and its "internal" counterpart (5). Finally, the described mechanism of internal reference based on matching the contextual representation with concepts attached to language signs supports a distinction between the surface of the internal sign representation (5) and its meaning (4).

Another important point illustrated by the color reader concerns the notion of **similarity**, which is central to our approach to pragmatics. In order to define a similarity relation, three things are required: (i) an object that serves as the classification pattern (e.g., literal meaning), (ii) a range of objects that are being classified (e.g., internal subcontext), and (iii) a similarity metric which determines which of the objects in (ii) is most similar to the object in (i).[8]

The main prerequisite for building successful pattern matching systems is the specification of small, clearly structured domains for the matching algorithm. Chapter 11 explained how the STAR-point of the sign identifies a limited subcontext, and how the linear structure of the sign severely delimits the range of possible referents at each interpretation step (Linear Path Hypothesis, see also Chapter 5). Given these structural restrictions, there is no reason why the principle of the color reader cannot be expanded into systems capable of modeling the speaker-hearers pragmatic interpretation relative to more and more complex context structures.

In summary, the modeling of similarity in terms of pattern matching does not require a universal "theory of similarity", but concrete domain-specific structures which provide a clear basis for the systematic implementation of correspondences. Such systems are in principle capable of recognizing new objects—as illustrated by the color reader. Furthermore, the power of these systems may be greatly enhanced by complementing their pattern matching algorithm with simple, domain-specific inferences.

12.4   Intensional and Extensional Meaning Analysis

As illustrated by the color reader, a theory of meaning may choose to describe "meaning" as an **internal** or as an **external** relation. A Paradigm I approach to meaning chooses to describe the relationship between the external sign (6), and the external referent (1) (cf. 12.3.1), while a Paradigm II approach to meaning chooses to describe the relationship between the internal meaning representation of the sign (5) and the internal context representation (2).

Another important alternative in meaning analysis is the choice between an **intensional** and an **extensional approach** to meaning. This choice is also exemplified by the color reader (cf. 12.3.1). The relationship between the external sign (6) and the external referent (1) is an instance of an extensional meaning relation because it is direct, without a mediating sense or concept. The relationship between the internal representation of the sign (5) and the internal context representation (2) is an instance of an intensional meaning relation, because it is based on the mediating concept (4).

We call an approach to meaning "extensional" if it avoids the postulation of an intermediate level of concepts, and defines meaning as a direct relationship between expressions and "real objects." The extensional approach emphasizes a realistic attitude towards the entities admitted as referents of expressions. This attitude is motivated by the philosophical quest for "real" truth. After all, how can we arrive at reliable results with our logic if the objects referred to are not real?

The question of what is real, though, is notoriously controversial. One tradition is that of **nominalism**, which takes a "real" thing to mean a spatio-temporal thing, i.e., a thing we can potentially touch. As a consequence of this view, many noun and verb phrases of natural language (e.g., *hope, desire, pain*) do not have a denotation and thus cannot be assigned a meaning. In another tradition, that of **realism**, mathematical entities such as numbers are also admitted to be real. But there remain many expressions of natural language for which there are no real objects to serve as referents or meanings.

Proponents of the extensional approach are thus faced with a choice between the following two positions:

1. In order to assign meaning to expressions where no suitable objects are available, the range of referents is expanded by adopting a wide notion of what is considered to be real.

2. In order to maintain a strict notion of what is considered real, most expressions of natural language are simply assumed to have no meaning by themselves.

An extreme version of the first position was advocated by Meinong (1904), who took the view that every grammatically well-formed expression of natural language has a meaning. Meinong postulated "virtual objects" to serve as a referents in cases where no suitable real object is available. Note that Meinong's approach is extensional insofar as it does not assume an intermediate level of conceptual meaning.

An extreme version of the second position was defended by Russell (1905), in direct opposition to Meinong. According to Russell, "Denoting expressions never have any meaning in themselves, but...every proposition in whose verbal expression they occur has a meaning." Assuming that propositions denote truth values, Russell arrived at an extremely parsimonious ontology.

Besides the extensional notion of meaning, which Frege (1892) called "Bedeutung," there has traditionally been another notion according to which the meaning

---

[8]Any NLC-system based on the notions of literal meaning, internal subcontext, and pragmatic interpretation based on internal matching provides the general basic structure needed for implementing similarity relations. The implementation of specific similarity relations which model the communicative behavior of the speaker-hearer is an empirical problem. For example, a color reader simulating the color terms of an Inuit language will select different sections from the color spectrum than a color reader simulating the color terms of Warlpiri.

of an expression is a concept rather than an object. This conceptual notion of meaning, called "Sinn" by Frege, may be traced back to Plato. Let us call an approach to meaning "intensional" if the relation between an expression and its referent is mediated via the concept, or sense, associated with the expression. The definition of conceptual meanings provides a denotation if expressions lack a natural referent, or occur in "intensional contexts" where **substitutivity of identicals** and/or **existential generalization** fail to hold, and therefore the existence of an "extensional" referent cannot be guaranteed.[9]

While Meinong's assumption of non-existent real objects leads to contradictions, Russell's postulate—that only complete declarative sentences have a meaning—violates a basic linguistic intuition. An approach using intensions, on the other hand, is not subject to these objections. Frege, for example, avoids breach of the law of contradiction by distinguishing "in a denoting phrase two elements, which we may call the *meaning* and the *denotation*" (Russell (1905), p. 45)—or "Sinn" and "Bedeutung," respectively. According to Frege, expressions like *the present king of France*, *Pegasus*, or *the square circle* are meaningful in that they denote their respective "senses," but lack a natural referent and are therefore assigned the null class as referent.[10]

Regarding the question of what these "senses" are exactly, Frege was not specific. He assumed senses to be real abstract entities like the natural numbers. But Carnap (1947) proposed an ingenious formal reconstruction of Frege's dichotomy between "sense" and "reference" in terms of *intensions* and *extensions*. A formal intension is defined as a function from possible worlds (or indices) into extensions. The sense of a word like *table* is identified with an intension, i.e., the function which at each index renders the set of all tables as its value. The set of tables at an index is called the *extension* of *table* at that index.[11]

In many respects, Carnap's construction serves its purpose: If extensions are not appropriate as denotations because of failure of substitutivity of identicals or existential generalizations, the intension functions are available as alternative denotations with suitable formal properties. But the reconstruction of the Fregean "sense" in terms of Carnap's intensions does not provide us with an intuitively acceptable notion of a concept or **sense**. Carnap's construction consists merely of a relativization of denotations to points of reference (indices). The question of whether or not a certain model-theoretic object, e.g., a_0, is in the extension of, e.g., 'table' at indices (i_1,i_1), (i_2,j_2), (i_3,j_3), etc., does not contribute in any way to characterize the **sense** of, e.g., 'table' as a concept.[12] We are thus led to classify the reconstruction of

---

[9]See Section 13.4 for further discussion.

[10]Russell's objection to Frege's intensional theory of meaning is that Russell regards the null-class as an "artificial" referent. Russell preferred assigning no referent in these cases, which led him to do without senses.

[11]The model-theoretic term "index," used to refer to a point of reference, is distinct from the sign-theoretic term, as defined in Section 11.1.

[12]See Putnam (1975), chapter 12, who points out that the notion of an intension as a concept, on

Fregean senses in terms of formal intensions (Carnap (1947), Montague (1974)) as a **-sense** approach, while Frege's original proposal represents a **+sense** approach to meaning analysis.[13]

12.5   Four Basic Approaches to Meaning

While an external approach to natural-language meaning cannot be constructive,[14] an internal approach **must** be constructive[15] if it is to be implemented in a robot processing natural language. Let us therefore represent the choice between an internal and an external meaning analysis with the binary feature ±**constr**. Furthermore, let us represent the choice between an intensional and an extensional meaning analysis with the binary feature ±**sense**.[16] Combination of these two binary features renders four possible approaches to meaning, namely <-constr,-sense>, <-constr,+sense>, <+constr,-sense>, and <+constr,+sense>. Which traditions in philosophy and cognitive science are associated with which of these approaches to the analysis of natural-language meaning?

The **-constr** alternative is the choice of analytic philosophy, which rejects +constr approaches as "psychologistic." The <-constr,-sense> alternative is found in "nominalism" (e.g., Quine) and is incorporated in standard model theory as represented by Tarski, Davidson, and Montague. A <-constr,-sense> theory of meaning and reference describes the relationship between the external symbol token (6) and the

---

the one hand, and the notion of an intension as an extension determining function, on the other, are two different notions which are incompatible. The reason, according to Putnam, is that concepts are something mental and thus in the head of the speaker-hearer. Since Putnam chooses to define meaning as an extension-determining function (cf. op.cit, p. 270), he is led to the counterintuitive conclusion that "meanings just ain't in the head" (op.cit., p. 227).

[13] Another aspect supporting the classification of Carnap's intensions as **-sense** (or extensional) is the fact that one may define a "strictly intensional logic" where expressions always denote intensions and are therefore not ambiguous between a "sense" and a "referent." Such a system, called IL_1, was presented in Hausser (1979b, 1984a) and is described by Peregrin and Sgall (1987) as follows: "...the recursion of the logical rules operates uniformly on the level of intensions; consequently there is no operator ' ^ ' in IL_1 and no basic emphasis on the concept of extension. It is worth noting that if we accept the definition of the concept of intensional logic as given, for example, by T.M.V. Janssen, then IL_1 is *not* intensional, since the rule of intersubstitutivity of identicals holds without restriction." A presuppositional variant of IL_1 is defined in 15.5.1.

[14] That is because it assumes that meanings, like numbers, exist even without people who know about them.

[15] Our notions of +constr or -constr approaches to *meaning* are distinct from the mathematical notions of a constructive approach to *proof theory*.

[16] Hausser (1984b) uses the feature ± **ext** rather than ±**constr**. Let us adopt ±**constr** because the feature used earlier is unclear in distinguishing between "external" and "extensional." Similar considerations motivate our choice of the feature ±**sense**.

Fillmore (1977), p. 60, uses the term *internal semantics* to refer to "the inner structure of a clause," in contrast to *external semantics*, which he uses to refer to "truth or entailment or illocutionary force," i.e. properties of the clause as a whole. Thus, internal as well as external semantics in Fillmore's sense are compatible with a -constr approach—though Fillmore (1975) seems to favor a +constr ontology. How Fillmore would choose between the +sense and the -sense alternative, however, is not obvious.

-sense> theory takes pains to avoid postulating an intermediate level of concepts which would mediate the relationship between the sign and the referent. A <-constr, -sense> approach tries to define everything in terms of real objects (signs as well as referents) and sets or classes of real objects.

The <-constr,+sense> alternative may be found in Frege, and has recently been revived in a more formal mode in "situation semantics."[17] and "discourse semantics"[18] It postulates an intermediate level of external, platonic senses in order to handle certain phenomena in connection with modals (possibility, necessity) and other phenomena which are regarded as troublesome for a purely extensional <-constr,-sense> approach.

The **+constr** alternative, on the other hand, is the choice of cognitive science and artificial intelligence. Newell and Simon (1972), for example, argue explicitly for the distinction between a "task environment" (external reality) and a "problem space" (internal representation), where the formal system is defined to describe the latter.

With respect to the choice between -sense or +sense, Newell and Simon advocate the possibility <+constr,-sense>. They argue that a +sense approach would result "in an unnecessary and unparsimonious multiplication of hypothetical entities that has no evidential support" (Newell and Simon (1972), p. 66). Many systems in A.I., such as SHRDLU (Winograd (1972)), HEARSAY (Reddy et al. (1973)), and MARGIE (Schank et al. (1975)) agree with Newell and Simon on this point. The "mental models" of Johnson-Laird (1983) also represent a <+constr,-sense> approach.[19]

It should be noted, however, that <+constr,-sense> systems which have been actually implemented are characterized by the absence of a perception component, and the use of a highly-specialized context (block world, chessboard). It is for this reason that the language expressions may be defined to refer to contextual structures without an intermediate concept level. For example, as soon as SHRDLU would be implemented as an actual robot with vision, and capable of handling unfamiliar blocks, a -sense approach would be unsuitable because it "glues" the language surfaces to specific contextual referents, thus preventing reference to new contextual objects.[20]

---

[17]Barwise and Perry (1983). See Pollard and Sag (1987, pp. 1 – 6) for a description. An "idealistic," <+constr,+sense>, reinterpretation of situation semantics is proposed in Ishimoto (1987). Such a reinterpretation, however, runs counter to the most fundamental motivation of situation semantics, which is an attempt to maintain (a version of) mathematical realism in the analysis natural language semantics: situation semantics adopts an extremely wide notion of external reality in order to avoid description of the speaker-hearer internal information processing. Instead, the external platonic structures postulated by situation semantics are supposed to "classify" internal states (see Barwise and Perry (1983), p. 226).

[18]Kamp (1981a).

[19]See the description of "translating an assertion into a mental model," Johnson-Laird (1983), pp. 249f.

[20]This point is emphasized by McDermott (1976), who notes that the possible referents of an expression cannot be fixed in advance. "The uses of reference in discourse are not the same as those

A <+constr,+sense> approach, finally, is taken by Anderson and Bower (1973, 1980). They are interested in a general psychological model of language understanding, and arrive at a matching procedure similar to that outlined in Section 2.2 and Chapter 11. A <+constr,+sense> has also been proposed in the context of a philosophically oriented meaning analysis resulting in the definition of a strictly intensional logic.[21] A <+constr,+sense> theory chooses to describe the relationship between the internal symbol (5) and the internal context representation (2) of 12.3.1. It is a **+sense** theory because it explains reference in terms of an intermediate level of concepts (4).

We see that all four approaches have been explored in the literature. Given that the <-constr,-sense> (Paradigm I) and the <+constr,+sense> (Paradigm II) approaches are both represented in the schematic representation of the color reader 12.3.1, let us consider how these two basic approaches are related.

If we assume that verbal processing in the <+constr,+sense> system is so accurate that the distinction between the real token and the token representation can be neglected; and that perception is so accurate that the distinction between the real world situation and its representation in the context model can be neglected; and that the use of language consists only of the most simple-mindedly literal use so that the distinction between the token-model and the context-model can be neglected; then we end up with a <-constr,-sense> system. In other words, the <-constr,-sense> systems may be regarded a special (simplified) case of the <+constr,+sense> approach.

There is another way to compare <-constr,-sense> systems and <+constr,+sense> systems. Both <-constr,-sense> systems and <+constr,+sense> systems relate the real token to the real object. But while <-constr,-sense> systems treat the real-token/real-object relation as a direct relation (with the result that the model structure is treated as a representation of reality of which the speaker-hearer(s) is (are) a part), <+constr,+sense> systems take this relation apart into several submappings by routing it through the speaker-hearer. The result is that the model structure is used to describe something conceptual which is part of the speaker-hearer.

The special case of a <-constr,-sense> system is the appropriate choice in systems of mathematical logic or simplified models of scientific knowledge, where reference (i.e., the relation between elementary constants and the corresponding objects in the model-theoretic simulations of the real world) can be assumed to be accurate, and logic serves only to check consistency of the theory. But this idealization is

---

of naming in internal representation...In discourse, a speaker will introduce a hand and easily refer to 'the finger'. Frame theorists and other notation-developers find it marvelous that their system practically gives them 'the finger' automatically as a piece of the data structure 'at hand'. As far as I can see, doing this automatically is the worst way of doing it. First, of course, there are four or five fingers, each with its own name, so 'the finger' will be ambiguous. Second, a phrase like 'the finger' can be used in so many ways that an automatic evaluation to **Finger109** will be wasteful at best. ...It seems much smarter to put knowledge about translation from natural language to internal representation in the natural-language processor, not in the internal representation."(McDermott, (1976), pp. 149f.)

[21]Hausser (1979b, c, 1981, 1983a,b, 1984a,b).

inappropriate when the goal is a computational implementation of communication in a natural language.

This conclusion raises the following question: If a truth-definition *à la* Tarski is not appropriate for natural language[22] how can we accommodate the intuition that there is a clear denotation-conditional aspect to natural language?[23] According to the proposal of Section 13.2 below, we use the meta-language definitions of predicate calculus to *construct* finite denotation-conditional prototypes, also called set-theoretic icons of the literal meaning. These structures are *used* by the pragmatics relative to the internal utterance context, in the sense of the matching procedure described in Chapter 11. In this way, we retain the intuitions and results of formal logic in a <+constr,+sense> system without the original ontological assumptions and idealizations.

---

[22]Tarski expressed this opinion very strongly. See Section 14.1 for further discussion.

[23]This intuition seems to be the driving force behind the work of Montague and Davidson.

13. Model Theory and Artificial Intelligence

This chapter continues the discussion of referential semantics by explaining the construction of semantically-interpreted languages which are not dependent on a hierarchy of externally-defined metalanguages. The reason for this independence from a metalanguage hierarchy is that the definitions of the metalanguage have been **operationalized**. This result permits the use of semantically-interpreted languages in computers and robots.

Section 13.1 begins with a reconstruction of the central notion of **truth** in the context of the color reader outlined in 12.3.1. Section 13.2 shows that a **constructive**, rather than the standard interpretive, approach to model-theoretic semantics results in an autonomy from the metalanguage. Section 13.3 explores the consequences of this move for the definition of semantics and reference. Rather than defining semantics as describing the relationship between "the language and the world," the task of semantics is the construction of robot-internal literal meanings. Section 13.4 summarizes why the assumption that *meanings just ain't in the head* (Putnam (1975)) is unacceptable for a theoretical approach to meaning which is intended for the construction of NLC-robots. Section 13.5 explains the steps necessary to expand the color reader into a speaker-simulation device.

13.1   Reconstructing Truth in a Robot

In theory, mathematical logic provides the foundations for both computer programming and philosophical theories of natural-language meaning. But in practice, it is not clear how the assumptions and results of philosophical theories based on logic are related to those of the computational environment. What is the theoretical relationship between Tarski's <-constr, -sense> truth definition and a <+constr,+sense> theory exemplified by the color reader?

Let us consider the circumstances in which the color reader would say something false. First, its perception might be faulty, leading to an inaccurate internal context representation. Second, its internal reference mechanism which matches the color concepts of the words with the color readings of the context may be faulty. And third, the mechanism which articulates the result of the color classification by triggering a certain stretch of the tape may pick out the wrong sentence. If everything is working properly, on the other hand, the color reader's utterances are true.

This robot-based definition of truth may be classified as an "idealistic" approach because it models the inside of the agent. But the external reality is not denied or disregarded. On the contrary, the color reader requires an external environment in order to work. Furthermore, for the builders of the robot, the external environment and the inside of the robot are equally real.

The color reader describes the relationship between the real symbol and the real referent in terms of three operationalized matching procedures. Tarski, on the other hand, uses a metalanguage to describe the relation between the real symbol token (6) and the real referent (1) in 12.3.1. This metalanguage takes the viewpoint of an external observer, though no observer (or speaker of the metalanguage) is required in order for Tarski's theory to function. Is there a role for the metalanguage in the functioning of a robot or computer? Can computers use semantically-interpreted languages?

The language used by the builders of the robot is not a metalanguage because it evolved naturally and has been learned rather than constructed. Also, it does not have clear logical or mathematical meanings, as Tarski requires. But most importantly, once the robot has been built, the characterization of truth and meaning by the robot is independent of a Tarskian metalanguage.

This autonomy from a metalanguage is characteristic for all computers. A pocket calculator, for example, performs arithmetic operations reliably and without overt reference to an external metalanguage. Does this mean that computers are limited to "uninterpreted" systems of logic, i.e., systems which are purely syntactic?[1]

No. Overt use of an external, predefined[2] metalanguage—or an infinite hierarchy of such metalanguages—is not a necessary condition for a language to be semantically interpreted. We call a formal language syntactic (or uninterpreted) if it is defined as a one-level system, such that derivations are based on substitutions of equivalent terms. In contrast, a formal language is called semantically interpreted if it is defined as a two-level system, such that each operation on the syntactic level is accompanied by a corresponding semantic operation characterizing the impact of the surface operation on the underlying meaning level.

The crucial feature of a semantically-interpreted language is the systematic correlation of the two levels. A Tarskian metalanguage is only one possible method to connect the surface level of the object-language with the level of things (i.e., the "world") referred to. The object-language is represented in the metalanguage in the form of "structural descriptive names," while the level of the referents (or the "model") is represented in the metalanguage in terms of signs which are explicitly enumerated and have a clear meaning (Tarski (1935), p. 172).

The relation between the level of the language and the level of the referents was specified further by Montague (1974, UG), who formally defined it as a **homomorphism**. In 3.3.2 we described this homomorphism as follows:

---

[1]The question of a mathematical semantics for computer languages is explored in Scott and Strachey (1971). Our approach to the problem is concerned with the different question of a computational modelling of communication. For us, the role of model-theoretic denotation conditions is a concern only insofar as they relate to the meaning analysis of natural language.

[2]Or preexisting—according to the viewpoint of mathematical realists.

13.1.1 The Homomorphism between Syntax and Semantics

1. For each syntactic category there is a corresponding semantic object.
2. For each syntactic operation there is a corresponding semantic operation.

The homomorphism condition strengthens the structural relationship between the object-language and the level of referents. The question now is this: What is required for a semantically interpreted language (i.e., a formal two level system satisfying the homomorphism condition) to become autonomous from the metalanguage? And what is the intuitive function of such a language in a robot simulating natural-language processing?

13.2 Autonomy from the Metalanguage

The truth conditions of a semantically-interpreted language such as predicate calculus may be interpreted in two different ways. The semantic definitions may be used to **check** whether the language expression is true relative to a given model structure and an index (called the interpretive approach), or they may be used to **construct** a model that makes the language expression true—or false—(called the constructive approach).[3] Consider for example 13.2.1.

13.2.1 A Montague-style Definition of "Functional Application"

$F(a)^{@,i,j,g}$ is true if and only if $a^{@,i,j,g} \; \varepsilon \; F^{@,i,j,g}$.[4]

For example, *John walks* may be represented semantically as *walk(john)*. According to 13.2.1, $walk(john)^{@,i,j,g}$ is true iff $john^{@,i,j,g} \; \varepsilon \; walk^{@,i,j,g}$. As long as the model structure tells us the extension of $john^{@,i,j,g}$ and $walk^{@,i,j,g}$, we can determine the truth value of the complex expression *walk(john)* relative to the index @,i,j,g on the basis of 13.2.1.

But where does the model structure @ come from? The theory only tells us that @ is defined as a quintuple <A, I, J, $\leq$, F>, where A, I, J are sets, $\leq$ is a linear ordering on J, and F is a denotation function which assigns denotations to the words of the language. These denotations are set-theoretic constructions built from A, I, and J.

Given these definitions, one may build a concrete model structure—but there is little point in actually doing so (except for purposes of illustration). After all, the truth values of the sentences interpreted relative to a model structure will be no

---

[3]The distinction between the interpretative and the constructive approaches to model theory was introduced in Hausser (1979b).

[4]Like 12.2.1, 13.2.1 is proper instance of a Tarskian definition. The truth-conditions of the complex expression $F(a)$ are defined in terms of the extension of F (a set) and the extension of a, where F and a are metalanguage names for object language expressions, ε is a metalanguage operator (for set membership), and "if and only if" and "is true" are further metalanguage expressions.

surprise; they will be the direct result of how the model structure was defined by
the logician. And furthermore, reality is much too complex to seriously consider
depicting it as a model structure in the cumbersome notation of set theory.[5]

Thus, the interpretative approach to model-theoretic semantics, based on the assumption that (i) the model structure represents reality and that (ii) the purpose
of the interpretation is checking the truth value of sentences relative to the model
structure, remains stuck in a posture of the potential. Logicians are satisfied that the
theory in principle can determine the truth value of any sentence (logical formula)
relative to any well-defined model structure. Their goal is the abstract modeling of
what it means for a sentence to be true, not the large scale application of the theory
with respect to the messy details of reality.

The constructive approach to model theory, on the other hand, uses truth definitions like 13.2.1 to **build** small, finite model structures (rather than checking relative
to presupposed model structures). For example, the logical aspect of the meaning
of *All girls sleep* may be represented by the truth-values relative to the following
model structure @:[6]

$$@ =_{def} <A,I,J,\leq,F>$$
$$A =_{def} \{a_0, a_1\}$$
$$I =_{def} \{i_0, i_1, 2\}$$
$$J =_{def} \{j\}$$
$$F(girl)(i_0,j) =_{def} \{a_0, a_1\}$$
$$F(girl)(i_1,j) =_{def} \{a_0, a_1\}$$
$$F(sleep)(i_0,j) =_{def} \{a_0, a_1\}$$
$$F(sleep)(i_1,j) =_{def} \{a_0\}$$
$$F(sleep)(i_1,j) =_{def} \emptyset$$

value of $\forall x [girl(x) \rightarrow sleep(x)]^{@,i_0 j,g}$: 1

value of $\forall x [girl(x) \rightarrow sleep(x)]^{@,i_1 j,g}$: 0

value of $\forall x [girl(x) \rightarrow sleep(x)]^{@,i_2 j,g}$: 0

The sentence *All girls sleep* is pragmatically true if the "true" model (i_0,j) most
closely resembles the corresponding structure in the subcontext. But if any of the
"false" models (i_1,j) or (i_2,j) resembles the corresponding structure in the subcontext
most closely, then the sentence is false on a literal pragmatic interpretation.

---

[5]Even with small finite sets A, I, and J, and a small set of words, e.g., each set containing five
elements, manual definition of a model structure is almost prohibitively complex.

[6]The definition of a model structure is provided in 15.5.1, (2.2).

These constructed model structures are not regarded as a representation of reality, but as **set-theoretic icons**[7] of the literal meaning of the sentence. Given the purpose of characterizing the meaning of the sentence in terms of its truth conditions, set-theoretic icons are defined as constructed model structures which are **minimal but exhaustive** representations of the logical properties of the sentence; they are denotation-conditional prototypes.

In its most basic form, the system will represent the meaning of *John walks and (John) talks* by a model structure consisting of four models, such that the sentence is true relative to one, and false relative to the other three. These four models are a direct reflection of the truth conditions of **&** (i.e., the logical connective representing conjunction). Tautologies (contradictions) are defined as sentences which are true (false) with respect to all models in their set-theoretic icon. Furthermore, we may demonstrate the logical consistency of a sequence of sentences by constructing a model structure which will make all the sentences true. By the same token, we may show the logical inconsistency of a text by demonstrating that no such model structure can be constructed.[8]

The systematic construction of set-theoretic icons has a straightforward operational implementation. That is, one can define procedures which use the existing truth definitions to construct the set-theoretic icon for any formula of predicate calculus or intensional logic. Furthermore, one can define a program which will accomplish the incremental construction of "model structures for texts" which represent the meaning of any given sequence of logically-consistent sentences, based on the set-theoretic icons of the sentences. We have thus arrived at a formal language system which is semantically interpreted in the sense that it is a homomorphic two-level system, yet this system is autonomous in the sense that the definitions of the metalanguage have been completely **operationalized**.

Once tense and modal aspects,[9] semantic presuppositions,[10] and pronouns[11] are taken into account, the constructive approach to model-theoretic semantics provides a highly-differentiated representation of (the compositional aspect of) the literal meaning of sentences and texts.[12] Because the existing formalism of model-theoretic

---

[7]Our notion of a meaning icon is discussed in chapter 11.

[8]The consistency or inconsistency of denotation-conditional prototypes does not imply that these finite constructs are viewed as the place of mathematics or logic. On the contrary, mathematics and logic must be thought of as lying outside the speaker-hearer. Just as there are no chairs and tables in the speaker-hearer's head, there are no infinite sets or infinitely long lines in his head. But we may well imagine that the denotation-conditional prototypes of natural-language meanings help to build the mental structures which *define* the mathematical objects in the subcontext.

[9]Montague (1974), PTQ.

[10]Hausser (1973, 1976).

[11]Hausser (1979b,c).

[12]For a more extensive discussion see Hausser (1983a,b). Johnson-Laird (1983) resembles this approach insofar as both approaches advocate explicit construction of model structures for (i) for methodological reasons (explicit procedures) and (ii) for explaining certain phenomena of language use. However, Johnson-Laird (1983) describes constructed models for the logical quantifiers and is concerned with the explanation of **inferences** (syllogisms) based on the them. Hausser (1983a,b), on

semantics lends itself equally well to the interpretive and the constructive approach, a constructive approach to model theory requires no changes in the formal theory, and inherits all its mathematical results.

13.3   Semantics and Reference

The switch from an interpretative to a constructive approach to model theory has profound consequences on the intuitive role of the theory. Models and model structures are no longer viewed as representations of the world, but as constructed conceptual meanings. Therefore we must reconsider the nature of truth and reference, i.e., the relationship between the concepts and their real external counterparts.

It has been shown in Chapter 11 that there are two fundamental notions of meaning, namely the literal meaning of an expression or sentence (meaning$_1$) and the speaker meaning of an utterance (meaning$_2$). An expression like *The weather is wonderful* can be used literally relative to the context of a beautiful summer day, but also ironically relative to the context of a rainy November morning. The literal meaning (meaning$_1$) of the tokens used in these two utterances is exactly the same, but the utterance meanings (meanings$_2$) are quite different.

In a <-constr,-sense> system like conventional model theory, on the other hand, the semantic analysis of meaning$_1$ and the pragmatic analysis of meaning$_2$ cannot be separated. The reason is that this approach defines **semantics** as the theory describing the relationship between the language and the "world." This relationship between particular classes of words and the corresponding objects in the world (or rather the set-theoretically defined model structure) is called **reference** or **denotation**.

For example, the denotation (referent, meaning) of a name like *John* is defined extensionally as the person so-named, or intensionally (in the sense of Carnap) as the function which has this person as its value in all possible worlds. Similarly, the denotation (reference) of a one-place verb like "sleep" or a noun like "man" is defined extensionally as the set of sleepers or men, respectively, or intensionally as the function which has these sets as its value in all possible worlds. And the denotation of a sentence is defined extensionally as its truth value, or intensionally as the function which determines its truth value in all possible worlds.

A <-constr,-sense> approach like model-theoretic semantics provides an account of reference or denotation in terms of explicit metalanguage definitions. This means

---

the other hand, describes constructed models for the logical connectives, functional application, and quantifiers in a presuppositional logic, and is concerned with the explanation of **reference**. Besides certain technical differences between the two approaches, the main difference resides in the alternative interpretation of the constructed models. Johnson-Laird (1983) takes a <+constr,-sense> approach and postulates only one level of model-theoretic construction, called mental models, which are interpreted as representations of the speaker internal context. Hausser (1983a,b), on the other hand, takes a <+constr,+sense> approach and assumes two levels of model-theoretic construction, i.e., set-theoretic icons of literal meaning and set-theoretic context-representations.

that the denotation of all non-logical expressions used in a sentence must be defined by the logician before the interpretation of the sentence can begin. By assigning the task of defining denotations to the logician, the whole aspect of **language use** by speaker-hearer is effectively eliminated from the theory. Furthermore, as shown in the previous chapter, metalanguage definitions in their <-constr,-sense> interpretation are not suitable for use in a natural-language processing robot if we demand that the robot (like a speaker-hearer) should be able to refer spontaneously to new objects in its surroundings.

In our alternative <+constr,+sense> interpretation of the model-theoretic formalism, semantics ceases to describe the relationship between language and the world. Instead, the task of semantics is the construction of **literal meanings**. By limiting model-theoretic semantics to the more modest task of building minimal but exhaustive model-structures we gain an important advantage for the purpose of building a natural-language processing robot: The process of semantic interpretation can be fully operationalized.

But what about the relation between the language and the world? The answer to this question is provided by the color reader described in Section 12.3. The literal meanings (e.g., the color sample (4)) relate to an internal context (e.g., the color measurement (2)) on the basis of a **matching procedure**. Furthermore, by linking the internal context to the external environment via perception/manipulation, and by linking the internal language surface to the external sign via recognition/verbalization, the relationship between the external sign and "the world" is reconstructed in a <+constr,+sense> approach in terms of three (robot internal) submappings (cf. 12.3.2).

By building internal representations of literal meaning which are matched with a context representing what the speaker-hearer perceives and remembers at the moment of interpretation, we arrive at a natural distinction between semantics (construction of literal meanings) and pragmatics (matching literal meanings with the context). The importance of this distinction for a surface-compositional semantics (cf. Section 2.3), on the one hand, and a highly-structured theory of pragmatics (cf. Chapter 11), on the other, cannot be exaggerated.

Intuitively, we view the pragmatics of language as the theory of language use by the speaker-hearer. We assume that natural-language expressions have a **use potential** just like tools and other "real" objects.[13] A screw driver, for example, may be used "literally" to put in or take out screws, but it may also be used "non-literally" to put wholes into a juice can, or even as a letter weight, etc. The use potential of a screwdriver is limited by its form, size, and material.

Similarly, the use potential of a natural-language expression is limited by its literal meaning.[14] Just as a screwdriver cannot be used to sew a regular button to a normal

---

[13]This viewpoint was emphasized by Bühler (1934).

[14]In the special use of **mentioning** (cf. Section 13.4), e.g., *"Cicero" has six letters*, the use potential of an expression is determined by its form rather than its meaning.

shirt, the word "table" cannot normally be used to refer to a baseball bat.

The difference between a tool like a screwdriver and the literal meaning of a word is, of course, that screwdrivers exist in the external environment, whereas the literal meanings of a language exist in the minds of the people speaking it. Accordingly, screwdrivers can only be used in the external environment, while meanings can only be used in the internal environment of the mind.

13.4   Why Meanings are in the Head

Our definition of semantics as the theory for the automatic construction of set-theoretic icons homomorphic with the syntactically-analyzed language surface is motivated by several reasons. One is the desire to use semantically-interpreted language in a natural-language processing robot. A second reason is the theoretical necessity to distinguish between semantics and pragmatics. A third reason is that natural language doesn't always refer to the facts of the "world." This simple fact argues strongly against defining semantics as describing the relationship between "language and the world" directly in terms of metalanguage definitions.

Consider a speaker reporting a pain in his chest. While **-constr** theories go through the laborious machinations of a "double aspect" theory in order to make this pain "real" in an external ("objective") sense,[15] our <+constr,+sense> approach treats this kind of pain as an internal sensation. For the purposes of reference, internal sensations like pain are on a par with external sensations like seeing a red box.[16] The literal meaning of "pain" is defined in terms of a class of extreme readings of preception parameters which may "measure" the external as well as the internal environment. It follows from our definition of pain as a property of sensory readings that this concept will not have any external counterparts.

Similar considerations hold for the interpretation of language referring to events long past, far away, or fictitious. When we talk with someone about J.S. Bach, the primary reference are structures in our respective internal contexts. The correspondence of internal contextual structures representing J.S. Bach with the real individual living from 1685 to 1750 in Europe is a fragile chain of historical tradition that occurred entirely speaker-hearer internally. If humanity were wiped out except for a small neolithical tribe, J.S. Bach as a topic of conversation would disappear. The assumption that J.S. Bach remains as a "true fact" whether or not there are people who know about him, may be comforting those who believe that "meanings just ain't in the head" (Putnam (1975)), but it is at best irrelevant (and at worst misleading)

---

[15]By measuring brain waves.

[16]There is no difficulty in providing a robot with internal as well as external sensory input, e.g., measurement of internal and external temperature. Furthermore, each parameter of sensory input may have a range of degrees which are interpreted by the robot as extremely undesirable (pain). They may even be coupled with involuntary reflexes such as flight or "fainting."

for a scientific account of the functioning of natural-language communication.

Many semanticists (e.g., Frege, Putnam) defend the thesis that meanings are real external entities because they feel the need to give meanings an **objective** quality. I agree that the literal word meanings should not be treated as something personal left to the whim of each individual. But simply declaring meanings to be real external entities is an irrational method for making them "objective."

The real reason why meanings are well-defined "objective" entities shared by the speech community is that **otherwise communication wouldn't work**. A description of communication, e.g., in the form of interacting NLC-robots, requires an explicit construction of internal contexts and internal meanings. If these internal meanings and contexts are sufficiently similar, communication between the robots will succeed; otherwise it will fail. Postulation of external meanings does not contribute to the actual working of communication.

But couldn't one compromise and say that just as there are real surfaces corresponding to the internal surface representations, there are real external ("platonic") meanings corresponding to the internal meanings? The answer is "no." First of all, there is no evidence that the external surfaces of the signs have external meanings attached to them.[17] Thus, postulating external meanings would violate the philosophical principle of Occam's razor. More importantly, however, postulating external meanings would miss the whole point of natural-language communication among people, which accomplishes the task of transmitting internal meanings **without** the need to rely on external counterparts of the internal meanings.

A speaker uses the literal meanings to depict a relevant internal context structure, and he transmits this depiction by way of the surfaces to which the literal meanings are attached. The hearer understands the external sign by going from the surfaces to his corresponding literal meanings. This process requires the pairing of meanings and surfaces in both the speaker and the hearer, but it does not require a pairing of meanings and surfaces in the external sign which is used to transmit the meanings.

13.5   The Speaker-Simulation Device

Our iconic view of language meaning and reference may be traced back at least to John Locke (1632 – 1704), who said that a person seeing a tree has an image of that tree in his head. This position does not commit us to assume a particular form of the image. Information can be stored in many forms, some of which are immediately obvious to us, whereas others have to be decoded in order to be recognizable.

For example, we immediately recognize a photograph of a close friend. However, if we store the visual information of the photograph in a computer in the form of sequences of zeros and ones, we are unable to understand the information in that

---

[17]We sympathize here with the ontological assumptions of nominalism.

form. Yet we may say that the computer **contains the image** because the information stored in the computer may be **recovered**. i.e., the sequences of zeros and ones may be transformed back into a picture which we can recognize and which is equivalent to the original photograph.

It is similar in the case of Locke's example. We do not know exactly how the image of the tree is stored in the person's head, though we may presume that it is some neurological brain code. But because the person will be able to draw a picture of the tree from memory, we conclude with Locke that he has an image of the tree in his head.

The assumption that concepts in general and language meanings in particular are like images or icons has been widely held throughout history.[18] At the same time it has been consistently derided as naive and overly simplistic.[19] A fellow empiricist, Bishop Berkeley (1685 – 1753), attacked Locke's proposal that a triangle is recognized on the basis of an internal concept or "idea" of a triangle, by asking what kind of triangle *exactly* this idea should be: an isosceles, equilateral, or scalene triangle?

Today we would have little problem in building an extended color reader capable of recognizing geometric shapes. The concept of a triangle would be represented by a robot-internal procedure capable of generating **all** possible kinds of triangles. The recognition of triangles and non-triangles proceeds as follows. A contextual object is approximated with the robots flexible triangle scheme. The quality of the overlap between the contextual object and the schematic approximation determines whether the object is classified as a triangle or not. If the contextual object is recognized as a triangle, then the structure of approximating scheme indicates whether the contextual object is an isosceles, equilateral, or scalene triangle.

A more recent rejection of an iconic definition of meaning may be found in Ogden and Richards (1923). However, calling the use of icons—or "images" — in the analysis of meaning "hazardous," "mental luxuries" and "doubtful" does

---

[18]To say that concepts are *like* images is not the same as saying that concepts *are* images. Our position is in agreement with Chafe (1970), who carefully distinguishes between concepts and images: "But a mental image, in the sense of an imagined visual experience—a kind of internal photograph of some arrangement of visually perceptible objects—is not a concept. For the most part one cannot draw pictures of concepts or imagine them as specific objects. I would assert that speakers of English, and speakers of perhaps every other language, have in their minds a piece of knowledge which can be called the concept *dog*. This particular kind of knowledge is not an image of a particular dog on a particular occasion, but rather an underlying unity of which images of dogs are only particular and accidental manifestations. There are certainly many concepts which are not related to visualizable phenomena even in this way. Those which underlie words like *truth* and *succeed* are random examples." (op.cit., p. 75) Our notion of an icon is not restricted to visualizable phenomena. All we are claiming is that the Chafe'ian concept of *dog*, however it is represented internally, refers on the basis of a similarity relation—*like* a picture. It seems that part of the controversy between pro- and anti-imagists is caused by a difference in the interpretation of the term "image": The anti-imagists seem to interpret "image" in a strong sense of *visual* image, while the pro-imagists proceed on a much more abstract notion of "image."

[19]Ogden and Richards (1923) call it a "potent instinctive belief being given from many sources" (op.cit., p. 15).

not amount to a scientific argument.[20] A more moderate account of images, and a more articulate reasoning against their possible role in terms of the "homunculus argument,"[21] is given by Johnson-Laird:[22]

> No one doubts the conscious phenomena of imagery. Many people report that they can use their imagination to form a visual image of an object or scene. ...What is problematical is the ultimate nature of images as mental representations. They cannot be pictures-in-the-mind, because a picture requires a homunculus to perceive it, and this requirement leads to the slippery slope of infinite regress—big homunculi need little homunculi to perceive their pictures-in-the-mind, and so on *ad infinitum*.

Fortunately, the homunculus argument does not apply to our iconic theory of meaning. The assumption of constructed literal meanings interacting with an internal context dispenses not only with the infinite hierarchy of metalanguages (cf. Section 13.2), but also with the infinite hierarchy of homunculi. The color reader, for example, has an internal image of the color of the external box under analysis. Yet it can recognize colors without a homunculus because it is based on **matching** the image with a set of other images, i.e., the color samples representing the literal meanings.

The color reader described in Section 12.3 is of course primitive. For one thing, it is not capable of logical inferences. Furthermore, it can only process a small, finite set of sentences, and its internal context is capable only of representing (an interval of) the electromagnetic spectrum. But the basic method of reference in terms of matching perception data with internal meaning concepts is completely general and may be used in a large scale-expansion of the color reader, called a speaker-simulation device, or NLC-robot.

In order to handle a potentially infinite number of sentences, we replace the color reader's primitive two-level system attaching elementary meanings (color samples) to unanalyzed sentences (tape stretches) by a **grammar**, consisting of a lexicon, a set of syntactic rules, and a set of semantic rules. The grammar may be assumed to be model-theoretically interpreted: it constructs homomorphic meanings (set-theoretic icons) for all recognized input sentences. The color reader's internal representation of electromagnetic frequencies, furthermore, is replaced by a model-theoretically defined context which allows a differentiated representation of episodic and non-episodic knowledge.

For the construction of literal meanings and the internal context in model theoretic terms, a definition of the non-logical constants is required. These are provided by (abstractions from) elementary perceptions (colors, shapes, sounds, temperature,

---

[20]Ogden and Richards (1923), p. 59

[21]The homunculus-argument goes back to Hume (1711 – 1776) and has been recently revived by Dennett (1978).

[22]Johnson-Laird (1983), pp. 146,7.

tactile input, etc.) of the robot, and higher-order constructs built from these. For example, the meanings of the non-logical constants "red," "green," and "blue" are defined as specific intervals in the perception of the color spectrum, while the non-logical constant "color" is defined as the **set** containing "red," "green," and "blue" as its elements.

Our basic position is close to the viewpoint of recent work in psychology.

> Moreover, language eventually facilitates the development of abstract conceptual structures that appear far removed from the description of intermediate perceptual experience. By this and other similar means, language plays a central role in our capacity for abstract thought. ... Even the most abstract structures seem capable of being reduced to perceptual data. ... real languages always remain close to their perceptual base in their interpretation. The perceptual derivation of even abstract concepts is almost so obvious as to be missed. Many of these abstract concepts arise from metaphors that use perceptual terms (Asch, 1961), such as the "depth" of thought, a "piercing wit," a "heated debate," a "raging passion," a "well-tuned" car, a "stormy meeting," etc.

> Anderson and Bower (1980), p. 83.

In other words, the speaker-simulation device, like the color reader, is **perceptionally grounded** in that its basic non-logical concepts are all built from operationally-defined perceptions. But in contrast to the color reader, the NLC-robot may be programmed to have complex concepts, constructed from basic concepts by means of the logical quantifiers and connectives. The higher concepts are connected in a semantic hierarchy, which provides the basis for certain logical inferences.

With present technology, context recognition and symbol recognition in an NLC-robot will leave much to be desired. But for limited domains, a functioning NLC-robot can be built even today. Furthermore, prototypes may differ in the choice and implementation of basic perceptions and corresponding elementary concepts, as well as in the choice and implementation of a logical framework for building higher-order concepts (e.g., set theory vs. frames).

Our reference to set theory (set-theoretic icons) is motivated mainly by the fact that set theory is general. For the actual construction of an NLC-robot, we are primarily interested in computational methods which do the job, even if the relationship of these methods to set theory may not always be immediately obvious. In other words, it is not necessary to know "the ultimate nature of the images" or concepts in order to build an NLC-robot, because the overall design can be implemented in many alternative ways. This is not to say that the coding of mental structures in humans should not be investigated. Within psychology it is a legitimate question whether syllogistic inferences by humans are based more likely on Euler circles or Venn diagrams,[23] or whether images should be analyzed in terms of an "imagist" or a

---

[23]Johnson-Laird (1983), Chapters 4 – 6.

"propositionalist" theory.[24]

The goal of building natural-language processing robots may be compared to the historic efforts of man to learn how to fly. Throughout history, man diligently studied the flight of birds, and tried to achieve his goal with methods closely resembling the actions observed (i.e., flapping wings). Today's airplanes are airborne on the basis of the same principle as birds, namely the air foil. But a sparrow and a jumbo jet achieve air foils with very different techniques.

By analogy, the goal of our research into natural-language processing is not building a bird, but building a "Kitty Hawk" and ultimately a jumbo jet. Just as building a jumbo jet is much easier and much more useful than building a sparrow, building an NLC-robot is easier and more useful than a low-level simulation of the information-processing in humans. And just as the experience and growing body of theoretical knowledge concerning the building of air planes led to a deeper understanding of the principles of flight in animals, experience and growing theoretical knowledge in building NLC-robots will lead to a new and deeper understanding of human information processing.

An airplane is evaluated by its ability to fly, not by how closely it resembles ones favorite bird. Similarly, an NLC-robot is evaluated by its ability to communicate in natural language, not by its degree of "psychological reality." But, like an airplane, an NLC-robot must be adapted to its human user.

If the robot is to serve practical functions, it must understand language, deduce the speakers intentions, store the information correctly, retrieve information and express it clearly in natural language. While the physical material and structure of an NLC-robot (electronic hardware) are quite different from those of a human speaker-hearer (biological "wetware"), the behavioral properties of the robot on the level of information-processing are narrowly constrained by its human model.

---

[24] See Johnson-Laird (1983), pp. 147f, for a discussion. For a summary of the pro- versus anti-imagist debate between Pylyshyn, Kosslyn, and Shepard see Miller (1986), pp. 224 – 232.

14. Reference and Denotation

The <+constr, +sense> interpretation of model-theoretic semantics proposed in Chapter 13 differs from the <+constr, -sense> interpretation of predicate calculus found in many A.I. applications.[1] We motivated the level of literal meanings by the desire to model spontaneous reference to new objects by the robot, and by the necessity to distinguish between the literal meaning of expressions and the speaker meaning of utterances.

In the present and the following chapter we investigate the consequences of the <+constr, +sense> interpretation on the analysis of certain classic puzzles in philosophy, namely the Epimenides Paradox, the Sorites Paradox, the status of semantic presuppositions, and the handling of intensional contexts. Given the close connection between logical semantics and techniques in A.I., the present and the following chapter may again be read as a reanalysis of certain well-rehearsed questions of logic and language philosophy, and as a study of "epistemological problems in Artificial Intelligence" (McCarthy 1977).

Section 14.1 explains the Epimenides Paradox and evaluates proposals for constructing object languages with a truth predicate. Section 14.2 presents an alternative solution based on the distinction between reference and denotation. Section 14.3 shows how the Epimenides Paradox may be reconstructed within the pragmatics of the Paradigm II approach. Section 14.4 investigates the phenomenon of vagueness in natural language. Section 14.5 proposes a solution to the Sorites Paradox.

14.1 The Epimenides Paradox

Are natural languages logically consistent? The answer depends on whether we use "natural language" to refer to the level of expressions or to the level of utterances. On the level of expressions and their set-theoretically represented literal meanings, natural language is consistent. On the level of utterances, however, many different uses of an expression are possible (cf. 11.5.1).

In Paradigm II, the theory of language use (by the speaker-hearer) falls outside the realm of traditional logical analysis. Therefore, the question of logical consistency for **utterances** does not arise as an issue of formal semantics. Paradigm I systems, on the other hand, do not distinguish between the literal meaning of expressions (denotation) and the speaker meaning of utterances. Therefore, they permit constructing

---

[1]A <+constr, -sense> interpretation predicate calculus may found in Nilsson (1980). See Sections 12.5 and 15.5 for discussion.

certain semantic inconsistencies based on self-reference. These are usually referred to as the Epimenides, Eubolides, or Liar Paradox.

The Epimenides Paradox must be addressed by any theory of natural-language meaning. Natural languages all over the world contain words corresponding to *true* and *false* in English. Yet according to Tarski, a metalanguage will not be consistent if the object language (e.g., the natural language to be analyzed) contains a truth predicate. But consistency is a precondition for logical analysis, and thus for the model-theoretic analysis of natural language. Tarski concludes:[2]

> The attempt to set up a structural definition of the term 'true sentence'— applicable to colloquial language—is confronted with insuperable difficulties.

Tarski's student Montague, on the other hand, was unperturbed by this assessment, and begins the paper "English as a Formal Language"[3] as follows:

> I reject the contention that an important theoretical difference exists between formal and natural languages. ... Like Donald Davidson I regard the construction of a theory of truth—or rather the more general notion of truth under an arbitrary interpretation—as the basic goal of serious syntax and semantics.

Of course, Montague is aware of the Epimenides Paradox and mentions it in other contexts, but he never discusses its possible consequences in connection with his approach to the semantics of natural language. Davidson, however, is explicit:[4]

> Tarski's ... point is that we would have to reform natural language out of all recognition before we could apply formal semantic methods. If this is true, it is fatal to my project.

Quoting Leśniewski, Tarski (1935) reconstructs the paradox as follows:

14.1.1 Tarski's Formulation of the Epimenides Paradox

> For the sake of greater perspicuity we shall use the symbol 'c' as a typological abbreviation of the expression 'the sentence printed on this page, line 28 from the top'. Consider now the following sentence:
>
> *c is not a true sentence*
>
> Having regard to the meaning of the symbol 'c', we can establish empirically:
> (a) 'c is not a true sentence' is identical with c.
> For the quotation-mark name of the sentence c we set up an explanation of type (2):
> (b) 'c is not a true sentence' is a true sentence if and only if c is not a true sentence.

---

[2]Tarski (1935), page 164.
[3]Montague (1974), p. 188.
[4]Davidson 1967.

The premises (a) and (b) together at once give a contradiction:
c is a true sentence if and only if c is not a true sentence.

Since "no rational ground can be given why substitution should be forbidden in principle," Tarski concludes that a definition of truth for natural languages is impossible.

The point of 14.1.1 is not that we can formulate contradictions in natural language—we can do that in logic too (e.g., 'A & ¬A'). It is rather that substitution of equivalent terms is a general inference rule of logic. 14.1.1 constitutes a logical inconsistency because the contradiction is derived from a true premise (i.e., the instance of the general T-condition given in (b)) by means of a valid inference rule (substitution based on equation (a)).

The self-reference comes about because the word *true* occurs both in the formulation of the T-condition in the metalanguage (cf. 12.1.1), and the object-language sentence. The inconsistent metalanguage sentence resulting from the self-referential substitution described in 14.1.1 has the following structure.

14.1.2 Structure of the Inconsistent Metalanguage Sentence

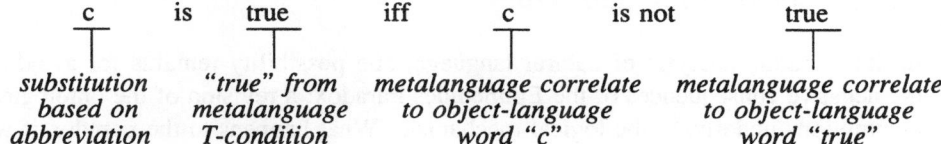

The presence of the word *true* in natural language, and the use of substitution in logic are of a simple and basic nature. Therefore, the status of the paradox must be clarified. After all, if the formal metalanguage is inconsistent, any falsehood can be proved. And with the loss of a theory of truth we lose the basis for an analysis of natural language in terms of truth conditions. Yet Davidson and Montague simply ignore the paradox. Hacking (1975, p. 136) describes Davidson's position as follows:

> Without denying the interest of these paradoxes Davidson suggests that we should ignore them for the time being. Even if there is no consistent set of rules for the whole of English, we should expect a consistent set for almost all of it, excluding a few rather unimportant devices that allow for self-reference.

Others accept Tarski's conclusion that a formal semantics for natural language is ultimately impossible, because they share his attitude (held also by Russell, Quine, and many others) that natural language is not susceptible to a logical analysis.[5]

The question of whether model-theoretic semantics for natural language is generally possible can't be fully answered until the role of Epimenides Paradox has been

---

[5]This did not stop them, however, from producing intricate theories for formal structures inspired by natural language.

clarified. Instead of accepting the paradox, or ignoring it (which is also a form of acceptance), one can only reanalyze the problem.

What are the possibilities of reconstructing the paradox in another form—without the disastrous consequences for a formal semantic analysis of natural language? One possibility is a revision of the logic, specifically the mechanism of valuations. Kripke (1975), Gupta (1982), and Herzberger (1982) propose logic systems which seem to avoid the paradox. These systems resemble each other in that they define formal object languages (first-order predicate calculus) which contain truth predicates, yet they are not inconsistent. The common bases of this feat are recursive *valuation schemes* for their respective truth predicates.

Valuation schemes are based on large numbers of valuations (transfinitely many in the case of Kripke (1975)). These valuations are arbitrary value assignments by the model structure. Yet the Epimenides Paradox is a problem of reference: A symbol can refer on the basis of its meaning, and at the same time be a referent on the basis of its form. Valuation schemes do not address this problem because they are based on an *ad hoc* treatment of reference.

14.2 Consistency and Truth

In the semantic analysis of natural language, one possibility remains for avoiding the negative consequences of the Epimenides Paradox: a revision of the ontological assumptions underlying the logical mechanism. What happens to the paradox if we assume Paradigm II instead of the Paradigm I approach of Tarski, Montague, Davidson, Kripke, Gupta, and Herzberger? In a Paradigm II system, reference and denotation are completely different notions: reference is defined as a matching process between the literal meaning (denotation) and the internal context, while denotations are minimal model structures representing the truth conditions of the expression (see Section 13.2).

The differentiation between reference and denotation in Paradigm II leads naturally to a distinction between the object-language predicate *true* and the metalanguage predicate *true*. The model-theoretic notion of truth (represented by $\{\emptyset\}$ or 1) is used in the metalanguage for the construction of formal denotations. The object-language word *true*, on the other hand, is analyzed as "corresponds to reality." In the NLC-robot, "corresponds to reality" may be formally interpreted as a procedure of comparing relevant sections of the internal context with the external referent.

For example, we could ask an advanced version of the color reader "Is it true that this box is red?" The robot would measure the electromagnetic input from the external referent and compare its measurements with his concept of red, i.e., with the interval of the spectrum defined as *red*. If the measurement and the concept agree, the answer would be "yes"; otherwise it would be "no."

It follows that the Epimenides sentence "c is not true" has quite different translations, depending on whether we use the abstract notion of truth, i.e., $\{\emptyset\}$ or 1, or the new notion of truth defined by comparing language meanings with sense data (or data from the long-term memory). In a Paradigm I system, only the first possibility exists. In a Paradigm II system, the second possibility is intuitively more plausible.

14.2.1 Two Different Analyses of 'C is not true'

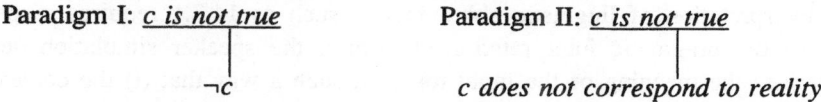

Paradigm I: *c is not true*

$\neg c$

Paradigm II: *c is not true*

c does not correspond to reality

Consider the different meanings of these translations. "$\neg c$" denotes 1 only if c denotes 0. "*c does not correspond to reality*," on the other hand, represents a non-logical meaning and denotes a speaker-hearer internal procedure.

Now, if the meaning of the word "true" in the object-language **differs** from the formal notion of truth (defined as '1') in the metalanguage, then the Epimenides Paradox no longer results in the inconsistency of the metalanguage. Instead of Tarski's contradiction (1)

1. 'A' is true if and only if 'A' is not true.

we get

2. 'A' is 1 (*model-theoretic truth*)

   if and only if

   'A' is not true (*pragmatic truth in the sense of* "[does not] correspond to reality").

Thus, the Epimenides Paradox is eliminated from the natural object language, and the Montague/Davidson program of constructing a theory of truth for natural language is vindicated at least insofar as there are no necessary inconsistencies. The basis for this result, however, is the transition from Paradigm I of Tarski and Montague to Paradigm II of Artificial Intelligence. Only the Paradigm II framework provides a procedural analysis of non-logical meanings of the object language in general, and the object-language word "true" in particular.

14.3 Reconstructing Epimenides Pragmatically

Inconsistencies (or rather indeterminacies based on infinite recursion of the pragmatic interpretation process) are possible within the **pragmatics** of the Paradigm II approach. Thus, the Epimenides Paradox may be reconstructed within the Paradigm II. But the infinite recursions are not necessary, because they depend on a blind "use of literal meaning" in the interpretation of a linguistic abbreviation.

Consider the details of a reconstruction of the Epimenides Paradox in a Paradigm II system. We begin by describing the systems operation in the case of a normal (i.e. nonself-referential) interpretation of "Sentence A is not true," whereby sentence A happens to be the following abbreviation:

14.3.1   *A = The blue box is on top of the red box.*

The interpretation of linguistic abbreviations such as 14.3.1 requires a special routine of the pragmatic interpretation algorithm: the speaker simulation device characterizes the meaning of the input token in such a way that (i) the contextual referent of A is determined, and (ii) a procedure is initiated to check whether A corresponds to reality. Since A is the abbreviation of a linguistic sign, the NLC-robot determines what A abbreviates and enters the equation "A = The blue box is on top of the red box" into the context.

The sentence on the right side of this equation is run through the language interpretion system of the NLC-robot, its meaning is characterized in terms of a set-theoretic icon, and the icon is copied into the context and compared with external reality. Since the representation of meaning in the sentence "The blue box is on top of the red box" corresponds to external reality, the sentence "Sentence A is not true" must be false.

14.3.2 A Normal Instance of Linguistic Abbreviation

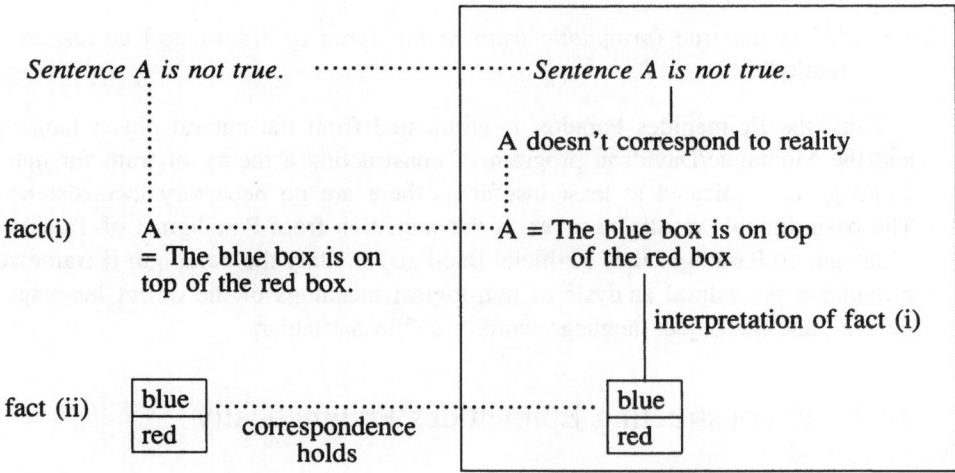

The external context must contain two objects for the correct evaluation of the truth of "Sentence A is not true": (i) a specification of what A actually says, and (ii) a specification of the situation which sentence A claims to obtain.

The Epimenides Paradox, on the other hand, is obtained by replacing sentence 14.3.1 with sentence 14.3.3.

14.3.3   *A = Sentence A is not true.*

In other words, the sentence to be interpreted is "Sentence A is not true," whereby "A" abbreviates "Sentence A is not true."

Again, the NLC-robot translates the input token, determines the contextual referent of "sentence A " and enters the equation "A = sentence A is not true" into the context. So far, everything is like example 14.3.2. Next, the NLC-robot runs the sentence through the language interpretation system in order to compare its meaning with the external reality (as in example 14.3.2). Now a strange thing happens: the sentence whose meaning is supposed to correspond to reality turns out to be "Sentence A is not true." So the system looks for sentence A in the external context, finds "A = Sentence A is not true." and the same recursion starts over again. What appears as an inconsistency in Paradigm I turns out to be an infinite recursion in Paradigm II.

14.3.4 A Devious Instance of Linguistic Abbreviation

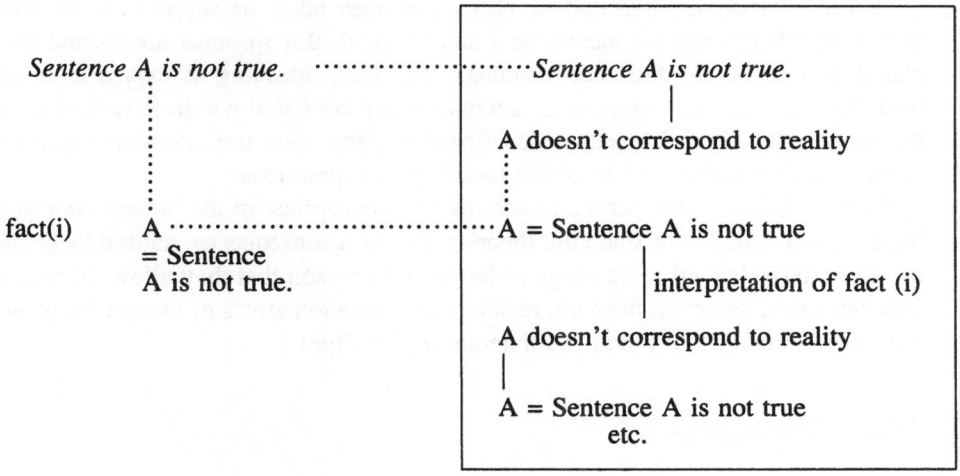

This infinite recursion comes about in 14.3.4 because there is only **one** external referent, namely "A = Sentence A is not true." This external referent performs simultaneously the distinct roles of (1) and (2) in 14.3.2, repeated below for convenience:

1. A = The blue box is on top of the red box (*linguistic abbreviation*)

2. | blue | *(Contextual referents described by the long version of (1))*
     | red |

Clearly, the paradox has reappeared in Paradigm II—not in the object language, not in the metalanguage, but in the interaction of form, meaning, context, and external reality. Instead of a logical inconsistency (as in Paradigm I), the Epimenides Paradox has the form of an infinite recursion in Paradigm II. This infinite recursion in the pragmatics, however, does not affect the consistency of natural-language semantics.

Furthermore, an infinite recursion based on one particular use interpretation may be avoided in an appropriate theory of pragmatics. The purpose of such a theory is to make sense out of the relation between the content of the sign and the associated subcontext. Just as people sometimes have trouble figuring out the intended meaning of an utterance, one valid conclusion of the pragmatic interpretation algorithm may be that the utterance simply doesn't make sense. And in the case illustrated in 14.3.4, this is indeed the most appropriate response.

The Epimenides Paradox, constructed by means of an inappropriate choice of a use interpretation, is not the only example used to support the spurious claim that natural languages are not susceptible to a strictly logical analysis. Each of the other use alternatives indicated in 11.5.1 has been taken as support for the view that natural languages are inconsistent and illogical. But we must understand these claims in light of the fact that meaning$_1$ (the literal meaning of expressions) and meaning$_2$ (the speaker meaning of utterances) are conflated within Paradigm I. For this reason, Paradigm I is incapable of handling any other use alternative than that of sincere, literal, precise use of the meaning of expressions.

The restriction to this particular use may be appropriate in the limited context of logical reconstruction of scientific theories. But as a consequence, natural languages are ultimately claimed to be illogical for the sole reason that they allow other uses. The weakness, however, does not reside in the use alternatives of natural languages, but in the limitation to literal use inherent in Paradigm I.

14.4   Vagueness

The flexibility of natural languages (such as English or German) leads to the claim that they are inherently vague, whereas formal languages (like propositional calculus or predicate calculus) are precise and consistent. This view is not limited to logicians, who regard the formal languages as a means to escape what they perceive as the pitfalls and irregularities of natural languages; it may also be found among linguists whose primary concern is the analysis of natural language. For example, Lakoff (1972, p. 183) claims that "natural-language concepts have vague boundaries and fuzzy edges and that, consequently, natural-language sentences will very often be neither, true nor false, nor nonsensical, but rather true to a certain extent and false to a certain extent, true in certain respects and false in other respects."

Let's illustrate this viewpoint with a few examples. When one observes the process of a door slowly closing, then, we are told, this raises the question at what point is the sentence "The door is open" still true and at what point is the sentence false. One may even feel impelled to ask to what *degree* the sentence is true or false at various stages of closing the door— and similarly for the sentence "The door is closed."

The same considerations may be applied in the evaluation of an adjective like *big*. How much bigger than the average fly must Xerxes be in order for the sentence "Xerxes is a big fly" to be true?[6]

Another situation in which logicians and linguists have found vagueness is the classification of colors. If an object is called *red* in one context, but non-*red* in another, doesn't it follow that the natural-language concept *red* is vague? Indeed, if we consider applying the predicates "x is red" and "x is orange" to the transition from red to orange on a color spectrum, the problem is similar to the first example.

What are the consequences of this widely accepted view? If sentences are true or false only to a certain degree, then the traditional two-valued logic systems do not suffice, and must be extended into many-valued logics. Indeed, different proposals for treating vagueness, such as those by Lakoff (1972), Kamp (1975), Blau (1977), Pinkal (1981), and Kindt (1983), accept the premise inherent in Lakoff's formulation quoted above. The concern of these authors is the construction of different multi-valued logic systems.

In a multi-valued logic a sentence is not either true or false (as in a traditional two-valued—or bivalent—logic), but the truth values are identified with the the real numbers between zero and one. Thus, a sentence may have the truth value 0.615. How sentences get these "vague truth values" is never addressed, however. Rather, the concern is to find an intuitively plausible value assignment for complex formulas like 'A & B', where A and B have been assigned vague truth values (by the logician).

There are numerous multi-valued logics. Some use valuation schemes (supervaluations) rather than vague truth values. Thus, instead of giving a sentence a vague value like 0.615, systems based on valuation schemes assume that a sentence always has a bivalent truth value. By evaluating a sentence many times rather than just once, and by allowing the values of these valuations to vary, one obtains vagueness on the basis of a different technique. In short, multi-valued logics differ mainly in that they

---

[6]The question of degrees of truth and the related question of vagueness of certain words must be clearly distinguished from certain other issues frequently brought into the discussion, namely the intensionality of certain adjectives. The fact that "Xerxes is a big fly" does not entail "Xerxes is a big entity" has nothing to do with the vagueness of *big*. After all, there are completely extensional predicates like *red* which are also considered vague. Thus, "Xerxes has red eyes" clearly entails "Xerxes' eyes are red entities." And conversely, there are adjectives like *alleged* and *fake* which are intensional but not vague.

borrow motivation and/or formal proposals from other areas—such as probability or measurement theory *à la* Kolmogorov (Kamp), mathematical topology (Kindt), supervaluations (Pinkal, Kamp), fuzzy logic *à la* Zadeh (Lakoff), or three-valued logic in the tradition of Łukasiewicz (Blau).

But there is no need for devising logic systems which will "treat vagueness." The depiction of semantic vagueness in the above examples is an absurd artifact of a misguided ontological interpretation of model-theoretic semantics. For us, the meaning of "The door is open" nor of "This stone is red" is not vague. Vagueness does not arise in the literal meaning concepts of natural language (*pace* Lakoff), but rather in the pragmatic process of reference, which we define as the matching relation between the sharply defined concepts of natural-language meanings (icons), and the contextual objects to which these icons refer.

Thus, we propose to treat vagueness through the pragmatic notion of language use (reference) rather than through the semantic notion of truth- or denotation-conditions. This intuitive concept of vagueness is quite different from the widespread view that "natural-language concepts have vague boundaries and fuzzy edges." Attempts to treat vagueness through extensions of traditional logic not only vastly complicate the logic—either by assuming a large number of truth values (fuzzy logic) or by assuming a large number of valuations of a predicate at a point of reference (supervaluations)— but also completely miss the intuitive essence of linguistic vagueness.

Consider the analysis of the slowly closing door in Paradigm II. The sentence "The door is open" has a clearly defined literal meaning, formally specified by a set-theoretic icon representing its truth conditions. The slowly closing door is not a problem concerning the literal meaning of the sentence, and therefore is not a logical problem. The question is how the sentence is *used* relative to the indicated situation. And here it seems that a normal speaker will simply use another sentence—like "The door is closing"—or wait a few moments and say "The door is closed."

Next, consider the sentence "Take the red stone," interpreted in the following two situations. In one situation the hearer is confronted with a grey stone and a pale pink stone. Obeying the utterance "Take the red stone," he will pick the pale pink stone. In the other situation the hearer is confronted with the pale pink stone and a bright red stone. In this case he will not pick the pale pink stone, but the bright red stone. Within Paradigm I model theory it follows that the word *red* is vague: sometimes *red* is true of the pale pink stone and sometimes it is false of this very same stone.

Nunberg (1978) has suggested that predicates referring to different objects in different contexts can be handled in terms of "context-dependent functions." Thus the word *chicken* has the set of live chickens as its extension in one context, but the set of chicken meat batches in another context. This proposal remains firmly within the Paradigm I approach in that it incorporates "context dependency" (of expressions which are clearly not indexicals) into the semantics and treats the relation between, e.g., *chicken*, and its real referents as a direct semantic relation. In Paradigm II, on the other hand, the word *chicken* denotes one and the same icon in the two interpretation contexts, and the different real world referents are accounted for in terms of different uses.

The same is true in the case of the pale pink and the red stones. The sentence "Take the red stone" is not ambiguous, and neither is the word *red*. For the sake of simplicity let's assume that the iconic content of *red* is represented in the form of a little red card of bright red color (regarded as the NLC-robot internal prototype of *red*). The interpretation of the two situations described above is described as follows:

14.4.1

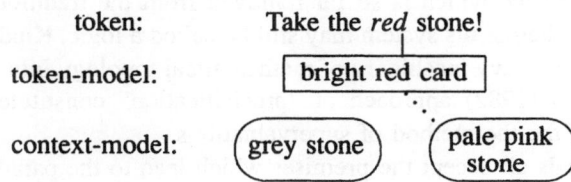

If we change to a context where the grey stone is replaced by a dark red one, the pale pink stone ceases to be the one that best matches the icon. Thus, we have a situation as indicated in 14.4.2:

14.4.2

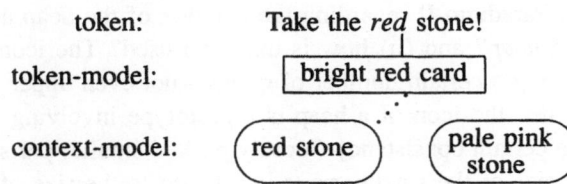

So what happens to the be "red stone" in 14.4.1 happens to be the "non-red stone" in 14.4.2. The point is that it is not the meaning of *red* that is vague or which changes; it is the **context** which changes—and thus the instances of best match.

14.5   The Sorites Paradox

The essence of the Paradigm I approach to vagueness is contained in a classical paradox, namely the Sorites Paradox or "paradox of the heap," which has received considerable attention by contemporary Paradigm I logicians interested in vagueness. The paradox is described as follows: One grain of sand does not form a heap. If we add one grain, we still don't have a heap. If n grains don't form a heap, then adding an $n + 1$ grain will not result in a heap. Yet at some point, when enough grains are added, we arrive at something that is undeniably a heap.

The recent proposals to resolve this paradox all accept it as a semantic paradox, and thus stay within the traditional framework of semantics. But the price paid for these "semantics of vagueness" is considerable. Kamp (1981b) arrives at a notion of semantic inference which is so far removed from the traditional notion that he himself doubts whether his system may still be called a logic. Kindt (1983) proposes to incorporate the heavy machinery of mathematical topology into formal semantics, whereas Pinkal's (1982) approach of "precisification" constitutes a sophisticated development of the the method of supervaluations.

These proposals all accept the premises which lead to the paradox. But when we look at another classical paradox—that of Achilles and the turtle—which today is regarded as solved, we see that one acceptable resolution of a paradox is to revise its premises in an intuitively convincing way. Indeed, this may be the only way to solve a genuine paradox. The moment we accept that a heap is to be defined as having a certain number of grains (e.g., 1 grain: no heap; 100,000 grains, properly arranged: heap) we are trapped. Because now comes the inevitable question: How many grains make the difference between a heap and a non-heap?

Let us look at the problem in a different way. As illustrated by our discussion of the slowly closing door, and of the pale pink versus dark red stones, the crucial questions within Paradigm II regarding the paradox of the heap are: (i) what is the icon of the word *heap*? and (ii) how is this icon used? The icon *heap* should not be defined as having a certain number of grains—not even upper or lower limits of this number. Rather, the icon of a heap is a prototype involving (i) a certain form (cone-like), (ii) a certain consistency (loosely packed smaller parts), and (iii) certain proportions (the size of the smaller parts in relation to the size of the heap and the size of the heap in relation to the rest of the context).

Consider, for example, two people flying at 10,000 feet altitude. Pointing to what looks like a tiny speck on the ground, A says to B: "That heap wasn't there yesterday." In such a case, A would violate the proper use of the icon *heap* even if it should turn out later that the speck on the ground was indeed a "proper" heap of sand. A may be construed to be right in a narrow, pseudo-scientific sense, but that does not mean that A communicated in a natural and reasonable way.

Of course, A could also say:: "Do you see that tiny speck down there. That must be a heap of sand. I don't think it was there yesterday." This situation would be different (from a communication point of view). In the second case, A introduces a context change. A leads B from viewpoint 1 (10,000 feet altitude) to viewpoint 2 (at ground level, close by). It is of no consequence that B cannot *verify* A's conjecture. All that is required is that B is a cooperative partner in this communication in the sense that he is willing to provide a context which accommodates the icon *heap* (on the literal interpretation intended by A).

Now we can summarize the difference between the Paradigm I and the Paradigm II approaches to the Sorites Paradox. Paradigm I presumes a model-theoretic reality which provides various samples of heaps and non-heaps, starting from a single grain and going up to 100,000 grains. The supposed problem is to find a semantic definition of the logical constant *heap*, such that heap(x) is evaluated as 0 (false) if x denotes only one grain, heap(x) is evaluated as 1 if x denotes 100,000 grains, and which furthermore assigns the correct truth values for the critical transition from non-heap to heap. However, no semantic theory can fulfill this last desideratum, because the transition from non-heap to heap is intuitively unclear in a non-trivial sense. The traditional approach to vagueness presents an unsolvable problem, because it asks the wrong questions on the basis of the oversimplified, and as such mistaken, ontological assumptions of Paradigm I.

With the Paradigm II approach, on the other hand, there is no attempt to characterize the transition from non-heap to heap in the semantics. Rather, the icon *heap* is defined in a fixed way as a semantic prototype, just as the icon *red* was defined in terms of a little red card. The question of whether something is properly referred to as a heap is left to the pragmatic process of matching the icon with the context. What counts as a proper heap in one context may be a non-heap in another context (just by changing the relative proportions of the objects relative to each other and relative to the context). This is similar to our example of a pale pink stone, which turned out to be the red species in 14.4.1 and the non-red species in 14.4.2. A further possibility, never discussed in Paradigm I, is the metaphoric use of the icon *heap*, as when an old car is referred to as a "heap of scrap." In this case, the icon invokes an imagined future state of disintegration felt to be so immediately pending as to justify this manner of speaking.

15. Surface Compositional Semantics

The distinction between the literal meaning of expressions and the speaker meaning of utterances (see Chapter 11) is the communication-theoretic precondition for a **surface-compositional** syntax and semantics.[1] Adoption of the surface compositional approach to the syntax and semantics of natural language has two kinds of empirical consequences: (i) the semantic analysis of natural language is limited to structurally based literal meanings of the signs (based on fixed word meanings and systematic syntactic composition), and (ii) all other interpretation phenomena are explained in terms of language use, defined as the interaction between the fixed literal meaning of the sign and the internal utterance context.

The analysis of the Epimenides and the Sorites Paradoxes in the previous chapter illustrated the **second** empirical consequence of surface compositionality: Both paradoxes were analyzed without any change in the denotation-conditional semantics of the language expressions. Instead, the phenomena in question were explained by the interaction between the literal meanings and the utterance context.

The present chapter turns to the analysis of presuppositions and intensional contexts. These phenomena of natural language are traced to the presence of certain words. By providing a specific denotation-conditional meaning analysis of these words, we arive at a grammatical account which exemplifies the **first** empirical consequence of surface compositionality: The semantic properties of certain sentences are defined as the systematic compositional result of the semantic properties of their constituent words.

15.1 Presuppositions

Here and in the following sections we consider semantic phenomena which warrant a conservative extension of traditional logic: semantic presuppositions and intensional contexts. Both phenomena are described in Frege (1892). Presuppositions are introduced in connection with proper names:[2]

> That the name 'Kepler' designates something is just as much a presupposition
> for the assertion 'Kepler died in misery' as for the contrary assertion.

This *invariance under negation* of presuppositions is formally defined as follows:[3]

---

[1] The notion of surface compositionality was first used in the analysis of syntactic mood (Hausser 1978), but conceptually it goes back to the analysis of semantic presuppositions (Hausser 1973). An extensive discussion of surface compositionality may be found in Hausser (1984a).

[2] Frege (1892), in the translation by Black.

[3] After Fraassen (1968). Both 15.1.1 and 15.1.2 capture the intuitive notion of a presupposition

15.1.1 Formal Definition of a Presupposition (Formulation I)

Sentence A presupposes sentence B if and only if A is neither true nor false unless B is true.

This is equivalent to 15.1.2:

15.1.2 Formal Definition of a Presupposition (Formulation II)

Sentence A presupposes sentence B if and only if

1. if A is true then B is true; and

2. if ¬A is true then B is true.

For example, if A = *Kepler died in misery*, and B = *Kepler existed*, then A is bivalent only if B is true. In other words, A carries an *existential presupposition*, and unless this existential presupposition is satisfied, A is neither true nor false.

Frege described certain semantic properties of natural language, such as presuppositions and intensional contexts, with great insight and clarity. But his concern for "truth" led him to regard what distinguishes natural language from a logic system as the "imperfection of language." For Frege,

> languages have the fault of containing expressions which fail to designate an object (although their grammatical form seems to qualify them for that purpose). ... This lends itself to demagogic abuse as easily as ambiguity— perhaps more easily. 'The will of the people' can serve as an example: for it is easy to establish that there is at any rate no generally accepted reference for this expression.[4]

For a Paradigm I logician, the "problem" of presuppositions is to insure that expressions in question always denote. Frege achieved this by letting the expressions in question denote the null class if no suitable referent is available. In contrast, Russell (1905) analyzed sentences with existential presuppositions by means of existential assertions with wide scope over negation.

For a Paradigm II semanticist, on the other hand, the issue of guaranteeing denotations is of no concern. Of course, natural language can be misused to invoke impressions and emotions that are not warranted by the facts. (This is true for visual images, too.) Take, for example, a story beginning as follows: "It was a sunny Sunday afternoon. The city was completely quiet. Everybody had congregated by the river..." We accept the description as a piece of fiction. That we don't know which city, and which river, is of no concern—it is simply the city and the river in the story. That presupposing words can be used without actual counterparts is not a fault of natural language, but part of its expressive power.

---

described in Strawson (1950).

[4]Frege (1892), in the translation by Black.

The semantic analysis of presuppositions raises the following questions. First, what causes a sentence to have a presupposition? Second, what kinds of presuppositions are there in natural language? And third, what are their characteristic semantics in terms of their denotation conditions? The semantic definitions are used only to model the literal meaning. Whether there are any real referents to which these meanings refer (under some use interpretation) is not part of the semantic analysis of the expression, but part of the pragmatic interpretation of the utterance.

Since semantic presuppositions are formally defined by means of entailment relations between sentences (cf. 15.1.1 and 15.1.2), the definition only tells *when* a sentence has a presupposition, but not *why*. Comparison of 15.1.3 and 15.1.4, however, indicates that the presence of a presupposition is induced by certain lexical items.

15.1.3 An Existential Presupposition

(A) John ate the apple. > (C)
(B) John didn't eat the apple. > (C)
(C) There exists an apple.

15.1.4 An Existential Assertion

(A) John ate an apple. > (C)
(B) John didn't eat an apple. ≯ (C)
(C) There exists an apple.

In 15.1.3, sentences A and B entail C (formally 'A > C' and 'B >C'), whereas in 15.1.4, only A entails C, while B does not. Thus, according to the definitions 15.1.1 or 15.1.2, sentences A and B in 15.1.3 *presuppose* sentence C (formally 'A ≫ C' and 'B ≫ C'), while this is not the case in 15.1.4. Furthermore, since the only difference between the respective A and B sentences in 15.1.3 and 15.1.4 is the use of the determiner *the* versus the determiner *a*, we conclude that the presupposition in 15.1.3 is induced by the presence of *the*.

Since *the* induces an existential presupposition, it is called an "existential P-inducer" (Hausser 1973). Using the test illustrated in 15.1.3 and 15.1.4, it may be shown that other existential P-inducers of English are the determiners *every*, *all*, and *some*, whereas the determiners *one*, *two*, *three*, etc., as well as *any* are like *a(n)* in that they do not induce an existential presupposition.

As an example of a P-inducing verb consider 15.1.5:

15.1.5 A Factual Presupposition

(A) John regrets that Mary sold her bike. > (C)
(B) John doesn't regret that Mary sold her bike. > (C)
(C) Mary sold her bike.

If the verb *regret* is replaced by *conclude*, the sentences A and B in 15.1.5 do not presuppose sentence C. Adapting the terminology of Kiparsky and Kiparsky (1970), let us call the presupposition in question a "factual presupposition." Thus, *regret* is a "factual P-inducer" while *conclude* is not.

15.2 Restricted Quantification

Next let us consider the formal implementation of P-inducers in Paradigm II. The Paradigm II approach retains the formal results of model-theoretic semantics,— not for a characterization of truth by using certain logical meanings, but for a characterization of literal meaning by using differentiated denotation conditions. Thereby the model-theoretic objects 1 (true) and 0 (false) are treated on a par with elements of A (the set of individuals) or functions from A into $\{1,0\}$.[5]

The characteristic difference between an existential P-inducer like *the* and and an assertive quantifier like *a* may be treated by extending traditional bivalent predicate calculus to include **restricted quantification**.[6]

15.2.1 Non-Restricted and Restricted Quantification

1. Non-restricted existential quantification:
   $\exists x[f(x) \ \& \ g(x)]$
   This formula is 1 if there exists an x such that f(x) is 1 and g(x) is 1; otherwise it is 0.

2. Restricted existential quantification:
   $\exists x \varepsilon [f(x)]g(x)$
   This formula is 1 if there exists an x such that f(x) is 1 and g(x) is 1; it is 0 if there exists an x such that f(x) is 1, and g(x) is 0 for all x; otherwise it is undefined.

3. Non-restricted universal quantification:
   $\forall x[f(x) \rightarrow g(x)]$
   This formula is 1 if g(x) is 1 for every x for which f(x) is 1; otherwise it is 0.

4. Restricted universal quantification:
   $\forall x \varepsilon [f(x)]g(x)$
   This formula is 1 if g(x) is 1 for every x for which f(x) is 1; it is 0 if there exists at least one x for which f(x) is 1, and g(x) is 0 for all x; otherwise it is undefined.

The different denotation conditions of non-restricted and restricted quantification may be used to capture the meaning differences in the following examples:[7]

---

[5]See the definition of IL_2 in 15.5.1 for further details.

[6]For simplicity, the definitions in 15.2.1 omit the usual variable-value assignment machinery. For the standard formulation see 15.5.1, clauses (9) and (10).

[7]For simplicity, number distinctions (singular versus plural) are not treated in 15.2.2. A more differentiated analysis is given in Hausser (1976).

15.2.2 Examples Illustrating Existential Assertion Versus Presupposition

1. John ate an apple.
   $\exists x[apple(x)\ \&\ eat(j,x)]$

2. John didn't eat an apple.
   $\neg\exists x[apple(x)\ \&\ eat(j,x)]$

3. John ate the apple.
   $\exists x\varepsilon[apple(x)]\ eat(j,x)$

4. John didn't eat the apple.
   $\neg\exists x\varepsilon[apple(x)]\ eat(j,x)$

5. John didn't eat any apple.
   $\neg\forall x[apple(x)\ \rightarrow\ eat(j,x)]$

6. John didn't eat every apple.
   $\neg\forall x\varepsilon[apple(x)]\ eat(j,x)$

The definition of restricted quantification results in the possibility that a sentence may have an undefined truth value. Consequently, the sentential operators ¬, &, v, →, and = have to be redefined. Intuitively, the most straightforward definition of a propositional logic with undefined values is the three value system by Kleene (cf. Rescher (1969)).

15.2.3 Definition of Sentential Operators `a la Kleene

1. Negation: If ϕ is defined, then $\neg\phi$ has the usual definition; otherwise $\neg\phi$ is undefined.

2. Conjunction: $\phi\ \&\ \psi$ is 1 if ϕ is 1 and ψ is 1; $\phi\ \&\ \psi$ is 0 if ϕ is 0 or ψ is 0; otherwise no value is defined.

3. Disjunction: $\phi\ v\ \psi$ is 0 if ϕ is 0 and ψ is 0; $\phi\ v\ \psi$ is 1 if ϕ is 1 or ψ is 1; otherwise no value is defined.

4. Implication: $\phi\ \rightarrow\ \psi$ is 1 if ϕ is 0 or ψ is 1; $\phi\ \rightarrow\ \psi$ is 0 if ϕ is 1 and ψ is 0; otherwise no value is defined.

5. Equality: $\phi = \psi$ is 1 if ϕ and ψ are defined and equal; $\phi = \psi$ is 0 if ϕ and ψ are defined and not equal; otherwise no value is defined.

Kleene's extension of traditional propositional calculus has intuitive appeal. If a conjunction has one false conjunct, the conjunction is false no matter whether the other conjunct is true, false, or undefined. But if a conjunction has one true conjunct, while the other conjunct is undefined, nothing conclusive can be said about the value of the whole, i.e., the conjunction has no defined value. The same is true in case of disjunction. If one disjunct is true, we don't even have to determine whether the other disjunct is true, false, or undefined. But if one disjunct is false and the other is undefined, the disjunction has no defined value. And similarly for the other operators.

Our analysis of existential presuppositions based on restricted quantification and a definition of sentential connectives *á la* Kleene explains the meaning difference of the following complex sentences:

15.2.4 *If Jack has children, all of Jack's children are bald.*

15.2.5 *If baldness is hereditary, all of Jack's children are bald.*

Intuitively, 15.2.5 presupposes that Jack has children, while no such presupposition is carried by 15.2.4. In other words, 15.2.5 can be used literally only if the speaker assumes that Jack has children, while 15.2.4 can be used without this assumption.

What is the reason for this intuitive difference in the denotation conditions? Both sentences contain the same existential P-inducer *all of Jack's children*. Both sentences have the same conditional form. But in 15.2.4 the presupposition of the consequent occurs as the premise, while in 15.2.5 the premise is something unrelated to the presupposition of the consequent.

Given Kleene's definition of the conditional, 15.2.4 is always bivalent: If Jack doesn't have children, the sentence is true because the premise is false; if Jack does have children, on the other hand, the presupposition is fulfilled, and there is no reason for an undefined value. On the other hand, 15.2.5 is undefined if the consequent is undefined. Thus, the intuitive difference between 15.2.4 and 15.2.5 is explained as a straightforward consequence of their different logical structures.

The same phenomenon may be observed with the other logical connectives. Compare, for example, 15.2.6 and 15.2.7.

15.2.6 *Either Jack doesn't have children or all of Jack's children are bald.*

15.2.7 *Either baldness is not hereditary or all of Jack's children are bald.*

15.3   Tautologies, Presupposition Failure, and Vagueness

Kleene's definition of the sentential operators has not been generally accepted because tautologies like $\psi \lor \neg\psi$ are 1 only if ψ is defined; similarly, contradictions like $\psi \ \& \ \neg\psi$ are 0 only if ψ is defined. This property of Kleene's definition is plausible from the viewpoint of common sense intuition. But from a logician's point of view, tautologies should *always* be true, and contradictions should *always* be false, solely on the basis of their form.[8]

---

[8]The underlying distinction between analytic and synthetic statements has been attacked by Quine (1951). For discussion see Gochet (1986).

The most prominent attempt to permit undefined values while preserving the traditional concepts of tautologies and contradictions is the approach of **supervaluations**.[9] Supervaluations are based on a large number of standard or "classical" valuations. These classical valuations are always bivalent. The supervaluation of a sentence is true (false) if all classical valuations are true (false). But if some of the classical valuations are true and others are false, the supervaluation is undefined.

The concept of supervaluations is intuitively akin to a statistical approach to science. If a measurement consistently produces a certain value, it is considered reliable; otherwise its value is "undefined." Once we get to the level of supervaluations, van Fraassen's system assigns the same values as the three-valued system of Kleene, except that a sentence of a tautological form—e.g., $\psi \vee \neg\psi$—is undefined for Kleene if ψ is undefined. But for Van Fraassen the classical tautologies are valid whether or not their constituents are defined. (The corresponding result is true for contradictions.)

The question of whether the classical tautologies should be true always, or only if their constituents are defined, seems particularly important within Paradigm I. Because denotation and reference are not distinguished, the model-theoretic notion of truth is interpreted in an absolute way that does not take into account different possibilities of use.

In Paradigm II, on the other hand, the truth of a statement depends on the accuracy of verbal processing, the accuracy of perception and memory, and the proper pragmatic interpretation (the intended *use* of the expression relative to the context). It is a fact of nature that even logical contradictions may be used to make a true statement.

Consider the sentence "It rains and it doesn't rain," uttered in the dry desert where raindrops reach the hand but evaporate before they reach the ground. Statements like this are common and nobody would accuse the speaker of saying something nonsensical, or false. Now, given that a logically contradictory sentence may be pragmatically true, nothing is lost (as far as the characterization of truth in a Paradigm II system is concerned) if logical tautologies and contradictions are undefined when their constituents are undefined.

The basis of supervaluations is multiple evaluations of a sentence at an index. This procedure makes intuitive sense only if the model-theoretic evaluation is identified with the process of reference. Yet reference is handled in terms of *ad hoc* definitions within the Paradigm I approach.

In a Paradigm II system, on the other hand, there is no room for multiple evaluations. The purpose of the model-theoretic interpretation is the characterization of the literal meaning using denotation conditions (represented by a minimal, but exhaustive, model structure), whereas the process of reference is not part of the semantics.

---

[9]Fraassen (1966, 1968, 1969).

The desire of some logicians to avoid undefined truth values in tautologies and contradictions goes back to Frege and Russell, and was inspired metaphysically. When logical methods were first used in linguistic semantics in the early seventies, the campaign to "save the tautologies" was taken up by some linguists with a vengeance.[10] To avoid the consequences of possible presupposition failure, they proposed variants of Russell's entailment analysis, calling the result a theory of "pragmatics." Examples like 15.3.1[11] were presented as proof that definite noun phrases do not always require existence in order for the sentence to be bivalent.

15.3.1 *The king of France didn't visit the exhibition—France hasn't got a King.*

That sentences like 15.3.2

15.3.2 *The king of France didn't visit the exhibition.*

carry a "strong suggestion" of existence was explained as a pragmatic phenomenon (in the sense of Gricean principles of conventional implicitures (cf. Section 11.2)).

However, the appeal to pragmatics may also be turned into an argument *for* semantic presuppositions. The fact that 15.3.1 may be *used* at all has a pragmatic explanation: the sentence can be used only in a very specific type of speech act, which we might call a corrective speech act.[12] Since the purpose of a semantic analysis is the characterization of the literal meaning, special uses—like that illustrated in 15.3.1—do not constitute an argument against a denotation-conditional analysis of presuppositions. After all, even sentences of a contradictory form can be used in a pragmatically sensible way.[13]

Finally, consider the relation between presupposition failure and vagueness. In Paradigm I vagueness and presupposition failure are essentially indistinguishable: both arise when a sentence cannot be evaluated as either true or false. Therefore, the assignment of no truth value—or a third truth value—is assumed in either case (per definition of the model structure) and the whole interest is directed towards the question of what deductions are valid from premises with an undefined or third value, or how component sentences with an undefined or third value figure in the value of a complex sentence. The assumption that vagueness and presupposition failure are logically the same is made explicitly in Blau (1977). Implicitly, this assumption is made in Kamp (1975, 1981b), Pinkal (1981), and others who use supervaluations.

If presuppositions are a semantic property of expressions and vagueness is a pragmatic property of utterances, then it is a mistake to treat presupposition failure and

---

[10]Karttunen and Peters (1977).

[11]From Kempson (1975, p. 86).

[12]Speech acts are the central notion of ordinary language philosophy (Austin (1962), Searle (1969)). Unfortunately, this attempt to provide an alternative to truth-conditioanl semantics acts has remained an isolated effort because its ontological and methodological foundations were never sufficiently clarified. For the same reason, later attempts at a formalization added very little to the initial informal description.

[13]Kempson now accepts a semantic notion of presuppositions.

vagueness with the same formal system, i.e., a semantics based on multi-valued logic. The origin of this mistake is in the failure of traditional model-theoretic systems to distinguish between semantics, dealing with the truth- (or rather denotation-) conditional analysis of the literal meaning of natural-language expressions, and pragmatics, which analyzes the use of natural-language expressions by a speaker-hearer relative to a context.

When a theory is a special case of a more general theory, it is characteristic that certain distinctions which are well-motivated in the general theory collapse in the context of the special theory. In the case of Paradigm I systems, which are a special case of Paradigm II systems (as explained in Section 12.5 above), this phenomenon may be observed in a number of linguistically relevant instances. The most general notions at issue are those of semantic versus pragmatic interpretation, which are distinct processes in a Paradigm II system, but indistinguishable in a Paradigm I system. A more special case in point are the notions of vagueness and presupposition failure.

15.4   Intensional Contexts

While the analysis of existential presuppositions is based on the definition of the logical quantifiers, the analysis of factual presuppositions is connected with the definition of logical functors. Intuitively, *regret* denotes a function taking a sentence as its argument, such that the value of this function is undefined unless the argument has the value *true*. Thus, *John regrets that the present king of France is bald* has a truth value only if it is true that the present king of France is bald. In contrast, *discover* denotes a function of the same type which may be bivalent even if the argument has the value *false*. Thus, *John discovered that the present king of France is bald* may be bivalent if the complement sentence is false, i.e., if there is a king of France and he doesn't happen to be bald.

The semantic analysis of verbs like *regret* and *discover* is closely connected with the analysis of verbs creating intensional contexts. A sentence like *John believes that the present king of France is bald* is intuitively bivalent even if the value of the complement sentence is undefined (because of presupposition failure). Thus, *believe* denotes a function of the same type as *regret*, but it is bivalent no matter whether the argument is true, false, or undefined.

Intensional contexts are defined in contrast with extensional contexts.[14] In logic, extensional contexts are characterized by two rules: **substitutivity of identicals** and **existential generalization**. Substitutivity of identicals is illustrated as follows:

15.4.1 *John finds the morning star.*

---

[14]Intensional and extensional contexts are *verbal* contexts which must be clearly distinguished from speaker-hearer contexts and subcontexts (cf. 2.2.1).

Since the morning star happens to be the evening star, and 15.1.1 happens to be an extensional context, we may replace "the morning star" by "the evening star" *salva veritate*. That is, the substitution represented by the transition from 15.4.1 to 15.4.2

15.4.2 *John finds the evening star.*

does not result in a change in truth value.

Existential generalization is illustrated as follows:

15.4.3 *John finds a unicorn.*

15.4.3 entails 15.4.4

15.4.4 *There exists at least one unicorn.*

That is, whenever 15.4.3 is true, 15.4.4 is true.

The rules of **substitutivity of identicals** (SI) and **existential generalization** (EG) are important to the extensional approach to logical semantics, which characterizes meaning as a direct relation between expressions and referents, without the intermediate stage of a concept. It has long been noted, however, that in natural-language there are systematic exceptions to the rules of SI and EG. Those syntactic environments in which SI and EG fail are called *opaque contexts* (Quine 1960), or *intensional contexts* (Montague 1974). Consider 15.4.5 and 15.4.6:

15.4.5 *Necessarily, the morning star is the morning star.*

15.4.6 *Necessarily, the morning star is the evening star.*

While 15.4.5 is intuitively true, 15.4.6 is not, even though 15.4.7 happens to be true:

15.4.7 *The morning star is the evening star.*

Thus, the modal operator *necessarily* creates an intensional context which causes substitutivity of identicals to fail.

Turning to EG, consider 15.4.8.

15.4.8 *John seeks a unicorn.*

While 15.4.3 entails 15.4.4, 15.4.8 does not entail 15.4.4. Thus, *seek*—in contrast to *find*—creates an intensional context, causing existential generalization to fail with respect to the object term.

As long as expressions like *the morning star* or *a unicorn* denote their extensional referents (or are regarded as doing so), SI and EG must hold. In intensional contexts, however, where SI and EG do not hold, the expressions in question cannot denote their "natural" extensional referents. After all, 15.2.2 can be true whether or not any unicorns exist.

If we take the extensional approach as basic, intensional contexts force us to ask what kind of denotation (other than their extensional referents) expressions should denote. Within Paradigm I, most authors assume that in extensional contexts expressions denote "real objects." Since SI and EG do not hold in intensional contexts, these authors are forced to postulate that in intensional contexts expressions denote something else. Frege, for example, assumes a denotational ambiguity between "Bedeutung" and "Sinn," Russell between "primary occurrence" and "secondary occurrence," Quine betwen "proper occurrence" and "accidental occurrence," and Montague between "extensions" and "intensions."

In Paradigm II, on the other hand, the distinction between extensional and intensional contexts is one of differing denotation *conditions*. A denotation-conditional account of the respective failure, versus validity of SI and EG, does not require the use of different *kinds* of denotations. Instead, we define a logic system where expressions always and uniformly denote intensions, and where the difference between intensional and extensional contexts is handled in the definitions of the functions creating these contexts.

The question of what constitutes an extensional versus an intensional logic system is complicated by different uses of the terminology. The following properties have been used to characterize a system as extensional.

15.4.9 Different Definitions of Extensionality

A system may be called extensional if it

1. allows unrestricted substitution of equivalent expressions,
2. fails to treat the difference between intensional and extensional contexts, or
3. avoids the use of possible worlds.

The system presented in 15.5.1 is intensional in the sense of (2) and (3), i.e., it treats the difference between intensional and extensional contexts in terms of different denotation conditions, and it uses the notion of possible worlds. However, in Paradigm II the model structure is part of the NLC-robot (in contrast to Paradigm I, where the speaker/hearer is part of the model structure); therefore possible worlds are intuitively interpreted as belief-states of the NLC-robot, and not as possible states of the universe. We thus use the term "possible world" in a technical sense in order to maintain the traditional definitions of the modal operators and intensions. A similar reinterpretation holds of our notion of extension, which has the meaning "value of an intension function," but not "object of robot-external reality."

With respect to (1) in 15.4.9, the system defined in 15.5.1 may be called extensional in that it allows unrestricted substitution of logically equivalent terms. The reason is that expressions always denote intensions, defined as functions from world-time pairs to extensions.

Another "extensional" feature of the strictly intensional logic defined in 15.5.1 is the absence of an intension operator ' ^ '. Logically speaking, this is probably the most interesting property of the system. It simplifies the logic in that it removes one of the two restrictions on lambda conversion,[15] according to which $\lambda x_\alpha[A_\beta(x)]B_\beta \equiv A_\beta(B_\alpha)$ is not valid if x lies within the scope of ' ^ ' (unless B is modally closed).[16]

15.5   A Unified Semantic Account

There are several reasons why definition of a formal logic system in 15.5.1 is appropriate. First, it provides a coherent account of presuppositions and intensional contexts in a tradition of high formal standards. Second, it serves as a concrete example for many of the issues of semantic interpretation and ontology discussed in the previous chapters. Third, it provides us with a well-defined formal language which can be used in the discussion of semantic issues as long as no formal definition of frame-theoretic semantics has been provided.

15.5.1 Definition of the Strictly Intensional Presuppositional Logic IL_2

1. The IL_2 Lexicon
1.1 *Types*
Let e, t, and s be three objects (0, 1, and 2) that are distinct and not an ordered pair or triple. The TYPE, or set of types, of IL_2 is the smallest set of Y such that

1. e,t ε Y;
2. whenever a, b ε Y, $<a,b>$ ε Y, and
3. whenever a ε Y, $<s,a>$ ε Y.

1.2 *Basic Expressions*
We shall employ denumerably many variables and infinitely many constants of each type. In particular, if n is any natural number and a ε TYPE, we understand by $v_{n,a}$ the nth variable of type a, and by Con_a the set of constants of type a.

2. The IL_2-Interpretation
2.1 *Possible Interpretations*
Let A, I, J be any sets, which we may regard as the set of entities (or individuals), the set of possible worlds, and the set of moments of time, respectively. In addition, let a be a type. Then $D_{a,A,I,J}$, or set of possible

---

[15]Cf. Gallin (1975) pp. 18, 19, AS4.
[16]For a more extensive discussion of this particular feature of extensional systems with intension and lambda-operator—like PTQ—see Link (1979), pp. 106 and 158.

denotations of type a corresponding to A, I, and J, may be introduced by the following definition:

$$D_{e,A,I,J} = A$$
$$D_{t,A,I,J} = \{0,1\}$$
$$D_{<a,b>,A,I,J} = D_{b,A,I,J}{}^{D_{a,A,I,J}}$$
$$D_{<s,a>,A,I,J} = D_{a,A,I,J}{}^{I \times J}$$

2.2 Interpretation or Intensional Model
By an interpretation we mean a quintuple $(A,I,J,\leq,F)$ such that

1. A,I,J are non-empty sets;
2. $\leq$ is a simple (that is, linear) ordering having J as its field;
3. F is a function having as its domain the set of all constants; and
4. whenever $a \; \varepsilon$ TYPE and $\alpha \; \varepsilon$ CON, $F(\alpha) \; \varepsilon \; D_{a,A,I,J}$

2.3 Intension and Extension
Suppose that @ is an interpretation having the form $<A,I,J,\leq,F>$. Suppose also that g is an @ assignment (of values to variables)—that is, a function having as its domain the set of all variables, such that $g(u) \; \varepsilon \; D_{a,A,I,J}$ whenever u is a variable of type a. If α is a meaningful expression (i.e., a member of the set ME to be defined below) and α is of type $<s,a>$, we shall understand by $a^{@,g}$ the intension of α with respect to @ and g; if $<i,j> \; \varepsilon \; I \times J$, then $\alpha^{@,i,j,g}$ is to be the extension of α with respect to @,i,j, and g—that is, $\alpha^{@,g}(<i,j>)$ or the function value of the intension of α when applied to the point of reference $<i,j>$.

3. The Syntax and Semantics of IL_2
The set of meaningful expressions ME of IL_2 is recursively defined in the clauses (1-11), while the corresponding denotation conditions are recursively defined in clauses (1'-11'):

(1) Every constant of type $<s,a>$ is in $ME_{<s,a>}$.
(1') If α is a constant of type $<s,a>$, then $\alpha^{@,g}$ is $F(\alpha)$.

(2) Every variable of type $<s,a>$ is in $ME_{<s,a>}$.
(2') If α is a variable of type $<s,a>$, then $\alpha^{@,g}$ is $g(\alpha)$.

(3) If $\alpha \; \varepsilon \; ME_{<s,a>}$, then $(\check{\,}\alpha) \; \varepsilon \; ME_a$.
(3') If $\alpha \; \varepsilon \; ME_{<s,a>}$, and $(i,j) \; \varepsilon \; I \times J$, then $(\check{\,}\alpha)^{@,i,j,g}$ is $\alpha^{@,g}(i,j)$.

(4) If $\alpha \; \varepsilon \; ME_{<s,a>}$, and u is a variable of type $<s,b>$, then $(\lambda u \alpha) \; \varepsilon$ $ME_{<s,<<s,b>,a>>}$.
(4') If $\alpha \; \varepsilon \; ME_{<s,a>}$, and and u is a variable of type $<s,b>$, then $(\lambda u \alpha)$ is that function h from $I \times J$ to $D_{a,A,I,J}{}^{D_{<s,b>,A,I,J}}$ such that whenever x

is in the domain of $D_{<s,b>,A,I,J}$, $h(<i,j>)(x)$ is $(\check{}\alpha)^{@,i,j,g'}$, where g' is the @-assignment like g except for the possible difference that g'(u) is x.

(5) If $\alpha \; \varepsilon \; ME_{<s,<<s,b>,a>>}$ and $\beta \; \varepsilon \; ME_{<s,b>}$, then $\alpha(\beta) \; \varepsilon \; ME_{<s,a>}$.

(5') If $\alpha \; \varepsilon \; ME_{<s,<<s,b>,a>>}$ and $\beta \; \varepsilon \; ME_{<s,b>}$, then $\alpha(\beta)$ is a function from $I \times J$ to $D_{a,A,I,J}$ such that $(\check{}\alpha(\beta))^{@,i,j,g}$ is $(\check{}\alpha)^{@,i,j,g}(\beta)^{@,g}$.

(6) If $\alpha, \beta \; \varepsilon \; ME_{<s,a>}$, then $(\alpha = \beta) \; \varepsilon \; ME_{<s,t>}$.

(6') If $\alpha, \beta \; \varepsilon \; ME_{<s,a>}$, then $(\alpha = \beta)$ is a function from $I \times J$ to $D_{t,A,I,J}$ such that $(\check{}\alpha)^{@,i,j,g}$ is $(\check{}\beta)^{@,i,j,g}$.

(7) If $\phi \; \varepsilon \; ME_{<s,t>}$, then $(\neg\phi) \; \varepsilon \; ME_{<s,t>}$.

(7') If $\phi \; \varepsilon \; ME_{<s,t>}$, then $(\neg\phi)^{@,g}$ is a function from $I \times J$ to $D_{t,A,I,J}$ such that $(\check{}\neg\phi)^{@,i,j,g}$ is 1 iff $(\check{}\phi)^{@,i,j,g}$ is 0, and $(\check{}\neg\phi)^{@,i,j,g}$ is 0 iff $(\check{}\phi)^{@,i,j,g}$ is 1; otherwise no value is defined.

(8) If $\phi, \psi \; \varepsilon \; ME_{<s,t>}$, then $(\phi \; \& \; \psi)$, $(\phi \; \& \; \psi)$, $(\phi \; v \; \psi)$, $(\phi \rightarrow \psi) \; \varepsilon \; ME_{<s,t>}$.

(8') If $\phi, \psi \; \varepsilon \; ME_{<s,t>}$, then $(\phi \; \& \; \psi)^{@,g}$ is a function from $I \times J$ to $D_{t,A,I,J}$ such that $(\check{}(\phi \; \& \; \psi))^{@,i,j,g}$ 1 iff $(\check{}\phi)^{@,i,j,g}$ and $(\check{}\psi)^{@,i,j,g}$ is 1; $(\check{}(\phi \; \& \; \psi))^{@,i,j,g}$ is 0 iff $(\check{}\phi)^{@,i,j,g}$ or $(\check{}\psi)^{@,i,j,g}$ is 0; otherwise a value is not defined.

$(\phi \; v \; \psi)^{@,g}$ is a function from $I \times J$ to $D_{t,A,I,J}$ such that $(\check{}(\phi \; v \; \psi))^{@,i,j,g}$ 0 iff $(\check{}\phi)^{@,i,j,g}$ and $(\check{}\psi)^{@,i,j,g}$ is 0; $(\check{}(\phi \; \& \; \psi))^{@,i,j,g}$ is 1 iff $(\check{}\phi)^{@,i,j,g}$ or $(\check{}\psi)^{@,i,j,g}$ is 1; otherwise a value is not defined.

$(\phi \rightarrow \psi)^{@,g}$ is a function from $I \times J$ to $D_{t,A,I,J}$ such that $(\check{}(\phi \rightarrow \psi))^{@,i,j,g}$ is 1 iff $(\check{}\phi)^{@,i,j,g}$ and $(\check{}\psi)^{@,i,j,g}$ is 0. $(\check{}(\phi \; \& \; \psi))^{@,i,j,g}$ is 1 iff $(\check{}\phi)^{@,i,j,g}$ is 0 or $(\check{}\psi)^{@,i,j,g}$ is 1; otherwise a value is not defined.

(9) If $\phi \; \varepsilon \; ME_{<s,t>}$ and u is a variable, then $\exists u\phi$ and $\forall u\phi \; \varepsilon \; ME_{<s,t>}$.

(9') If $\phi \; \varepsilon \; ME_{<s,t>}$ and u is a variable of type $<s,a>$, then $\exists u\phi^{@,g}$ is a function from $I \times J$ to $D_{t,A,I,J}$ such that $(\check{}\exists u\phi)^{@,i,j,g}$ is 1 if and only if there exists $x \; \varepsilon \; D_{<s,a>,A,I,J}$ such that $(\check{}\phi)^{@,i,j,g'}$ is 1, where g' is as in 4; and similarly for $\forall u\phi$.

(10) If $\phi, \psi \; \varepsilon \; ME_{<s,t>}$ and u is a variable, then $\exists u\varepsilon[\phi]\psi$ and $\forall u\varepsilon[\phi]\psi \; \varepsilon \; ME_{<s,t>}$.

(10') If $\phi, \psi \; \varepsilon \; ME_{<s,t>}$ and u is a variable of type $<s,a>$, then $\exists u\varepsilon[\phi]\psi^{@,g}$ is a function from $I \times J$ to $D_{t,A,I,J}$ such that $(\check{}\exists u\varepsilon[\phi]\psi^{@,i,j,g}$ is 1 if there exists an x in $D_{a,A,I,J}$ such that $(\check{}\phi)^{@,i,j,g'}$ is 1 and $(\check{}\psi)^{@,i,j,g'}$ is 1, where g' is as in 4; and $(\check{}\exists u\varepsilon[\phi]\psi^{@,i,j,g}$ is 0 if there exists an x in $D_{a,A,I,J}$ such that $(\check{}\phi)^{@,i,j,g'}$ is 1 and for every x in $D_{a,A,I,J}$ $(\check{}\psi)^{@,i,j,g'}$ is 0; otherwise a value is not defined.

If $\phi, \psi \; \varepsilon \; ME_{<s,t>}$ and u is a variable of type $<s,a>$, then $\forall u\varepsilon[\phi]\psi^{@,g}$ is a function from $I \times J$ to $D_{t,A,I,J}$ such that $(\check{}\forall u\varepsilon[\phi]\psi^{@,i,j,g}$ is 1 if and only if for each x in $D_{a,A,I,J}$ if $(\check{}\phi)^{@,i,j,g'}$ is 1 then $(\check{}\psi)^{@,i,j,g'}$ is 1, and for some x $(\check{}\phi)^{@,i,j,g'}$ is 1, where g' is as in 4; $(\forall u\varepsilon[\phi]\psi^{@,i,j,g}$ is 0 if for some x in $D_{a,A,I,J}$ $(\check{}\phi)^{@,i,j,g'}$ is 1 and $(\check{}\psi)^{@,i,j,g'}$ is 0; otherwise a value is not defined.

(11) If $\phi \,\varepsilon\, ME_{<s,t>}$, then $\Box\phi$, $W\phi$, $H\phi \,\varepsilon\, ME_{<s,t>}$.

(11') If $\phi \,\varepsilon\, ME_{<s,t>}$, then $\Box\phi^{@,g}$ is a function from I × J to $D_{t,A,I,J}$ such that $(\check{}\Box)^{@,i,j,g}$ is 1 if and only if $(\check{}\phi)^{@,i',j',g}$ is 1 for all i' ε I and j' ε J; and similarly for W and H.

Nothing is in any set ME_a except as required by (1-11). If ϕ is a formula (that is, a member of $ME_{<s,t>}$), then $(\check{}\phi)$ is true with respect to @,i,j if and only if $(\check{}\phi)^{@,i,j,g}$ is 1 for every @-assignment g.

The strict intensionality of IL_2 is based on an unusual type structure. In PTQ (Montague 1974), functors are defined as functions from intensions to extensions, e.g., $<<s,a>,b>$. In order to apply such a function to an argument β of type $<a>$, the argument has to be "intensionalized" in the syntax, e.g., $\alpha(\hat{}\,\beta)$. In IL_2, on the other hand, functors are defined as functions from intensions to intensions, e.g., $<s,<<s,a>,b>>$. Since all expressions are defined as intensions in IL_2, there is no need to define an intension operator '$\hat{}$', though the extension operator is still available.

15.5.2 The Type Structure of IL_2 compared with PTQ

		Functor	Argument	Result
PTQ:	Syntax	α	β	$\alpha(\hat{}\,\beta)$
	Types	$<<s,a>,b>$	$<a>$	$<b>$
IL_2:	Syntax	α	β	$\alpha(\beta)$
	Types	$<s,<<s,a>,b>>$	$<s,a>$	$<s,b>$

A strictly intensional logic has an advantage in that it avoids the switching between the intensional and the extensional level characteristic of PTQ. Thus, there is no need for the PTQ conventions associated with curly brackets, sub-stars, etc. Furthermore, the system has the intuitive advantage that sentences denote propositions (and not truth values, as in PTQ), noun phrases denote properties (and not sets), etc. The absence of an intension operator formally incorporates the intuition, expressed already by Frege and Russell, that there is no way back from an extension to the original intension.

The formalism of IL_2 may be interpreted ontologically according to all four possibilities described in Section 12.5.

The first possibility of interpreting IL_2 is a $<$-constr, -sense$>$ approach, such as a standard logical interpretation `a la Montague. Thus, the sets A, I, and J are taken to represent real objects, and the purpose of the system is a modelling of the world by the logician. That such a model cannot even begin to describe reality in all its complexity is not taken as a serious objection because the goal is merely to account for the *principles* of semantic interpretation in general, and a characterization of "truth" in particular.

The second possibility of interpreting IL_2 is a $<$+constr, -sense$>$ approach, such as a simplified A.I. interpretation `a la SHURDLU. Thus, the sets A, I, and J are interpreted as objects in a database which are manipulated by the computer program. Such an approach is +constr because the metalanguage definitions of the logical expressions are implemented as mechanical (electronic) operations; it is -sense because no attempt is made to arrive at an analysis of *meaning concepts*.[17]

The third possible interpretation of IL_2 is a $<$-constr, +sense$>$ approach. According to "situation semantics," for example, the calculus is interpreted as describing an "abstract situation." This approach is -constr because the abstract situations are assumed to be real, external, platonic entities; it is +sense because the abstract situations are regarded as "meanings," and truth is defined somewhat indirectly by way of embedding the abstract situations in the "real situations."

The fourth possible interpretation of IL_2 is a $<$+constr, +sense$>$ approach. As explained in Section 12.5, such an interpretation is motivated by the desire to model spontaneous reference to new objects. Use of IL_2 in the color reader described in Section 12.3, for example, would constitute a +constr approach because the metalanguage definitions of the logical expressions are implemented as mechanical (electronic) operations; it constitutes a +sense approach because the sets A, I, and J are used not as objects in the robots internal knowledge representation (context), but for defining the literal meaning of language expressions in terms of minimal but exhaustive model structures.

Because a $<$+constr, +sense$>$ approach defines the relation between the "set theoretic icon" and the context as a speaker-hearer internal process, it can model different types of pragmatic interpretation (cf. Section 11.5.) in terms of different speaker-hearer internal matching operations. But if the interpretation is restricted to literal use and a predefined domain (as in SHURDLU, for example), a $<$+const, +sense$>$ and a $<$+constr, -sense$>$ approach turn out to be equivalent.

In Artificial Intelligence, the formal properties of a logical calculus cannot be completely separated from questions of proper ontological interpretation. Development of the basic ontological alternatives, specified above in terms of the features

---

[17] As explained in Section 5.4, the formal treatment of intensions in the style of Carnap and Montague does not amount to a description of meaning concepts. Hence the -sense classification.

±constr and ±sense, may prove more useful for the design of better inference systems in Artificial Intelligence than modifications of traditional logical calculi based on exotic valuation schemes.

Conclusion

This book presented a formal theory of *possible continuations*, and applied it to the analysis of natural language. Incorporating possible continuations into natural language analysis required extensions and revisions of current linguistic, computational and philosophical theory of natural language, which were described in Parts I, II, and III, respectively.

Our analysis of natural language is based on the following premises:

1. the syntax is time-linear (or left-associative),
2. the semantics is surface-compositional (or constructive), and
3. the pragmatics consists of matching surface-compositional literal meanings with the utterance context.

These premises are clear structural hypotheses which support each other in a unified model of communication. This model is designed for computational implementation, and it is, as such, testable. Furthermore, each of the three premises may be justified in its own right.

I.

The *left-associative derivation order* is psychologically well motivated because it is input-output equivalent with the speaker-hearer. It is heuristically optimal in computational linguistics because it results in absolutely type-transparent parsers and generators.[1]

Beyond the conceptual justification, however, a new approach to syntactic analysis has to demonstrate empirical coverage and formal transparency. We showed that LA-grammar provides powerful, linguistically well-motivated syntactico-semantic analyses of natural language by presenting sizable fragments of English[2] and German.[3]

We reconstructed the traditional PS-grammar based analysis of generative capacity in LA-grammar,[4] and presented explicit LA-grammars for numerous formal languages familiar in the literature. Furthermore, we analyzed the computational complexity of LA-grammar, and proved that LA-grammars are more efficient computationally than systems which are not left-associative.[5] Also, we were able to

---

[1]Cf. Sections 3.5 and 8.1.
[2]Cf. Appendices.
[3]Cf. Hausser (1986).
[4]Cf. Chapter 7.
[5]Cf. Chapter 10.

obtain decidability results[6] for a new class of grammars, called D-LAGs, which covers many context-free as well as context-sensitive languages.

II.

The premise of *surface compositionality* affects syntax, semantics, and pragmatics. In semantics, surface compositionality results in a structurally based notion of literal meaning. This has the effect of a clean separation between expression meanings (meaning$_1$) and utterance meanings (meaning$_2$). The surface-compositional approach is conceptually simple because it limits semantics to the automatic conversion of surface structures into literal meanings based on operationalized meta-language definitions.[7]

In syntax, surface compositionality results in a system based solely on the composition of concrete entities, i.e., categorially analyzed word forms. However, while the principle of surface compositionality provides a strong formal link between syntax and semantics in the form of the homomorphism condition,[8] it does not suffice as the sole structural basis of syntactic analysis. Without the additional assumption of a time-linear derivation order, surface-compositional syntax is underspecified.

Conventional approaches have attempted to motivate the composition of words and phrases on the basis of semantic considerations and intuitions. This strategy, which does not utilize the surface order in a basic, systematic fashion, results in inadequate constraints on syntactic derivations and creates artificial problems.[9]

As long as derivation order is treated as a performance phenomenon left to the procedural aspect of the implementation, there are just too many ways for words to be put together in a sentence. On the other hand, utilizing the surface order in the form of a time-linear derivation order results in surface compositional systems which are highly constrained combinatorially. Also, it provides a sound basis for the simultaneous derivation of semantic hierarchies which not only capture the relevant intuitions, but are suitable for pragmatic interpretation.

---

[6]Cf. Chapter 9.

[7]Cf. Section 13.2.

[8]Surface compositional semantics extends a well-established formal technique pioneered by Montague, consisting of the simultaneous derivation of surface and meaning structures, whereby the latter are homomorphic with the former.

[9]Constituent-structure analysis, for example, requires transformations and/or feature components to handle discontinuous constituents. A categorial grammar approach based on functor-argument structures, on the other hand, either generates an enormous number of equivalent derivations (e.g., Lambek (1958), Geach (1972)), or constrains the combinatorics at the cost of high lexical ambiguity (Hausser 1984a). Semantically motivated approaches to motivating (or constraining) syntactic composition also necessitate postulation of zero-surfaces or "traces."

III.

Internal-matching pragmatics provides an operational notion of language use, defined as the speaker-hearer's internal matching of literal meanings and the utterance context. This treatment of language use is founded on structurally based literal meanings, yet is capable of handling metaphor, irony, and vagueness.[10] We showed, furthermore, that traditional <-constr,-sense> approaches in formal logic may be viewed as a special case of the <+constr,+sense> ontology required for the construction of NLC-robots.

From the viewpoint of pragmatics, a surface-compositional approach to semantics provides the highly structured tools (literal meanings) without which a theory of use cannot get off the ground. Once we have the tool and the object to be worked on (context), however, we need a strategy for performing the task.

The pragmatic matching process is accomplished in accordance with the Linear Path Hypothesis:[11] the literal meanings of the natural-language expressions and the utterance context are closely coordinated on the basis of the time-linear structure of the sign. The starting point of the pragmatic interpretation is determined via the STAR-point of the sign. After that, the pragmatic interpretation follows the sequential surface order in the form of a two-level path.

Without the assumption of a time-linear derivation order, the pragmatics would be structurally underspecified — just as the surface-compositional syntax. But the STAR-point isolates the small contextual substructure relevant for the interpretation, and the Linear Path Hypothesis severely delimits the set of potential matching candidates accessible at each combination step.

Thus the matching task is greatly facilitated: Because there are only a few matching candidates at any given point in the incremental pragmatic interpretation, a relatively simple meaning structure of the sign suffices for proper reference. The syntactico-semantic theory of possible continuations is equally suitable for incremental pragmatic interpretation (analysis) and connected meaning extraction (generation).[12]

---

[10]Cf. Sections 11.5, 14.4, and 14.5.
[11]Cf. Section 5.3.
[12]Cf. Sections 5.4, 5.5.

Appendices

Appendices

Introductory Remarks

The following appendices describe different aspects of the LA-grammar for English, called ECAT. Appendix A lists the category segments and categories used by ELEX (the lexicon of ECAT) and the ECAT-derivations. Appendix B presents seven sample derivations, illustrating the handling of different constructions in English. Appendix C presents the current set of sample sentences.

In LA-grammar, the syntactic analysis of a sentence is explicitly stated in the history sections of its linear derivation. Each history section represents a left-associative combination between a sentence start and a next word.

A left-associative combination is defined by the input categories, the output category, and the rule name. The relation between the input categories and the output category represents an instantiation of the categorial operation of the respective rule.

The linguistic motivation underlying the categorial operation depends largely on the conceptual interpretation of the category segments involved. As an example, consider the following history section:

```
    (GQ) THE
    (SH) MAN
 *DET+NOUN_2
 2
    (S) THE MAN
```

This information may be paraphrased as follows: Given a general quantifier (GQ) like *the*, and a singular human noun (SH) like *man*, the rule DET+NOUN renders a singular noun phrase (S) with the surface *the man*.

In other words, the history section provides an explicit instantiation of the rule DET+NOUN, which may be notated as follows:

DET+NOUN: [(GQ)(SH)] ⇒ [*DET+NOUN (S)]

Based on the explicit instantiations of categorial operations in the history sections, and the interpretation of the category segments (Appendix A), the reader may reconstruct the linguistic motivation of each left-associative composition in the sample derivations of Appendix B (as well as the derivations presented in the previous text).

Appendix C contains 421 sentences, each exhibiting different syntactic constructions. This set evolved during the design and expansion of ECAT. After the addition of a new construction to the grammar, the entire sample set is parsed automatically, and the derivations are written into a file. This file is printed in hard copy (currently comprising more than 600 pages), and proofread for parsing errors. After the grammar has been amended, the process is repeated until all derivations are correct. In addition, the derivation file may be processed in the manner illustrated in 4.1.7.

A. ECAT Category Segments and Categories

In ECAT/ELEX the name of a category segment indicating a valency position is usually different from that of the segment indicating a compatible argument. For example, the nominative valency position N in the category (N A V) of *ate* may be filled by a noun phrase of category (S), (P), (S3), etc. In other words, in ECAT the category segments used to indicate the 'slot' differ from those indicating the 'filler'; compatibility between a given valency position and an argument is specified in the linguistic rules of the grammar. In some instances, the valency position has the same name as the argument, e.g., *John has* of category (HV V) combines with *given* of category (HV D A) into *John has given* of category (D A V). But such cases of categorial correspondence with identity are the exception in ECAT/ELEX.

A.1 Alphabetical List of Category Segments

1. **A** [accusative]

   indicates valency position for a noun phrase, e.g., (SAW (N A V).

2. **ADJ** [adjective]

   represents elementary adjective, e.g., (BEAUTIFUL (ADJ)).

3. **ADP** [ad-phrase]

   represents result category of an adverbial phrase, e.g., (AFTER (ADP NP)).

4. **ADV** [adverb]

   represents elementary adverb, such as (ALREADY (ADV)).

5. **B** [be]

   indicates valency position for a present participle, e.g., (AM (S1 B V)), and represents result category of present participle verb forms, e.g., (GIVING (B D A)).

6. **BY** [by]

   indicates valency position for an optional by-phrase, e.g., *John was given a book* of category (BY V).

7. **CADJ** [comparative adjective]

   represents comparative form of adjective, e.g., (FASTER (CADJ)).

8. **D** [dative]

indicates valency position for a noun phrase, e.g., (GAVE (N D A V)).

9. **DECL** [declarative]

result category of a complete declarative sentence, e.g., (%. (V DECL)).

10. **DO** [do]

second segment of verb forms in the *do* paradigm, e.g., (DOES (S3 DO V)).

11. **GN** [genitive noun]

represents the genitive form of singular and plural nouns such as (UNCLE'S (GN)) and (UNCLES' (GN)).

12. **GNQ** [genitive noun quantifier]

represents the genitive form of proper names, such as (BILL'S (GNQ)), which function as determiners.

13. **GQ** [general quantifier]

represents determiners which have no agreement restrictions on whether the noun is singular or plural, e.g., (the (GQ)) as in *the man, the men*.

14. **HV** [have]

indicates valency position for a past participle, e.g., (HAVE (NOM HV V)), and represents result category of past participles, e.g., (GIVEN (HV D A)).

15. **IMP** [imperative]

result category of a complete imperative sentence, e.g., (! (VIMP IMP)).

16. **INF** [infinitive]

indicates valency position for infinitive form of a verb, e.g., *John promised Mary to* of category (INF V).

17. **INF&A** [infinitive binding accusative]

indicates valency position for an infinitive whose underlying subject is coreferential with the indirect object (A) of the higher sentence, e.g., (PERSUADE (NOM A INF&A V)) as in *John persuaded Mary to sleep*.

18. **INF&N** [infinitive binding nominative]

indicates valency position for an infinitive whose underlying subject is correferential with the subject (NOM) of the higher sentence, e.g., (PROMISE (NOM D INF&N V)) as in *John promised Mary to sleep*.

19. **INT** [intensifier]

represents modifiers like (VERY (INT)) which can recursively modify adjectives and adverbs.

20. **INTERROG** [interrogative]

result category of a complete interrogative sentence, e.g., (? (V INTERROG)).

21. **M** [modal]

second segment of modal verbs, e.g., (COULD (N M V)).

22. **MR** [more]

represents the comparative modifier (MORE (MR)).

23. **MST** [most]

represents the comparative modifier (MOST (MST)).

24. **N** [nominative]

indicates valency position for noun phrases of all persons and numbers, e.g., (GAVE (N D A V)).

25. **NH** [name human]

represents singular noun phrases denoting a person, e.g., (JOHN (NH)), for proper names.

26. **N-H** [name non-human]

represents singular noun phrases denoting a non-person, e.g., (FIDO (N-H)).

27. **NM** [nominative]

indicates valency position for noun phrases of all numbers and persons except the first and third person singular, e.g., (ARE (NM B V)).

28. **NOM**

'nominative', indicates valency position for noun phrases of all persons and numbers except the third person singular, e.g., (GIVE (NOM D A V)).

29. **NP** [noun phrase]

indicates noun phrase valency position which does not assign a case, e.g., (TO (ADP NP)).

30. **P** [plural]

represents noun phrases of third person plural without case marking, e.g., (THE MEN (P)).

31. **P1** [plural first person]

represents noun phrase of first person plural marked for nominative, e.g., (WE (P1)).

32. **:P1** [oblique plural first person]

represents first person plural noun phrases which cannot fill a nominative valency position, e.g., (US (:P1)).

33. **P3** [plural third person]

represents noun phrases of third person plural marked for nominative, e.g., (THEY (P3)).

34. **:P3** [oblique plural third person]

represents noun phrases of third person plural which cannot fill a nominative valency position, e.g (THEM (:P3)).

35. **PH** [plural human]

represents plural nouns denoting persons, e.g., (MEN (PH)).

36. **P-H** [plural non-human]

represents plural nouns denoting things, e.g., (CARS (P-H)).

37. **PQ** [plural quantifier]

represents plural indefinite determiners, e.g., (ALL (PQ)).

38. **S** [singular]

represents singular noun phrases without case marking, e.g., (THE MAN (S)).

39. **S1** [singular first person]

indicates a valency position for first person singular nominative, e.g., (AM (S1 B V)), and represents first person singular noun phrases marked for nominative case, e.g., (I (S1)).

40. **:S1** [oblique singular first person]

represents first person singular noun phrases which cannot fill nominative valency position, e.g., (ME (:S1)).

41. **S3** [singular third person]

indicates a valency position for third person singular nominative, e.g., (gives (S3 D A V)), and represents third person singular noun phrases marked for nominative case, e.g., (HE (S3)) and (SHE (S3)).

42. **:S3** [oblique singular third person]

represents third person singular noun phrases which cannot fill a nominative valency position, e.g., (HIM (:S3)) and (HER (:S3)).

43. **SADJ** [superlative adjective]

represents superlative form of adjective, e.g., (FASTEST (SADJ)).

44. **SC** [subordinate clause]

indicates valency position for subordinate clauses which may be open or closed, e.g, *John read + that...* versus *John read + who....*

45. **SC&C** [closed subordinate clause]

indicates a valency position for a closed subordinate clause, e.g., *Mary believes* of category (SC&C V), and represents subordinating conjunctions, e.g., (THAT (SC&C)).

46. **SC&O** [open subordinate clause]

indicates a valency position for an open subordinate clause, e.g., *Mary wonders + who....*

47. **SC-INF&N** [closed subordinate clause or infinitive binding nominative]

indicates a valency position for an subordinate clause or infinitive, e.g., *Mary deserves + what ...* or *Mary deserves + that ...* or *Mary deserves + to ...*

48. **SH** [singular human]

represents singular nouns beginning with a consonant and denoting a person, e.g., (MAN (SH)).

49. **S-H** [singular non-human]

represents singular nouns beginning with a consonant and denoting a thing, e.g., (CAR (S-H)).

50. **SNP** [sentence or noun phrase]

represents valency position for a sentence or a noun phrase in certain prepositions like (BEFORE (ADP SNP)), which can be used as sentential conjunctions, as in *Before John ate the apple*, and as prepositions, as in *Before the movie*.

51. **SP2** [singular-plural second person]

represents second person pronoun (YOU (SP2)), which can fill nominative and oblique case positions in singular and plural, e.g., *I·see you*, *You see me*, etc.

52. **SQ** [singular quantifier]

represents singular indefinite determiners, e.g., (A (SQ)).

53. **TO** [to]

indicates a valency position for a to-phrase, e.g., (GAVE (N A TO V)).

54. **V** [verb]

indicates a valency position for a declarative sentence, e.g., (DECL V), and represents the result category of finite verbs, e.g., (was (S3 B V)), and sentence starts containing a finite verb, e.g., *John was* of category (B V).

55. **VI** [verb interrogative]

indicates a valency position for an interrogative sentence, e.g (VI INTER-ROG), and represents result category of sentence starts marked for interrogative mood, e.g., *Was John* or *Who was* of category (B VI).

56. **VIMP** [verb imperative]

indicates a valency position for an imperative sentence, e.g (VIMP IMP), and represents result category of sentence starts marked for interrogative mood, e.g., *Give John* of category (A VIMP) or (TO VIMP).

57. **WH** [w-phrase human]

represents interrogative noun phrases used as relative and interrogative pronouns, e.g., (WHO (WH)).

58. **:WH** [oblique w-phrase human]

represents interrogative noun phrases used as relative and interrogative pronouns (WHOM (:WH)).

59. **W-H** [w-phrase non-human]

represents interrogative noun phrases used as relative pronouns, e.g., (WHICH (W-H)) and (WHAT (W-H)).

60. **WP** [w-phrase plural]

represents plural interrogative noun phrases, e.g., *which books* or *which men* of category (WP).

61. **WQ** [w-phrase quantifier]

represents interrogative determiners without agreement restrictions on the first letter of the next word or on whether it is singular or plural, e.g., (WHICH (WQ)) in *which man, which men, which autos*, etc.

62. **WS** [w-phrase singular]

represents singular interrogative noun phrases, e.g., *which book* or *which man* of category (WS).

63. **WT** [w-phrase topicalized]

represents topicalized w-phrase as in *Who did John ..* of category (DO WT VI).

In addition to the 63 segments listed above, ECAT/ELEX use the markers &, 0, %, *, as well as an open-ended set of word surfaces and prepositions to handle idiomatic expressions, phrasal verbs, and discontinuous constituents. The present treatment of these expressions is just a first try. A systematic lexical analysis may have to explore alternative means of coding; for example, one might want to define "cover"-segments which represent different sets of phrasal continuations.

The marker & is used in **idiomatic phrases**, e.g.,

```
("GANG" (NOM A V & "UP" "ON") GANG-UP-ON)
```

The remaining parts of the idiomatic surface are listed to the right of &. See example B.7.1 for an explicit derivation.

The treatment of **phrasal verbs** is based on optional valency positions for prepositional phrases. For example, the following analysis of *agree* indicates that besides the nominative there may be a *with*-phrase, as in *John agreed with Mary*. The "0" in (0 WITH) indicates that this position may be empty, as in *John agreed*. The second non-nominative valency position specifies possible *on-*, *upon-*, and *about*-phrases, as in *John agreed (with Mary) on the contract*.

```
("AGREE" (NOM (0 WITH) (0 ON UPON ABOUT INF&N) V) AGREE)
```

Another possible use of *agree* is with a nominative-binding infinitival object (INF&N), as in *John agree (with Mary) to cooperate*.

The treatment of **discontinuous constituents** uses the marker "%":

```
("LOOK" (NOM A UP% V) LOOK)
```

The % in UP% indicates that this preposition does not require a noun phrase argument. See example 3.3.4 for a complete derivation.

The treatment of "stranded prepositions" uses the marker "*":

```
    (B WT VI) WHO WAS THE BONE
    (HV A TO) GIVEN
*OBJ+VERB_12
5
    (TO* BY VI) WHO WAS THE BONE GIVEN
```

As indicated by the above history section, the "*" marker is introduced by a syntactic rule. Like "%", the "*" indicates that the preposition does not take a noun phrase argument in the surface—though one is provided in the semantics (see derivation B.4.1).

A.2   List of ELEX categories

The following lexical categories evolved during the development of the current ECAT version, and underly the fragment characterized in Appendix C. What holds for the ECAT analysis of English in general applies also to the ECAT categories: their list is still partial and experimental.[1]

The categories are grouped into (1) substantives, (2) verbs, (3) auxiliaries and modals, (4) adverbs, (5) determiners, (6) adjectives, (7) intensifiers, (8) prepositions, (9) conjunctions, (10) interrogative and relative pro-forms, and (11) mood markers. The first three groups are subdivided. The total of distinct ELEX categories is ninetyfour.

1. SUBSTANTIVES:

- **nouns:** (SH), (S-H), (PH), (P-H), (GN)

```
("MAN"   (SH)  MAN)
("CAR"   (S-H) CAR)
("MEN"   (PH)  MAN)
("CARS"  (P-H) CAR)
("MAN'S" (GN)  MAN)
("MENS'" (GN)  MAN)
```

- **proper names:** (NH), (N-H), (GNQ)

```
("JOHN"   (NH)  JOHN)
("FIDO"   (N-H) FIDO)
("BILL'S" (GNQ) BILL)  ·
```

- **pronominal noun phrases:**
  (S1), (:S1), (SP2), (S3), (:S3), (P1), (:P1), (P3), (:P3)

```
("I"   (S1)  I)
("ME"  (:S1) I)
("YOU" (SP2) YOU)
("HE"  (S3)  HE)
("SHE" (S3)  SHE)
("IT"  (N-H) IT)
("HIM" (:S3) HE)
("HER" (:S3) SHE)
("WE"  (P1)  WE)
```

---

[1]Specifically, we consider abandoning the H versus -H distinction in nouns and proper names, because the relevant agreement information may be obtained directly from the pragmatics (contextual referent). Thus SH and S-H would collapse into SN (for singular noun), PH and P-H would collapse into PN (plural noun), and NH and N-H would collapse into PN (proper name). In relative pronouns, i.e., *who* and *which* the distinction would remain.

```
("US"  (:P1) WE)
("THEY" (P3) THEY)
("THEM" (:P3) THEM)
```

2. VERBS[2]

- **intransitive verbs:** (NOM V), (S3 V), (N V), (HV), (B)

```
("WALK"  (NOM V) WALK)
("WALKS" (S3 V) WALK)
("WALKED" (N V) WALK
          (HV) WALK)
("WALKING" (B) WALK)
```

- **transitive verbs:**

  o noun-phrase objects:

  (NOM A V), (S3 A V), (N A V), (B A), (HV A)

```
("EAT"  (NOM A V) EAT)
("EATS" (S3 A V) EAT)
("ATE"  (N A V) EAT)
("EATING" (B A) EAT)
("EATEN" (HV A) EAT)
```

  o noun-phrase or sentential objects:

  (NOM SC V), (S3 SC V), (N SC V), (B SC), (HV SC)

```
("KNOW"  (NOM SC V) KNOW)
("KNOWS" (S3 SC V) KNOW)
("KNEW"  (N SC V) KNOW)
("KNOWING" (B SC) KNOW)
("KNOWN"  (HV SC) KNOW)
```

  o noun-phrase or closed sentential objects:

  (NOM SC&C V), (S3 SC&C V), (N SC&C V), (HV SC&C), (B SC&C)

```
("BELIEVE"  (NOM SC&C V) BELIEVE)
("BELIEVES" (S3 SC&C V) BELIEVE)
("BELIEVED" (N SC&C V) BELIEVE
            (HV SC&C) BELIEVE)
("BELIEVING" (B SC&C) BELIEVE)
```

  o open sentential objects:

  (NOM SC&O V), (S3 SC&O V), (N SC&O V), (B SC&O), (HV SC&O)

```
("WONDER"  (NOM SC&O V) WONDER)
("WONDERS" (S3 SC&O V) WONDER)
("WONDERD" (N SC&O V) WONDER
           (HV SC&O) WONDER)
("WONDERING" (B SC&O) WONDER)
```

---

[2]For reasons of perspicuity, irrelevant lexical readings are not shown (for example, the lexical analysis of WALK as a verb does include the corresponding noun).

o noun-phrase or sentential object or nominative-binding infinitival objects:

(NOM SC-INF&N V), (S3 SC-INF&N V), (N SC-INF&N V),
(B SC-INF&N), (HV SC-INF&N)

```
("DESERVE" (NOM SC-INF&N V) DESERVE)
("DESERVES" (S3 SC-INF&N V) DESERVE)
("DESERVED" (N SC-INF&N V) DESERVE
           (HV SC-INF&N) DESERVE)
("DESERVING" (B SC-INF&N) DESERVE)
```

o noun-phrase or nominative-binding infinitival objects:

(NOM INF&N V), (S3 INF&N V), (N INF&N V), (B INF&N),
(HV INF&N)

```
("TRY" (NOM INF&N V) TRY)
("TRIES" (S3 INF&N V) TRY
("TRIED" (N INF&N V) TRY
         (HV INF&N) TRY)
("TRYING" (B INF&N) TRY)
```

- **ditransitive verbs:**

  o dative and accusative noun-phrase objects

  (NOM D A V), (S3 D A V), (N D A V), (B D A), (HV D A)

  or accusative noun-phrase object and *to*-phrase

  (NOM A TO V), (S3 A TO V), (N A TO V), (B A TO), (HV A TO)

```
("GIVE" (NOM D A V) GIVE
        (NOM A TO V) GIVE)
("GIVES" (S3 D A V) GIVE
         (S3 A TO V) GIVE)
("GAVE" (N D A V) GIVE
        (N A TO V) GIVE)
("GIVING" (B D A) GIVE
          (B A TO) GIVE)
("GIVEN" (HV D A) GIVE
         (HV A TO) GIVE)
```

o dative and nominative-binding infinitival (or noun-phrase) objects:

(NOM D INF&N V), (S3 D INF&N V), (N D INF&N V), (B D INF&N),
(HV D INF&N)

or accusative noun-phrase object and *to*-phrase

(NOM A TO V), (S3 A TO V), (N A TO V), (B A TO), (HV A TO)

```
("PROMISE" (NOM D INF&N V) PROMISE
           (NOM A TO V) PROMISE)
("PROMISES" (S3 D INF&N V) PROMISE
            (S3 A TO V) PROMISE)
("PROMISED" (N D INF&N V) PROMISE
            (N A TO V) PROMISE
            (HV D INF&N) PROMISE
```

```
                    (HV A TO) PROMISE)
("PROMISING" (B D INF&N) PROMISE
                    (B A TO) PROMISE)
```

o accusative and accusative-binding infinitival objects:

(NOM A INF&A V), (S3 A INF&A V), (N A INF&A V), (B A INF&A),
(HV D INF&A)

```
("PERSUADE"  (NOM A INF&A V) PERSUADE)
("PERSUADES" (S3 A INF&A V) PERSUADE)
("PERSUADED" (N A INF&A V) PERSUADE
                    (HV D INF&A) PERSUADE)
("PERSUADING" (B A INF&A) PERSUADE)
```

- **phrasal verbs: (N A V & " " ...)**

```
("GANG"   (NOM A V & "UP" "ON") GANG-UP-ON)
("GANGS"  (S3 A V $ "UP" "ON") GANG-UP-ON)
("GANGED" (N A V & "UP" "ON") GANG-UP-ON
                (HV A & "UP" "ON") GANG-UP-ON)
("GANGING" (B A & "UP" "ON") GANG-UP-ON)
```

3. AUXILIARIES and MODALS:

- *have*-paradigm: **(NOM HV V), (S3 HV V), (N HV V), (B A)**

```
("HAVE"   (NOM HV V) HAVE)
("HAS"    (S3 HV V) HAVE)
("HAD"    (N HV V) HAVE)
("HAVING" (B A) HAVE)
```

- *be*-paradigm: **(S1 B V), (NM B V), (S3 B V), (N B V), (B B)**

```
("AM"    (S1 B V) BE)
("ARE"   (NM B V) BE)
("IS"    (S3 B V) BE)
("WAS"   (S1 B V) BE (S3 B V) BE)
("WERE"  (N B V) BE)
("BEING" (B B) BE)
```

- *do*-paradigm: **(NOM DO V), (S3 DO V), (N DO V), (B DO)**

```
("DO"    (NOM DO V) DO)
("DOES"  (S3 DO V) DO)
("DID"   (N DO V) DO)
("DOING" (B DO) DO)
```

- modals: **(N M V)**

```
("SHOULD" (N M V) SHALL)
```

4. ADVERB: (ADV)

```
("BEAUTIFULLY" (ADV) BEAUTIFUL)
```

5. DETERMINERS: (SQ), (PQ), (GQ)

```
("A" (SQ) A)
("ALL" (PQ) ALL)
("THE" (GQ) THE)
```

6. ADJECTIVES: (ADJ), (CADJ), (SADJ)

```
("FAST" (ADJ) FAST)
("FASTER" (CADJ) FAST)
("FASTEST" (SADJ) FAST)
```

7. INTENSIFIERS: (INT), (MR), (MST)

```
("VERY" (INT) VERY)
("MORE" (MR) MORE)
("MOST" (MST) MOST)
```

8. PREPOSITIONS: (ADP NP), (ADP SNP)

```
("BY" (ADP NP) BY)
("AFTER" (ADP SNP) AFTER)
```

9. CONJUNCTIONS: (SC&C), (ADP SNP), (ADP SC&O)

```
("THAT" (SC&C) THAT)
("AFTER" (ADP SNP) AFTER)
("WHY" (ADP SC&O) WHY)
("WHERE" (ADP SC&O) WHERE)
        etc.
```

10. INTERROGATIVE and RELATIVE PRO-FORMS: (WH), (:WH), (W-H), (WQ)

```
("WHO" (WH) WHO)
("WHOM" (:WH) WHO)
("WHICH" (W-H) WHICH)
("WHICH" (WQ) WHICH)
```

11. MOOD MARKERS: (V DECL), (VI INTERROG), (VIMP IMP)

```
("/." (V DECL) DECLARATIVE)
("?" (VI INTERROG) INTERROGATIVE)
("!" (VIMP IMP) IMPERATIVE)
```

A.3 Derived ECAT categories

Of the sixtythree category segments listed in Section A.1, the following do not occur in any lexical categories: BY, S, P, WS, WP, INF and WT. Instead, these segments are introduced by certain syntactic rules. Specifically, BY is introduced by ADD-VERB, as illustrated in the following history section.

```
    (B V)  THE BONE WAS
    (HV SC) FOUND
 *ADD-VERB_6
 4
    (BY V)  THE BONE WAS FOUND
```

The segments S, P, WS, and WP are introduced by the rule DET+NOUN:

```
(GQ) THE            (GQ) THE             (WQ) WHICH           (WQ) WHICH
(S-H) BONE          (P-H) BONES          (S-H) BONE           (P-H) BONES
*DET+NOUN_2         *DET+NOUN_2          *DET+NOUN_2          *DET+NOUN_2
2                   2                    2                    2
(S) THE BONE        (P) THE BONES        (WS) WHICH BONE      (WP) WHICH BONES
```

The segment INF is introduced by the rule START-INF:

```
    (INF&N V) JOHN TRIED
    (ADP NP) TO
 *START-INF_7
 3
    (INF V) JOHN TRIED TO
```

Once the underlying subject of the infinitive, specified by the verb (e.g., INF&N), has been coded in the semantics, the addition of *to* results in the simplified infinitive segment INF. See example B.3.1 for an explicit derivation.

The segment WT is introduced by the rule MAIN+AUX:

```
    (WH) WHO
    (S3 B V) WAS
 *MAIN&W+AUX_11
 2
    (S3 B WT VI) WHO WAS
```

See example B.4.1 for an explicit derivation.

Parsing the 421 sample sentences presented in Appendix C results in 250 distinct sentence-start categories, e.g., (GQ A V), (SQ A V), (PQ A V), etc. Given that sixtythree category segments (cf. Appendix A.1) result theoretically in 63^2 (= 3969) 2-segment categories, or 63^3 (= 250 047) 3-segment categories, a total of 250 different sentence start categories is a small number.

B. Sample Derivations

In the following examples, two timings are specified at the top of the derivation. The 'real time' and 'run time' on the left indicate the parse time of the derivation with the "frames switched off", while the timings of the semantically interpreted system are given on the right. Addition of a frame-theoretic semantics to an LA-grammar results in run times which are ten to fifty times slower than the syntactic analyses alone. This is due to the fact that the present system *copies* the frames at each combination step. The faster alternative of using *views* instead of frame-copying has not yet been implemented.

For comparisons with other parsers only the timings on the left are relevant, unless the other system also generates both a syntactic analysis and a minimal database. In the sample set of the current system (cf. Appendix C), no syntactic derivation takes longer than 0.2 seconds. The indicated timings are those of a Hewlett-Packard 9000 machine.[1]

B.1   Yes/No Interrogative

B.1.1 *Did Fido find the bone?*

```
*  (z Did Fido find the bone ?)
Real time:      0.04 s                        Real time:      1.10 s
Run time:       0.04 s                        Run time:       0.64 s

    Linear Analysis:

    *START_0
    1
        (N DO V)  DID
        (N-H)  FIDO
    *FVERB+NOM_10
    2
        (DO VI)  DID FIDO
        (NOM SC V)  FIND
    *ADD-VERB_6 ·
    3
        (SC VI)  DID FIDO FIND
        (GQ)  THE
    *FVERB+MAIN_4
    4
        (GQ VI)  DID FIDO FIND THE
        (S-H)  BONE
    *DET+NOUN_2
```

---

[1]Common Lisp, release Rev. 1.01, 14-May-87.

```
5
    (VI) DID FIDO FIND THE BONE
    (VI INTERROG) ?
*CMPLT_13
6
    (INTERROG) DID FIDO FIND THE BONE ?
```

Hierarchical Analysis:

```
(PROPOSITION-6_10_8
 (MOOD (INTERROGATIVE-6_10_8))
 (PROP-CONTENT
  ((SENT-1_10_8
   (SUBJ ((NP-2_10_8 (NAME (FIDO-2_10_8)))))
   (AUX (DO-1_10_8))
   (PREDICATE
    ((NFV-3_10_8
     (INF (FIND-3_10_8))
     (DIR-OBJ
      ((NP-4_10_8 (REF (THE-4_10_8 SG-5_10_8)) (NOUN ((BONE-5_10_8)))))))))
    ))))))
```

The first rule in example B.1.1, i.e., FVERB+NOM changes the V-segment in the
ss-category of history section 1 into VI (cf. history section 2). This ensures that the
sentence must end with a question mark.

B.2   Ambiguity in a Passive Sentence

LA-grammar analyzes passive as the combination of an auxiliary of paradigm *be*
and a past participle, e.g., ((the bone was)(B V)) ((given)(HV A TO)). As shown in
history section 4, the result category is (TO AG V). Example B.2.1 is ambiguous
between an interpretation of *by the man* as postnominal modifier of *dog* and as agent
phrase of the passive verb.

B.2.1 *The bone was given to the dog by the man.*

```
* (z the bone was given to the dog by the man \.)
Real time:    0.14 s                         Real time:    2.24 s
Run time:     0.12 s                         Run time:     2.12 s

2    Linear Analysis:

    *START_0
    1
        (GQ) THE
        (S-H) BONE
    *DET+NOUN_2
    2
        (S) THE BONE
        (S3 B V) WAS
    *NOM+FVERB_3
```

```
3
    (B V)  THE  BONE  WAS
    (HV A TO)  GIVEN
*ADD-VERB_6
4
    (TO BY V)  THE  BONE  WAS  GIVEN
    (ADP NP)  TO
*FVERB+MAIN_4
5
    (NP BY V)  THE  BONE  WAS  GIVEN  TO
    (GQ)  THE
*PREP+NP_5
6
    (GQ BY V)  THE  BONE  WAS  GIVEN  TO  THE
    (S-H)  DOG
*DET+NOUN_2
7
    (BY V)  THE  BONE  WAS  GIVEN  TO  THE  DOG
    (ADP NP)  BY
*FVERB+MAIN_4
8
    (NP V)  THE  BONE  WAS  GIVEN  TO  THE  DOG  BY
    (GQ)  THE
*PREP+NP_5
9
    (GQ V)  THE  BONE  WAS  GIVEN  TO  THE  DOG  BY  THE
    (SH)  MAN
*DET+NOUN_2
10
    (V)  THE  BONE  WAS  GIVEN  TO  THE  DOG  BY  THE  MAN
    (V DECL)  .
*CMPLT_13
11
    (DECL)  THE  BONE  WAS  GIVEN  TO  THE  DOG  BY  THE  MAN  .
```

Hierarchical Analysis:

```
(PROPOSITION-11_19_9
  (MOOD (DECLARATIVE-11_19_9))
  (PROP-CONTENT
    ((SENT-3_19_9
      (SUBJ
        ((NP-1_19_9 (REF (THE-1_19_9 SG-2_19_9)) (NOUN ((BONE-2_19_9))))))
      (AUX (BE-3_19_9))
      (PASSIVE-PREDICATE
        ((NFV-4_19_9
          (PAST-PART (GIVE-4_19_9))
          (PREPOSITIONAL_OBJ
            ((PREP-5_19_9
              (PREPOSITION (TO-5_19_9))
              (PREPOSITIONAL-ARG
                ((NP-6_19_9 (REF (THE-6_19_9 SG-7_19_9)) (NOUN ((DOG-7_19_9)))))
                ))))
          (AGENT-PHRASE
            ((PREP-8_19_9
              (PREPOSITION (BY-8_19_9))
```

```
        (PREPOSITIONAL-ARG
          ((NP-9_19_9
            (REF (THE-9_19_9 SG-10_19_9))
            (NOUN ((MAN-10_19_9)))))))))))))))))
```

1   Linear Analysis:

```
    *START_0
    1
        (GQ) THE
        (S-H) BONE
    *DET+NOUN_2
    2
        (S) THE BONE
        (S3 B V) WAS
    *NOM+FVERB_3
    3
        (B V) THE BONE WAS
        (HV A TO) GIVEN
    *ADD-VERB_6
    4
        (TO BY V) THE BONE WAS GIVEN
        (ADP NP) TO
    *FVERB+MAIN_4
    5
        (NP BY V) THE BONE WAS GIVEN TO
        (GQ) THE
    *PREP+NP_5
    6
        (GQ BY V) THE BONE WAS GIVEN TO THE
        (S-H) DOG
    *DET+NOUN_2
    7
        (BY V) THE BONE WAS GIVEN TO THE DOG
        (ADP NP) BY
    *ADD-ADP_14
    8
        (NP BY V) THE BONE WAS GIVEN TO THE DOG BY
        (GQ) THE
    *PREP+NP_5
    9
        (GQ BY V) THE BONE WAS GIVEN TO THE DOG BY THE
        (SH) MAN
    *DET+NOUN_2
    10
        (BY V) THE BONE WAS GIVEN TO THE DOG BY THE MAN
        (V DECL) .
    *CMPLT_13
    11
        (DECL) THE BONE WAS GIVEN TO THE DOG BY THE MAN .
```

Hierarchical Analysis:

(PROPOSITION-11_18_9

```
(MOOD (DECLARATIVE-11_18_9))
(PROP-CONTENT
 ((SENT-3_18_9
   (SUBJ
    ((NP-1_18_9 (REF (THE-1_18_9 SG-2_18_9)) (NOUN ((BONE-2_18_9))))))
   (AUX (BE-3_18_9))
   (PASSIVE-PREDICATE
    ((NFV-4_18_9
      (PAST-PART (GIVE-4_18_9))
      (PREPOSITIONAL_OBJ
       ((PREP-5_18_9
         (PREPOSITION (TO-5_18_9))
         (PREPOSITIONAL-ARG
          ((NP-6_18_9
            (REF (THE-6_18_9 SG-7_18_9))
            (NOUN ((DOG-7_18_9)))
            (PNM
             ((PREP-8_18_9
               (PREPOSITION (BY-8_18_9))
               (PREPOSITIONAL-ARG
                ((NP-9_18_9
                  (REF (THE-9_18_9 SG-10_18_9))
                  (NOUN ((MAN-10_18_9)))))))))))))))))
      (ADVERB ("PREP-8_18_9"))))))))))
```

As in 3.3.8, the different readings in B.2.1 stem from applications of different rules.
Up to history section 6 (*the bone was given to the dog*) the two derivations are
syntactically and semantically identical. But in history section 7 of the first reading
the rule FVERB+MAIN applies, while in the second reading it is the rule ADD-ADP.
Note that ADD-ADP handles both the adnominal and the adverbial interpretation of
the by-phrase. In this way an excessive number of readings is avoided, while the
pragmatic interpretation still has two choices to interpret the PREP-8_18_9 frame.
The example *The bone was given to the dog by the man by the woman* is generated
with three readings, in accordance with our intuition.

B.3   Recursion of Control

Example B.3.1 illustrates the recursive handling of "control". In a sentence like *Fido
promised Eddie to bark* the subject of the infinitive is Fido, but in *Fido persuaded
Eddie to bark* the underlying subject is Eddie. This difference is encoded in the
category segments INF&N versus INF&D representing the valency of the infinitival clause of the verbs. For example, *promise* has the category (N D INF&N V),
while *persuade* has the category (N D INF&D V). In order to provide for the correct semantic interpretation, the hierarchical analysis must indicate the "underlying"
subjects of the infinitival clauses.

B.3.1 *Fido tried to persuade Eddie to try to persuade Felix to try to promise Zach to steal the book.*

```
* (z Fido tried to persuade Eddie to try to persuade Felix to try to
    promise Zach to steal the book \.)
```

Real time: 0.16 s   Real time: 6.72 s
Run time: 0.16 s   Run time: 6.26 s

Linear Analysis:

```
*START_0
1
    (N-H) FIDO
    (N INF&N V) TRIED
*NOM+FVERB_3
2
    (INF&N V) FIDO TRIED
    (ADP NP) TO
*START-INF_7
3
    (INF V) FIDO TRIED TO
    (NOM D INF&A V) PERSUADE
*ADD-VERB_6
4
    (D INF&A V) FIDO TRIED TO PERSUADE
    (N-H) EDDIE
*FVERB+MAIN_4
5
    (INF&A V) FIDO TRIED TO PERSUADE EDDIE
    (ADP NP) TO
*START-INF_7
6
    (INF V) FIDO TRIED TO PERSUADE EDDIE TO
    (NOM INF&N V) TRY
*ADD-VERB_6
7
    (INF&N V) FIDO TRIED TO PERSUADE EDDIE TO TRY
    (ADP NP) TO
*START-INF_7
8
    (INF V) FIDO TRIED TO PERSUADE EDDIE TO TRY TO
    (NOM D INF&A V) PERSUADE
*ADD-VERB_6
9
    (D INF&A V) FIDO TRIED TO PERSUADE EDDIE TO TRY TO PERSUADE
    (N-H) FELIX
*FVERB+MAIN_4
10
    (INF&A V) FIDO TRIED TO PERSUADE EDDIE TO TRY TO PERSUADE FELIX
    (ADP NP) TO
*START-INF_7
11
    (INF V) FIDO TRIED TO PERSUADE EDDIE TO TRY TO PERSUADE FELIX
    TO
    (NOM INF&N V) TRY
*ADD-VERB_6
12
```

```
    (INF&N V) FIDO TRIED TO PERSUADE EDDIE TO TRY TO PERSUADE FELIX
    TO TRY
    (ADP NP) TO
*START-INF_7
13
    (INF V) FIDO TRIED TO PERSUADE EDDIE TO TRY TO PERSUADE FELIX
    TO TRY TO
    (NOM D INF&N V) PROMISE
*ADD-VERB_6
14
    (D INF&N V) FIDO TRIED TO PERSUADE EDDIE TO TRY TO PERSUADE FELIX
    TO TRY TO PROMISE
    (N-H) ZACH
*FVERB+MAIN_4
15
    (INF&N V) FIDO TRIED TO PERSUADE EDDIE TO TRY TO PERSUADE FELIX
    TO TRY TO PROMISE ZACH
    (ADP NP) TO
*START-INF_7
16
    (INF V) FIDO TRIED TO PERSUADE EDDIE TO TRY TO PERSUADE FELIX
    TO TRY TO PROMISE ZACH TO
    (NOM A V) STEAL
*ADD-VERB_6
17
    (A V) FIDO TRIED TO PERSUADE EDDIE TO TRY TO PERSUADE FELIX
    TO TRY TO PROMISE ZACH TO STEAL
    (GQ) THE
*FVERB+MAIN_4
18
    (GQ V) FIDO TRIED TO PERSUADE EDDIE TO TRY TO PERSUADE FELIX
    TO TRY TO PROMISE ZACH TO STEAL THE
    (S-H) BOOK
*DET+NOUN_2
19
    (V) FIDO TRIED TO PERSUADE EDDIE TO TRY TO PERSUADE FELIX
    TO TRY TO PROMISE ZACH TO STEAL THE BOOK
    (V DECL) .
*CMPLT_13
20
    (DECL) FIDO TRIED TO PERSUADE EDDIE TO TRY TO PERSUADE FELIX
    TO TRY TO PROMISE ZACH TO STEAL THE BOOK .


Hierarchical Analysis:

(PROPOSITION-20_26_10
  (MOOD (DECLARATIVE-20_26_10))
  (PROP-CONTENT
    ((SENT-2_26_10
      (SUBJ ((NP-1_26_10 (NAME (FIDO-1_26_10)))))
      (VERB (TRY-2_26_10))
      (DIR-OBJ
        ((COMP-3_26_10
          (COMP (TO-3_26_10))
          (INF
            ((SENT-4_26_10
```

```
(SUBJ ("NP-1_26_10"))
(VERB (PERSUADE-4_26_10))
(INDIR-OBJ ((NP-5_26_10 (NAME (EDDIE-5_26_10)))))
(DIR-OBJ
 ((COMP-6_26_10
    (COMP (TO-6_26_10))
    (INF
     ((SENT-7_26_10
        (SUBJ ("NP-5_26_10"))
        (VERB (TRY-7_26_10))
        (DIR-OBJ
         ((COMP-8_26_10
            (COMP (TO-8_26_10))
            (INF
             ((SENT-9_26_10
                (SUBJ ("NP-5_26_10"))
                (VERB (PERSUADE-9_26_10))
                (INDIR-OBJ ((NP-10_26_10 (NAME (FELIX-10_26_10)))))
                (DIR-OBJ
                 ((COMP-11_26_10
                    (COMP (TO-11_26_10))
                    (INF
                     ((SENT-12_26_10
                        (SUBJ ("NP-10_26_10"))
                        (VERB (TRY-12_26_10))
                        (DIR-OBJ
                         ((COMP-13_26_10
                            (COMP (TO-13_26_10))
                            (INF
                             ((SENT-14_26_10
                                (SUBJ ("NP-10_26_10"))
                                (VERB (PROMISE-14_26_10))
                                (INDIR-OBJ
                                 ((NP-15_26_10 (NAME (ZACH-15_26_10)))))
                                (DIR-OBJ
                                 ((COMP-16_26_10
                                    (COMP (TO-16_26_10))
                                    (INF
                                     ((SENT-17_26_10
                                        (SUBJ ("NP-10_26_10"))
                                        (VERB (STEAL-17_26_10))
                                        (DIR-OBJ
                                         ((NP-18_26_10
                                            (REF (THE-18_26_10 SG-19_26_10))
                                            (NOUN ((BOOK-19_26_10))))))))))))))))))))
)))))))))))))))))))))))))))))))))
```

The hierarchical analysis above shows that LA-grammar assigns the infinitive subjects correctly in accordance with the category of the higher verbs. "Underlying subjects" are represented as strings, e.g "NP-10_15_10", in order to avoid another expansion of the substructure dominated by, e.g., NP-10_15_10.[2]

---

[2]Such secondary expansions of a frame may in fact lead to infinite loops.

B.4   Unbounded Dependency

Example B.4.1 is a wh-interrogative with an "unbounded dependency". In *Who does Eddie believe that Fido bit?* the fronted *who* serves as the object of an embedded verb, e.g., *bit.* This relation is called an unbounded dependency, because the verb may be arbitrarily deeply embedded, e.g., *Who does Eddie believe that Zach believes that Felix believes that Fido bit?.* In order to provide for the correct semantic interpretation, the hierarchical analysis has to specify the relation between the embedded verb and the topicalized wh-word. In the following derivation, the wh-word is the underlying argument of a prepositional phrase. This construction is also called "preposition stranding".

B.4.1 *Who does the young dog believe that the beautiful woman gave the bone to?*

```
* (z who does the young dog believe that the beautiful woman gave the
     bone to ?)
```

Real time:	0.16 s		Real time:	17.40 s
Run time:	0.16 s		Run time:	6.66 s

```
    Linear Analysis:

    *START_0
    1
        (WH) WHO
        (S3 DO V) DOES
    *MAIN&W+AUX_11
    2
        (S3 DO WT VI) WHO DOES
        (GQ) THE
    *FVERB+NOM_10
    3
        (GQ DO WT VI) WHO DOES THE
        (ADJ) YOUNG
    *DET+ADJ_1
    4
        (GQ DO WT VI) WHO DOES THE YOUNG
        (S-H) DOG
    *DET+NOUN_2
    5
        (DO WT VI) WHO DOES THE YOUNG DOG
        (NOM SC&C V) BELIEVE
    *ADD-VERB_6
    6
        (SC&C WT VI) WHO DOES THE YOUNG DOG BELIEVE
        (SC&C) THAT
    *START-SUBCL_8
    7
        (WT VI) WHO DOES THE YOUNG DOG BELIEVE THAT
        (GQ) THE
    *ADD-NOM_9
    8
        (GQ $ WT VI) WHO DOES THE YOUNG DOG BELIEVE THAT THE
        (ADJ) BEAUTIFUL
    *DET+ADJ_1
    9
```

```
      (GQ $ WT VI) WHO DOES THE YOUNG DOG BELIEVE THAT THE BEAUTIFUL
      (SH) WOMAN
*DET+NOUN_2
10
      (S WT VI) WHO DOES THE YOUNG DOG BELIEVE THAT THE BEAUTIFUL
      WOMAN
      (N A TO V) GAVE
*OBJ+VERB_12
11
      (A TO* VI) WHO DOES THE YOUNG DOG BELIEVE THAT THE BEAUTIFUL
      WOMAN GAVE
      (GQ) THE
*FVERB+MAIN_4
12
      (GQ TO* VI) WHO DOES THE YOUNG DOG BELIEVE THAT THE BEAUTIFUL
      WOMAN GAVE THE
      (S-H) BONE
*DET+NOUN_2
13
      (TO* VI) WHO DOES THE YOUNG DOG BELIEVE THAT THE BEAUTIFUL
      WOMAN GAVE THE BONE
      (ADP NP) TO
*FVERB+MAIN_4
14
      (VI) WHO DOES THE YOUNG DOG BELIEVE THAT THE BEAUTIFUL
      WOMAN GAVE THE BONE TO
      (VI INTERROG) ?
*CMPLT_13
15
      (INTERROG) WHO DOES THE YOUNG DOG BELIEVE THAT THE BEAUTIFUL
      WOMAN GAVE THE BONE TO ?


Hierarchical Analysis:

(PROPOSITION-15_24_11
  (MOOD (INTERROGATIVE-15_24_11))
  (PROP-CONTENT
   ((SENT-2_24_11
     (TOP ((NP-1_24_11 (W-PRO (WHO-1_24_11)))))
     (AUX (DO-2_24_11))
     (SUBJ
      ((NP-3_24_11
        (REF (THE-3_24_11 SG-5_24_11))
        (ADJ ((ADJ-4_24_11 (ADJECTIVE (YOUNG-4_24_11)))))
        (NOUN ((DOG-5_24_11))))))
     (PREDICATE
      ((NFV-6_24_11
        (INF (BELIEVE-6_24_11))
        (DIR-OBJ
         ((COMP-7_24_11
           (COMP (THAT-7_24_11))
           (SENT
            ((SENT-8_24_11
              (SUBJ
               ((NP-8_24_11
                 (REF (THE-8_24_11 SG-10_24_11))
```

```
         (ADJ ((ADJ-9_24_11 (ADJECTIVE (BEAUTIFUL-9_24_11)))))
         (NOUN ((WOMAN-10_24_11))))))))
     (VERB ((GIVE-11_24_11)))
     (DIR-OBJ
      ((NP-12_24_11
        (REF (THE-12_24_11 SG-13_24_11))
        (NOUN ((BONE-13_24_11))))))
     (PREPOSITIONAL_OBJ
      ((PREP-14_24_11
        (PREPOSITION (TO-14_24_11))
        (NP ("NP-1_24_11")))))))))))))))))))))
```

LA-grammar handles unbounded dependencies for arbitrary levels of embedding.

B.5   Relative Clauses

Example B.5.1 contains two kinds of relative clause. In the first the head noun serves as the subject of the relative clause, and in the second it serves as the direct object. Note that the second relative clause doesn't have a relative pronoun.

B.5.1 *The dog which bit Eddie likes the bone Fido dug up.*

```
* (z The dog which bit Eddie likes the bone Fido dug up \.)
Real time:      0.16 s                    Real time:     2.74 s
Run time:       0.14 s                    Run time:      2.66 s

    Linear Analysis:

    *START_0
    1
        (GQ) THE
        (S-H) DOG
    *DET+NOUN_2
    2
        (S) THE DOG
        (W-H) WHICH
    *START-RELCL_15
    3
        (WS S) THE DOG WHICH
        (N A V) BIT
    *NOM+FVERB_3
    4
        (A S) THE DOG WHICH BIT
        (N-H) EDDIE
    *FVERB+MAIN_4
    5
        (S) THE DOG WHICH BIT EDDIE
        (S3 SC-INF&N V) LIKES
    *NOM+FVERB_3
    6
        (SC-INF&N V) THE DOG WHICH BIT EDDIE LIKES
        (GQ) THE
    *FVERB+MAIN_4
    7
        (GQ V) THE DOG WHICH BIT EDDIE LIKES THE
```

```
        (S-H) BONE
    *DET+NOUN_2
    8
        (V) THE DOG WHICH BIT EDDIE LIKES THE BONE
        (N-H) FIDO
    *START-RELCL_15
    9
        (N-H WS V) THE DOG WHICH BIT EDDIE LIKES THE BONE FIDO
        (N A UP% V) DUG
    *OBJ+VERB_12
    10
        (UP% V) THE DOG WHICH BIT EDDIE LIKES THE BONE FIDO DUG
        (ADP NP) UP
    *FVERB+MAIN_4
    11
        (V) THE DOG WHICH BIT EDDIE LIKES THE BONE FIDO DUG UP
        (V DECL) .
    *CMPLT_13
    12
        (DECL) THE DOG WHICH BIT EDDIE LIKES THE BONE FIDO DUG UP .
```

```
Hierarchical Analysis:

(PROPOSITION-12_17_12
 (MOOD (DECLARATIVE-12_17_12))
 (PROP-CONTENT
  ((SENT-6_17_12
    (SUBJ
     ((NP-1_17_12
       (REF (THE-1_17_12 SG-2_17_12))
       (NOUN ((DOG-2_17_12)))
       (REL-CLAUSE
        ((COMP-3_17_12
          (COMP ((WHICH-3_3_12)))
          (SENT
           ((SENT-4_17_12
             (SUBJ ("NP-1_17_12"))
             (VERB (BITE-4_17_12))
             (DIR-OBJ ((NP-5_17_12 (NAME (EDDIE-5_17_12)))))))))))))))
    (VERB (LIKE-6_17_12))
    (DIR-OBJ
     ((NP-7_17_12
       (REF (THE-7_17_12 SG-8_17_12))
       (NOUN ((BONE-8_17_12)))
       (REL-CLAUSE
        ((SENT-9_17_12
          (SUBJ ((NP-9_17_12 (NAME (FIDO-9_17_12)))))
          (VERB ((DIG-10_17_12)))
          (DIR-OBJ ("NP-7_17_12"))
          (DISCONTINUOUS-ELEMENT ((UP-11_17_12)))))))))))))))
```

The underlying grammatical relations of the two relative clauses are characterized correctly in the hierarchical analysis.

B.6   Genitive Recursion

Genitive recursion like the one illustrated in B.6.1 is problematic for many PS-grammar based top-down parsers, because it is analyzed as left-recursive structure.

B.6.1 *John kicked the beautiful girl's old mother's intelligent brother's ugly dog.*

```
* (z John kicked the beautiful girl's old mother's intelligent brother's
ugly dog \.)
Real time:     0.08 s                          Real time:     1.80 s
Run time:      0.08 s                          Run time:      1.56 s

    Linear Analysis:

    *START_0
    1
       (NH) JOHN
       (N A V) KICKED
    *NOM+FVERB_3
    2
       (A V) JOHN KICKED
       (GQ) THE
    *FVERB+MAIN_4
    3
       (GQ V) JOHN KICKED THE
       (ADJ) BEAUTIFUL
    *DET+ADJ_1
    4
       (GQ V) JOHN KICKED THE BEAUTIFUL
       (GN) GIRL'S
    *DET+NOUN_2
    5
       (GQ V) JOHN KICKED THE BEAUTIFUL GIRL'S
       (ADJ) OLD
    *DET+ADJ_1
    6
       (GQ V) JOHN KICKED THE BEAUTIFUL GIRL'S OLD
       (GN) MOTHER'S
    *DET+NOUN_2
    7
       (GQ V) JOHN KICKED THE BEAUTIFUL GIRL'S OLD MOTHER'S
       (ADJ) INTELLIGENT
    *DET+ADJ_1
    8
       (GQ V) JOHN KICKED THE BEAUTIFUL GIRL'S OLD MOTHER'S INTELLIGENT
       (GN) BROTHER'S
    *DET+NOUN_2
    9
       (GQ V) JOHN KICKED THE BEAUTIFUL GIRL'S OLD MOTHER'S INTELLIGENT
       BROTHER'S
       (ADJ) UGLY
    *DET+ADJ_1
    10
       (GQ V) JOHN KICKED THE BEAUTIFUL GIRL'S OLD MOTHER'S INTELLIGENT
       BROTHER'S UGLY
       (S-H) DOG
    *DET+NOUN_2
```

```
11
    (V) JOHN KICKED THE BEAUTIFUL GIRL'S OLD MOTHER'S INTELLIGENT
    BROTHER'S UGLY DOG
    (V DECL) .
*CMPLT_13
12
    (DECL) JOHN KICKED THE BEAUTIFUL GIRL'S OLD MOTHER'S INTELLIGENT
    BROTHER'S UGLY DOG .
```

```
Hierarchical Analysis:

(PROPOSITION-12_15_1
 (MOOD (DECLARATIVE-12_15_1))
 (PROP-CONTENT
  ((SENT-2_15_1
    (SUBJ ((NP-1_15_1 (NAME (JOHN-1_15_1)))))
    (VERB (KICK-2_15_1))
    (DIR-OBJ
     ((NP-3_15_1
       (REF
        ((NP-8_15_1
          (REF
           ((NP-6_15_1
             (REF
              ((NP-4_15_1
                (REF (THE-3_15_1))
                (ADJ ((ADJ-4_15_1 (ADJECTIVE (BEAUTIFUL-4_15_1)))))
                (NOUN ((GIRL-5_15_1))))))
             (ADJ ((ADJ-6_15_1 (ADJECTIVE (OLD-6_15_1)))))
             (NOUN ((MOTHER-7_15_1))))))
          (ADJ ((ADJ-8_15_1 (ADJECTIVE (INTELLIGENT-8_15_1)))))
          (NOUN ((BROTHER-9_15_1))))
        SG-11_15_1))
       (ADJ ((ADJ-10_15_1 (ADJECTIVE (UGLY-10_15_1)))))
       (NOUN ((DOG-11_15_1)))))))))))
```

The left-recursive structure is clearly reflected in the shape of the hierarchical analysis.

B.7   Idiom

Finally consider the treatment of an idiomatic expression.

B.7.1 *Who was John ganged up on by?*

```
* (z Who was John ganged up on by ?)
Real time:    0.12 s                    Real time:    0.56 s
Run time:     0.12 s                    Run time:     0.54 s

    Linear Analysis:

    *START_0
    1
        (WH) WHO
```

```
    (S3 B V) WAS
*MAIN&W+AUX_11
2
    (S3 B WT VI) WHO WAS
    (NH) JOHN
*FVERB+NOM_10
3
    (B WT VI) WHO WAS JOHN
    (HV A & UP ON) GANGED
*OBJ+VERB_12
4
    (UP ON & BY* VI) WHO WAS JOHN GANGED
    (ADP NP) UP
*CONT-COMPOUND_16
5
    (ON & BY* VI) WHO WAS JOHN GANGED UP
    (ADP NP) ON
*CONT-COMPOUND_16
6
    (BY* VI) WHO WAS JOHN GANGED UP ON
    (ADP NP) BY
*FVERB+MAIN_4
7
    (VI) WHO WAS JOHN GANGED UP ON BY
    (VI INTERROG) ?
*CMPLT_13
8
    (INTERROG) WHO WAS JOHN GANGED UP ON BY ?


Hierarchical Analysis:

(PROPOSITION-8_10_3
 (MOOD (INTERROGATIVE-8_10_3))
 (PROP-CONTENT
  ((SENT-2_10_3
    (TOP ((NP-1_10_3 (W-PRO (WHO-1_10_3)))))
    (AUX (BE-2_10_3))
    (SUBJ ((NP-3_10_3 (NAME (JOHN-3_10_3)))))
    (PASSIVE-PREDICATE
     ((NFV-4_10_3
       (PAST-PART (GANG-UP-ON-4_10_3))
       (AGENT-PHRASE
        ((PREP-7_10_3 (PREPOSITION (BY-7_10_3)) (NP ("NP-1_10_3")))))))))))))
```

The particles *up* and *on* are treated like valency positions in the lexical analysis of *gang*. In the semantics, *gang up on* is treated as a unit.

The hierarchical analyses presented above are intended for the interpretation relative to a knowledge base. There is no preconceived notion of what kinds of structures are or are not permissable, except for the simple distinctions between frames, slots, and fillers imposed by FrameKit. But there are two basic constraints: (i) the hierarchical analysis must be surface-compositional in the sense that it may only contain elements contributed by specific left-associative combinations, and (ii) the hierarchical analysis must be build up incrementally during the left-associative parse. These two assumptions follow from the fact that the semantic representation is homomorphic with the syntactic analysis.

C. The Current Example Set of ECAT

C.0 The Examples Explicitly Derived in Part I.

1. Peter gave Fido the bone. (3.2.2)
2. * The young man give Fido the bone. (3.2.3)
3. Fido dug the bone up. (3.3.4)
4. Who did Eddie try to bite? (4.1.4)
5. Did Eddie try to bite Fido? (4.1.5)
6. John bought a beautiful old house. (4.2.2)
7. John kissed the girl who slept. (4.2.11)
8. The man has eaten an apple. (4.3.5)
9. I am happy. (4.5.4)
10. John slept after he ate an apple. (4.5.5)
11. After John ate an apple he slept. (4.5.11)
12. Near him John saw a snake. (4.5.13)
13. The man who gave the paycheck to his wife is wiser than the man who gave it to his mistress. (4.5.14)
14. The man who deserves it will get the prize he wants. (4.5.15)
15. What did John give to Sue? (8.4.4)
16. The meeting was scheduled for Wednesday. (8.4.6)
17. John was believed to be happy. (8.4.8)
18. John ate the apple on the table behind the tree in the garden. (9.5.7)
19. John drank the beer. (10.5.3)
20. John drank beer. (10.5.4)
21. John likes these beers. (10.5.5)
22. John likes beers. (10.5.6)

C.1 The Examples Explicitly Derived in Appendix B

23. Did Fido find the bone? (B.1.1)
24. The bone was given to the dog by the man. (B.2.1)
25. Fido tried to persuade Eddie to try to persuade Felix to try to promise Zach to steal the book. (B.3.1)
26. Who does the young dog believe that the beautiful woman gave the bone to? (B.4.1)

27. The dog which bit Eddie likes the bone Fido dug up. (B.5.1)

28. John kicked the beautiful girl's old mother's intelligent brother's ugly dog. (B.6.1)

29. Who was John ganged up on by? (B.7.1)

C.2 Active Voice Constructions

30. John drank wine.

31. John likes to try wines.

32. John drank old wine.

33. John likes to drink different very old wines.

34. John's beautiful sister will read the book.

35. The man could have read the book.

36. * The man could has read the book.

37. The smiling man gave the girl the book.

38. The man gave the book to the smiling girl.

39. A very old man has given smiling girls the book.

40. The man might have given John's beautiful sister the book.

41. * The man have might given the girl the book.

42. The man might have given a very beautiful book to smiling girls.

43. Beautiful women could have given the book to the smiling girl.

44. Smiling men could give the girl a book.

45. The man could be giving the girl a book.

46. * The man could giving the girl a book.

47. The man could be giving beautiful books to smiling women.

C.3 Passive Voice Constructions

48. The beautiful old book was given the girl by the man.

49. A book was given John.

50. A book was given John by Mary.

51. A book might have been given to John by Mary.

52. A book might have been given to John.

53. The man was given a book by Mary.

54. The man might have been given a book.

55. The book has been given the girl by the man.

56. The book was given to the girl.

57. The book might have been given to the girl.

58. The book was given to the young girl by the man.

59. The girl was given the book by the man.

60. * The girl was given the book to by the man.

61. The girl will be given the book by the man.

62. The girl could have been given the book by the man.

63. The girl was given the book by the man by the woman.

64. Mary says that John was given a book by Susi.

65. The man who was given a book by Mary is intelligent.

C.4 Genitive Constructions

66. John's book is beautiful.

67. * John's book are beautiful .

68. John's books are beautiful.

69. * John's books is beautiful.

70. The old man's book is beautiful.

71. The beautiful girl's old mother's intelligent brother's ugly dog was kicked by John.

C.5 Auxiliaries Taking Quantified Noun Phrases as the Second Argument

72. Mary is beautiful.

73. * Mary are beautiful.

74. You are beautiful.

75. You are a beautiful young woman.

76. Mary is reading a book.

77. Mary is reading books.

78. John has many beautiful books.

79. John has a beautiful book.

C.6 Nominative Agreement in the Case of the Auxiliary "be"

80. You are women.

81. He is a good doctor.

82. * You is good doctors.

83. We are good doctors.

84. * We are a good doctor.

85. You are beautiful women.

86. I am a collector of old beautiful books.

87. * I know that these boys are a good doctor.

88. I know that these boys are good doctors.

89. * John is good doctors.
90. John is a good doctor.
91. John is good.
92. The book which John bought is beautiful.
93. * The book which John bought are beautiful.
94. The books which John bought are beautiful.
95. * The books which John bought is beautiful.

C.7 Adverbs as Subjects and Predicates of Auxiliaries

96. There are many problems.
97. There has been an accident.
98. * There has been accidents.
99. There have been accidents.
100. * There have been an accident.
101. There is a book.
102. * There is books.
103. There are books.
104. * There are a book.
105. Read the book there!
106. On the table was a book.
107. I am on the table.
108. I am here.
109. I am here on the table.
110. * Here am I.
111. Here is Jonny.
112. He is good.
113. * Here is good.
114. Here it is good.
115. He has been good.
116. * Here has been good.
117. Here has been a table.
118. They could have been good.
119. * There could have been good.
120. There could have been good tables.

C.8 Yes/No-Interrogatives and Related Declaratives

121. Did John read the book?

122. * Did John read the book.

123. Did the young man read the book?

124. Mary said that.

125. Mary said that?

126. Does John love Mary?

127. * Does John love Mary.

128. John loves Mary?

129. John loves Mary.

130. Did Mary give John the book?

131. Did Mary give the book to John?

132. Has Mary given John the book?

133. Has Mary given the book to John?

134. Did Mary read the book?

135. Has Mary read the book?

136. Could Mary have read the book?

137. Was Mary reading a book?

C.9 Wh-Interrogatives

138. Who does Mary love?

139. Who doesn't love Mary?

140. Who loves Mary?

141. Whom doesn't Mary love?

142. * Whom loves Mary?

143. Mary said what?

144. * Mary said what.

145. Who gave what to whom?

146. Who did Mary give a book?

147. Who was given the book by Mary?

148. Who was the book given to by Mary?

149. * Who was given the book to by Mary?

150. Whom did Mary give a book?

151. Who did Mary give a book to?

152. Who did Mary give to John?

153. What did Mary say?

154. Who could Mary have seen?

155. Who could have seen Mary?

156. Who could Mary have given the book?
157. Who could Mary have given the book to?
158. Which book did John read?
159. Which beautiful book may John read?
160. John gave who a book?
161. John read which beautiful book?
162. * John read which book.
163. What did you do?
164. Why did you do it?
165. Where did you go afterwards?
166. Why did you do this movie?

C.10 Imperatives
167. Sleep!
168. Try to sleep!
169. Read the book!
170. Give the old man a kiss!
171. * Gave the old man a kiss!
172. Give me a kiss!
173. * Give I a kiss!
174. Don't touch this dial!

C.11 Unbounded Dependendies
175. Who does John believe?
176. Who does John believe Mary loves?
177. Who does John believe that Mary loves?
178. Who could John be seeing?
179. Who could John have been seeing?
180. What is John reading?
181. Who was the book written by?
182. Who was the book written by Bill given to?
183. What did John talk about?
184. Who did they agree on?
185. Who does Mary say that John loves?
186. * Who says Mary that John loves?
187. Who says that Mary loves John?

188. Who says Mary loves John?

189. Who did Mary say that John doesn't like?

190. * Who says Mary that Bill believes that John loves?

191. Who does Mary say that Bill believes that John loves?

192. Who does the old man believe that the beautiful young woman could be?

193. Who does the old man believe that the beautiful young woman could be loving?

194. Who does John believe that Mary gave the book to?

195. Who does the young man believe that the beautiful woman gave the book to?

196. Who does John believe that Mary said that Bill will love?

197. Who does John believe that the beautiful young woman said that Bill loves?

198. Who does John believe Mary said Bill loves?

199. Who does John believe the beautiful young woman said Bill loves?

200. Which book did Mary say that John doesn't believe that Susi read?

201. Who did Mary tell the answer?

202. * Who has Mary told the answer?

203. Who did Mary tell that Bill had been reading the book?

204. Who could Mary have told that the book was given to John?

205. Who could Mary have told the book was given to John by Suzy?

206. Who did John persuade to walk?

207. Who did John try to persuade to walk?

208. Who did John promise to drink the wine?

209. Who did John try to promise to drink the wine?

C.12 Subordinate Clauses with and without Complementizer

210. Mary says John loves Susi.

211. Mary says that John loves Susi.

212. Mary believes John said Susi was reading a book.

213. Mary believes that John said that Susi was reading a book.

214. John knows who loves Mary.

215. * John believes who loves Mary.

216. John knows who Mary loves.

217. * John believes who Mary loves.

218. The man knows who the beautiful young woman loves.

219. The man didn't know who the beautiful young woman will love.

220. The man knows whom the beautiful young woman loves.

221. The man didn't know whom the beautiful young woman will love.

222. John knows Mary read a book.

223. John knows that Mary read a book.

224. John knows who read a book.

225. John knows where Mary read a book.

226. John knows why Mary read a book.

227. John knows when Mary read a book.

228. John could have known that the beautiful young woman would be reading a book.

229. John could have known where the beautiful young woman would be reading a book.

230. John knows that Mary believes that Bill read the book.

231. * John knows that Mary believes where Bill read the book.

232. John would know that Mary believes that Bill gave the book to Peter.

233. John believes Mary knows Bill read the book.

234. John knows the beautiful young woman read a book.

235. John knows Mary believes Bill gave the book to Peter.

236. John believes that the book was given to the girl by the man.

C.13 Relative Clauses Modifying Sentence Final Noun Phrases

237. I know the man who loves Mary.

238. I know the man who has read the book.

239. I know the man who will be reading the book.

240. I have the book which Mary didn't read.

241. I have the book which Mary didn't give to John.

242. I have the book that Mary didn't give to John.

243. I have the book which Mary didn't give Jchn.

244. I have the book that Mary didn't give John.

245. John likes us who read the book.

246. John doesn't like ants which are in his pants.

C.14 Relative Clauses Modifying Mid-Sentence Noun Phrases

247. John gave the girl who read the book a cookie.

248. John didn't give the girl who didn't read the book a cookie.

249. John gave the girl who gave the man a book a cookie.

250. John didn't give the girl who didn't give the man a book a cookie.

251. John gave the girl who Mary gave a cookie a book.

252. John gave you who read the book a cookie.

C.15 Relative Clauses Modifying Sentence Initial Noun Phrases

253. The man who gave Mary a book loves Susi.

254. The man who didn't read the book loves Mary.

255. The man who could have been reading the book loves Mary.

256. * I who has read the book was given a cookie by John.

257. I who have read the book was given a cookie by John.

C.16 Reduced Relative Clauses

258. The man reading a book is happy.

259. The man reading a book was given to Mary by Bill is happy.

260. The child eating an apple was given to Mary by Bill.

261. John gave the child reading a book a cookie.

262. The book read by the man is interesting.

263. The man Mary gave a book loves Susi.

264. * The man gave Mary a book loves Susi.

265. The man Mary gave a book to loves Susi.

266. The man Mary didn't give a book loves Susi.

267. The man Mary didn't give a book to loves Susi.

268. John is a man women like.

269. John is a man women like to kiss.

270. John is a man liked by women.

C.17 The Relative Pronoun "Who" as Subject and as Object

271. The man who loves Mary is reading a book.

272. The man who Mary loves is reading a book.

273. The man who doesn't love Mary is reading a book.

274. The man who Mary doesn't love is reading a book.

275. The man who gave Mary a book loves Susi.

276. The man who didn't give Mary a book loves Susi.

277. The man who Mary gave a book loves Susi.

278. The man who Mary gave a book to loves Susi.

279. The man who Mary didn't give a book loves Susi.

280. The man who Mary didn't give a book to loves Susi.

C.18 Mixing Relative Clauses and "that"-Clauses

281. The man who saw that John loves Mary is reading a book.
282. The man who said that Mary loves him sleeps.

C.19 Unbounded Dependencies with Relative Pronouns

283. I know the man who John says Mary loves.
284. I know the man who John says that Mary loves.
285. I know the man who John says Mary gave the book.
286. I know the man who John says Mary gave the book to.
287. I know the man who John says Mary gave the book is sleeping.
288. I know the man who John says Mary gave the book to is sleeping.
289. I know the man who John says that Mary gave the book.
290. I know the man who John says that Mary gave the book to.
291. I know the man who John said Mary believes.
292. I know the man who John said Mary believes that Susi loves.
293. I know that the man who John said that Mary believes that Susi loves is reading a book.
294. Who did the man who Mary gave the old book to say that Susi gave the new book to?

C.20 Wh-Interrogatives with Relative Clauses

295. Who loves the man who gave Mary a book?
296. Who loves the man whom Mary gave a book to?

C.21 Recursion of 'Control'

297. John tried the cookies.
298. John tried to read the book.
299. John could have tried to read the book.
300. John promised the book.
301. John promised Mary the book.
302. * John persuaded Mary the book.
303. John didn't promise Mary the book.
304. John promised Mary to read the book.
305. John has promised Mary to read the book.
306. John promised to read the book.
307. John promised to try to have read the book.
308. John promised the woman to read the book.
309. John could have promised the beautiful young woman to read the book.

310. * John persuaded to read the book.

311. John persuaded Mary to read the book.

312. John didn't persuade Mary to read the book.

313. John persuaded the woman to read the book.

314. John has persuaded the woman to read the book.

315. John could have persuaded the beautiful young woman to read the book.

316. John tried to promise Mary to read the book.

317. John has tried to promise Mary to read the book.

318. John tried to persuade Mary to read the book.

319. John has tried to persuade Mary to read the book.

320. John tried to persuade Mary to promise Bill to read the book.

321. John tried to promise Mary to persuade Bill to read the book.

322. John tried to persuade Mary to promise Bill to try to read the book.

323. John could have tried to persuade Mary to try to persuade Bill to try to promise Peter to read the book.

C.22 Mixing Unbounded Dependency and Recursion of Control

324. What did John say that Fido tried to persuade Eddie to steal?

325. What did John say that Fido tried to persuade Eddie to try to persuade Felix to try to promise Zach to steal?

C.23 Sentential Adverbs

326. There are ants in my pants.

327. In my pants are ants.

328. In my pants there are ants.

329. After John read the book Mary ate an apple.

330. Mary ate an apple after John read the book.

331. For three days John sat by the window.

332. John sat by the window for three days.

333. John sat by the window for three days without sleeping.

334. Already we have seen six movies.

335. We have already seen six movies.

336. We have seen six movies already.

337. John is already on the table.

C.24 Phrasal Verbs

338. John agreed with Mary on the contract.

339. John agreed on the contract with Mary.

340. What did John agree on?

341. Who did John agree with?

342. What did John agree on with Mary?

343. Who did John agree with on the contract?

C.25 Idioms

344. His brothers ganged up on John.

345. John was ganged up on by his brothers.

346. John ate a few apples.

347. John has seen many a movie.

348. Suzy looks down on Mary.

349. Mary is looked down on by Suzy.

350. Who is Mary looked down on by?

C.26 "Tough-Movement"

351. John is eager.

352. John is very eager.

353. John is eager to please.

354. John is very eager to please.

355. John is eager to please Mary.

356. John is very eager to please Mary.

357. It is eager to please John.

358. John is eager to try to read the book.

359. John is eager to promise Mary to read the book.

360. John is eager to persuade Mary to read the book.

361. John is eager to try to promise Mary to read the book.

362. John is easy to please.

363. John is very easy to please.

364. It is easy to please.

365. It is easy to please John.

366. * John is easy to try to read the book.

367. To please John is easy.

368. To try to please John is easy.

369. To please John is eager.

370. To try to please John is eager.

371. John read the letter to please Mary.

372. John read the letter to Mary.

373. To please Mary John read the letter.

C.27 Comparative Constructions and Intensifiers

374. John is quick.

375. John is very quick.

376. John is as quick as Mary.

377. * John is as quick than Mary.

378. John is quicker than Mary.

379. * John is quicker as Mary.

380. John wrote the letter quickly.

381. John wrote the letter very quickly.

382. John wrote the letter as quickly as Mary.

383. * John wrote the letter as quickly than Mary.

384. John wrote the letter more quickly than Mary.

385. * John wrote the letter more quickly as Mary.

386. John read the book slowly.

387. John read the book very very slowly.

388. John reads slowly.

389. John reads more slowly.

390. John reads more slowly than Mary.

391. John reads more than Mary.

392. John read the book more than Mary.

393. John is more intelligent than Mary.

394. * John is more intelligent as Mary.

395. * John is most intelligent than Mary.

396. John talks more intelligently than Mary.

397. John talks more intelligently as Mary.

398. John has more apples.

399. John has more apples than Mary.

400. * John has more apples as Mary.

401. John has the most apples.

402. John likes most dogs.

403. John is the tallest man.

404. John is the most intelligent man.

405. John has the most apples.

406. * John is the most most intelligent man.

407. John is a rather intelligent man.

408. * John is a rather rather intelligent man.

409. John is a very intelligent man.

410. John is a very very intelligent man.

411. John is a most intelligent old man.

412. John is an old more intelligent man.

413. John is a more intelligent old man.

414. John is an old most intelligent man.

415. John is the old fastest man.

416. John is the fastest old man.

417. * John is the more fastest old man.

418. * John is the more faster old man.

419. * John is the most fastest old man.

420. * John is the most faster old man.

C.28 Noun Noun Compounds

421. the book table

References

Aho, A.V., and J.D. Ullman (1972) *The Theory of Parsing, Translation, and Compiling. Vol.I: Parsing*. Prentice Hall, Englewood Cliffs, New Jersey.

Aho, A.V., and J.D. Ullman (1979) *Principles of Compiler Design*. Addison-Wesley, Reading, Massachusetts.

Ajdukiewicz, K. (1935) *"Die syntaktische Konnexität,"* Studia Philosophica, 1:1-27.

Alt, F.L. and I. Rhodes (1961) *"Recognition of Clauses and Phrases in Machine Translation of Languages,"* Proc. of the First International Conference on Machine Translation of Languages and Applied Language Analaysis.

Anderson, J.R. (1976) *Language, Memory, and Thought*. Lawrence Earlbaum Associates, Hillsdale, New Jersey.

Anderson, J.R. (1983) *The Architecture of Cognition*. Harvard University Press, Cambridge, Massachusetts.

Anderson, J.R. and G.H. Bower (1973) *Human Associative Memory*. V.H. Winston, Washington, D.C.

Anderson, J.R. and G.H. Bower (1980) *Human Associative Memory: A Brief Edition*. Lawrence Earlbaum Associates, Hillsdale, New Jersey.

Appelt, D. (1982) *Planning Natural-Language Utterances to Satisfy Multiple Goals*. Technical Note 259, SRI-International, Menlo Park, California.

Asch, S.E. (1961) *"The Metaphor: A Psychological Inquiry,"* M.Henley (ed.), Documents of Gestalt Psychology, University of California Press, Berkeley.

Austin, J.L. (1962) *How to do Things with Words*. Clarendon Press, Oxford.

Bar-Hillel, Y. (1953) *"A Quasi-arithmetical Notation for Syntactic Description,"* Language 29.

Barthes, R. (1986) *The Rustle of Language*. Hill and Wang, New York.

Barton, G.E., R.C. Berwick, and E.S. Ristad (1987) *Computational Complexity and Natural Language*. The MIT-Press, Cambridge, Massachusetts.

Barwise, J. and J. Perry (1983) *Situations and Attitudes*. The MIT-Press, Cambridge, Massachusetts.

Beneviste, E. (1971) *Problems in General Linguistics*. University of Miami Press, Coral Gables, Florida.

Berwick, R.C. (1985) *The Aquisition of Syntactic Knowledge*. The MIT-Press, Cambridge, Massachusetts.

Berwick, R.C., and A.S. Weinberg (1984) *The Grammatical Basis of Linguistic Performance: Language Use and Aquisition*. The MIT-Press, Cambridge, Massachusetts.

Black, M. (1979) *"More about Metaphor,"* Ortony (ed.), Metaphor and Thought, Cambridge University Press, Cambridge, England.

Blau, U. (1977) *Die dreiwertige Logik*. Berlin.

Bloch, B. (1953) *"Linguistic Structure and Linguistic Analysis,"* Report on the Fourth Annual Round Table Meeting on Linguistics and Language Teaching, p.40-44, A. Hill (ed.), George Town University, Washington, D.C.

Bloomfield, L. (1933) *Language*. Holt, Rinhart and Winston, New York.

Bolinger, D. (1968) *Aspects of Language*. Harcourt, Brace, and World, Inc., New York.

Brachman, R.J. (1979) *"On the Epistemological Status of Semantic Networks,"* Associative Networks: Representations and Use of Knowledge by Computers, p. 3 - 50, N.V. Findler (ed.), Academic Press, New York. Reprinted in Brachman and Levesque (eds.) 1985.

Brachman, R.J. and H.J. Levesque (eds.) (1985) *Readings in Knowledge Represenation*. Morgan Kaufmann Publishers, Los Altos, CA.

Bresnan, J. (ed.) (1982) *The Mental Representation of Grammatical Relations*. The MIT-Press, Cambridge, Massachusetts.

Bühler, K. (1934) *Sprachtheorie*. Fischer, Jena.

Carbonell, J.G. (1981) *Subjective Understanding: Computer Models of Belief Systems*. UMI Research Press, Ann Arbor, Michigan.

Carbonell, J.G., and R. Joseph (1986) *"FrameKit+: A Knowledge Representation System,"* Carnegie-Mellon University, Department of Computer Science.

Carnap, R. (1961) *Der Logische Aufbau der Welt*. 2nd edition, Felix Meiner, Hamburg.

Carnap, R. (1947) *Meaning and Necessity*. University of Chicago Press, Chicago and London.

Cassirer, E. (1923) *Die Philosophie der Symbolischen Formen*. Hamburg. Translated by R. Manheim as *The Philosophy of Symbolic Forms*. Yale University Press, New Haven and London 1955.

Chafe, W. (1970) *Meaning and the Structure of Language*. The University of Chicago Press, Chicago.

Chafe, W. (1979) *"The Flow of Thought and the Flow of Language,"* T. Givon (ed.), Syntax and Semantics, Vol. 12, Academic Press, New York.

Chomsky, N. (1957) *Syntactic Structures*. Mouton, The Hague.

Chomsky, N. (1965) *Aspects of the Theory of Syntax*. The MIT-Press, Cambridge, Massachussetts.

Chomsky, N. (1981) *Lectures on Government and Binding*. Foris Publications, Dordrecht, Holland.

Church, A. (1951) *"A Formulation of the Logic of Sense and Denotation,"* in F. Frankfurter (ed.), Structure, Method, and Meaning, Essays in Honor of Henry M. Sheffer, The Liberal Arts Press, New York.

Clocksin, W.F., and C.S. Mellish (1984) *Programming in Prolog*. Springer-Verlag, Berlin.

Collins, A.M. and E.F. Loftus (1975) *"A Spreading-Activation Theory of Semantic Processing,"* Psychological Review 82-6:407-428.

Damerau, F. (1971) *Markov Models and Linguistic Theory*. Mouton, The Hague/Paris.

Daneš, F. (1974) *"FSP and the Text Organization,"* F. Daneš, (ed.).

Daneš, F. (ed.) (1974) *Papers in Functional Sentence Perspective*. Mouton, The Hague/Paris.

Davidson, D. (1967) *"Truth and Meaning,"* Synthese, VII:304-323.

Dennett, D. (1980) *Brainstorms*. Harvester Press, Brighton.

Dijk, T.A. van (1977) *Text and Context. Explorations in the Semantics and Pragmatics of Discourse*. Longman, London and New York.

Dionysious of Halicarnassus (1910) *On Literary Composition*. Edited with introduction, translation, notes, glossary, and appendices by W. R. Roberts, MacMillan and Co., London.

Dretske, F. (1981) *Knowledge and the Flow of Information*. Bradford Books/MIT-Press, Cambridge, Massachusetts.

Earley, J. (1970) *"An Efficient Context-Free Parsing Algorithm,"* CACM 13(2):94-102.

Ebbinghaus, H.D., J. Flum, W. Thomas (1984) *Mathematical Logic*. Springer-Verlag, New York.

Eco, U. (1975) *A Theory of Semiotics*. Indiana University Press, Bloomington.

Fillmore, C. (1968) *"The Case for Case,"* E. Bach and R. Harms (eds.), Universals in Syntactic Theory, Holt, Rinehard, and Winston, New York.

Fillmore, C. (1977) *"The Case for Case Reopened,"* P. Cole and J. Sadock (eds.), Syntax and Semantics, Vol. 8, Grammatical Relations, Academic Press, New York.

Fillmore, C. (1982) *"Frame Semantics,"* Linguistics in the Morning Calm, edited by the Linguistic Society in of Korea, Hanshin, Seoul.

Firbas, J. (1964) *"On Defining Theme in Functional Sentence Analysis,"* Traveaux Linguistiques de Prague 1:267-280.

Fodor, J. (1975) *The Language of Thought*. MIT Press, Cambridge, Massachusetts.

Fraassen, B. van (1966) *"Singular Terms, Truth-Value Gaps and Free Logic,"* Journal of of Philosophy LXIII.

Fraassen, B. van (1968) *"Presupposition, Implication, and Self-Reference,"* Journal of Philosophy 65:136-152.

Fraassen, B. van (1969) *"Presuppositions, Supervaluations, and Free Logic,"* K. Lambert (ed.), The Logical Way of Doing Things, Yale University Press, New Haven, N.J.

Frege, G. (1892) *"Über Sinn und Bedeutung,"* Zeitschrift für Philosophie und Philosophische Kritik 100:25-50.

Frisch, K. von (1946) *"Die Tänze der Bienen,"* Österr. zool. Z. 1:1 - 48.

Gallin, D. (1975) *Intensional and Higher-Order Modal Logic*. North Holland, Amsterdam and Oxford.

Gazdar, G., E. Klein, G. Pullum, and I. Sag (1985) *Generalized Phrase Structure Grammar*. Harvard University Press: Cambridge, Massachusetts, and Blackwell: Oxford.

Geach, P. (1972) *"A Program for Syntax,"* D. Davidson and G. Harman (eds.), Semantics of Natural Language, Reidel, Dordrecht, Holland, p. 483-497.

Geach, P. and M. Black (ed.) (1970) *Translations from the Philosophical Writings of Gottlob Frege*. Basil Blackwell, Oxford.

Givon, T. (1985) *"Iconicity, Isomorphism, and Non-Arbitrary Coding in Syntax"* in J. Haiman (ed.) 1985a, Iconicity in Syntax.

Gochet, P. (1986) *Ascent to Truth*. Philosophia Verlag, Munich.

Goodman, N. (1951) *"The Structure of Appearance,"* Harvard University Press, Cambridge, Massachusetts.

Grice, P. (1957) *"Meaning,"* Philosophical Review, 66:377-388.

Grice, P. (1965) *"Utterance's Meaning, Sentence-Meaning, and Word-Meaning,"* Foundations of Language, 4:1-18.

Grice, P. (1975) *"Logic and Conversation,"* P. Cole and J.L. Morgan (eds.), Syntax and Semantics, Vol. 3: Speech Acts. Academic Press, New York.

Griffith, T., and Petrik, S. (1965) *"On the Relative Efficiencies of Context-Free Grammar Recognizers,"* CACM 8, p. 289-300.

Grosz, B. and C. Sidner (1986) *"Attention, Intensions, and the Structure of Discourse,"* Computational Linguistics, Vol. 12.3:175-204.

Grosz, B., K. Sparck Jones, and B.L. Webber (eds.) (1986) *Readings in Natural Language Processing*. Morgan Kaufmann Publishers, Los Altos, CA.

Gupta, A. (1982) *"Truth and Paradox,"* Journal of Philosophical Logic, 11:1-60.

Hacking, I. (1975) *Why Does Language Matter to Philosophy*. Cambridge University Press, Cambridge, England.

Haiman, J. (ed.) (1985a) *Iconicity in Syntax*. Typological Studies in Language 6, John Benjamins Publishing Company, Amsterdam/Philadelphia.

Haiman, J. (1985b) *Natural Syntax, Iconicity and Erosion*. Cambridge University Press, Cambridge, England.

Halliday, M.A.K. (1967) *"Notes on Transitivity and Theme in English,"* Journal of Linguistics 3:37-81, 199-244, 4:179-215.

Halliday, M.A.K. (1976) *System and Function in Language*. Oxford University Press, Oxford.

Halliday, M.A.K. and R. Hasan (1976) *Cohesion in English*. Longman, London.

Harris, Z. (1951) *Structural Linguistics*. The University of Chicago Press, Chicago.

Haugeland, J. (ed.) (1981) *Mind Design*. MIT Press, Cambridge, Massachusetts.

Hausser, R.   (1973) *"Presuppositions and Quantifiers,"* Papers from the Ninth Regional Conference, Chicago Linguistics Society, Chicago.

Hausser, R.   (1976) *"Presuppositions in Montague Grammar,"* Theoretical Linguistics 3:245-279.

Hausser, R.   (1978) *"Surface Compositionality and the Semantics of Mood,"* Groenendijk, Stokhof, and Bartsch (eds.), Amsterdam Papers in Formal Grammar, Vol. II, 1978. Reprinted in Searle, Kiefer, and Bierwisch (eds.), Speech Act Theory and Pragmatics, Reidel, Dordrecht, 1980.

Hausser, R.   (1979a) *"How do Pronouns Denote?"* Schnelle and Heny (eds.), Syntax and Semantics, Vol. 10, Academic Press, New York.

Hausser, R.   (1979b) *"A Constructive Approach to Intensional Contexts,"* Language Research, Vol. 18, No. 2, Seoul, Korea, 1982.

Hausser, R.   (1979c) *"A New Treatment of Context in Model-Theory,"* Sull' Anaphora, atti del seminario Accademia della Crusca, Florence, Italy, 1981.

Hausser, R.   (1981) *"The Place of Pragmatics in Model-Theory,"* Groenendijk et al. (eds.), *Formal Methods in the Study of Language.* Mathematical Center Tracts 135, University of Amsterdam.

Hausser, R.   (1982) *"A Surface Compositional Categorial Grammar,"* Linguistic Journal of Korea, Vol 7.2.

Hausser, R.   (1983a) *"Vagueness and Truth,"* Conceptus, Zeitschrift für Philosophie, Jahrgang XVII, Nr. 40/41.

Hausser, R.   (1983b) *"On Vagueness,"* Journal of Semantics 2:273-302.

Hausser, R.   (1984a) *Surface Compositional Grammar.* Wilhelm Fink Verlag, Munich.

Hausser, R.   (1984b) *" The Epimenides Paradox,"* presented at the Fourth Colloquium on Formal Grammar, Amsterdam.

Hausser, R.   (1985) *"Left-Associative Grammar and the Parser NEWCAT,"* Center for the Study of Language and Information, Stanford University, IN-CSLI-85-5.

Hausser, R.   (1986) *NEWCAT: Parsing Natural Language Using Left-Associative Grammar.* Lecture Notes in Computer Science, Springer-Verlag, Berlin.

Hausser, R.   (1987a) *"Left-Associative Grammar: Theory and Implementation,"* Center for Machine Translation, Carnegie-Mellon University, CMU-CMT-87-104.

Hausser, R.   (1987b) *"Modelltheorie, Künstliche Intelligenz und die Analyse der Wahrheit,"* in L. Puntel (ed.) Der Wahrheitsbegriff, Wissenschaftliche Buchgesellschaft, Darmstadt.

Hausser, R.   (1988a) *"Left-Associative Grammar, an Informal Outline,"* Computers and Translation, Vol. 3.1:23-67, Kluwer Academic Publishers, Dordrecht.

Hausser, R.   (1988b) *"Algebraic Definitions of Left-Associative Grammar,"* Computers and Translation, Vol. 3.2, Kluwer Academic Publishers, Dordrecht.

Hayes, P.   (1979) *"The Logic of Frames,"* D. Metzing (ed.) *Frame Conceptions and Text Understanding.* Walter de Gruyter, Berlin. Reprinted in Brachman R. and H. Levesque (eds.) *Readings in Knowledge Representation.* Morgan Kauffman Publishers, Los Altos.

Herzberger, H. (1982) *"Notes on Naive Semantics,"* Journal of Philosophical Logic, 11:61-102.

Hockett, C.F. (1966) "Language, Mathematics, and Linguistics," T.A. Sebeok (ed.), Current Trends in Linguistics, Vol. III, Mouton, The Hague, Paris.

Hopcroft, J.E., and Ullman, J.D. (1979) *Introduction to Automata Theory, Languages, and Computation.* Addison-Wesley Publishing Company, Reading, Massachusetts.

Hovy, E.H. (1987) *"Some Pragmatic Decision Criteria in Generation,"* G. Kempen (ed.), p. 3-17.

Householder, F.W. (1981) *The Syntax of Apollonius Dyscolus.* John Benjamins B.V., Amsterdam.

Hutchins, W.J. (1986) *Machine Translation – Past, Present, Future.* Ellis Horwood Limited, Chichester, England.

Hymes, D. and J. Fought (1975) *American Structuralism.* Mouton, The Hague/Paris.

Ishimoto, A. (1987) *"An Idealistic Approach to Situation Semantics,"* M. Nagao (ed.), p. 401-416.

Johnson-Laird, P.N. (1983) *Mental Models.* Harvard University Press, Cambridge, Massachusetts.

Joshi, A.K., K. Vijay-Shanker, and D.J. Weir Forthcoming . *"The convergence of mildly Context-Sensitive Grammar Formalisms,"* T. Wasow and P. Sells, Eds., *The Processing of Linguistic Structure.*

Kamp, J.A.W. (1975) *"Two Theories about Adjectives,"* E.L. Keenan (ed.), Formal Semantics of Natural Language, Cambridge University Press, Cambridge, England.

Kamp, J.A.W. (1981a) *"A Theory of Truth and Semantic Representation,"* Groenendijk et al. (eds.), *Formal Methods in the Study of Language.* Mathematical Center Tracts 135, University of Amsterdam.

Kamp, J.A.W. (1981b) *"The Heap Paradox,"* unpublished manuscript.

Kaplan, D. (1969) *"Quantifying In,"* Synthese 19:179-214.

Karttunen, L. (1973) *"Presuppositions and Linguistic Context,"* Theoretical Linguistics I.

Karttunen, L. (1977) *"Whichever Antecedent,"* paper submitted to the Chicago Linguistics Society Squib Antology.

Karttunen, L. and S.P. Peters (1977) *"Requiem for Presuppositions,"* Proceedings of the third annual meeting, Berkeley Linguistics Society, pp. 360 - 371.

Kasami, T., and Torii, K. (1969) *"A Syntax-Analysis Procedure for Unambiguous Context-Free Grammar Recognizers,"* JACM 16, p. 289-300.

Kempen, G. (ed.) (1987) *Natural Language Generation.* Martinus Nijhoff Publishers, Dordrecht, Holland.

Kindt, W. (1983) *"Vagueness as a Topological Problem,"* T.T. Ballmer and M. Pinkal (eds.), Approaching Vagueness, Amsterdam.

Kiparsky, P. and C. Kiparsky (1970) *"Fact,"* M. Bierwisch and K. Heidolph (eds.), Progress in Linguistics, The Hague, Mouton.

Kleene, S.C. (1938) *"On a Notion for Ordinal Numbers,"* Journal of Symbolic Logic 3: 83-94.

Kleene, S.C. (1952) *Introduction to Metamathematics.* Amsterdam.

Knuth, D.E. (1968) *"Semantics of Context-Free Languages,"* Mathematical Systems Theory 2:127-145. Errata: Mathematical Systems Theory 5:95-6 (1971).

Kolmogorov, L. (1970) *Foundations of the Theory of Measurement.* New York.

Kosslyn, S.M. (1981) *Image and Mind.* Harvard University Press, Cambridge, Massachusetts.

Kripke, S. (1963) *"Semantical Considerations on Modal Logic,"* Acta Philosophica Fennica 16:83-94, reprinted in L. Linsky (ed.) Reference and Modality, Oxford University Press, London.

Kripke, S. (1975) *"Outline of a Theory of Truth,"* Journal of Philosophy, 72:690-715.

Kuno, S. (1972) *"Functional Sentence Perspective — A Case Study from Japanese and English,"* Linguistic Inquiry 3:269-320.

Kuno, S. (1987) *"Anaphora and Discourse Principles,"* M. Nagao (ed.), p. 87-111.

Kuno, S. and A. Oettinger (1963) *"Multiple Path Syntactic Analyzer,"* Information Processing-62, p. 306-312. Preceedings of the ISIP Congress 1962, C.M. Popplewell (ed.), Amsterdam, North-Holland Publishing Company.

Lakoff, G. (1968) *"Pronouns and Reference,"* University of Indiana Linguistics Club, Bloomington, Indiana.

Lakoff, G. (1972) *"Hedges: a Study in Meaning Criteria and the Logic of Fuzzy Concepts,"* in P.M. Peranteau, J.N. Levi, and G.C. Phares (eds.): Papers from the Eights Regional Meeting of the Chicago Linguistic Society. p. 183 - 228. Chicago.

Lakoff, G. and M. Johnson (1980) *Metaphors we Live by.* The University of Chicago Press, Chicago and London.

Lambek, J. (1958) *"The Mathematics of Sentence Structure,"* American Mathematical Monthly 65:154-170.

Lees, R. B. and E. S. Klima (1963) *"Rules for English Pronominalization,"* Language 39:17-28.

Leśniewski, S. (1929) *"Grundzüge eines neuen Systems der Grundlage der Mathematik,"* Fundamenta Mathematicae, Warsaw.

Levesque, H.J. and R.J. Brachman (1985) *"A Fundamental Tradeoff in Knowledge Representation and Reasoning,"* (revised version), R.J. Brachman and H.J. Levesque (eds.) 1985.

Lewis, D. (1972) *" General Semantics,"* D. Davidson and G. Harman (eds.), Semantics of Natural Language, Synthese Library, Reidel, Dordrecht and Boston.

Lindauer, M. (1961) *Communication Among Social Bees.* Havard University Press, Cambridge, Massachusetts.

Link, G. (1979) *Montague Grammatik.* Wilhelm Fink Verlag, Munich.

Locke, J. (1690) *An Essay Concerning Human Understanding.* In four books. Printed by Eliz. Holt for Thomas Basset, London.

Longacre, R. E. (1983) *The Grammar of Discourse.* Plenum Press, London and New York.

Łukasiewicz, J. (1935) *"Zur vollen dreiwertigen Aussagenlogik,"* Erkenntnis 5:176.

Mann, W. and S.A. Thompson (1987) *"Rhetorical Structure Theory: description and construction of text structures,"* G. Kempen (ed.) 1987.

Marcus, M. (1978) *"A Computational Account of Some Constraints on Language,"* Theoretical Issues in Natural Language Processing-2, D. Waltz (ed.), p. 236-246, Urbana-Champain, Association for Computational Linguistics.

Marcus, M. (1980) *A Theory of Syntactic Recognition for Natural Language* Cambridge, Massachusetts, The MIT-Press.

Markov, A.A. (1954) *Theory of Algorithms.* Academy of Sciences of the USSR, Moscow.

McCall, S. (ed.) (1967) *Polish Logic 1920 - 1939.* Oxford University Press, London.

Mathesius, V. (1928) *"On Linguistic Characterology with Illustrations from Modern English,"* J. Vachek (ed.), A Prague School Reader in Linguistics, Indiana University Press, Bloomington and London, 1964.

McCarthy, J. (1977) *"Epistemological Problems of Artificial Intelligence,"* IJCAI 5:1038-1044. Reprinted in Webber and Nilsson (eds.) 1981.

McCarthy, J. (1980) *"Circumscription - A Form of Non-Monotonic Reasoning,"* Artificial Intelligence 13:27-39. Reprinted in Webber and Nilsson (eds.) 1981.

McDermott, D. (1976) *"Artificial Intelligence Meets Natural Stupidity,"* SIGART Newsletter No. 57, reprinted in Haugeland (ed.) 1981.

McDonald, D.D. (1984) *"Description Directed Control: Its implications for natural language generation,"* N. Cercone (ed.) Computational Linguistics, Plenum Press, New York. Reprinted in Grosz et al. (eds.) 1986.

McDonald, D.D. (1987) *"Natural Language Generation: Complexities and Techniques,"* Nirenburg, S. (ed.) 1987.

McDonald, D.D. and L. Bolc (eds.) (1988) *Natural Language Generation Systems.* Springer Series Symbolic Computation - Artificial Intelligence, Springer-Verlag, New York.

McDonald, D.D., M.M. Vaughan, and J.D. Pustejovsky (1987) *"Factors Contributing to Efficiency in Natural Language Generation,"* G. Kempen (ed.) 1987.

McKeown, K. (1985) *Textgeneration.* Studies in Natural Language Processing, Cambridge University Press, Cambridge.

Meinong, A. (1904) *"Über Gegenstandstheorie,"* A. Meinong (ed.), Untersuchungen zur Gegenstandstheorie und Psychologie, Johann Ambrosius Barth, Leipzig.

Miller, A.I. (1986) *Imagery in Scientific Thought.* The MIT-Press, Cambridge, Massachusetts.

Miller, G., and N. Chomsky (1963) *"Finitary Models of Language Users,"* Handbook of Mathematical Psychology. Vol. 2, R. Luce, R. Bush, and E. Galanter, (eds.), John Wiley, New York.

Montague, R. (1974) *Formal Philosophy.* Yale University Press, New Haven, CT.

Moravscik, J.M.E. (1974) *"Competence, Creativity, and Innateness,"* J.M.E. Moravscik, (ed.).

Moravscik, J.M.E. (ed.) (1974) *Logic and Philosophy for Linguistics.* Mouton, The Hague.

Nagao, M. (ed.) (1987) *Language and Artificial Intelligence.* North-Holland, Amsterdam.

Newell, A. and H.A. Simon (1972) *Human Problem Solving.* Prentice Hall, Englewood Cliffs, N.J.

Nilsson, N. (1980) *Principles of Artificial Intelligence.* Tioga Publishing Company, Palo Alto and Springer-Verlag, Berlin (Symbolic Computation – *Artificial Intelligence*).

Nirenburg, S., J.H. Reynolds, and I. Nirenburg (1986) *"Studying the Cognitive Agent: A Theory and Two Experiments,"* Research Report COSC9, Colgate University, New York.

Nirenburg, S. (1987) *"Knowledge and Choices in Machine Translation,"* S. Nirenburg (ed.) 1987.

Nirenburg, S. (ed.) (1987) *Machine translation.* Cambridge University Press, Cambridge, England.

Nirenburg, S., V. Raskin and A.B. Tucker (1987) *"The Structure of Interlingua in Translator"* in Nirenburg (ed.) 1987.

Nunberg, G. (1978) *The Pragmatics of Reference.* Indiana Linguistics Club, Bloomington, Indiana.

Nyberg, E. (1988) *"The FrameKit User's Guide, Version 2.0,"* CMU-CMT-MEMO.

Oettinger, A. G. (1961) *" Automatic Syntactic Analysis and the Pushdown Store,"* Proc. of Symposia in App. Math., Amer. Math. Soc. 12.

Ogden, C.K. and I.A. Richards (1923) *The Meaning of Meaning.* Routledge and Kegan Paul LTD, London.

Ortony, A. (ed.) (1979) *Metaphor and Thought.* Cambridge University Press, Cambridge, England.

Paul, H. (1920) *Grundzüge der Grammatik.* Halle 1880; fifth edition 1920.

Peirce, C.S. (1940) *The Philosophy of Peirce: Selected Writings.* J. Buchler (ed.), London.

Peregrin, J. and P. Sgall (1987) *"Review of Hausser 1984a,"* The Prague Bulletin of Mathematical Linguistics, 47:56-62.

Peters, S., and Ritchie, R. (1973) *"On the Generative Power of Transformational Grammar,"* "Information and Control," 18:483-501.

Phillips, E.A. (1971) *Basic Ideas in Biology.* Macmillan Company, New York.

Pinkal, M. (1981) *"Konsistenz und Kontextwechsel: das Sorites Paradox,"* Universität Düsseldorf, mimeo.

Pollard, C. (1984) *Generalized Phrase Structure Grammars, Head Grammars, and Natural Language.* Ph.D. Dissertation, Stanford University.

Pollard, C. and I. Sag (1987) *An Information-Based Syntax and Semantics*. Vol. 1, CSLI Lecture Notes No. 13, Stanford, CA.

Popper, K. (1959) *The Logic of Scientific Discovery*. Harper and Row, New York.

Post, E. (1936) *"Finite Combinatory Processes — Formulation I,"* Journal of Symbolic Logic, I.

Putnam, H. (1975) *Mind, Language, and Reality 2*. Cambridge University Press.

Pylyshyn, Z.W. (1980) *"Computation and Cognition: Issues in the Foundations of Cognitive Science,"* The Behavioral and Brain Sciences 3:11-169.

Quine, W.V.O. (1951) *"Two Dogmas of Empiricism,"* Philosophical Review 60:20-43.

Quine, W.V.O. (1960) *Word and Object*. MIT Press, Cambridge, Massachusetts.

Rabin, M.O. and D. Scott (1959) *"Finite Automata and their Decision Problems,"* IBM J. Res., 3:2, 115-125. Reprinted in Sequential Machines: Selected Papers, E.F. Moore (ed.), Addison-Wesley, Reading, Massachusetts, (1964).

Ratcliff, R. and G. McKoon (1981) *"Does Activation Really Spread,"* Psychological Review 88-5:545-462.

Reddy, D.R., L.D. Erman, R.D. Fennell, and R.B. Neely (1973) *"The Hearsay Speech Understanding System: An Example of the Recognition Process,"* Proceedings of the Third International Joint Conference on Artificial Intelligence, Stanford, California.

Reddy, M.J. (1979) *"The Conduit Metaphor - A Caseof Frame Conflict in Our Language about Language,"* Ortony (ed.) 1979.

Rescher, N. (1969) *Many-valued Logic*. MacGraw-Hill, New York.

Rhodes, I. (1959) *A New Approach to the Mechanical Translation of Russian*. NBS Report No. 6295.

Riemsdijk, H. van and E. Williams (1986) *Theory of Grammar*. The MIT-Press, Cambridge, Massachusetts.

Rumelhart, D.E. (1977) *Introduction to Human Information Processing*. John Wiley and Son, New York.

Rumelhart, D.E. and J.L. McClelland (eds.) (1986) *Parallel Distributed Processing*. Vol. 1: Foundations, Vol. 2: Psychological and Biological Models, The MIT-Press, Cambridge, Massachusetts.

Rumelhart, D.E., P. Smolensky, J.L. McClelland, and G.E. Hinton (1986) *"Schemata and Sequential Thought Processes in PDP Models,"* Rumelhart et al. (eds.) 1986.

Russell, B. (1905) *"On Denoting,"* Mind 14:479-493.

Salton, G., and M.J. McGill (1983) *Introduction to Modern Information Retrieval*. McGraw-Hill Book Company, New York.

Sampson, G. (1980) *Schools of Linguistics*. Stanford University Press, Stanford, California.

Saussure, F. de (1960) *Course in General Linguistics*. Peter Owen, London.

Schank, R.C., and the Yale A.I. Project (1975) *SAM - A Story Understander*. Research Report No. 43, Yale University, Committee on Computer Science.

Schank, R.C. and R. Abelson (1977) *Scripts, Plans, Goals, and Understanding*. Lawrence Earlbaum, Hillsdale, New Jersey.

Scott, D. and C. Strachey (1971) *"Toward a Mathematical Semantics of Computer Languages,"* Technical Monograph PRG-6, Oxford University Computing Laboratory, Programming Research Group, 45 Branbury Road, Oxford.

Searle, J.R. (1969) *Speech Acts*. Cambridge University Press, Cambridge.

Sells, P. (1985) *Lectures on Contemporary Syntactic Theory*. CSLI Lecture Notes Number 3, Stanford.

Sgall, P. (1974) *"Zur Stellung der Thema-Rhema-Gliederung in der Sprachbeschreibung,"* F. Daneš (ed.), p. 54-74, 1974.

Sgall, P., E. Hajčová, and J. Penevová (1986) *The Meaning of the Sentence in its Semantic and Pragmatic Aspects*. edited by J.L. Mey, Reidel, Dordrecht, Holland.

Shannon, C.E. and W. Weaver (1949) *The Mathematical Theory of Communication*. University of Illinois Press, Urbana.

Shepard, R.N. and L.A. Cooper (1982) *Mental Images and their Transformations*. The MIT-Press, Cambridge, Massachusetts.

Shepardson, J.C., and H.E. Sturgis (1963) *"Computability of Recursive Functions,"* JACM, Vol. 10, pp. 217-255.

Sherry, M. (1961) *Comprehensive Report on Predictive Syntactic Analysis*. Mathematical Linguistics and Automatic Translation, Report No. NSF-7, Section I, Harvard Computation Laboratory.

Shieber, S. (1983) *"Direct Parsing of ID/LP Grammars,"* Linguistics and Philosophy, Vol. 7.2:145-152.

Shieber, S., S. Stucky, H. Uszkoreit, and J. Robinson (1983) *"Formal Constraints on Metarules,"* in *Proceedings of the 21st Annual Meeting of the Association for Computational Linguistics*. Cambridge, Massachusetts.

Shoenfield, J. (1967) *Mathematical Logic*. Addison-Wesley, Reading, Massachusetts.

Smolensky, P. (1986) *"Information Processing in Dynamical Systems: Foundations of Harmony Theory"* in Rumelhart and McClelland (eds.), 1986.

Sowa, J.F. (1984) *Conceptual Structures: Information Processing in Mind and Machine*. Addison-Wesley Publishing Company, Reading, Massachusetts.

Strawson, P.F. (1950) *"On Referring,"* Mind 59:320-344.

Tarski, R. (1935) *"Der Wahrheitsbegriff in den Formalisierten Sprachen,"* Studia Philosophica, Vol. I, 262 - 405.

Tarski, R. (1944) *"The Semantic Concept of Truth,"* Philosophy and Phenomenological Research 4:341-375.

Tomita, M. (1986) *Efficient Parsing for Natural Languages*. Kluwer Academic Publishers, Boston-Dordrecht.

Uszkoreit, H., and S. Peters (1982) *"Essential Variables in Metarules,"* presented at the 1982 Annual Meeting of the Linguistic Society of America, San Diego.

Vijay-Shanker, K., D.J. Weir, and A.K. Joshi (1987) *"Characterizing Structural Descriptions produced by Various Grammatical Formalisms,"* Proceedings of 25th Meeting of the Association of Computational Linguistics.

Webber, B.L. and N.J. Nilsson (eds.) (1981) *Readings in Artificial Intelligence.* Morgan Kaufmann Publishers, Los Altos, CA.

Weizenbaum, J. (1966) *"ELIZA - a Computer Program for the Study of Natural Language Communication between Man and Machine,"* Comm. ACM 9:36-45.

Wells, R.S., (1947) *"Immediate Constituents,"* Language 23:81-117.

Weyhrauch, R. (1980) *"Prolegomena to a Formal Theory of Mechanical Reasoning,"* Artificial Intelligence. Reprinted in Webber and Nilsson (eds.) 1981.

Wilks, Y. (1975) *"An Intelligent Analyzer and Understander of English,"* CACM 18(5):264-274. Reprinted in Grosz et al. (eds.) 1986.

Winograd, T. (1972) *Understanding Natural Language.* Cognitive Psychology 1:1-191.

Winograd, T. (1983) *Language as a Cognitive Process: Syntax.* Addison-Wesley Publishing Company, Reading, Massachusetts

Wittgenstein, L. (1921) *Logisch-Philosophische Abhandlungen.* Annalen der Naturphilosophie 14:185-262.

Wittgenstein, L. (1953) *Philosophical Investigations.* Blackwell, Oxford.

Woods, W.A. (1970) *"Transition Network Grammars for Natural Language Analysis,"* CACM 3(10):591-606.

Yngve, V.H. (1955) *"Syntax and the Problem of Multiple Meaning,"* W.N. Locke and A.D. Booth (eds.), Machine Translation of Languages, The MIT-Press, Cambridge, Massachusetts.

Younger, D.H. (1966) *"Context-Free Language Processing in n^3,"* General Electric R & D Center, Schenctady, N.Y.

Zadeh, L. (1971) *"Quantitative Fuzzy Semantics,"* Information Science 3:159-176.

Name Index

Subject Index

Springer Series
SYMBOLIC COMPUTATION – *Artificial Intelligence*

N. J. Nilsson: Principles of Artificial Intelligence. XV, 476 pages, 139 figs., 1982

J. H. Siekmann, G. Wrightson (Eds.): Automation of Reasoning 1. Classical Papers on Computational Logic 1957–1966. XXII, 525 pages, 1983

J. H. Siekmann, G. Wrightson (Eds.): Automation of Reasoning 2. Classical Papers on Computational Logic 1967–1970. XXII, 638 pages, 1983

L. Bolc (Ed.): The Design of Interpreters, Compilers, and Editors for Augmented Transition Networks. XI, 214 pages, 72 figs., 1983

M. M. Botvinnik: Computers in Chess. Solving Inexact Search Problems. With contributions by A. I. Reznitsky, B. M. Stilman, M. A. Tsfasman, A. D. Yudin. Translated from the Russian by A. A. Brown. XIV, 158 pages, 48 figs., 1984

L. Bolc (Ed.): Natural Language Communication with Pictorial Information Systems. VII, 327 pages, 67 figs., 1984

R. S. Michalski, J. G. Carbonell, T. M. Mitchell (Eds.): Machine Learning. An Artificial Intelligence Approach. XI, 572 pages, 1984

A. Bundy (Ed.): Catalogue of Artificial Intelligence Tools. Second, revised edition. IV, 168 pages, 1986

C. Blume, W. Jakob: Programming Languages for Industrial Robots. XIII, 376 pages, 145 figs., 1986

J. W. Lloyd: Foundations of Logic Programming. Second, extended edition. XII, 212 pages, 1987

L. Bolc (Ed.): Computational Models of Learning. IX, 208 pages, 34 figs., 1987

L. Bolc (Ed.): Natural Language Parsing Systems. XVIII, 367 pages, 151 figs., 1987

N. Cercone, G. McCalla (Eds.): The Knowledge Frontier. Essays in the Representation of Knowledge. XXXV, 512 pages, 93 figs., 1987

G. Rayna: REDUCE. Software for Algebraic Computation. IX, 329 pages, 1987

D. D. McDonald, L. Bolc (Eds.): Natural Language Generation Systems. XI, 389 pages, 84 figs., 1988

L. Bolc, M. J. Coombs (Eds.): Expert System Applications. IX, 471 pages, 84 figs., 1988

C.-H. Tzeng: A Theory of Heuristic Information in Game-Tree Search. X, 107 pages, 22 figs., 1988

Springer Series
SYMBOLIC COMPUTATION – *Artificial Intelligence*

H. Coelho, J. C. Cotta: Prolog by Example. How to Learn, Teach and Use It. X, 382 pages, 68 figs., 1988

L. Kanal, V. Kumar (Eds.): Search in Artificial Intelligence. X, 488 pages, 67 figs., 1988

H. Abramson, V. Dahl: Logic Grammars. XIV, 234 pages, 40 figs., 1989

R. Hausser: Computation of Language. An Essay on Syntax, Semantics, and Pragmatics in Natural Man-Machine Communication. XVI, 425 pages, 1989